THE LONG ARC
OF THE UNIVERSE

THE LONG ARC
OF THE UNIVERSE

Travels Beyond the Pale

KATHLEEN STOCKING

STOCKING PRESS

Lake Leelanau, MI

©2016 Kathleen Stocking
All rights reserved

Published by Stocking Press, Lake Leelanau, MI

Text illustrations ©2016 Lynne Rae Perkins
Map illustration ©2016 Tom Woodruff
Cover art ©1994 Gaia Somweba

ISBN 978-0-692-69308-7

First Edition, 2016

Book Design by Saxon Design, Inc.
Printed in the United States of America

Library of Congress Control Number 2016905884

*This book is dedicated to all
those brave and benevolent
souls working in refugee camps,
war zones, non-governmental
organizations, public libraries,
charity thrift stores, and
environmental non-profits—
both here at home and around
the world—ordinary people
trying to make the world a better
place by being kind.*

Contents

EUROPE

HOME

EPILOGUE

AMSTERDAM

THAILAND.

ROMANIA

ISTANBUL

Acknowledgements

Individuals don't exist without their communities. I am profoundly thankful for all the people out there, both at home in Lake Leelanau and in faraway lands, who have supported, encouraged, and helped with my existence and with this book. They have been my community.

They range from early readers of first drafts to proof readers and artists, reference librarians, book sellers, employers, old friends, car repair people, wood cutters, neighbors, snow shovel guys, total strangers, a little boy in Guatemala who rescued me when I was hopelessly lost, a woman who gave me a rib eye steak for Christmas because she thought I would like it and would find it amusing, people who helped with my computer, and people who took me to supper or made me laugh. The people who made me laugh are important; without them I wouldn't have lasted.

Because the community is so large, I'm going to simply list them alphabetically, as follows: Stephen Arens, Josephine Arrowood and family, Alvie and Helene, Joyce Bahle, Cristi Bardenhagen, Bobby and Kenny, Sue Boucher, Mike Buhler, Mary and Brian Bush, Traverse Area District Library reference librarians Amy Barritt, Bryce Bush, Katheryn Carrier and Betsy Myers, Alan Campbell, Laurie Carroll, Cathy Carter, Lydia, Laura and Sorin Cazacu, Chuck Chimosky, Noam Chomsky, Lucy Crandall, Ditto Couturier, Laurie Davis, the Scott and Ashley Denoyer family, Tricia Denton, librarians Ryan Deery and David Diller, Cynthia Dougal, Mary Ann Duperon, Carolyn Faught, Bradley Fewins, Cymbre, Eliza, and Chloe Foster, Deb Freed, Grace Glynn, Charles Godbout, David and Pamela

Grath, Donald Hall, Marlene Hahnenberg, Carrie Hansen, Scott Herrington, Adam Hochschild, Florence "Chip" Jermyn, Bronwyn Jones, Kevin, Kitty Knight, Lilah Koski, Jimmy and Suki LaForrest, Penny Larcom, Tony Lentych, Kyla Lightfoot, April Messias, James and Marilyn McCormick, George Moreno, Ruth Morgan, Angela Murphy, Nitaya and family, Naomi Shihab Nye, Julie Nowland, Midge Obata, all the members of Occupy Traverse City, Susan and Richard Och family, Anne-Marie Ooman, Teddy Page, Lori Park, Marti Pacquette, Lynne Rae Perkins, Anneke (Wegman) and Guy Plamondon, Jonah Powell, William Rastetter, Dwight and Barbara Reed, Amy Reynolds, Suzanne Rogers, Jeffery Ross, Jesse and Van Rozay, George Saunders, Olloriak Sawade, Angela and Erik Saxon, Mike Shell, Barbara Siepker, Christopher and Susann Schaberg, Leslee Spraggins, Gaia Somweba, Gretchen Sprout, Debbie Stabenow, Michael Steinberg, Mark Stone, Mary Sutherland, Becky Thatcher, Jill Tewsley, Theron, Lori Wegener, Jacob Wheeler, the Wheelock Boys, Tom Woodruff, the dedicated staff of the Resolve to Stop the Violence Program at the San Francisco Jail from the fall of 1999 to the late spring of 2000, my many brilliant and fun-loving fellow Peace Corps volunteers in Thailand and Romania, secret saviors everywhere (you know who you are), and all the peninsula volunteers with whom I worked between 2015 and 2016 at Samaritans' Closet in Lake Leelanau. All the considerable expert help I received notwithstanding, all of the errors of fact or language in my book are my own.

The cover art was done by Gaia Somweba, my daughter, when she was fourteen, in response to the e.e. cummings poem, *after all white horses are in bed*. You can see the *somewhat city* in the background. Gaia would go on to study for four years at the Interlochen Center for the Arts. Writer Cymbre Foster prevailed upon her lovely daughters, Eliza and Chloe, to help with the book's final stages. Artist Laurie Davis, a woman I've known for more than forty years, designed the cover of this book, as she had the covers of my first two books; she encouraged me, moreover, and that was invaluable. Northport artist Tom Woodruff, following a conversation about my adventures, drew what he called "a mind map" showing the places I'd been. Illustrator and writer, Lynne Rae Perkins, a Newberry Award winner and 2015 National Book Critics Circle Award winner, is a wonderful person, a neighbor I've only just met, did the inside illustrations. Naomi Shihab Nye, also a 2015 National Book Critics Circle Award winner, although I've never met her, has been a favorite poet of mine for years and I've often used her work in the classroom. Nye gave me permission to use her poem, "Kindness" and would accept no fee but a copy of the book and "something grown or made on the Leelanau Peninsula." I sent her morel mushrooms three years before the book was finished.

Many of the people in this book, including two of my nieces, other relatives and several friends, have been given other names in order to protect their privacy. Some of the people in the prisons and in the countries where I worked have been given alternate names or not named at all, or are composites, also for the sake of their privacy and sometimes for the sake of their safety. Everything I recount in the essays, to the best of my ability to recall and relate, is based on actual events.

Some of the essays in this book have appeared in substantially different forms in Peace Corps magazines in Thailand and Romania. Others have appeared in some form in northern Michigan or Leelanau County publications, including the *Lake Country Gazette, Blue Magazine, Leelanau Enterprise, Traverse Magazine, Glen Arbor Sun,* and Sleeping Bear Press, and are reprinted with permission.

Introduction

The waters of the big lake surround me. There's no other place like the Leelanau Peninsula, except maybe the Bosporus. You're never far from a view of the water so that even when you don't see it, you can easily imagine it.

Over the span of almost twenty years, successively traveling far and then returning, over and over again, I was mapping, like a bee charting the distance from the flowers to the hive, the world as I was discovering it. I was finding a world that is now without borders, or without meaningful borders. The Internet, like the printing press before it and ocean sailing before that, has changed the boundaries of the known world.

This is what I learned in all my travels: there's no escaping anything anymore. Your heavily guarded Manhattan apartment and my remote Michigan peninsula are no longer sufficient barriers to toxic miasmas and the rabble at the gate. The people in Flint are getting sick from drinking the poisoned waters of their river just like the people who live along the Danube. The children arriving at our southern border and the toddler's body washed up on the gravel of a Turkish beach are no different from our own children.

If the third world countries I visited sometimes seemed to be three hundred years behind the United States in democracy and enlightenment, the Dutch seemed to be that far ahead. Their system of making sure all people have enough food, medical care, and education to give them a chance to be useful members of the community, a system that allows all members of the Dutch society to achieve the highest level of learning of which they are capable, has created a country that is more fair and livable than ours.

Increasingly as I traveled I became aware of how America and the rest of the world are invisibly intertwined. The third world countries I visited seemed to have a dictatorship, or oligarchy, or monarchy, all thinly disguised as democracies, horribly corrupt governments violating all kinds of human rights, governments often being supported by, or maybe having even been put in place by, behind the scenes machinations of United States power and money.

Every time I go into Staples, where the young computer techs are trying to survive on minimum wage, working two jobs, sometimes trying to raise kids—while the CEOs are making millions a year—I feel I'm right back in El Salvador. Democracy prevention starts with making people so afraid of not surviving that they're incapable of protesting.

You don't need to try to imagine the third world. Just take a look around you. We're gaining on it. Our inequality is catching us up to every gun-toting, pot-holed, child-neglecting, violent, corruption-ridden, polluted, toxic backwater on the face of the earth.

The Internet was new when I first left Michigan; over the span of time during which I was traveling, it became a key part of the global culture. The Internet had just become available in 1999 in the library of the little coastal California town where I lived when I worked in the prisons of California. By 2001, in El Salvador and Guatemala, there were fly-specked Internet cafes, often in people's homes, even in the smallest towns. Cell phones, too, were becoming common. In Thailand in 2007 I saw a man walking through a rice paddy, naked except for a loincloth and carrying a rifle that looked like it was from the American Revolutionary War, and talking on his cell phone.

As I continued to come and go from my village of Lake Leelanau, to and from villages overseas, the whole world was becoming an Internet-connected village. Computers changed everything. It happened so fast and spread so far, it was hard to take it in.

When I told a twenty-four-year-old fellow Peace Corps volunteer in 2011 in Romania that I had been a reporter back in the 1970s, when we still used typewriters, got the news off the wire service, and used real scissors and real paste to reconfigure and rearrange our news stories, he was thunderstruck. He said, "Wow! So that's where they got *cut and paste*!" as if reconstructing an ancient Hebraic idiom.

Except for rare moments, some encounter like the one above, where I shocked a young person who seemed to think I was from the Stone Age because I hadn't grown up with computers, I never thought of myself as old.

Old age is freeing, especially I think it freed me as a woman. As an old woman I traveled all over parts of Latin America, Asia, and Europe. I was mostly in third world countries; sometimes there were dangers. Because I was an old woman, I got a pass. I went everywhere alone, unarmed, and remained safe.

Old age is not some cliff that appears suddenly out of nowhere at the bottom of which is: adult diapers, hearing aids, and dentures in a glass of water on the nightstand. It's more gradual than that; and, really, it's not even about that. It's less physical and more intangible.

I love to see my adult children and people of all ages running and working out in the gyms, not like my generation where we stopped where childhood left off and settled down to hard work and slow disintegration. But, as old age reveals to anyone who lives long enough, life's about developing strength, and not just of the quadriceps, biceps, and triceps. If one works at it, the muscles of courage, confidence, integrity, and caution increase in power over time. These are the muscles that do not atrophy. Pass through the veil of any culture's preconceived notions about anything, and you are suddenly in a world where it feels like you can fly. With age, one becomes more aerodynamic.

I would sometimes feel slightly whiplashed with all the

travel, metaphorically jet-lagged. Where was I? What century was it? Istanbul, between the Aegean and the Black Sea, reminded me achingly of Michigan's Manitou Passage, Sleeping Bear Bay, and the Manitou Islands. Something about the mist rising from all that surrounding water seems to make the air pink. Would I ever go home again?

I missed the songbirds in Michigan wherever I went. In many third world countries the birds, even the songbirds, have all been eaten. The Leelanau Peninsula is part of the flyway between Mexico and Canada. In the spring and summer the woods are filled with songsters. The sound of the hermit thrush, America's nightingale, in the deepest woods, is a sound that, once you hear it and know the clear, spirit-filled tones, you want to hear it again.

The Internet is new, but basic human nature is much the same on the other side of the world as it is on this one. People everywhere are capable of falling in love, like to spend time with their families, and cry when someone dies. People like to be out-of-doors in fine weather, cherish natural beauty, and make incredible art no matter where you go. Fresh flowers are an appropriate gift the world over.

Once in a hole-in-the-wall restaurant in Thailand, after serving me my bowl of noodles, the woman put a Johnny Cash CD on the CD player, looked over at me and smiled, as if to say, "Hi, you're not alone. You're human. So am I."

In 2011 the area in Michigan where I grew up around the Sleeping Bear Dunes was named by ABC's *Good Morning America* the most beautiful place in America (for that year). Suddenly the place where I had been "a local," a pejorative term when I was growing up, a term that signified that I was an unfortunate sub-human who lived in a place that was hopelessly backward, was now a sought-after place, a rare and beautiful place. Presumably my status has been elevated accordingly.

Beneath these surface changes I noticed things that were more profound. In Lake Leelanau, between bouts abroad, the men who helped me cut trees and haul brush, naturally getting younger as I got older because it was a young man's job, were no longer racist or homophobic, much more tolerant than the men had been in their father's and grandfather's generations.

In my experience it takes about six months—both in the coming and in the going—to enter the new culture, become comfortable enough to function and, also, on the return, to readjust to one's own culture. Each time I would have to do a kind of *tabula rasa*, erase all thoughts, and accept without contemplation what was happening around me.

As I came and went, people would sometimes ask me what I was after in all of this, the underlying question in this being, why would someone leave Paradise and visit Hell, since where I had always lived was beautiful and easy-going and the places I visited were often so difficult and fraught. At first I didn't know, but eventually I came to see that what I seemed to be going for was a bone-deep understanding of basic human nature—the kind of understanding that I'd had where I'd lived all my life but didn't have for the larger world—that I could only get by going out there and seeing for myself.

If the world was now an Internet-connected village, instinctively I'd felt I had to have some sense of the parameters, the human dimensions of this new world. What's required for all of us in the twenty-first century, no matter where we live on the earth, is a re-thinking of how we are going to share the resources without killing each other. Since killing seems to be our default mode, it's suddenly a very small place. Compassion for others, I discovered, was the only thing that made life bearable, no matter where I went. All people are capable of it.

And then one day I came back to the Leelanau Peninsula. My travels were over. Just as one late summer day I'd felt the need to go out and see the world, one day I felt the need to come home and stay. I was satisfied that I could trust what I had found out about people and how they had figured out how to live in this world, and I didn't need to go out seeking to know through experience anymore.

Prologue

MY GRANDMOTHER, MY COMPASS

Dear Grandmother,

I think I would have written before, but when you died I was too young and then later when I was a little older, I was overly concerned about doing things right, things like how to address the envelope and where to put the stamp, which was unfortunately about the same time I learned one is not supposed to write letters to the dead.

But now I'm at that stage in life where I don't pay too much attention to what one is supposed to do. Anyway, the line between living and dying seems arbitrary. I've decided to ignore it.

I still can see the bedroom we shared in Cadillac, the pine paneling, the way you would take your hair down at night and brush it. We were often silent, yet it felt like we were talking. I think I talked to you in my head, which is maybe the reason I still do.

You were in your nineties but still had some strands of hair that were black. You wore it braided and wrapped around your head, like a tiny nest, an invitation to birds. At night you took it down and combed and brushed it, putting it into one braid down your back. Even as an ancient, deeply wrinkled, blue-veined lady you had a palpable femininity, as if you were mysteriously part of everything that lived.

When we performed our nightly ritual of teeth-brushing and feet-washing, I can remember feeling privileged to be there with you in that ancient golden light, the infinite privacy of thoughts shared, unspoken, evening light, a privacy and intimacy that was itself part of infinity. When we were all done, I would go and get a book and you would read to me. Finally I would say the prayers I'd learned in the Congregational Sunday School. You never said them with me. Once I asked you why and you said you prayed in silence in your head.

Remember the wasps who built their nests under the eaves? One night, already in our bare feet, we discovered one crawling across the floor. I was terrified, having nearly died the summer before from multiple stings. You took one of your brown, high-topped, side-buttoned leather boots and hammered the wasp with the heel. You hammered long after the wasp was dead, never saying anything. I watched, secretly pleased, as you flushed the residue down the toilet. I fell asleep that night feeling safe, protected not just for the moment but for all time, my fear vanquished.

When school got out the summer I turned seven, we moved a hundred and twenty miles north to my father's biggest sawmill, the one by the Sleeping Bear Dunes. You stayed behind, being too old then to leave the only life you'd ever known. Or perhaps my parents didn't want to take you with us. I've had to try to piece this together since then.

As a child all I knew was that first it was winter and you were there, then it was summer and we had moved to a new place and you were gone. The loss, treated matter-of-factly by others, was for me like the loss of oxygen when the wasps stung me, only worse, because no one could see that I'd stopped breathing. I was told you had moved across town to your daughter's, my Aunt Margaret's place.

One night in July, soon after we moved, I dreamed you were climbing a ladder to the sky. As you reached the top, a man who looked like Abraham Lincoln, wearing a black stovepipe hat, tried to get you to go back down again.

I awoke worried about you. I wanted you there beside me, to tell you my dream, the way I had in Cadillac, and then you would tell me yours and, although different kinds of dreams, we would find in telling them to each other in the early morning that interplay of different kinds of harmonies, and I would feel again how everything distills and calibrates, transforms around the inside of a Mobius strip, that unseen ouroboros of the soul of the universe, just the way I did when you taught me that hanging the wash on the line and making paper dolls had a different but similar aesthetic.

At supper with my parents and sisters that evening, with some trepidation since I was not used to telling my dreams to anyone but you, I finally told my nightmare. My sisters were uninterested, but my parents looked stricken. Only later did I learn that you had died that afternoon. They did not tell me then, but at your funeral I learned you had decided to walk the railroad tracks back to your old Hoxeyville homestead.

It wasn't until we celebrated Abraham Lincoln's birthday in school that February twelfth that I realized that you and Abraham Lincoln shared a birthday. You were alike somehow, too. Maybe he was trying to get you to go back down the ladder because it wasn't time yet for you to come be with him in heaven; but naturally you had your own ideas of when it was time. It would be another thirty years before it would occur to me that the ladder in my prescient nightmare had been the dreaming mind's transliteration of the tracks.

You had walked the railroad tracks and, in the July heat, made it halfway before you collapsed. Your farm had been sold long since, but you were too old to remember, the relatives said, talking about it while they buried you in Clay Hill Cemetery.

Or maybe, and this is what I think, like birds migrating thousands of miles by measuring the position of the stars against the time of day and year, you were navigating by your own constellation of metaphors and you wanted to die that way, with your boots on, halfway to a home that was no longer your home, giving new meaning to the phrase, 'she bought the farm,' with your brown cardboard suitcase by your side, although, and here I should stop lest this letter become an end-less recitation of every dream and wasp sting and rainy spring since we were last in each other's physical presence.

There's no way to start at the beginning and so I'm just go-ing to start with today. When I came back into the house this morning, from hanging the clothes on the line outside on the slope above the creek, where the old-fashioned fuchsia-colored roses and bright orange poppies and purple bearded irises were blooming around the posts that hold up the clotheslines, col-ors and scents that call out to the world that life has just begun anew, no stopping it, my phone was ringing.

It was a friend calling who, after thirty-three years of mar-riage, tells me she's getting a divorce from the man she loves. She lived in fabulous luxury all those years, all over the world, in Paris, Belgium, Manhattan. Now she has a home in the hills above Lake Michigan, a place filled with original art, all of which she will have to sell. He'd brought the Thai airline hostess home to their palatial Paris apartment. He'd wanted his young and beautiful lady friend to see the high ceilings, the golden walls, the original artwork, the things his money could buy.

"But it was *Christmas*," my friend said, "our *children* were there." He had always philandered and she had always known, but they'd had an unspoken agreement that he would keep his paramours out of the house.

This was the story she'd told when she'd come home to Mich-igan six months earlier. Now she says she's been thinking about her sweet and beautiful grandmother, so many years ago down in Illinois, on another pioneer farm not too far from the Mis-sissippi River, and I say, well then, and why not, come with me down to Hoxeyville to see my grandmother's old farmhouse?

I'm leaving Michigan, I tell my friend. I have to leave to find work. I'm not sure where I'll end up or how long I'll be gone, but I want to see my grandmother's farm before I go. I want to take her with me, symbolically maybe, have her with me in spirit. She is my talisman, my standard-bearer, my grandmother.

The farm is all weeds now, I tell my friend. Wrack and Ruin. Pine flats, I say, barren land.

"Perfect," she says, "I'll pack a picnic lunch for us."

The day, which had dawned so bright and cool and clear, is becoming muggy and overcast by the time I pick her up, the clouds tangled and gray. Her grandmother, she tells me as we wend our way down through Grawn and Buckley along the back roads, past honeysuckle in bloom and lilacs with their heart-shaped leaves and purple blooms turning brown, had been lucky in those times to marry the well-read son of a prominent and wealthy farmer.

Our grandmothers, we decide, have given us a connection; but more than that, a capacity for connection. We are alike, and not alike, like friends. On this trip we talk and find we share an uncomfortable ability to feel compassion not only for the person who's been harmed but for the person who's done the harming, the Nazi as well as the Jew, Judas as well as Jesus, the Thai whore as well as the legal wife.

My friend is a person at ease with solitude, comfortable with contradiction: in art it's called negative space. I see her looking at the fields of long grass beside the road. The grass is shiny and lush after all the rain and when the wind moves through, it looks like the water on a calm day far out in the sea when you can see a wave moving just under the surface.

We crest the high hill above the Manistee River, a quick magnificent panoramic view of the river before the steep incline takes us abruptly down into Sherman. I tell my friend Sherman was one of the only two towns on this side of Michigan in the 1880s, along with Hoxeyville.

This is the road on which you, grandmother, and your young, blond husband, so handsome and so strong, came north by oxcart in 1888, newly married, along what was then called, and still is, the Old Indian Trail, that ran between Newaygo in the center of the state, a hundred miles south, and Northport, a hundred miles farther north, at the tip of the Leelanau Peninsula. You would have left the trail and headed for Hoxeyville about twenty miles south of here, down near the Pine River. You walked, but people walked in those days.

You yourself were visibly dark, rumored to be part-Indian, but it wouldn't have been something your grandmother would have bandied about in the 1800s, seeing as how Andrew Jackson and the U.S. cavalry were still rounding up the Native peoples and herding them onto reservations out west.

I knew, grandmother, that your grandmother had come to Michigan with the Mormons from a place called Palmyra in New York State, near where the Seneca and Oneida had once fought and died, trying to hang onto their land. Once in the 1960s my oldest sister and I, coming from Buffalo in a snowstorm, stopped not far from Niagara Falls, and stayed in a run-down old hotel that, we didn't discover until the next day, had bedbugs.

In the late 1800s, the buffalo out west were almost all gone. The Indians were starving. The Apache were still fighting but signed off on the vast Oklahoma Territory in 1901. Sitting Bull, who lost everything after defeating Custer, agreed to go to Europe with Wild Bill Cody and do his astonishing horse tricks, drinking his brains out the while, as anyone would; he returned to the reservation where he was shot by a U.S. soldier. Geronimo died in 1909, the same year Harvard trustees refused to let the first woman applicant into law school on the grounds that she would distract the young men from their studies.

The passenger pigeons would soon all be slaughtered, the last one dying in a Cincinnati zoo in 1914. In Petoskey in 1889, the year your first son was born, a billion pigeons from a single nesting site—forty miles long and ten miles wide— were killed when men set fire to the trees to frighten the birds (flightless when nesting), asphyxiating them with pots of burning sulfur. By this time, too, most of the virgin timber in Michigan had been clear-cut from Saginaw to Mackinac, the tree stumps, you told me, "like yellow plates" from one side of the state to the other.

An oxcart goes about two miles an hour so you must have walked along beside it, dancing along beside it, is how I imagine you. The oxcart would have been piled high with your belongings and your two youngest children. You would have needed to let them walk sometimes, too, just to get them tired enough to finally stay in the oxcart and, hopefully, fall asleep.

You might make twenty miles a day, two miles an hour for ten hours on uneven ground with the children and the cart would have been a good pace, stopping for lunch, and at the end of the long day camping in the summer evening as the sky in the west turned that peculiarly Michigan shade of tangerine. You would have been joyous, in love, on an adventure with your tall, strong husband with whom you had nine children and with whom you held hands at the dinner table until the day he died. He was so good-humored and big, and you were so little and brave.

In those old tintypes where everyone invariably looks so stiff (like Audubon's birds, sketched from corpses) he looks relaxed, jaunty, free in every sense of the word, even challenging; in long underwear winter and summer, no shirt with a collar for him; an unruly beard, like the first hippie.

They said he could always make you laugh. He must have loved you, his own female genius, although you once complained to my mother that he never let you go to town to pick out your own dress material.

Perhaps he knew what a rare woman had alighted in his life and so that's why he kept you hidden and, on the outside chance that any man should ever make it to Hoxeyville, happen upon your pioneer homestead and espy you working in your garden, among your beautiful fuchsia-colored roses, and purple bearded irises, and bright orange poppies—kept you dressed head-to-toe in gray-and-brown wallpaper stripes, nondescript as a red-eyed vireo, a hermit thrush, an ovenbird.

I'm guessing, based on how you were with me when I was a child, that you were one of those unusual women who comes along every so often, not just a beauty, but love goddess and shaman, so powerful in your perceptive abilities it would have seemed like magic to anyone with you, so able to connect to your man and connect him to everything else as well, that he was determined to protect you with everything he had. You were the chalice and he was the blade. You were the tinder and he was the flame. You were the dot and he was the line. You were the blossom and he was the hummingbird.

This mythic union of male and female is rare. It was codified in the geisha system of Japan and the rituals of European courtesans for countless ages, with customs that brilliantly mirrored the natural, the eternal and the mystical, but were not even close, like the jeweler's nightingale compared to the real one. Historically the children born of this carefully contrived allure, Agrippina's son Nero, or Olympias's son Alexander the Great, were scarcely full human beings. Driven and powerful, yes, but also beasts, progeny of the wiles and subterfuge required by desperate survival, not love.

You were lucky and my grandfather was lucky. My friend and I are less lucky. Though we may have found powerful protectors, it was at a price, a price we ultimately could not or would not pay.

You and I were both born at the ends of wars, you at the end of the Civil War and I at the end of the Second World War. Your grandmother was born just before the War of 1812 and her parents came of age during the Revolutionary War. How the generations just go on and on, like a ball bouncing down endless flights of steps.

My friend's grandmother also taught her how to hang wash on the line, also taught her how to put all the like items together. Her homestead was down in Bond County, Illinois only fifty miles from the great Mississippi River. All the traffic and goods were carried down to St. Louis and New Orleans. There was a little stop on the big river, a day's horseback ride from the farm.

My friend is unusually competent. She's practical, too, able to make her own preserves. By the time all of her various ancestors, and yours and mine, too, got off some boat in New York or Boston, the emerald and ruby cities of India were only legends, the pyramids had drifted over with sand, China had long since fallen into obscurity, and the ancient civilizations of Greece and Rome had fallen to ruins. But in America, as they said, the world was new.

My Aunt Mary said you could read, knit, and breast-feed all at the same time. You would prop your book on a music stand and cradle the baby first in the crook of one arm and then in the other, all the while your knitting needles were clicking away. Nursing a baby was a chance to sit, and if you could sit, why not read and knit? Nine babies in twenty years meant that pregnancy and breast-feeding were alternate states, your body waxing and waning like the moon.

You survived with your beauty intact, although my mother said your house still smelled like piss twenty years after the last toddler was grown. You toilet trained your children by letting them go around without diapers; with nine of them, one can understand.

Your garden was a showplace. After your husband was injured in a logging accident, you supported the family with your garden, your cows and your chickens. People came all the way from Cadillac, my Aunt Reva said, to get what you had: vegetables, butter, milk, cream, eggs.

We turn at Mesick onto M-115. There's a lot of roadkill. We pass several dead opossums with their dirty-gray coats and prehensile tails, crows finishing them off. Opossums are North America's only marsupial, some kind of throwback to animals that existed sixty-five million years ago, and they look it. Then up-turned coons, swollen, or pregnant, poor babies. We pass the turn to Meauwataka, a place I once picked blueberries with my father.

This grandfather, my friend goes on, had been an alcoholic and once, in a drunken rage, split her grandmother's head open. As soon as her youngest child was five, the grandmother left and, living in a time when women couldn't support themselves except by cleaning other people's houses, that's what she did. And so, my friend says, "I feel that's been done, my grandmother did it for both of us."

My friend is brave, able to stand her ground, able to get a divorce, the way she'd get a hair-do, to embrace adversity, as if it, too, were a friend. In her Swiss family, she said, when she researched it one day in Berne, she found documents where family members were disputing the dispensation of the dovecote; most Swiss families kept doves, as we keep chickens.

Her ancestors had come more recently from Europe than mine, at least on my father's side, coming out of Switzerland and Germany during the Napoleonic Wars when Europe was in chaos and America beckoned as a place of wealth and, at least on the east coast where the Indians had been eradicated, a place of peace. I slow around a curve and then glance over at her when the car's on the straight-away. She knows my question. "The guano," she says, "in the dovecote. For fertilizer. For the gardens. It was more valuable than gold."

Those early settlers in the Midwest came mainly from New York State, into the fertile valleys of Ohio, Indiana, and Illinois where my friend's family had stayed, a land of big rivers— while my relatives kept going, into the cedar swamps and pine woods, the northern rains and the snows, a place of lakes and clouds, and a wind that comes almost always from the northwest, across Lake Michigan from Wisconsin and Minnesota, out of the Rocky Mountains. In a day and age when many children died, my friend and I marvel together at how our grandmothers had kept theirs alive.

You, grandmother, had your last two babies, when you were forty-five, almost as old as I am now. You must have been surprised. Twins, my father and his sister, who were "small as squirrels" my Uncle Hale said. You kept them alive in shoe boxes on the back of the woodstove, steam rising constantly from the old wood burner, keeping those babies warm in your homemade incubator. They would live. You would see to it.

The expression on your face in the photo I have of you holding my father and his twin sister is that of a Sioux dog soldier, protecting with a fierce will power (palpable even through the faded photograph) the delicate new spirits inside your babies—as if they were candles and the world a wind waiting to blow them out.

We turn off M-115 toward Boon. The land is scrub pine here, sandy, no fertile farms. We pass the house where the white-haired woman has her permanent yard sale of knick-knacks—empty cobalt blue Vick's bottles and empty dark blue Evening in Paris bottles and empty turquoise canning jars— under the bright blue plastic tarps.

Today the tarps have small pools of water in their little sunken indentations, like tiny swimming pools for warbler and finch. My friend says the old woman is probably hoping someone will come and buy the whole thing. We pass homes with overturned, rusted cars lying around like shipwrecks. We pass the sound of a dozen dogs barking somewhere in the distance and—close to the road, lid up—marigolds planted in a gold-toned toilet bowl.

"My grandmother," my friend says, as we dip into a hollow on the outskirts of Boon and pass the U.S. Post Office with its American flag, and in the surrounding streets, wood stacked against the back sheds of old houses, "used to let me cut her hair. She had black, naturally curly hair, like mine. I think of the ways she had of letting me know I was loved, of giving me self-confidence. She never said 'love.' She let me cut her hair."

"My grandmother, too," I tell her. "I don't remember ever

hearing the word, but it was there." My friend is like her grandmother, able to watch things unfold, to trust how they will
turn out; to wait. A decade ago my friend survived a rare and
terrible disease where her body went on a rampage, producing
so much collagen her organs began to fuse together. The disease went away, leaving my friend with the skin of a teenager.
Now, in her art and in her life, she refuses to isolate the event
from its narrative.

The roads here are straight, as if someone laid them out
with a string and a compass. Pine plantations put in during the
Depression by men in the Civilian Conservation Corps, line
the roads. As we speed by it seems they are moving, the way it
is when you are small and run by a head-high picket fence, or
like the repeated image of a chicken pecking grain at the bottom of a page in a book when you riffle the pages looking for
something and you think you see the chicken moving its head
up and down; dizzying.

"This is strange country," my friend says. The tone of voice
says, "A place where you imagine murders being committed
and never discovered." We pass a tiny, overgrown cemetery in
the pines, then an entirely rusted-out, once red-and-white con-
vertible in an abandoned yard and a sign that excitedly proclaims, "1968 Pontiac!!! $1,800!!!" We know the car is old,
but is the sign new? Farther on a sign in the window of a small,
leaning house reads, "Hair Wacker." Then, an arrow pointing
south, down a dirt road and a hand-lettered sign, "Bucktail
Taxidermy."

How did you teach yourself all the names of the plants,
grandmother, the songs of the birds? How did you find time to
learn how to play the flute, read all those books? Your daughter, Minnie, passed the state test to teach with nothing more
than what you'd taught her at home.

"My grandmother had all her teeth almost until the day she
died," I say out loud to my friend. "My mother stayed with my
father's parents, Walt and Edith Stocking, when she taught at

the one-room Stocking School. She said, G'ma Stocking got up early every morning and went out and brushed her teeth at the well. Winter and summer."

Dug into the sandy banks of the back roads are woodchuck holes, big as culverts; usually they come in pairs about thirty feet apart, a back entrance and a front entrance, visible a long way off because of the bright sand around the openings.

"My grandmother bought a house," my friend says, "with her earnings from house cleaning and ironing. She loaned money to her children. She visited the sick. I would go with her. She used to put Vicks up our noses so we wouldn't catch their germs."

Galvanek's Auto Auction. I tell my friend that the Stockings and the Galvaneks are related somehow, back when my grandfather, Erastus Stocking, had a daughter who married one of the Galvaneks. The sky is now a thick curtain of gray, dense as the fur on a mole. We have gone from a day of strong shadows to no shadows.

We stop at Stocking Corners where the brick house still squarely fronts the road. The cement walk leads straight out from the front porch into the lawn, ending abruptly as if going to meet company halfway.

The log cabin you loved and lived in first, grandmother, has returned to earth, a jumble of old logs overgrown by lilacs and honeysuckle. The windmill, the well, the granary, the woodshed, the corncrib, the smokehouse, the outhouse, the chicken coop, the fox kennels, the pig sty, all gone. Where the large barn used to be, stands only the silo.

Someone from Chicago has turned your old homestead into a bed and breakfast. They've put up a pole barn for snowmobiles and dirt bikes next to the house, a giant jukebox in the living room, a plush acrylic bear on the wall of the dining room, posters of Elvis and Marilyn in the parlor.

"Labor Day weekend," I tell my friend, "was when they got their wood for the winter. My Cousin Glenn said everyone came home and cut and stacked wood for grandma and grandpa. Grandpa wanted her to have this big, red-brick house, but she wanted to stay in the log home."

"Easier to clean," my friend says.

"My father built her a log cabin next to our house in Cadillac, like that first log home. She lived there after grandpa died and then with us until we moved."

Remember, grandmother, how you made cookies inside at the woodstove while you had us making cookies outside in the sandbox? Same pans, same aprons, same spatulas and our "stove" an old board on a sawhorse where we pretended it was real. Everything you taught us was like a mirrored dance of the imagined and the real.

I look at the upstairs windows and think I see something move. "What if we see an apparition?"

My friend says, "I won't see it. You might. I brought the picnic to have on the porch. I thought we should do that. Soft-shelled crab and Rothschild wine. My husband loved soft-shelled crabs. He always bought them. He would cook them, too. He was an excellent cook." She pauses, then says, "My husband didn't like picnics. And he would never approve of using this wine here. He would be shocked."

"Good," I tell her, "that's good."

Everything we do changes us, changes the world. A hand lifted here, a breath taken there, shifts the universe. On the other side of the globe the quality of light in the Bosporus is noticeably different than it was in the moments before my friend unpacked the soft-shelled crabs and the Rothschild wine.

We sit on the porch and she pulls wine glasses from a beautiful wicker picnic basket, a gift from her son. "He has good taste, too," she says, "like his father." She spreads out a blue-and-white-checked tablecloth on the crumbling cement. It's overcast, the air dense with moisture. It rains a few drops and then stops.

My friend pours us each a glass of this wine, each swallow more costly than the gold necklace I saw and coveted in the Metropolitan Museum catalog, more costly than a used auto from Galvanek's, and tells me these soft-shelled crabs can only be harvested for a few days at exactly this time of year and have to be flown in fresh from the coast. The parchment-colored label on the bottle shows a chateau in France surrounded by a wall, and inside the wall, a series of walled and terraced gardens. But here in America we're free.

People say, "Nothing lasts." But they're wrong. The fact is, everything lasts. Out of the chemical soup, the primordial mud, we make meaning, we make ourselves.

My friend and I finish our repast of crab and wine. She says she wants to pick some of your rhubarb and goes off toward a patch beyond where the windmill used to be. I see old-fashioned, fuchsia-colored roses, the same shade as the ones by my clothesline at home in Leelanau County, and then further on, bright orange poppies under the gray sky, a bearded purple iris.

She is picking things to take back. An artist at heart, she instinctively wants the visual. I'm grateful that you were in my life and that somehow you are still in my life. Lives laced with love are never lost. I'm taking you back with me, and then on, and on, who knows where, but you'll be there, I think, since you always have been, more than a memory, something not tangible, not definable, but real and lasting, nevertheless, more real and more lasting maybe than this discernable world.

The day drains the color from the land. The light is the light in a diorama, or a garden under glass. My friend puts the rhubarb and a few of the flowers on the back seat of the car and when I glance at them there, their colors seem to hold—like a talisman of the past—the farm, as we head back to the Leelanau Peninsula and the present.

CALIFORNIA

Soledad

The state prison at Soledad, out in the Central Valley where all the lettuce is grown, is at least three hours south of where I live in California, so during the days of training I stay at a cheap motel over on the coast, close to the Valley but not in it. The training takes place in a flimsy, single-story, pre-fabricated building on the prison grounds adjacent to the main administration building.

We are told that it costs more to have a man in prison than it does to send him to Harvard for a year. We are told that only ten percent of prisoners are women and most of those are in for helping some guy. We are told that in Spain a prisoner has to pay for his own incarceration. We are told we should always say, "Correctional Training Facility" and not use the word *prison*. We are told to bring our own water and not to drink from the drinking fountains in the correctional training facility since tuberculosis and other diseases are rampant in this and all correctional training facilities.

Things that a few people in the general population knew anecdotally, by word of mouth, things that have since been documented, weren't widely known then. Most of the people I knew back in Michigan would have had no idea, for example, that in 1999 the United States had almost two million people in prison, close to one in a hundred Americans, an astonishing number, more people in prison than any country anywhere, more than Russia. And if they had known this, it wouldn't have meant anything to them. According to an editorial in *The New York Times* December 29, 2014, there are now 2.4 million people in prison in the United States.

We are not told at the training session that a thicket of bureaucratic rules—rules that are constantly being changed—made it difficult for family members to visit their relatives in prison and to give and receive the emotional support necessary to keep the family together and prevent recidivism. We are not told that it's hard for felons to find work once they are released from prison. We are not told that thousands of prisoners are serving life terms for non-violent crimes.

These things would have been known by the trainers in 1999 but they aren't brought up and questions were not invited. Since that time the situations for prisoners and their families, and the conditions in prisons, have been reported and well-documented. *The New York Times* in the past three or four years has had articles about many aspects of incarceration by reporters Timothy Williams, Binyamin Applebaum, Erik Eckholm and others.

There are many books now about prisons and there are even programs on TV, so I've heard. (I don't have a TV.) The eighty-year-old reporter, James Ridgeway, began in 2010 publishing excerpts of letters from people in solitary confinement on his web site, *Solitary Watch*. Ridgeway's latest book, *Hell Is a Very Small Place*, co-edited with Jean Casella and Sarah Shourd, was published in February 2016.

In 1999 the stories about these things were mostly anecdotal. Somebody who knew somebody who knew somebody had talked about it. That was one of the ways I'd heard things about the prisons, when I was on a fellowship at the Blue Mountain Center for Artists and Writers in the Adirondacks in 1998. One of the artists there had been teaching art in a prison near Los Angeles. The conversations I had with that artist and with some other people I met at Blue Mountain had ultimately led me to accept an appointment from the William James Foundation in Palo Alto to come out to teach in the California prisons.

We are not told by the trainers that, although people of

color only make up one-quarter of the population in the United States, more than half of the people in prison are African American, Native American or Hispanic, something that is now common knowledge. Several scholars, including but not limited to Ruth Wilson Gilmore, author of the *Golden Gulag* published in 2007, and Michelle Alexander, author of *The New Jim Crow* published in 2010, have done decades of research and produced excellent books about the incarceration and justice system in the United States.

We are not told, although it was known then, that in 1999 more than a hundred thousand juveniles were incarcerated, according to the United States Office of Juvenile Justice and Delinquency Prevention, or that more than half would return to prison at some point as adults. We are not told that even imprisoned children are held in solitary confinement. We are not told children in foster care age out when they're eighteen, often then becoming involved in drug dealing or other crimes to support themselves because they lack the skills, family support and good judgment to do otherwise. John Otis, reporting in *The New York Times* December 9, 2013 has covered this issue, as have many others.

Wikipedia didn't exist in 1999. It wouldn't be launched until January 2001 and even then, the articles and entries were few and far between compared to what is there now. It would be another ten years before people could Google and find information that was well-documented, and could be cross-referenced, about prisons and everything else. The technology that has created an information explosion was still being developed. The video recording of the black man, Eric Garner, saying, "I can't breathe," in 2015, and the video following the shooting by a policeman of Michael Brown, a young black man in Ferguson in 2014, were still in the future. Although cameras are still not allowed in prisons and journalists aren't welcome inside the gates, things like James Ridgeway's blog with the letters from people in solitary confinement can be found online.

Everything that's wrong with the prison system now, in 2016, was wrong in 1999, but no one talked about it then. If something appeared in the newspapers, it was about a particular prison riot, maybe, or some prisoner who had committed suicide, as if these things were isolated incidents. It was like the early days of slavery in America when, to whatever extent there were any stories at all, word of mouth or in the newspapers, it was about a badly managed plantation in one place or a few rowdy slaves in another place, it was never about the whole system being an abomination.

Joan Didion, that brilliant woman and California native, wrote about all the prisons springing up in economically desperate towns in California in her book, *Where I Was From*, published in 2003. But her writing was in the context of her lucky, wealthy, and richly endowed California childhood, it never got to be about other people's childhoods or children in general, or how people all across America were struggling to raise children while lacking good-paying jobs, time for their families, and decent schools in safe neighborhoods. Her book wasn't about society's lack of support for families and the negative impact this was having on children, children who were going to be lucky to get an education, find work, stay out of jail, and in some parts of the country, stay alive.

When I was sitting in the training session at Soledad in 1999, there were few studies on the number of foster care children who ended up in prison. A study conducted by the University of Chicago in 2005, based on three Midwestern states, concluded that thirty-five percent of children who were once in foster care will spend time behind bars as adults, but there was almost nothing in the 1990s beyond obscure studies somewhere or other and what there was never became public knowledge.

Most people I knew in my community back home believed then, and still do, that how children are raised and nurtured is crucial to their becoming good citizens. On the rural Leelanau Peninsula, which is only about thirty miles long and just about that wide at its base, there are four well-endowed public libraries with special rooms for children and special programs; most people take their children to the library every other week or so. They teach them about the beauty of nature by taking them to the beach and going for walks in the woods. Kids are taught how to swim or play baseball, how to cook and take care of animals, shown how to do carpentry or fix a car. Children are encouraged to find jobs when they're old enough to work and parents drive them to those jobs and let them keep the money they earn. These parents spend years nurturing their children, with the overall goal being that their children will become adults who have a good work ethic and marketable skills, become loving parents to their own children, and make a contribution to society.

The prison system, on the other hand, and the foster care system seem to be based on a much older idea about human life. This older paradigm, the one that created the caste system and the feudal system, seems to be based on the view that people are born the way they are going to be. In this view, parents are responsible for providing food and shelter but not a whole lot more. It was to be expected, as part of the natural scheme of things, that some people would grow up and do bad things. Who knows why? And these bad people, who did bad things for no discernable reason, would be executed or put in prison. The whole point of prisons was to keep the bad people away from the good people.

Back in Michigan I had read everything I could get my hands on about incarceration, everything from Calderon de la Barca's *Life Is a Dream*, and Nelson Mandela's accounts of his imprisonment up through famous prisoners such as Julian Hawthorne (son of Nathaniel), Jack London, George Jackson, Leonard Peltier, and Mumia Abu-Jamal as well as the barely fictionalized autobiographical accounts of prison life in Janet Fitch's *White Oleander*, and Edward Bunker's *No Beast*

So Fierce. One of the best books was a Penguin anthology of prison writings, *Prison Writings in 20ᵗʰ Century America*, edited by A. Bruce Franklin and with a foreword by *The New York Times* journalist Tom Wicker. I was planning on using it as a textbook.

George Jackson's book, *Soledad Brother: the Prison Letters of George Jackson*, is banned at Soledad for the inmates. Perhaps Jackson's book is off limits for the presenters, too. It doesn't appear that they have read it, or much of anything about their line of work. Jackson was transferred from Soledad to San Quentin where he was shot while trying to escape. Jackson became a folk hero, mythologized in story and song, including a ballad by Bob Dylan with the line, "They cut George Jackson down...he wouldn't bow down or kneel, authorities they hated him, because he was just too real."

State-wide budget cuts, loss of programs, overcrowding, increasing incidences of deadly contagious diseases, riots, and routine violence were already making California prisons some of the most dangerous in the nation, a nightmare for guards and prisoners alike, but there was little public awareness of this, and none of the trainers, who certainly must have known about it, mention these things, and any discussion of issues is not part of the training.

The first morning I listen, making a show of taking careful notes. At noon my supervisor asks to see my notes and I show him. "What are you taking notes for?" he wants to know. I tell him I'd thought we might be tested. I tell him I'll be happy not to take notes.

Training, beyond some statistics, is about things like how to work a fire extinguisher, and how to spy on the prisoners although what they actually say is, "how to report anything unusual to the guards." I'm sitting there thinking that naturally I'll be reporting anything unusual, and probably not just about the prisoners and probably not just to the guards, but about the whole place to everyone I know. It may be their prison, but it's my country. I think it is unusual—in fact amazing—that they spend three, mind-numbing hours showing us how to use a fire extinguisher.

Fortunately or unfortunately, depending, but fortunately in this case, my looks are deceiving. I look like the most spaced-out, uncoordinated, naturally physically awkward, sheltered, poetry-loving, middle class, not-a-thought-in-my-head, straight-laced and inattentive person in the world. It's just the way I come across, or it's one of the ways I can come across: the middle-aged lady from the Garden Club in dowdy clothes and flat shoes, the last person in the world to smell smoke in a burning building. A friend once imitated me, portraying me as the Scarecrow in *The Wizard of Oz*, "Oh the thoughts that I'd be thinkin', I'd be like Abraham Lincoln, if I only had a brain," with my legs flopping out and my hands dangling at the ends of my arms. All I need to say usually, to have people totally drop their defenses and see me as completely unthreatening, is a sweet and heartfelt, "Oh, my."

I call to mind the woman-artist who'd first told me about the William James Foundation's art and writing programs in the California prisons, when we'd both been at Blue Mountain. She had told me that if I applied, I should emphasize the poetry and creative writing part of my background, and not to let anyone know I had a background in journalism. This woman taught in the prisons near Los Angeles and also made art about the prisons.

One of her paintings, a large canvas, all grays and blues except for the whitish-blackish, fluorescent-light-shadowed, naked bodies of men, all lined up against the wall in a long arsenic-colored corridor, all looking out of the canvas, perhaps fifty men, half on each side of the narrow corridor, like a line of telephone poles with scared eyes and bare buttocks, all diminishing in the distance, like a lesson on perspective. The painting was called, *Strip Search during Lockdown*. She said she had seen this, and in order to get the image out of her mind, had to paint it. The bodies looked dead.

"The people who work in the prisons don't want anyone to know how frightened they are," the artist had said. "They're terrified of being killed. It's a war zone. There are gang wars. There are guards who are good people, but there are also guards who dehumanize the prisoners in any way they can in order to get the upper hand. They withhold privileges. They change the rules all the time for no reason. The whole prison system, the court system, too, is badly broken and they have no idea how to fix it."

She was a tall, thin woman with a brusque manner and a mannish walk. "Ninety-nine percent of the people in prison are not nice people, are guilty as charged," she said. "Don't ask questions. Watch your back."

Now I sit through the hours of training with about thirty other people—future guards, secretaries, and the random writing teacher from Michigan—all of us with "pleasant" and noncommittal expressions on our faces.

At noon I find a Mexican restaurant on the town's Main Street: the best shrimp gazpacho I've ever had in my life. I will eat it so often over the next few weeks that I'll learn how to make it. My supervisor and some of the trainers are there, but they pretend not to see me. I finish my food quickly so I don't have to pretend that I don't see them pretending not to see me.

It's hot outside at noon, but clear and sunny in that California way. I decide to walk around the center of town. The sun is so bright that wherever there is any shade at all, the shade looks almost black.

The white people in the town of Soledad in the Central Valley in the fall of 1999 look uncannily like extras from a 1950s cowboy movie. The men are tall with ropey muscles and weather-worn faces. Some of the men look like it's been days since they had a bath. I overhear one actually saying, "MAY-am" for ma'am, and another saying "little lady." The white women are dressed in cotton house dresses, and the Hispanic women are similarly dressed but I see only a few Hispanic women. I see just one Hispanic man. He's sleeping under a giant sombrero with his back against a white stucco wall. At first I think he's a prop, a yard ornament, and then he shifts in his sleep: he's real. There are lots of small, young Hispanic children playing on the sidewalks.

The afternoon's session is all about women guards and teachers, and especially women artists and writers, who'd fallen in love with prisoners. The fear that it might happen, at least in my sense of it as they're talking about it, seems to far exceed the few times that it appears to have actually happened. Also, if AIDS and all those other diseases were as prevalent as they say, wouldn't that act as a deterrent?

During our lunch break the second day, my supervisor and I eat quickly in the prison cafeteria and then he gives me a tour. I learn he's a musician. He teaches a class in music and is in charge of the art, writing, and music programs. His wife is an elementary school teacher. He shows me the gym at the prison, now closed. He shows me the music room but says they don't have the money to replace old or broken instruments. I ask him if he plays in a band when he's not working at the prison and he says he does. My supervisor seems like a genuine lover of music. He must have taken this job at a time that it seemed like he could indulge his love of music, inspire others, and pay the bills. Now he's stuck in a decaying institution where the idealism has gone rancid.

He shows me the library, now closed. He introduces me to the prisoner who works as the librarian. I ask why they have a librarian if the library is closed, and my supervisor says prisoners can request books off a list and they need the librarian to handle the paperwork. My supervisor says that when he had first come to the prison twenty years earlier, there were all kinds of programs for education and rehabilitation but the public now objects to paying for such programs for prisoners.

Most of the programs have been reduced to almost nothing or discontinued altogether. This is a hardship for the prison staff, my supervisor says, since without programs the prison population is more difficult to manage. For example, he tells me, Soledad recently had a prison-wide protest about the food. My supervisor says that the food is no different than it ever was and if the prisoners had had something else to occupy their minds, they wouldn't have found fault with the food.

He's a small, fit, tense man, the kind of person we'd call high strung back in Michigan. It's hard to tell how old he is. He seems to be somewhere in his late fifties or early sixties. He has a smile, but it's never quite in response to anything. It always makes me want to do a double-take, which I have to consciously keep myself from doing. For anyone who's ever watched Richard Nixon on TV, where Nixon would raise his finger to make a point a few seconds after he'd made the point, that's what my supervisor's smile is like.

Before I leave on the last day of training they give me a large beeper and a heavy man's belt on which to wear it. In my car, I try to use the beeper. It's clear I'll need lessons. The belt, a bit like one of my son's tool belts, makes me look like Annie Oakley or Calamity Jane. They also have given me a huge, hideous fluorescent-orange whistle to wear around my neck; it looks like Donald Duck's beak in children's cartoons. The whistle is self-explanatory, but when I pull off to a place above the ocean to try it out, it's not particularly loud. In a riot, who would hear me?

Instinct tells me that the visible whistle and the beeper are a bad idea. Montaigne, quoting Seneca, said, "Locked places invite the thief. The burglar passes by what is open." Montaigne lived during a time of civil war. Once he invited a troop of soldiers in, only to learn they were planning to take over his home. They didn't, as it turns out, because, the leader said, he was charmed by his host's "face and frankness."

You don't need to have one of history's great minds to figure out this kind of thing. Common sense would tell just about anyone that when hopelessly out-numbered and out-gunned, as well as physically inept, it's better to rely on compassion and transparency, even if it's subterfuge. A friend who was in the Peace Corps in Nigeria during a civil war got to a border at night in a jeep. The driver decided to run the blockade. Men with AK-47s shot out the jeep's tires and the jeep, naturally, went into a ditch. My friend, who knew Swahili, jumped out of the jeep, hands up, and said to the guard, in Swahili, "How is your family?" The guard, thinking he must somehow know this man, put down his gun and said, "My family's fine."

When I get back to San Francisco, I decide to stop and visit my son on the way out to my apartment at Stinson Beach. I don my new accessories in the car and walk into his house.

I look so ridiculous he can't stop laughing. I'm little and old and plump and the beeper and the orange whistle are so out of character that anyone looking at me would wonder about my judgment. The outfit says, "I'm a little old lady, folks, but I think I'm a cop. Put that in your pipe and smoke it." My daughter-in-law says I look like I'm in security guard drag, like someone at Halloween. All I need to complete the outfit is an orange Afro-wig, a too-large pink bow and floppy, green shoes.

That weekend in San Francisco I buy a small purse with a long strap so the beeper can hang at waist level and be relatively unobtrusive. I put the whistle on a nondescript string and find that, if my blouse is very loose, I can tuck the whistle inside. I want to blend in. I don't want to call attention to myself. "Hi, here I am. Come and get me if you dare. Don't I look like I'd make a good hostage?" I have pictured in my mind being in a prison riot. I imagine the panic and terror. I imagine some violent, not very bright prisoner seeing the large fluorescent orange whistle around my neck on its thick fluorescent orange string, and deciding to use it to choke me within an inch of my life and holding me in front of him as a human shield.

I want my students to think I'm their friend. Maybe I am, and maybe I'm not, but it's in my best interests to have them *think* I'm their friend. Having the whistle is one thing; I might need it. But wearing it where all the prisoners can see it, especially the ones who are not in my classes, the ones who don't know me and have no reason to like me, and giving some moron several weeks head start to plan how to disable the big, orange whistle and me, is not smart.

I live near Point Reyes so I have a long drive to Soledad. I get up at three in the morning so I can arrive by the time the gates open at 8 A.M. As time goes by, I develop a routine. I stop at the McDonald's in Soledad before driving out to the prison in the Salinas Valley. This gives me time to mentally prepare myself for the work and arrive a few minutes early, relaxed and ready for the day.

THE CENTRAL VALLEY

California's climate is warmer than Michigan's, but some things are the same. In the autumn in the Central Valley—where all the food is grown—they have the same short days and thin fall light that we have back in Michigan. In Michigan we have the same sky but with cold, sleet, and snow under it, and trees with bare black branches. We don't have rows of iceberg lettuce growing under the pale light and we don't have tule fog. At first I thought tule fog was like the tulle net for wedding dresses but one of the guards said the word comes from a native word for the reeds that used to grow in the Valley. Many of the guards grew up in the Valley, where their families had been doing back-breaking, poorly-paid field work for generations.

The first prison building went up in the late 1940s and more were added up through the 1990s. Some of the guards have fathers or even grandfathers who were guards. A symbiotic relationship has developed over the years between the people in the prison and the people in the town, a consciousness of an "*us*" and a "*them*" that to me, as a newcomer, seems out of proportion. I'm wary of it.

Salinas, I learn, means salt works in Spanish. The Salinas River is a river in sand and dries up in the summer. In the winter water runs through it from the mountains. Along the edges are salt marshes and that's where the tule reeds grow. The Valley during the 1930s was the setting for John Steinbeck's *Of Mice and Men* where the field workers fought and drank and, I suppose, still do.

The prison work is dangerous—at least four guards have died in the line of duty at The Salinas Valley Correctional Training Facility over the years—but the work pays enough to support a family, and it isn't stoop work out in the hot sun with constant exposure to agricultural pesticides. There are worse jobs than being a prison guard and everyone who works in the prison knows it, because they pass by the field workers every day on their way to the prison.

OVER THE WALL

The Salinas Valley Correctional Training Facility is a large prison, almost six thousand people crammed together in a space meant for three thousand, spread out over several separate buildings. I teach a morning class in one building and an afternoon class in another. Only the best-behaved and the most qualified are allowed writing classes so my students are the best of six thousand. They are some of the best students I've ever had. In composite form, with distinguishing characteristics changed, I'll describe some of them.

There's the self-taught twenty-five-year-old who carries his "library" around: dog-eared copies of Nietzsche, Sun Tsu's *The Art of War*, Machiavelli, Frederick Douglass, Mandela, Martin Luther King, Jr., Malcolm X, Freud, Jung, Julian Jaynes.

He wants me to see what he's reading. His mother sends him the books. He's a young African American who talks about his strong and loving mother—a nurse—and his five-year-old daughter.

There's the African American who's also Native American and talks about how much his black grandfather loved his Indian grandmother and about "the men on the money"—Washington, Jefferson, Jackson—and their enslavement of black Americans and genocide of Indian Americans. He compares them to Pol Pot and Hitler.

There's the quiet intellectual writing a treatise on the prisons as slave labor camps, making the connection between the history of slavery and the history of incarceration in the United States. He says—and it's true—that during the Reconstruction Era after the Civil War, many former slaves were captured and put into chain gangs after having been arrested on some pretext such as vagrancy. He's a sixty-year-old man who would have been paroled, but the rules had changed from twenty-five-to-life to simply, life, by the time he came up for parole. At his request, he says his wife divorced him when they learned he was never coming up for parole. It was just too hard to continue.

There's the smooth-talking Jamaican with a lilting accent who tells about his Oxford-educated English friend, a homeless man, who'd invited him for "breakfast" at his dumpster in Detroit.

There's the wild-eyed Scot, an ex-marine, who tells about his love for his Hispanic step-father, a calm and gentle man who was never without a camera to photograph all his children, a man who told him he would be able to roll his r's if he ate more jalapenos.

And there are many more, all ages, all different. Most are African American, many are Hispanic, some are white and some are American Indian. To the best of my knowledge none of my students are Asian. With a few exceptions, all the men are bulked up because they work out in their cells so they will be able to defend themselves and also because they have nothing else to do. I start the first day with a dozen or so students in each class, morning and afternoon, and end up with about twice that many in each class by the end of the next week.

None of the men seem to be friends with each other. I learn that friendships are discouraged in the prisons since any friendship could be seen as a conspiracy, an attempt to form an alliance that might threaten or undermine the prison authorities. None of the men make overtures of friendship toward me. There is great distance between me and my students, and among themselves, as well.

Some of my students are a little off, like the seventy-year-old white doctor called 'Doc' by the other students. Doc constantly nods off in class. I ask my supervisor if I can expel Doc from my class and he says I can't. Doc's behavior is the reason I ask my supervisor if I can read my students' jackets, which is what their files are called. My supervisor says I can, and he comes with me. I learn Doc really had been a doctor in Florida. He'd killed his wife in front of his children, his neighbors, and a TV crew, but insists he's innocent. My supervisor is bored. After letting me read three files, he says, "That's enough."

I believe, along with the artist I'd met at Blue Mountain who had worked in the prisons, that most of the prisoners are not innocent. But I also believe that even the worst person has good qualities. It's my job as a writing teacher to find those good parts and expand on them, and I can do that more readily if I know the back-story.

I spend a lot of time building my students up, trying to empower them. For my African American, Native American, and Hispanic students I tell them about all the famous writers down through history of their own ethnic or racial background. Yes, I tell them, most of the famous writers you hear about in school are white, but that doesn't mean that's all there is. I remind my black students of famous intellectuals such as Aesop, Pushkin, Eratosthenes, St. Augustine (North African/

Berber), Alexandre Dumas, James Baldwin, Alice Walker, Nelson Mandela, and Martin Luther King, Jr. For the Hispanic students there's Calderon de la Barca, Cervantes, Marquez, Neruda, Isabelle Allende. Native American students have Leonard Peltier, James Welch, Scott Momaday, Leslie Silko and Sherman Alexie. I tell them I think the racism and sexism in their prison—and in our society—is stupid; very, very stupid. I don't tolerate it in my class. "Think what you want," I say, "but keep your thoughts to yourself."

They love knowing that Shakespeare was a regular guy. "His mother was illiterate," I tell them. "He comes up to London and he starts to cross London Bridge, and there's his uncle's head on a spike—gang warfare—Protestants and the Catholics killing each other: craziness. And if you changed sides, or if they *thought* you'd changed sides, woe betide." They love *woe betide* and want to know what it means, "Bad things coming your way," I say. They want it written on the board.

Every cook loves to cook for hungry eaters and every teacher loves to teach eager learners. I had been told that this would be one of the best teaching gigs I'd ever have and it's true.

Read, I tell them, you may be in a benighted system but you can enlighten yourselves. "Get the books and read them," I say, quoting Lincoln, "your ability to read and comprehend is the same in all places." I tell them that less than a hundred thousand years ago we were all in Africa, that skin color is only one of hundreds of pieces of DNA. I tell them about the volcano Toba that exploded and darkened the sky seventy thousand years ago and killed off all but about ten thousand of us. "Expand your awareness," I tell them. "There's more than this. There's more than you. Think about it."

Doc is a problem. He's insolent, and doesn't participate, and pretends to sleep. How did he get through medical school? Is he in the early stages of dementia? I don't like him. He's messing with my class. His smile is a crooked wire where his mouth should have been. I wonder if he knows I can't expel him. He has age-spotted arms attached to a fat belly. His amphibious legs dangle off his chair. I don't usually like or dislike people because of their physical appearance but because he's playing head games, I'm beginning to loathe him. He's a horrible human frog. I try to control my revulsion by treating him as if he's normal, but anyone with any sensitivity has surely figured this out: too normal is not normal.

I tell Doc he probably needs to be somewhere else, maybe somewhere he can sleep. At this the other students laugh and tell me Doc's nodding-off is a ruse: Doc's building a case to get out of 5 A.M. kitchen duty. For the first time I realize the other students don't like him either. Group dynamics will take care of this. "Hear what they're sayin', Doc, my friend? Cat's out of the bag." After that he stays awake.

We are together for three hours and it feels like thirty minutes. I run my writing classes the way many are run, with in-class assignments using prompts from great literature. The men work hard. These are men who already know, for the most part, that "the life of the mind" is probably the only life they're ever going to have. It's a sad truth, but it's good for my writing classes. I say to them, "My mom always told me that my education is something no one would ever be able to take away from me. So read. Educate yourselves. Learn. Write." I'm part-preacher, part-teacher and they seem to thrive with that. I wonder if they ever had anyone tell them how to live.

Students, if they wish, read their work out loud. It's never a requirement. I have one requirement, I tell all my students the first day: be kind. This means that when someone is reading we sit and listen politely: no sniggering, no eye-rolling, no rude slouching. Courtesy in all things. Students can only comment if the reader invites comments and the comments have to be positive.

I tell my students that they can't swear in their writing or use explicit sexual scenes because we're in mixed company. I also tell them that I've been teaching writing for years and that people—all people: inmates, old ladies, and young children—often produce alarmingly explicit sexual or gory or scatological scenes in their writing and that they shouldn't be at all concerned if they do this: the creative parts of the brain and the creative parts of the body are connected. However, one of the things a writer learns, as part of the skill set, is about audience and also how to edit. The rule: write it, but don't share it in class if it's too sexual or too gory. Don't be ashamed of your human nature but don't throw it in people's faces. Spare us. No profanity. At the end of every class, I give an out-of-class assignment. I tell them they can write as much as they want, but to only turn in five pages because I won't have time to read more than that.

When you're in a room with twenty guys the size of refrigerators, and you know half of them are killers from the low letters on their numbers, and the huge stoic guy who is reading is so choked up he has to give his writing to someone else to read, and several of the guys have tears in their eyes, and the writing is stunningly good and honest—about the cause of the Zapatistas, about the father who died in prison, about the wife he loves and will never be able to hold in his arms again—all you can do, like being in church, is sit quietly.

These are men who've been taught not to speak, but in my class they are free. It's as if they are, somehow, somewhere else. The guards come by sometimes and look in, as if worried that we are being too quiet and are up to something. I always give them my best 'Mrs. Kindhead from the Community Chest' smile. And then we go back to work.

In order to get people to write, and share their writing, I'd learned over the years of teaching, it's my job to create a safe space and also, as needed, reroute the group away from anything awkward. One day a man who was in for rape (which I knew because his was one of three jackets I was allowed to read) reads a piece that, while not sexual, has an underlying current of misogyny. I can see the men sitting more stiffly than usual, perhaps wondering how I will handle this. I thank the student for his reading and then say, "I have a story I'd like to read to you, if that's ok?"

They all nod yes. I probably could have read them the New York City telephone book at that point and it would have been a welcome relief. I pull the children's book, *Amos and Boris* by William Steig, from my things, and read it to them. The story is about a friendship between and whale and a mouse, well-written and well-illustrated. I tell them sometimes a friendship—for example between a woman and a man, or a mouse and a whale—can require a leap of faith, but it's in that leap that we discover beauty, transcendence, the truth of our own and another's spirit. I read slowly. I show them the drawings, too. I finish just as the class ends. I ask the students to each write five pages on friendship for the next class, and tell them I'll write something, too.

One of the students, a quiet and polite bilingual Hispanic man, a man who the week before had borrowed a Spanish edition of *News of a Kidnapping* by Gabriel Garcia Marquez, passes by my desk very close after that class and says, in the hubbub and cover noise of everyone moving their desks and walking out, almost under his breath, "We think you're a genius, Miss, don't quit."

RETURNING TO STINSON BEACH

It doesn't occur to me until I'm driving home that night and going back over the events of the day, like a blind person touching an unfamiliar object, feeling for every nuance that might tell me where I am and what is happening, and trying to make sense of things, that I again see the way the student passed by my desk when he was leaving the classroom, with his head down, and the way he spoke out of the corner of his mouth. In thinking about when and where he spoke and how he kept his voice low, I finally realize there are almost certainly cameras in the room and probably audio tapes too, recording every word.

Not knowing anything about people in prison, I learn as the weeks go by that my students are hungry for normal life. This makes perfect sense, but I would have had no way of knowing that until I was there. I instantly give up on the idea of using the Penguin *Prison Writings in the 20th Century* as a textbook in the classroom. I'm learning that what they like best are my descriptions of the ocean, the sea otters, the calla lilies, and the wind on the coast. They love to write about food and how to prepare it.

My students want me to teach them about grammar as if it's some deep mystery. I tell them grammar is about consistency and clarity and that in Shakespeare's time there was no standardized spelling or grammar. I tell them about the parts of speech, about driving west and having trouble with my car. "The man is on one of those skateboard things and he slides out from under the car and he says, "The F'ing F'er is F'd." It takes them a minute. I say. "He has used the F-word as every part of speech." I write it on the board, reminding them we can't swear, and ask them to say which word is the noun, or subject, which is the verb, or action word, and which is the adjective, or descriptive word. They understand quite quickly. Grammar, demystified.

I write, "Snuffy could not walk any farther and he refused to discuss it further" on the board and ask them to define the difference between farther and further. They do this, too, determining that farther is definite and physical and further is abstract or in the mind, metaphysical. When they ask me what metaphysical means I tell them to find a dictionary and look it up. "Words mean something," I tell them. "Sometimes their meaning is subtle. Knowing the difference between further and farther might be important."

I tell them grammar can be fun, a game, but that good writing, writing that lasts, and writing that moves people, is very little about grammar and a whole lot about honesty, courage, and having ideas that will help people know how to live in this world. Ideas are imbedded in stories in order to trick and lull people into listening. A writer can only keep an audience with narratives. Storytelling is as old as humanity. I tell them there are hundreds and hundreds of things to know about grammar and that I cannot teach them in the little time we have. What I will do, I tell them, is if I notice several students making the same mistake, like conflating and confusing "its" the possessive, and "it's" the contraction, I will take a few minutes during every class to address grammar, probably no more than one issue per class. I don't want to take up class time going over things they can find in a book.

I tell them they should get a standard book on grammar, if they are serious about writing. Any grammar book will do the job. Grammar is something they can learn on their own. I recommend *The Elements of Style* by William Strunk Jr. and E. B. White. This is a slim, efficient volume, which I tell them is often assigned in college classes. If I can find free grammar books in the boxes of books public libraries in the Bay Area usually have available to give away, I'll bring some in.

One of the favorite anecdotes of my students is one I share about my friend's daughter's first day at kindergarten back in Michigan, where she writes down rules for school and one of them is to "not act up in circle." So the next time I see them, we spend a whole class writing rules to live by using Confucius, Walt Whitman, the Bible, Shakespeare, and John Irving's *Cider House Rules*, as patterns. We have the speech from *Hamlet* where old Polonius, the fuddy-duddy, the father of Hamlet's girlfriend, tells Hamlet how to do right and be right, the "to thine own self be true" and so on. We talk about "phony" rules, pedantic rules and meaningless or cliché rules. It's not as easy, they quickly learn, to write rules to live by that are sincere—and, equally important—sound sincere. Somewhat surprisingly, for a population of supposedly violent criminal types, the men talk about the importance of a society's taking care of children, the value of children, particular children in their lives, and the privilege of having children in one's life.

They want to learn about Shakespeare—Macbeth and Hamlet. We look at the "to be or not to be" speech from Hamlet, his mental confusion, and talk about times we've not been sure of our perceptions. We look at Lady Macbeth's "Out, damned spot! Out, I say!" speech about her guilt, and talk about it, talk about the relationship between Lady Macbeth and her husband and what it must have been like to want to kill a king. Part of their wanting to know this stuff is simply wanting to be at the intellectual table, to be a person who knows what it is to eat the cake they've only heard about, to not be left out.

I bring in Jonathan Swift's *A Modest Proposal* where he advises raising babies to eat them. The room is dead silent when I'm done reading. The men are flabbergasted.

Finally, I say, "What do you think of that?" After a minute or two goes by in numb silence, one of my most lethal students—all the men give him a wide berth—at last seems to find his voice and steps up to it, to speak for all of them. The first day of class I had recognized this man's ability to call out a hit on me or do it himself. I had also decided to let it go. I'm there to make things better. I'm there to try to figure out what's going on in our society. I'm not there to survive, at least not as my first purpose.

He says, slowly, "Now, that's some *cold* thinkin' you got there." They had thought it was real.

I explain satire. I explain Ireland and poverty, and England and a time three hundred and fifty years earlier. I tell them that at the time of the Roman conquest of England, two thousand years ago, the British were raising their children to sell them, a cash crop. I tell them that five thousand years ago gladiators— often noblemen captured in war—fought to the death for the amusement of their conquerors.

I tell them that moral behavior, like everything else that is human, has evolved over time. I tell them that Jonathan Swift, who was Irish, was so angry at the British that he wrote—tongue in cheek—to show them how barbaric the English were toward the Irish, to let the children of the Irish starve. Swift is fighting with words, I tell them. This is the hardest kind of fighting but, if you do it well, and you're lucky, it will last. Stories in the Bible, probably first oral and then written down, have lasted at least five thousand years. Why? Because, in most cases, they're really good stories.

At last, there are some smiles, then some giddy jokes.

At the end of the first few weeks my supervisor says, "The work you're getting out of the men is good. It could be published in a broadside. It'll make the program look good."

I wonder how he knows what kind of writing they're producing. I haven't shown it to him. Perhaps the men have shared it with him but this seems improbable.

"They think you have a lot of class." He pauses. He clears his throat, "But you need to be more careful about the signals you give. I don't want you touching them."

I tell him that, to the best of my knowledge, I have never touched a student. It won't occur to me until much later that in fact I am touching my students, but not physically. I'm reaching out to them and connecting simply by being a responsive human being. Although he probably couldn't have articulated this, I'm guessing he doesn't want me touching them metaphysically either.

My supervisor says, "Next week I want you to come at 8:15 A.M., instead of 7:50 A.M. I'm afraid you're trying to do too much."

The next week I come at 8:15 A.M. and my supervisor comes down to meet me at the gate at 8:20 A.M., saying in a harsh tone, "I was here at 8:10 A.M., where were you?"

I remind him that he'd told me not to come at 7:50 A.M., but to come at 8:15 A.M.

"Did I?" he asks. He smiles his tight, little smile.

NEW RULES

It's the end of another week at Soledad. My supervisor and I have gotten out of our cars at the same time in the parking lot. As he walks toward me he tells me I need to take all my papers, all my teaching materials, back to my car. He says he'll wait for me.

During my first week at Soledad, I'd purchased a wire basket on wheels, the kind I'd had years before in New York City for groceries. I use it to haul my teaching materials. Having learned what my students are interested in reading, I bring old Sunday *New York Times*, free books from the Bay Area's public libraries, and hand-outs for the class. My students are interested in the classics. Many times libraries will have extra copies of the classics from things people have donated. The books in my cart are Shakespeare, Homer, Socrates, Tolstoy, Chekhov and Dickens. The students love Shakespeare because Shakespeare is all about power relationships and so are their lives in the prison. My supervisor had complimented me on the cart when I'd first brought it. He'd asked where I'd found it and I'd told him at a K-Mart near Richmond.

Now my supervisor tells me I can't bring the cart with my teaching materials into the classroom. The newspapers are dangerous because prisoners might start fires in their cells. The books could be stolen and then the prison would be responsible.

I'm dumbfounded. "The books are free," I say. And then, "How am I going to teach without materials? Writing and literature go hand-in-hand. Writing is thinking. Writing is about having ideas. Books help with that."

For the first time I wonder if the logical processes of my supervisor's mind are working right. His nervousness has always been worrisome, but this glimmer of slipshod reasoning is more so. Would I want to take a long trip with this man? Say for example on the Jerusalem to Jericho road in the time of Jesus, a road known to be lined with brigands and thieves, murderers and highwaymen?

He says, "You have to realize you're in a prison. I want you to be using your powers of observation and your intuition to be alert for anything out of the ordinary." He pauses. "You're being too nice to them. They're going to get the wrong idea. You're supplying them with too many outside handouts and ideas. You need to be focusing on your teaching."

I begin to explain that outside ideas and handouts are part of my teaching, but he cuts me off. He says, "You are a gifted teacher. You have enough in your head to teach without ever looking at a book." I'm thinking to myself, *Could you teach someone how to play the clarinet without a clarinet?*

He looks me up and down and tells me I need to wear my orange whistle around my neck where it's visible and keep my beeper on my belt, also visible.

I remind him that he'd told me I could wear the beeper in a small shoulder bag and that I could keep the whistle on a string around my neck and tucked inside my blouse.

He says, "New rules."

After I come back from my car he says, "How much have you spent on materials?"

I'd been given a hundred dollar limit to spend on materials for which I could submit receipts and be reimbursed. I tell him that up to this point I've spent about fifty dollars on photocopies, all of which are returned at the end of every morning class, re-used for the afternoon class and collected at the end of the day.

He says, "I don't want you to spend any more. I still have to take you to the commissary so you can pay for the belt, beeper, and whistle. That's going to cost you about fifty dollars."

This is the first I learn that I will have to pay for those hideous accoutrements.

When we get to the initial guard station at the main entrance, where they check my identity papers and run their "wand" over me, I feel a little strange, like I'm coming down with the flu. There's a strange smell, like copper pennies when you're a kid and hold them in your hand too long, or like the smell from a child who has a high fever.

The smell doesn't seem to be coming from me. It's a mineral-y smell and I think maybe it's coming from the stones of the building, that they're "sweating" in the humid fog that fills the Central Valley at this time of year. It's a strange but also familiar smell. I think maybe it's the lye in the cleaning solution they use and I just hadn't smelled it before. We move through the corridors of the building where I have my afternoon classes and then out the back, across a parking lot, and toward the building where I have my morning classes.

My Coat at McDonald's

As we cross the open yard, there's a chill wind and I suddenly realize that I've left my coat at McDonald's. It's cold. There had been snow on the mountains that morning. I tell my supervisor I want to go back and get my coat. I tell him I need to call to make sure it's there and ask them to hold it for me until noon.

He doesn't respond.

I repeat my request. He keeps walking.

I'm thinking to myself as we walk that when we get inside the building I will have to call McDonald's and tell them to hold the coat. I have no money with me for a phone call. All my money, as per prison rules, is in my locked car and my car's in the parking lot back by the entrance to the gate, a long ways away.

We continue on toward the building. My supervisor still hasn't said anything.

Inside I think there's a pay phone. I ask him if he has fifty cents so I can call McDonald's. He says, "I have a quarter. I could *loan* you a quarter." His tone of voice is that of someone who thinks he's being panhandled. He takes a quarter out of his pocket and begins tossing it.

I say, "I need a phone number."

He says, "You could use the quarter to call information."

We're in a corridor outside a row of offices, some with their doors partly open. "Can I ask someone for a phonebook?" I can't use the quarter to call information. It takes two quarters even to call information, but I don't say this since everything he's said and done since we were in the parking lot near the gate has been making no sense to me. The coat is a London Fog raincoat with a removable wool lining. It was a hand-me-down from my older sister. It looks good on me. I would be sad to lose it.

My supervisor still hasn't responded.

I say, "It's a two-hundred dollar coat. It's the only one I have."

He says, "Well! That's more than you make here in a day. Do you want to cancel your classes?"

I look at him. Is he joking?

"No," I say levelly. I realize he's not attempting to be amusing. He's deliberately trying to see if he can rattle me. He's unhappy about something and he wants me to be unhappy, too. "I've already driven all the way down here. It's a long drive, as you know. I need this job. I need the income. I also need to stay warm and so I need my coat. I think the *logical* and *sane* thing here is for me to go get my coat on the lunch hour, not cancel my classes for the whole day."

I picture my coat over the back of the booth. My mind goes back to the gray, chilly McDonald's parking lot early that morning where several buses had come in while I was eating my Egg McMuffin.

Prison guards in full body armor and carrying weapons had come in for coffee while I was there. The buses were filled with prisoners. The inmates had told me of "punishment by bus" where those prisoners who were deemed trouble-makers, agitators, or leaders would be sent to another prison, among them the dreaded Pelican Bay, the maximum security prison six hours north of San Francisco on the California coast.

There had been major news articles, one in the *Los Angeles Times*, about the "caging" at Pelican Bay where prisoners were put naked in metal cages in cold weather. Prison gangs at Pelican Bay, self-segregated by race, might have been tricked into fighting each other while guards watched and placed bets, according to some newspaper reports. In September there'd been a riot at Pelican Bay, according to Bay Area news accounts. Several prisoners had been injured and a guard had been hospitalized with a broken jaw. No one wanted to be sent to Pelican Bay.

I begin walking toward one of the offices to retrieve a phonebook when my supervisor cuts in front of me and goes in and borrows a phone book from someone. When he comes back, I say, "I still need another quarter. Should I go to my car and get one?" '*If she goes to her car,*' I can see him thinking, '*she might go to McDonald's and if she goes to McDonald's, what's to stop her from going home? What's to stop her from not coming back? What'll I tell the prison administrators? Could I have her arrested? What can I threaten her with?*'

He looks more than peeved. He looks like he wants to club me to the floor. He wrestles with his anger and then, with jerky movements—he's always walked like a drum majorette and now it's more pronounced—walks back to the office and borrows a quarter and then returns and hands it to me with a pinched look on his face. He's not being nice, but he's not being nice like a not-nice club lady. It's all body language and acidic tone of voice and head games. I wonder what his mother was like.

I make my call and to my relief the coat is still there. The man at McDonald's agrees to hold it for me. I tell my supervisor I'll go at noon and pick up the coat.

A fellow artist arrives, a huge, friendly black man who instantly reminds me of a Bernese Mountain Dog. He's a teacher I've never met before. He teaches visual art. He's wearing baggy brown corduroys and a brown Harris Tweed jacket with leather elbow patches. He's pulling a cart with all his materials. We all walk together toward the next gate, this one with a camera scan and a guard to frisk us. I'm wondering why the artist is allowed a cart for materials while I'm not, and am about to ask when my supervisor says to the art teacher in a mean voice, "You're late."

"I'm not late, man..." the teacher begins.

My supervisor cuts him off. "I can't have you being late."

The man is not late. It's 8:25 A.M. and we will be in our classes before the students get there. Anyway, since when did they care if classes started on time? Until I'd told my students to be there exactly at 8:30 A.M., my students had drifted in—and sometimes out—over the first thirty minutes or so, and the "drifting" was even more pronounced in other teachers' classes.

My Chihuahua-sized supervisor continues to berate the Bernese-Mountain-Dog-sized artist. I stand there with my eyes averted, a book-smart Afghan Hound who has found herself in the wrong place at the wrong time.

I wonder if my supervisor's getting mad at the man because it'll keep him from getting mad at me, if the other teacher is my stand-in. I wonder if my supervisor's making a scene as a distraction, to keep me from asking why I can't have a cart, too.

An hour into the class an entire entourage of white people shows up, half of them women. There are about eight people. They file into the room and around the back and sit for a while and then leave. Some of them smile at me, which is how I know they are not typical prison people. I learn from the students that the people are from something like the California commission on prisons from Sacramento or Bakersfield or someplace like that.

When the class ends my supervisor comes in and is his old self, a cordial gentleman. He says the "board" had been very impressed with my teaching and wants me to join them for lunch in the cafeteria. I say I would love to eat lunch with them and will see him shortly, as soon as I get my coat from McDonald's. I hadn't realized it, but I had been looking forward to leaving the prison grounds and being alone in my car almost since I'd arrived, and can now hardly wait to escape.

I get back to the staff cafeteria at the prison just as everyone is finishing their lunch. I place two quarters next to my supervisor's plate. I explain to the people gathered that it had taken a while to get my coat but I'll join them in a minute. I go and get in line for food. I take as long as possible deciding what to put on my tray. By the time I'm through the line, it's time to go to my next class. I dump the food in the trash.

I teach in a stupor all afternoon, thinking about my supervisor. He's running hot and cold, one minute being almost abusive and the next almost charming. Is he trying to get me to quit? Is he trying to whip me into shape?

As I'm leaving, the black art teacher and my supervisor are walking out of the building together, laughing and talking, best of friends. Had that whole "you're late" thing been a show for the cameras? Had they planned it together? A way for my supervisor to show the guards watching him on some video that he was on their side and didn't take any guff from any art teachers?

TULE FOG

In the late afternoon, after I finish at the prison, I drive past fields of artichokes, out of the long valley and toward the coast with its eucalyptus trees. Usually the fog in the Valley would burn off by noon but today, because of the intermittent rain, it has lingered in a lazy way, a soft gray shroud. Like softly woven cobwebs in a loose weave, it hangs over the land, close to the ground, all around my car, making me feel claustrophobic and eager to get to the coast and home.

As I drive carefully in the tule fog, I ruminate about the day's events. I go back over everything, scanning and winnowing and revisiting the gray blur of the day. When I go back I can feel an undercurrent of anger and fear in the halls at Soledad. I see again one of the prisoners in a doorway, looking at me. I see the fear in his eyes, but why would he be afraid of me? He's not afraid of me; it's something else. There is something going on behind the scenes at this prison.

There seems to be a great divide between the prisoners and the people in charge. What about the prison board members? They seem like they are just nothing but show. For the real prison, the people who run it, my being there seems to be not about teaching at all but about "offering programs" as they had said during orientation, "to garner continued public support." I was window dressing. And while I was at it, I should do double-duty as a security guard, or a human shield.

The guards want to stay safe and to that end they want to control the prisoners. They want to keep the state prison board happy and they want a steady supply of prisoners. It's all about money. They can't afford to dwell on why they are doing what they're doing. They can't allow themselves to care about rehabilitation or what kind of person they are going to return to society. They care about their own survival. They need to eat. They have to earn a living and, under the circumstances, that means they probably shouldn't think too much about the work itself.

The whole "arts in corrections" program is beginning to remind me of a play I'd seen about the Holocaust. It was called something like, *I'll Never See Another Butterfly*. It was based on a true story. During the Second World War, the Nazis, knowing they would have to let the Red Cross enter the concentration camps to inspect, built one for that purpose, the Terezin camp in Prague. Although the people at Terezin would be shipped to Auschwitz or Treblinka and used as slave labor before being exterminated, neither the Red Cross nor the inmates were aware of this. The camp was an illusion of decency, a front for evil. At Terezin there was a fake kindergarten, on display for the Red Cross visitors. Some of the children's artwork and writing survived. The teacher hid it in the walls and it was found later by Allied soldiers.

That night I'm dead tired as I unload the car. I feel like I've been beaten. I ache all over. Maybe I am coming down with something. I take some aspirin. I take a hot shower. I drink half a bottle of Merlot. I take another hot shower and fall asleep.

An hour or so later I wake up and can't get back to sleep. Maybe it was the wine. And I hadn't eaten anything since the fake food at lunch and, come to think of it, the fake food for breakfast before that. Eating that day had been about calories, not nourishment, the four basic American food groups: salt, sugar, starch, and grease.

I get out some of the leftover beef pot roast from the refrigerator, perfectly good food that I'd been too tired to eat when I'd come home. I slice it thin. I make some whole wheat sourdough bread toast and tear it up and put it in a big bowl and sprinkle it with oregano, a little olive oil. I love this bowl. It's a blue, over-lapping hexagrams pattern that I'd bought in Chinatown my first week in the Bay Area. The blues remind me of the water in the ocean around San Francisco.

On a whim I decide to heat the toast a second time in a big cast iron frying pan. The second heating will deepen the flavor of the spices in the bread. I add a little more oregano, salt and pepper, a tiny bit more olive oil and stir it gently with a wooden spoon. I cut part of a red onion into tiny pieces. I get out a handful of Greek olives. I see some feta cheese on the shelf in the refrigerator and add a little bit of that. I chop up a delicious-smelling ripe tomato I'd bought on the street down in Soledad and salt it. I tear up a couple of leaves of romaine lettuce. I throw it all into the beautiful blue bowl, grind some pepper over it, sprinkle in some balsamic vinegar and stir it around. It smells good. Heating up the toast a second time had been the right idea. I'm suddenly famished.

I go out to the white plastic chair on my porch. I like this chair. I like my deck. My deck is about the same size as my apartment.

My studio apartment is a converted motel room with an efficiency kitchen. The raised deck is about three feet from the ground and next to a soggy cattail marsh. There's a faint and hazy quarter-moon. It's quite dark outside. I don't see any stars. It must be overcast. I can hear the ocean pounding the shore.

I've only taken two bites of my roast beef salad when I hear someone coming through the marsh from up near the road. I hear them walking, then they stop and there's no sound; then they're walking again. It's a noisy, unworried walk, someone who doesn't care if anyone knows they're there. Who is walking through the marsh at this hour and why? I hear them again, then nothing. I peer into the darkness.

I feel someone staring at me. Then I see a masked face at the edge of the deck floor and level with it, like someone at night during Mardi Gras.

"You impudent scamp," I say. I deliberately make my voice sound casual, relaxed. "For God's sake, go back where you came from." Just a raccoon, a very large one, probably also couldn't sleep and wanted to see what I was up to.

This raccoon, like most raccoons, is bold, prepossessing, brassy, and nonchalant. A hungry animal can be dangerous.

I'm not afraid to die, but I want to die, if possible, from old age, not from being too tired and stupid and focused on eating not to know enough to avoid a fight. I gently toss my food into the marsh, bowl included, as if it's an offering. My body language says, "Here's a gift, my lovely friend." I slowly and casually back my way into my apartment. I don't care about my wonderful salad. I don't care about my beautiful bowl.

Once inside, I quickly slide the glass door back in place and bolt it. I'm about to go back to bed when I realize I'm still ravenously hungry, too hungry to sleep. I put another piece of sourdough in the toaster. I wait for it to come up.

I chastise myself: if I wasn't naturally more curious than cautious, I could be eating a salad I want rather than a piece of toast I don't particularly want. Still, it was worth it. On some subliminal level I'd known that a sane criminal wouldn't be walking through the marsh, or an insane one, either. Too mucky. They would have come down the driveway. It had to be an animal, and I wanted to see for myself. I spread the toast with peanut butter and a little strawberry jam. I take a swallow of milk straight from the carton. It will do, after all, and I got to see a really large and interesting raccoon in the middle of the night.

A while later I'm awakened with a jolt from a dream in which I had been sleeping with my cheek on my dog's chest, which was somehow in the dream the size of the bed, and I was feeling his breathing, the rising and falling, when suddenly he'd had a spasm, like a seizure. When I'm more awake and lying there thinking about the dream, it takes me a while to realize that the breathing of my dog had probably been the sound and even the feeling of the ocean. I've never slept with my face on my dog's chest.

I wonder if the dream is a warning, if something has happened to my dog back in Michigan. My mattress is on the floor and the pounding of the surf seems to come through, not enough to notice when I'm awake and moving around, but when I'm sleeping, it seems to be there. Later that day, when I call home to see if my dog is okay, my renter tells me that everything's fine, the dog, too. A few days later, when I read in the news about a shift in the San Andreas Fault, I'll realize that there had been a small tremor in the tectonic plates deep in the earth and that is probably what I'd felt.

The next morning dawns cold and foggy. It's very early. I decide to go to Point Reyes and look for a whale. I have wanted to see a whale since coming to the coast. It's a bit of a hike out to the point. A bearded man with binoculars tells me he saw a whale spout just fifteen minutes before I got there. I sit for a long time listening to the ocean but never see a whale. Simply listening to the Pacific pound the shore, a soothing sound, a rhythmic sound, a soft yet strong and endlessly repeated sound, calms me.

I drive in to Mission Dolores. The fog is burning off. It's beautiful and sunny away from the wind off the ocean. I like the singing at the Mission Dolores church on Sunday morning and I like their rose garden. Parking on the streets of San Francisco is free on Sunday. Somewhere there's jasmine blooming, or maybe japonica. I will miss this place when I've moved on from here. A group of evangelical Christians on the corner is singing and passing out literature. *"Conceived out of wedlock, born in a manger, buried in a borrowed grave ..."* Words of the hymn float across the street to me. Something faint but fine, the familiar and good scent of coffee is on the breeze as I walk down the hill toward the little place on Valencia, anticipating the excellent coffee and the whole milk to put in it.

Sunday night I email my supervisor and tell him I won't be there on Monday morning. I write that I admire all the wonderful work he's doing as the Director of the Arts in the Salinas Valley Correctional Training Facility. I write that my background hasn't suited me to work in such a structured environment and it's not a good fit. I write that I feel I can't serve my students or the program in the way that I would like and think it is best for all concerned if he finds someone else. After I hit "send" I think I should have just said it was too far to drive. Simpler. Less fuss. More believable.

Monday afternoon the head of the California Arts in Corrections Program down in Bakersfield calls and wants to know why I'm not returning to the Salinas Valley Correctional Training Facility. He's not satisfied with the "too far to drive" answer. He has a lot of questions. I repeat the stock phrases I'd put in my email to my supervisor. The man from Bakersfield wants to explore these answers. Finally I say, sounding as much like a little old lady as possible, "Sir, I have a doctor's appointment. I'm sorry, I have to go. Really, sir, all I can say is that it wasn't a good fit. Too far to drive."

Over the next few days I'll learn that Soledad has been put on lockdown. It was apparently put on lockdown over the weekend right after I left. There had been a near-riot. The copper penny smell, it occurs to me, had been the smell of fear emanating from all the prisoners. The management, too, had been afraid, afraid of a riot like the big one at Pelican Bay back in September. That's why some prisoners had been bussed. I would not look up the word, *soledad*, until I was in El Salvador in 2001. I could have looked it up sooner but I guess I was too busy or not ready to learn Spanish. *Soledad* means loneliness.

I would not realize until many years later, when I was watching a movie where a hired gunman puts newspapers and paperback books around his ribs and then uses duct tape to attach them before an anticipated brawl, when he will be outnumbered and unarmed, that possibly the reason my supervisor didn't want me to bring in books or newspapers is that the prisoners might use them as padding to protect themselves from the guards during beatings.

The San Francisco Jail

The San Francisco Jail is brand new, glass and concrete, next to highway 101, at Seventh and Bryant downtown, close to the courthouse. I have a new gig, teaching writing to the most violent inmates in the San Francisco Jail.

I park under the overpass where homeless people push grocery carts filled with their bedding and belongings. I'm early, as I always am. I spy a McDonald's and decide to wait out my extra fifteen minutes there.

One might think that a McDonald's next to a courthouse would be clean and safe but this one feels like a place for drug deals. The room is wall-to-wall people, half of them borderline homeless with carts like mine. I get in line for coffee but when I see two men, a tall, thin black man and a shorter, fatter white man, come out of the ladies' bathroom I decide I'll just go on to the jail.

Through people I know in the Bay Area I've learned a little about the San Francisco Jail. The head of the jail's programs, Michael Marcum, killed his abusive father in 1966 when he was only nineteen, then spent seven years in federal prison, became a social worker, and was made assistant sheriff in 1993 by Sheriff Michael Hennessey, his friend. Marcum heads the jail's rehabilitation programs. My writing classes will be part of that. Hennessey, given a vote of no confidence by his deputies when he hired Marcum, has been popular with voters and hasn't lost an election since he first ran in 1979. Unbeknownst to me at the time, I had landed in probably the best incarceration program in the entire world there at the San Francisco Jail.

Education, job-training, theater activities, counseling, AIDS awareness, and even acupuncture for drug addiction were all programs instigated by Marcum and Hennessey. The jail's signature program, Resolve to Stop the Violence Program (RSVP), is brand new, the only one like it in the United States. Violent criminals in this program meet and apologize to their victims.

Former prisoners, those who have successfully rehabilitated themselves, are eligible to work as counselors in the RSVP program. Harvard came and did a study of it. My supervisor's partner is a substance abuse counselor in the RSVP program. Her daughter has worked in the program. She knows the people who set up this project, knows them both professionally and socially, and has for a long time.

I'm impressed my supervisor doesn't bat an eye when I say I want my first class to go all day. She doesn't ask why. She just says, "Okay." She shows me where the copy machine is that I can use free of charge. This program would seem to be everything the Soledad program should be and maybe used to be. But it could still be window dressing, just better window dressing.

She says the students can all have a brown bag lunch. She'll let me hold the class in the atrium. I know what an atrium is; I've seen them in movies. Atriums have lots of tall windows in gilt frames, beautiful flowering plants, and maids in uniforms who walk around with little teacakes on a silver tray.

I've planned this thing. In the morning I will give a speech which will tell my students about me and the work we will do together. We'll eat our brown bag lunches. For the afternoon I have readings from great literature for prompts and we'll spend that time writing and reading.

The Atrium

The atrium at the San Francisco Jail is not like the atriums in movies set in Newport. It's three stories high, like the atrium is in Grand Central Station, but there's no gold-and-blue-green painted ceiling. This atrium is iron grating painted orange. It has a flimsy feeling. When cars go by on Highway 101, a sliver of which we can see out the sliver of window, the whole place shakes.

These men, too, are the size of refrigerators, except that instead of being dressed in dull grays and blues, they're dressed in neon orange. There are about twenty-five of them. On the whole they're much younger than the men at Soledad. They are also mostly brown and black men with two or three white ones. The fluorescent lights and the orange-suited men and the orange-painted grating which trembles when a truck goes by, minus the flowering plants and the maids with teacakes, make it an uncomfortable environment.

I tell them about my childhood in Michigan, growing up in a lumber camp, not exactly the truth. I tell them about where I live at Point Reyes, not exactly the truth. I tell them I teach writing because it's work I can do, mostly the truth. I tell them a little about my time at Soledad and how I've come to see people in prison as being like the children in a dysfunctional family.

I do not tell them that I see the prisons and jails as a breeding ground for home-grown terrorism in America. All it would take to plunge the country into darkness would be a few guys to take out the electrical grid. The billion dollar transformers are made in China and would take a minimum of two years to replace. This was talked about, as science fiction in the 1990s, but some people with guns shot up a power substation in San Jose, California in 2013, and the shooters still haven't been found. This was covered in the *Wall Street Journal* at the time and revisited in journalist Ted Koppel's 2016 book, *Lights Out: A Cyberattack, Unprepared, Surviving the Aftermath*. The San Francisco Jail program was working to prevent that kind of thing, but the federal, state, and private prisons were doing anything but.

"Counselors know," I tell them, "that in a dysfunctional

family the one who acts out, when the family comes in for counseling, dragging the wild-assed kid, that the troubled kid is troubled for a reason. The troubled kid is often the strongest member of the family, the one least afraid of the system. I see America as one, big dysfunctional family, and the two million prisoners, the ones acting out—more than in Russia they now tell us—as a catalyst for change.

"The chance that this program, RSVP, has to change things is exciting. We're standing in a doorway. We're in a liminal state—a threshold state—a place where what's envisioned becomes reality, a place where what's subconscious becomes conscious. We are, literally, here in San Francisco, at the jumping off place, the place where the shore meets the sea.

"Joan Didion," I tell them, "a famous writer who grew up in Sacramento, said, 'We tell ourselves stories in order to live.' Annie Dillard, another writer, said, 'You should write as if you're dying and every member of your audience is dying, too,' because that is in fact the case.

"We have nothing to lose here. Nothing to lose. Nobody gets out of it alive, boys. What lives is only what we create that lasts beyond us.

"Life is short. Art is long. Knowledge is power. The pen is mightier than the sword. Writing is fun. But nothing happens without work. You don't start to have fun—like playing football or soccer or basketball—until you've mastered a few moves."

I speak for an hour. Since there are no security guards anywhere around, I'm guessing we're all on camera and being taped. In my speech I'm trying to ingratiate myself with the prison higher-ups. And, despite some shifting of facts to protect my privacy and safety, I'm telling the truth about what I think and feel. I want the people running the program, as well as my students, to know where I'm coming from.

I ask the men to introduce themselves, tell their names, ages, where they grew up, and tell what they expect to gain from a writing class. Soledad gives me street cred so I tell them that obviously I don't expect them to say what crime they're in for, that's a taboo in prison, a breach of etiquette.

I tell them the story of Irish playwright Brendan Behan, hanging out with his fellow Irishmen, some of whom are members of warring factions within the Irish Republican Army, pro-treaty and anti-treaty groups. Behan knows that the other man at the bar is charged with murdering someone, but he doesn't know who. Is it someone from his own gang or someone from the other side? He feels he needs to know this so he can know who might want to kill the man at the bar or, conversely, who might want to kill him. So he finally says, "Who was the other individual in the situation in which you were the one accused, if I might ask?" They laugh at this story, which is good. It had been a test. If they hadn't laughed I would have known that in the jail this kind of thing was no joke.

We are now ready for a writing exercise. This one will be the rules to live by. At noon a guard comes in with the inmates' brown bag lunches, the closest this atrium gets to maids with teacakes. I've brought my own brown bag lunch. Whether they know it or not, the afternoon will be devoted to having them tell me about life in the jail.

First I have them write about acupuncture, then their GED classes, then the drama classes, then the therapy. We do individual work for an hour. I have them describe things in detail. "Details convince," I tell them. "Write everything, as if you were telling someone from Mars." We learn about metaphors and similes. "The acupuncture needles feel like..." Or, "The atrium is a gilded cage." Or, "My computer class teacher reminds me of..." We learn about adjectives and adverbs. "Now add a color." I have them do group work where we learn about writing with the five senses. "Now add a sound. Now add a smell." It will seem to them like I'm teaching them about writing, but I'm really learning all about the jail and their programs.

Whatever they do, I tell them their work is wonderful. I

know that if I keep saying, "Your work is wonderful," eventually it will be.

ORANGE

I have decided to stay. I'm having acupuncture along with some of my students in the dimly lit "pod" which is the name for their quarters in the jail. This is a room laid out like a wheel with a security guard on a raised dais in the center, like the captain of a space ship. The room is awash in the color orange since that's what the men are wearing and there are a lot of them and they're large and they're moving.

The needles are long and they hurt a little as they poke into my ears which is where, if you are being treated for addiction, they put the needles. I'm addicted to coffee and wouldn't mind drinking less of it. According to the latest reports, remember this is still 1999, coffee is very bad for you.

But mainly I'm there getting acupuncture because I want the students to see that I'm interested in their lives. Virtually all of my students have addiction issues. After the first day my classes are no longer held in the atrium. They are held in a long, shoe-box-shaped, glass-walled room in the pod itself where the security guard can see us.

I THINK YOU ARE MARVELOUS

I tell my students I think they're marvelous. I tell them I want to hear their stories. Only two students have done the out-of-class assignment I'd given them the first day in the atrium and so after that I know we need to do all the writing in class.

They begin to write autobiographies, a few of which are quite good. I praise them all equally, but we all know good writing from bad—even bad writers know when writing is good: good writing makes you feel something. They want to be one of the good writers. These men are naturally competitive. "Tell me something I can't forget," I exhort them. The writing slowly gets better.

By and large these men have poor writing skills. They either can't or don't read. Their writing is the kind of thing you see from second graders. Worse, they have no life skills. No one ever taught them how to make a bed, cook supper, take care of a dog, drive a car, or balance a checkbook. They have no emotional resources. They are like seven-year-old boys in the bodies of twenty-five-year-old men. It's mostly not their fault.

They were not taken care of as children. Their families, if they had any, were dysfunctional, sometimes on drugs, and so violent that the kids were put in foster care. Childhood was a blur for most of these men. They became emotionally numb early, went through school unable to retain anything. Many have real learning disabilities: brain damage from concussions from beatings; brain damage from malnutrition; hyperactivity; dyslexia; you name it, they've got it. Some became addicted to drugs so young they couldn't learn; some became addicted in the womb. Now here they are in my class.

My technique for dealing with their dysfunction is to mother them. I praise them ceaselessly. I expect way more from them than they can manage, as if I think they can do it. They want to convince me that they are helpless, but I pretend that I think they aren't. In reality, I can't imagine how they will survive on the outside, and deep-down they must feel the same way.

It is still not their fault. They grew up poor, terribly poor, for the most part, and no one cared about them. They did not develop intellectually or emotionally and so they're stunted and deformed, always inside and sometimes outside. Our government does not provide support for families and children. Why? Probably money, but even the reasoning behind that thinking is not smart or correct.

The economic cost alone for incarceration has to be in the many, many trillions. The prison system is an example of stupid thinking. It's like treating people for burns, but never putting out the fire. There's the lost potential for the children, something that's hard to measure. Then there's the cost of incarceration, easier to measure, but hard to know exactly how much of it was avoidable. Probably a lot.

Sixteen million American children live in poverty, live in violent neighborhoods, and go to bad schools. Our government, with a more equal distribution of income, taxing more fairly and using the great wealth produced by corporations, could fix this, but it doesn't.

It's natural that children who grow up in bad places end up in prison. In the prisons, the cost of not taking care of them as children is a thousand times greater than if they'd received the care they should have had—the care every human being needs in order to thrive—when they were babies and youngsters.

Our nation calls itself a democracy but it's not, or this would not be happening. These men should be in a program, run like the army, for at least five years, and educated and trained, raised-up, as it were. They should be in a place to acquire skills and there should be jobs for them when they are released. If those are jobs where there is extra supervision, so be it. Everyone needs paying work or we will sprinkle thieves and killers throughout the society.

The United States should have a universal service army, like a military draft, that takes everyone from the age of eighteen and makes them serve two years and allows them to serve ten. Everyone needs to understand that they are part of a caring community, and they need to feel obligated to give back to that community and a national service army would do that. We are not taking care of our people.

I am miserable every day knowing that I cannot solve with one writing class the systemic problems of a country gone bad, a country that does not understand public good or common cause, a country that does not honestly care about democracy, about equality, liberty, and fraternity for all people.

The men want to know about me. I tell them lies. I am not

about to tell them where I really live or where my children live or even the real names of my children, and so I make it up. Details convince, as I've told them.

They don't suspect when I tell them that I sleep on an air mattress on the floor of a bunkhouse at a ranch near Point Reyes and babysit for the rancher's children in exchange for rent. I show them the spider bites on my arms, as proof. The stories are believable and since they're stuck in jail, they have no way of knowing otherwise.

These students, like the men at Soledad, want to hear about things from nature: the Blue moon and high tide that almost floated me and my air mattress out into the Pacific and over to Japan one night in February; the giant whale who washed ashore and died on the beach and had to be buried with a front-end loader; the calla lilies I picked and put all around my room in old pickle jars; the sea shells and beach glass I gathered along the shore; the masked bandit who came to my porch.

Sometimes when we want to take a break from heavy subjects, we write about food. All of them know how to cook something, even if it's only fried bologna or scrambled eggs. We learn about ingredients, steps, sequence. We write about how to make something and the setting and who is there. Characters are important. Sequence is important. Setting is important.

When I ask them to guess who the masked bandit is, it's one of my best writers who is able to guess it first. This is a man who grew up on an Indian reservation. His mother died giving birth to him and so, according to him, his father hated him most. In one of his stories, his father, in a drunken rage, tried to kill all his children. They ran for the hills. The kids could tell which way the shots were coming from by the light glinting off their father's whiskey bottle.

The jail, like the prison, is the land of bad childhoods. It's the land of bad choices that come out of the land of bad childhoods. Many of my students grew up on the streets, in dire poverty, in foster care. If they came from wealthy families, then the parents were phenomenally unloving. If their parents are still alive and if they even know who their parents are, those parents are likely to have been on drugs and involved in crime: mothers who were prostitutes and fathers who were in and out of prison.

One of my students, a prisoner they call "The Blue Man," is tattooed from head to foot. The students respect him because he has suffered terrible sexual and physical abuse since childhood. He only comes to one class. Another student was raised at least part of the time under the bushes in Golden Gate Park; until the kids were put in foster care, his mother kept her four children alive by working the streets.

My best writer is a heroin addict, the son of heroin addicts who died. Another student, a man who worked as a hit man, says if he hadn't been high on drugs, he would have been over the border into Mexico by the time the police came. My students tell me that if someone can make it to Latin America before they're arrested, they can find good-paying jobs there as hit men and body guards. All the rich people need them and so do all the hotels and video stores.

One of my students is a pedophile, according to one of my other students, and will go to a special prison for sex offenders. There are special prisons for sex offenders because they are at-risk of being killed by other inmates. I believe this student's a pedophile because of things in his writing and his artwork; I also believe he has about eight personalities.

SIR JOHN GIELGUD

My students, like students anywhere, are all different kinds of people. One large man, the father of nine children, loves Shakespeare. I bring in speeches which he reads beautifully.

Another man loves music, rap music, and I bring in some of that. I cater to their individual interests for a reason: I want them to know they *are* individuals. That they have a "self" or a soul in there; without that, they can't write, or can't write anything meaningful.

As much as possible, I get them to laugh.

One morning when I come in to make copies my supervisor says that one of the guards thought my students were laughing too often. This is the guard the men call Barney Fife. He looks like Barney Fife, they tell me, the policeman from the Andy Griffith show. I look up from the copy machine and over at her.

"I guess he doesn't like people laughing," she says.

Most of the guards at the jail are good guys. Smart, kind, many ex-military, most are black. Barney Fife is the exception. He's white, in a gray-white way, with poor posture. He's suspicious of everyone. He enjoys punishing the men by denying them their computer classes or visits from families. The men don't like him. Although they would never say this, for fear of being punished, it's obvious.

"Are you kidding?" I say, noncommittally, keeping my voice flat, not looking up. I have no idea what she's thinking. Maybe she doesn't think my students should be laughing either.

"No." She's smiling. She thinks it's as funny as I do.

That day I put Sir John Gielgud on the tape player. He's doing a scene from Hamlet.

Only the one student likes Shakespeare. The others are merely tolerant. And the reading is very dated, very stiff, and very British. It's not easy to understand the British accent.

I know that Barney Fife is going to come skulking around our glass shoebox at some point. It doesn't take long. I have already instructed the men—passing out the message in writing so that the audio won't pick it up; and then collecting the writing—that when he comes peering in through the windows, they should all in unison throw back their heads and fall about laughing as if the most wonderfully funny and delightful thing ever had just happened.

They do. And I do, too.

He can't resist. He comes into the room. "What's going on in here?" he asks. He sounds very tough. He needs to know.

I tell him that we're listening to Sir John Gielgud read a scene from Shakespeare's *Hamlet* and ask him to join our group to listen with us. "Many of these students love Shakespeare," I explain.

He looks confused, and more suspicious than ever. Not knowing what else to do, he leaves, head down and shoulders together, slinking out, as if he doesn't want to be seen.

My best writer looks at me and says, with total mock-sincerity, "I love Shakespeare."

"I love Shakespeare," echoes around the room as each student murmurs agreement. They're all sitting a little taller in their chairs with their shoulders more square. Some days, you just have to get back a little of your own.

THE SIX-WEEK DITCH

Just as the writing starts to get real, several students drop out. This has happened to me before; writing is hard work when it's honest, and these students have hit what I call the six-week ditch.

My classes are voluntary.

I see the men who had been in my class hanging out in the pod, talking to their friends. These are guys who are at loose ends generally and probably always have been, guys who would be happy most days with a babe and a beer. This is a macho crowd. They all talk about their inner "hit man." Even the guys who in a million years were never hit men, want to have been. It's important to them not to be perceived as sissies— and creative writing, the world over, does have that reputation.

That weekend I go home and dye my hair red. I go to K-Mart and get new clothes in bright fuchsia and blue-green, colors that go with the orange prison clothing and look good under fluorescent lights. I look like a Howard Johnsons. I wear a brilliantly-colored silk scarf. I put on eye make-up and lipstick.

I got the idea for this transformation when one of my beer-and-a-babe students objected to my reading a piece of writing on tule fog, an example of detailed description that I had written, but said was from one of my former students at Soledad. He said in a distinctly whiney voice, "We don't want to hear about your students at Soledad. This is *our* class." I knew several things from that remark: that they could be jealous of other men, especially those they thought were bigger and badder than they were; that no matter what I looked like or how old I was, I could make them crave my attention; that they gossiped among themselves; and that because of all of those things, I could play them and get them to write.

I NEED TO TELL YOU SOMETHING VERY PERSONAL

When I come in the next week I say in a soft, low-toned, husky, hesitant, honest-sounding voice that I want to tell them a little about my background. They have been so brave and honest in their writing, and I respect them so much for that; now it's only fair for me to share my own story. And I've made up one helluva story. I grew up in a lumber camp, took care of the horses for the mill, and became an excellent horsewoman. I was young and beautiful then, I tell them, but didn't know it.

I meet a Saudi Prince at the University of Michigan, go home with him on spring break, and ride horses with him all over the Arabian Desert. He's my best friend until I become deathly ill. Faisal abandons me in an underground house in the sand—literally, a sand pit, in Tunisia, that's the kind of house they have there—and says he'll be back for me.

While I'm convalescing in the sand pit, a handsome, wandering, hippie drug dealer takes pity on me. When I'm better we start traveling together, end up in Turkey, where I'm arrested for carrying hashish in my backpack; to this day, I swear, I didn't know it was there. I'm put in a jail that was basically stone huts with a waist-high stone fence.

In this story, I flirted with the guard (wink-wink, we all know I did more than flirt) and he let me escape, whereupon I fled to the American Embassy, and my father paid to get me back home. Details convince, as I had told them, and in this story there were lots of details. The next week, I would have all my defectors back in the classroom plus a few more. They liked me better now that I'd revealed my checkered past, now that I'm almost a criminal, like them. And now, too, there's less chance that they'll be seen as sissies if they come to creative writing class, now that they have an almost-hooker for a writing teacher.

I would have to work very quickly to get my students to produce something publishable by the middle of May. I'd already talked to a friend at KQED, the National Public Radio (NPR) affiliate in San Francisco, and she'd hooked me up with a reporter who would come to the jail and tape their work. I hadn't finalized it because the work, with the exception of one or two students, simply wasn't good enough.

My students in the jail, for the most part, would transition to other prisons by the end of May. They were, understandably, preoccupied. They were waiting to see what would happen next. Since they wouldn't write out of class, they would have to write in class. Lavish praise works with most people, especially men who aren't getting much of it. "I think you're marvelous. I love what you're doing. Keep up the good work. I'm amazed by your experiences," was my constant refrain. Some of the in-class work was bound to be good, if I could just keep them in the room and their pencil moving across the paper.

HEADING OUT

I arrive at Old Faithful in the Rocky Mountains just as the sun is going down. I can smell the sulfur from the geyser as I walk to the big, log hotel. I think I can smell balsam but maybe I'm only imagining it. The last time I was at Old Faithful was the summer of 1964 when I worked in the restaurant there. I love these mountains.

A reporter from the radio station KQED, the NPR affiliate in San Francisco, had come to the San Francisco Jail on my last day there and taped the men reading from their writing. It had been excellent work. The men were proud of what they'd accomplished and I was proud of them.

As I fall asleep in my mountain fastness, looking at all the old electrical outlets in walls of the old hotel, I'm wondering where the students would go next. I wonder where I'll go, too. I'm glad to be alive, glad to be heading home to Michigan. I'll arrive just as the wildflowers are blooming and the songbirds are returning.

Achates, Faithful Companion

I dreamed about him when I was working in the California prisons. I felt him one night in the room as I was falling asleep and thought I could smell him. I missed him at a subliminal, subconscious level all the time, but missed him consciously in ways I'd never anticipated. I missed him on the days after work when I was tired and saw no hope for my students, men who were most likely going to be behind bars for a long time and, if they got out, would have no families, no jobs, and no future.

The relationship with him was one that had snuck up on me, without my knowing. One November day, sometime in the early 1990s, with the weather one minute raining and hailing and the next sunny and bright, that strange, fitful weather we get at that time of year, I had finished an uneventful day of substitute teaching in Traverse City and had gone on the spur of the moment to the Humane Society. This was when it was still on South Airport, not the new glass and brick place on Lafranier Hill but the old, moldy-smelling, cinderblock building at the bottom of the hill.

This was back when people still talked about getting a dog or buying a dog, and did so without self-consciousness. There were no "rescue dogs" in those days, there were just dogs. This was before the word "adoption" came into vogue in conjunction with an animal.

There in the open corral behind the cinderblock building was a happy-looking creature, red-coated, with a ruff of fur around his face like a lion and a tail like a Fourth of July sparkler. I paid whatever the fee was. He walked with me out of the building and jumped into the front passenger seat beside me with a little chuff, or huff sound, like, "Let's go!"

When I brought him into the house my daughter said, "He's so noble. What's his name?"

"Maybe Red?" That had been the name of the dog on my grandparents' Hoxeyville homestead.

She had looked disgusted. "I can do better than that just going through the dictionary."

After a minute or two, still in the early part of the A's, she said, "Achates, Aeneas's faithful companion." The name is Greek and is pronounced Ah-kay-tees. In a short time we would be calling him "Ahkee" for short, or "Ahkee-Kahn" when we were being formal because he had a kind of regal-yet-wild Genghis Kahn persona.

I learned, by people noticing him with me and telling me, that he was a Chow-Chow. They often added, warning me, that Chows are known to be biters, sometimes saying that veterinarians wouldn't treat them because they bite. This made no sense to me since this dog was mild-tempered. I thought that the information must be wrong. A bad rap for a good dog was my idea about that.

Julius Bunek, the man who'd always fixed my furnace, came that first fall Achates was there in the house. Julius had stopped by to do the routine maintenance that he always did but that day decided not to come in. "Your dog just looked at me through the glass," Julius told me later when I saw him in the grocery store. "The look in his eyes was, 'I'm not going to bite you. I'm just going to kill you.'" And Julius, a large, outdoorsy man who had good instincts about animals, wisely decided that the furnace check could wait.

Achates arrived in a household that already had an old dog and a young cat. From the start Achates was polite about letting them have first shot at the food, the water, the love and attention. He was friendly with us, but not a lap dog. If we petted him too much or too affectionately he looked embarrassed and at the first chance to politely escape, he did.

He didn't want to play fetch. He never wanted to sit around

with us while we read books or visited with friends, and would just retreat to some private place, usually outdoors. He seemed to eat very little and, unlike most dogs, would only eat until he was full, never more than that. He refused all food from strangers. When the bank teller in the drive-through would hand me a dog biscuit he would take it, hold it in his mouth, and then the minute we were out of sight, would drop it on the floor. He liked riding in the car and liked going for walks, but with a kind of watchfulness, or on-the-look-out quality. He hated rain and going in the water.

He had golden eyes. He had a black tongue.

He never barked. We thought he couldn't. One day he did bark, a short barely audible, not unfriendly sound, like someone speaking who hasn't spoken in a long time. It was surprising. He seemed surprised by it himself. "He can bark," my daughter observed dryly. "He just prefers not to."

He was a member of the household. I seldom thought about him, as one doesn't when someone is a member of the household. I liked having him there but I wasn't too interested in him.

One night I woke up and found him standing over me, straddling me on the bed. This was totally out of character for him. Also, no dog I'd known had ever done this. In the years afterwards when I've spoken with other dog owners, they've said they've never heard of a dog doing this. I think it was unusual. The look on Achates' face that night as he stared down at me was, "You are not going to die." His fierceness and determination was like a force field. I'd never experienced anything like it. I didn't know it then, but this dog would always be with me. In some mysterious way, that to this day I don't understand, he is still a part of me.

When I managed to get out of bed that night, I realized I was drenched in perspiration. It seems I may have had a fever that finally broke. Perhaps I'd been delirious, thrashing in the bed, I don't know, but that was my first inkling of his protective instincts.

The next time was when he chewed through the car door. He apparently had decided while sitting in the car, that I'd been in the dentist office too long and he was going to come in and get me. He had ripped away the door upholstery and was working on the metal part when I emerged from the appointment.

But other than those rare times, he was so laid-back that I basically didn't think about him at all. He was there. I liked having him around. I like dogs. I like cats. I like horses. I pretty much like all animals. That's all there was to that. He went with me and stayed in the car when I ran errands or when I had to go out on the road doing research. If I got groceries and put them on the seat next to him, and then ran into the post office for a few minutes, he never touched the ground beef, for example, or anything else. He was easy to be with. No trouble.

After Achates had been with me for about three years, I took a teaching job in a summer program that was twenty-five miles from my home. I had to be gone all day, too long to take him with me. He couldn't stay in a hot car all day. I had Invisible Fence but since he disregarded it, I couldn't use it with him. I had a kennel, too, but since he hated it, I would leave him in the house. He never destroyed anything. He was good in the house.

That first Monday in July when I came home from teaching, Achates was waiting for me in the driveway. He'd gone through the screen in the living room window, not that hard to do but he'd had to have backed way up, gone to the far end of the living room, and then taken a long, powerful flying leap to do it.

Tuesday, I closed the windows. That day he was also waiting for me in the driveway. He'd gone through the double, plate-glass picture window, unscathed because of his thick fur.

Wednesday I left him in the garage. That day also he was waiting for me in the driveway, a big hole behind him in the fiberglass garage door.

Thursday I put him in the kennel, a roofed space about six feet by ten feet, with a chain-link fence, anchored into concrete. This day, too, he was waiting for me in the driveway. He'd pulled the supports out of the concrete, apparently by hurling himself at the chain-link fence so hard, repeatedly, that he eventually pulled it loose.

Friday morning came. I had no place else to put him, no way to contain him. There were dog-sized holes in all the places I'd had. I'd been working every day and there'd been no time to repair everything. I couldn't have a dog who destroyed things. That would never do. I was going to have to put him to sleep.

A friend of mine, I confess I wouldn't have thought of this, advised me to get down on his level, roll him over on his back, pat his stomach and explain to him that I had to go to work and he had to stay and take care of the house. This would be my last gambit. I was sure it was nonsense, but I did it. I had nothing left to lose. That Friday afternoon, I drove home, dreading what I would find. But he was in the house, where I'd left him. Nothing was destroyed. He could have easily gone through the hole in the plate glass picture window. It was still there. But he hadn't.

I bought a book on Chows. This was before you could Google everything. I discovered that Chow-Chows had been bred by the Mongolians to go into battle as a team: one man, one dog. They were known for never leaving the side of their assigned warrior, for fighting to the death. The Chinese, when they negotiated a treaty with the Mongolians, requested a number of these dogs as part of the settlement. Traditional training methods for this dog, reward and punishment, carrot and stick, the book said, did not work. The owner must spend time with the dog, bond with the dog, and the dog would intuit, almost psychically, what the owner wanted. Chows are the traditional stone dogs, spirit guardians, found like gargoyles on the steps in front of Buddhist temples and Chinese palaces. DNA tests show Chows to be an ancient breed, one of the earliest to evolve from the gray wolf, perhaps more than fifteen thousand years ago on the high steppes of Outer Mongolia and Siberia.

One summer Achates tangled with a porcupine. He had no problem with my pulling out all the quills, even the ones that were way back in his throat.

Another year I foolishly accepted the job of babysitting for an acquaintance's Chow-Chow, Abby, a female who'd been tied out in Detroit in the hot sun. This dog was crazy, like a Vietnam vet. "Her eyes," one of my friends observed, "are like 'Lucy in the sky with diamonds.'" But we worked with her. If she went off and started growling and snapping at things for no reason, Achates would get her by the throat and nail her to the ground with a definite, 'We don't do that here' message. Then Abby would be given her "time-out" in the kennel. Achates, gentle creature that he was at heart, then would go and sit outside the kennel to keep her company.

Abby was more aggressive than Achates and liked to chase raccoons. She would find a raccoon to irritate and then race back to the porch, while leaving poor Achates to actually do battle.

One early dawn, before daylight, I awoke to a terrible racket down on the edge of the swamp.

I went down, barefoot, still in my thin white summer nightgown, and in the dusky air, saw Achates fighting two raccoons at once. Raccoons are not as cute and cuddly as they look. They are formidable fighters, with lethal claws and teeth. Their manner of fighting is to jump on the head of their adversary and claw their eyes out while at the same time trying to sever their victim's jugular with their teeth. One raccoon is a dangerous combatant. Two raccoons, that's an unfair fight.

I went back to the house and changed into Levis, boots, and a heavy barn coat, and got out a pitch fork. But once down at the edge of the swamp again I realized I would be of no help to Achates. If I got in the middle of the fight, between me and two raccoons, it would be the end of me. I returned to the house and closed the windows so I couldn't hear the war screams of the coons. I waited for quiet. It seemed to take an eternity.

When it came, I went outside. There was my poor dog, in a heap on the porch, bleeding and exhausted. All torn up, he looked suddenly small. The coons had been dispatched but not before inflicting serious damage. Achates had a nasty gash in a hind leg and another in his throat. His windpipe was exposed, but he was alive. I cleaned his wounds and gave him a shot of whiskey. It took him three months to recover, but he did, and once again he was as good as new.

The year I went out to work in the prisons of California, I rented my house to a single mom with two teenagers, letting Achates stay with that family during the year I'd be away. The woman told me that for the first time since she'd been raising kids alone, she'd been able to sleep soundly. "I always knew he was there," she said. "I could sleep with the windows open in the summer and the doors unlocked in the winter. I felt totally safe. It never entered my mind that I wasn't. I didn't listen for those little sounds, the way you do, or wake up at 3 A.M., checking to make sure everything was okay. Nothing was going to get past that dog. You just knew it without even thinking about it." And, as he'd been with me, Achates was always sweet and discreet, there in the background. No drama.

The men in the San Francisco Jail told me one day at the end of a writing class, when our time together was almost over, that I was the scariest person they had ever known. I was taken aback by this and asked how this could be, since I thought I was a fairly nondescript and even reclusive person.

One of the inmates said, speaking for the rest, almost as if designated, "You just don't quit." He paused. "You're a fighter." It seemed they had discussed this among themselves. "We think you're fading, and then you're up, and you're coming from a different direction, and we didn't see you coming because you'd changed. You'd disguised yourself. Or maybe you're a different person. We don't know. We can't decide. You keep changing. That's what's scary. You just don't quit."

Yes, I thought, it was probably true. The men in orange sitting around the table that day under the fluorescent lights all nodded in agreement. They seemed to be in no doubt about it.

I said something like, "Well. Hmm," and changed the subject.

I've been in trouble all my life, and needed a bodyguard all that time, but never knew it until the universe brought me Achates. Sometimes a pet is more than that. And if it happens, you have to let it.

LATIN AMERICA

The Big Mouth of the Volcano

The flight from Miami delivers us to the El Salvador airport in the middle of the night. The airport is new, air-conditioned, modern, deserted. The usual twenty-four-hour, duty-free stores offering expensive perfumes and fancy leather *attaché* cases line a wide, heavily guarded, echoing corridor. The shops and the corridor are completely empty, except for clerks stiff as mannequins waiting for customers, so immobile it takes a second glance to make sure they're real, and men with guns, very young and somewhat skittish, who look all too real.

We cross a huge expanse of tiled floor and then take a series of escalators and elevators, seemingly sideways, through several obscure realms and are finally deposited, like salmon who've navigated a succession of fish weirs, at a gate. Here the airport is not modern. It's hot and crowded. It's dirty and has a bad smell and everywhere one looks there are men with guns, all kinds of guns.

A large man with military bearing and acne scars, a dead ringer for the Panamanian strongman and drug kingpin, Manuel Noriega (the go-between for the Central Intelligence Agency until his 1989 arrest and imprisonment in the United States), is there to meet us. He's a heavily muscled man wearing a flak jacket, bulky enough to be formidable, carrying a sign announcing he is from the school. He reminds me of the hit men I taught in the San Francisco Jail. He has an air of aggressiveness that reeks of bravado rather than confidence, the kind of cocaine-fueled aggression that is combined in equal measure with a lack of sound judgment. He wears the school's insignia on his shirtsleeve. For a fleeting moment I wonder if he really is from the school, but the moment passes.

I had read in a travel guide that it might take a few hours to get through customs, but our escort whisks us right through, moving like a tank in front of the three other teachers and me, flashing some kind of documentation. Before we know it we're in a chauffer-driven, air-conditioned black van with tinted windows, speeding through dark, deserted streets.

An hour later I hear the creaking of large iron gates. We disembark in what we're told is the school's housing complex, the *complejo*. There is a cobblestone walkway and old-fashioned street lamps. There are maybe fifteen white stucco houses—five on the left, five on the right, and five down the center—with the walkway in an oblong loop. The houses are of varying sizes; some have balconies. The houses are landscaped. I can see tile roofs that look like they'll be red clay in the daylight. None of us has had any idea of what to expect.

I can smell camellias and see the silhouettes of palm trees. We are all tired and disoriented. So this is the tropics? It's like a hot, humid night in August in the Midwest, sweet corn season, maybe ninety-five degrees, without a breeze. We're twelve hundred miles from the equator.

I'm taken up a flight of stairs to a bare studio apartment. The electricity's not turned on yet, but with the light coming through the windows from the old-fashioned lamps lining the walkway, I can see the outlines of a chair, a table and, in the bedroom, a bare mattress, and above the bed the outlines of a ceiling fan. It feels like it's reasonably clean. I'm in my bare feet and the floor feels clean under my feet. I can't smell anything bad.

I throw a sheet loosely over the bed and stuff a pillowcase with some clothes from my suitcase. I don't undress. I lie down and force myself to close my eyes and try to sleep but it's like sleeping sitting up in a chair in someone's hospital room. The surroundings are too unknown for real sleep.

It must be about 4 A.M., gray light, when I'm awakened by a pesky mosquito. Moonlight is coming in through the screen-less, open windows. It's an ideal time to have a cigarette. I don't smoke but on a whim had bought some cigarettes in the Miami airport. I rummage in my purse and find the unopened pack of Marlboro Reds but then realize I have no lighter, no matches. I hadn't thought of that.

From my balcony I can see the little guard house by the gate. The guard house looks like something you'd find in the Black Forest, like the toy guard houses at Christmas that come with toy tin soldiers.

I appear to be in a quiet, walled compound of about four acres. This is surrounded by thirty-foot high walls topped with razor wire and broken glass.

I can't seem to sleep. I'm still wearing the clothes I'd worn on the plane. I decide to go out and ask the guard for a light. Surely the guard will have a light. Guards are often smokers.

I speak no Spanish but show the man my unlit cigarette and pantomime striking a match. He is a small, tidy man with the softest brown eyes I've ever seen.

Por favor," I say and, getting out my tiny Spanish-English dictionary, "*Fuego. Lumina.*" Alas, he's not a smoker and has no matches. In a city the size of San Salvador there must be an all-night corner store.

To the guard's consternation, I unlatch the small door beside the gate. I look first, left, where I see at the end of the street, the silhouettes of half a dozen men with what looks like AK-47s, and then, right, toward the other end of the street, where there's another silhouetted group, similarly armed. I return to my bed and try to sleep until the sun rises.

We have several days before classes will start. I came early for the orientation required for new hires. The American director and the American principal are still away, the first on vacation in Brazil and the second still in the States with his family.

When I wake up, it's already hot. I've brought a small pan for boiling water and a jar of instant coffee, but the stove doesn't work. There's no hot water in the tap in the kitchen or in the bathroom. There's cold running water in the shower, but I'm not going to take a cold shower. I fill the bathroom sink with cold water, add some bleach, let it sit for thirty minutes and then wash my face and neck. I mix some of the bottled water I'd bought in the Miami airport with some of the Nescafe. I drink it like medicine.

That morning, we are taken in hand by the Dean of Students, a petite woman originally from California who might be in her sixties or even seventies but looks much younger. She wears her platinum blonde hair in a classic page boy, every strand absolutely in place. She wears a string of large, beautiful pearls, the kind that Barbara Bush often wore. She touches the pearls from time to time when she's talking. If anyone compliments her on the pearls she will say they were a gift from her mother.

By the second week of school we will all know the Dean of Student's mother was Margaret Bourke-White, the well-known *Life* magazine photographer. There's a coffee table book on display in the school library of Bourke-White's photos and on the back cover is a picture of Bourke-White. There's a striking resemblance to our Dean of Students, something feisty or brave, something Irish. She amazes the female teachers because she wears pantyhose in the 100-degree tropical heat and does not appear ever to perspire.

The entire area of the school is about seventy acres, including the housing compound at the top of the hill and the soccer field at the bottom. The school grounds are surrounded by a fence, which I will see weeks later when I have the courage to leave the compound; but from the inside we can't see the fence, all we can see is jungle. There are giant trees wrapped with serpentine vines and underbrush so dense it's impenetrable. Another teacher tells me there are poisonous snakes and tarantulas in the wooded areas.

We have all heard what sounded like gun shots during the night and we have all been told by the guard at the gate that what we had heard was firecrackers. "*Salvadorens como muchos los petardos*," we are told: Salvadorans like very much the firecrackers.

When we leave the housing compound proper we continue on a wide, cement walkway that crosses a large, open field where there's an auditorium. We see many Salvadoran gardeners and janitors as we continue through the school grounds. They smile shyly as we pass but don't say hello. I'm amazed by their sheer numbers. They are everywhere, like pollinating bees, painting, fixing, gardening, tiling, washing windows, mopping, and sweeping. They sweep the sidewalks with branches tied together.

El Salvador is about one-thirteenth the size of Michigan with many, many more people than Michigan has, people for the most part who are desperately poor, on the verge of starvation and crowded into small, violent communities. Much of the land is desert or eroded mountains. El Salvador is one hundred and fifty miles long and sixty miles wide, situated in the middle of the narrow, two thousand mile long land bridge that connects the continents of North and South America. It has two hundred miles of coast on the Pacific Ocean. Honduras is east, between El Salvador and the Caribbean. The northwestern border is the Sierra Madre de Chiapas Mountains, Guatemala, and the Paz River. The Goascoran River is south and west. Almost all of the fifty-eight rivers in El Salvador were largely impassible before bridges were built in the 1950s, about the same time commercial air travel and the Pan American highway opened up the country. Until then, El Salvador was a world unto itself.

From the school grounds we can see a volcano in the distance. Someone says it hasn't erupted in over a century. The volcano is variously called the Big Mouth or the Big Hole.

We are escorted down the walkway to a walled passageway, high above a highway, cross and immediately we are on the school grounds. We pass classrooms that look like rooms in a motel, a long string of small rooms called the chicken coops. I'm told that's where I'll be teaching.

There are hibiscus and bougainvillea blooming everywhere. There are flame trees in different colors, like fall colors in Michigan, scattered across broad expanses of lawn. The grass here is different from the grass in Michigan. The tropical grass is broad-leaved and grows in clumps tight to the ground. Later I will discover that the school is in a wealthy residential area called *Moscota* or *Escalon* on the western edge of the city. *Moscota* means mascot in English and *Escalon* means stepping stone.

Most of the new teachers found this job, as I did, through a job fair. For many this is their first teaching job. A few are the worldly and sophisticated "travelers who teach," who circulate around the globe from one international school to another, where the pay is usually excellent. Often there's no requirement that teachers of English have an official teaching certificate, previous teaching experience, or even knowledge of the subject area. A four-year degree, a two-week online class in teaching English as a second language, and a certificate of completion is all that many international schools require—that, and that you be a native English speaker. With the exception of one or two other teachers and me, all the teachers appear to be in their early to mid-twenties.

We cross what is called a *passarella*, a covered walkway at the second story. We are told that this will be rebuilt soon because of damage caused the year before by a major earthquake.

We are headed toward the older part of the school where the architecture and the ambiance speak of 1950s-style stability and staidness. Here we meet the Salvadoran office staff and sign the usual papers. All the people we meet in the office speak perfect English. They are gracious and warm.

Our school is the most prestigious in El Salvador, we're

told. The current president of the country is a proud graduate. It's for the very wealthiest, the fourteen families called the *Catorce Grande*, the Big Fourteen, installed by the Spanish in the 1500s. I had done some research on El Salvador when I was back in Michigan, before I'd accepted the job, and am surprised to discover that many of the names of generals and political leaders are the same as the names of school staff. When I'm given my student list, I see many of the same names again.

These ruling families, not wanting to lose control of money or power, have intermarried multiple times down through the years, according to one of the veteran teachers, and we will have more imbeciles than normal among our students because of inbreeding. The fourteen families hire Americans to run the school and pay them extremely well, but the *Catorce Grande* are always somewhere in the background.

The young man who will be teaching next to me in the chicken coops asks me, as we leave the last meeting on our first day of orientation, if I want to go for supper at the Princess Hotel, across the street from the school. He's reading the Herbert Mason translation of *Gilgamesh*, the five-thousand-year-old Sumerian epic, and wants to teach it to his students. From memory he quotes the opening, *"It's an old story, but one that can still be told, of a man who lost his friend to death, and learned he lacked the power to bring him back."*

He's from Louisiana, always has a well-worn backpack slung over one shoulder, wants to save enough to go to law school, and is fluent in Spanish. He's in his early twenties, is gregarious, curious, wants to explore everything and, having learned that I hadn't yet left the compound, is gallant enough to offer to escort me. He's one of those people you meet sometimes who's so intelligent they seem a little less than normal, almost slow, but then you figure it out: everything is easy for them. This boy reminds me of my son. He's already been all over the city and made friends with several Salvadorans.

We walk out through an iron gate down the hill behind

the school, past an ancient, beautiful white church. I ask if we can stop at the church and we go in where people are lighting candles. An old Indian woman is moving slowly in front of me. Without warning, she turns and shoots me a penetrating look, almost a clairvoyant look. I give her the money I was going to put at the altar, nudge my co-teacher, and we exit.

There's a horseshoe driveway in front of the several-story high Princess Hotel, complete with liveried guards. Inside there's gleaming dark woodwork that looks like mahogany, a small jewelry store with the most beautiful hand-crafted gold and tourmaline earrings I have ever seen, a well-appointed lobby, a bar, a restaurant.

Louisiana asks me—a polite gesture I'm guessing since surely he knows I will turn him down—if I want to go out with a group of teachers from the compound later. I say I'll be too tired, which is true. I'm also still reeling from all the changes—the heat, the proximity to violence—and can't take in too much at once.

We have meetings all week. A representative from the American State Department comes and speaks to us during our first week. He's a fast talker with expensive shoes. He tells us never to leave the compound unless we're with one of the school's guards. This makes perfect sense to all of us. We've read the books. We've seen the movies.

El Salvador had a civil war, the one where Bishop Romero was assassinated in 1980. The war officially ended in 1992, and the country is safer than it had been, but in 2001 it's still unsafe. They tell us people don't stop at stop signs because it makes them vulnerable to robbery.

A previous teacher at the school had been killed by a stray bullet, I learn at the pool. The word among the teachers was that this teacher had given a student from a prominent family a grade below a C. There's no way to verify this. We only speak of these things when we're seated around the swimming pool in our housing compound, and then only do so with the portable radios blaring. I decide to give nothing below a B.

The school will take us by van to a grocery store. We will all have the opportunity to have a maid at the incredible rate of ten dollars a day. Some of the school's veteran male teachers of science and math, all now on vacation, have maids come in every day to cook, clean, and do laundry. Most of us are giddy at the thought of having a maid. American teachers don't make enough money to have maids.

Housing is included in our wages, as is the travel to the school in early August and back home again at the end of the school year in mid-May. We all have a two-year contract, standard for overseas teaching. Wages range from twenty thousand dollars to sixty thousand dollars for the school year. I will be able to save most of what I earn. Every payday one of the school guards will drive us in the school van to the bank and to the grocery store.

The country has just switched from the *colon* to the dollar. El Salvador, I've already learned, is a place where there's literally blood on the money. The first time I see it, I bring the money home and run it through the washing machine in a little net bag I'd previously used only for lingerie. I won't continue to launder my dollars; it would be a never-ending chore.

The little store, the *bodega,* on campus is out of eggs. I have only coffee, bananas, rice, and canned milk in my apartment. I need protein. I find a Salvadoran teacher at the school who is walking to the nearby store and ask if I can go with her. She walks with me and then goes into a nearby house and says she'll see me in fifteen minutes.

The little store is not much bigger than the one on campus. I look for the eggs. Surely they'll have eggs.

I go up to the clerk and make the shape of an egg. I remember how I could order "*heuvos rancheros*" in California and say, "Way-vos." She looks mystified. Maybe I'm pronounc-

ing it wrong. Maybe that's not the word for "eggs" in El Salvador. Maybe she doesn't expect an American to be speaking
Spanish and so it's just not coming across as anything she's able
to recognize.

I flap my elbows at my sides, the way I've seen my neighbors'
chickens do back home in Lake Leelanau. I say, "Bawk, bawk,
bawk, bawk," and, in pantomime of a chicken, dip my body as
if I had a beak and was pecking for grain. I repeat, "Way-vos."
By this time I have an audience. They are clearly amazed.

Finally, someone who is bilingual steps forward and asks
me what I want.

"Eggs," I say.

She takes me by the arm and shows me the way, down another aisle, to a big display of eggs, three dozen to a carton
and stacked waist-high, in the center of the aisle. They don't
refrigerate their eggs in El Salvador, so I had not thought to
look for eggs there. I had been looking in the small, refriger-
ated glass case.

I'm paying for six eggs when the Salvadoran teacher from
my school returns to meet me outside the store.

Once outside with her, I say, mystified, "I couldn't get them
to understand that I wanted eggs." I tell her how I had said
heuvos and imitated a chicken, saying "bawk, bawk," and everything; going the limit.

She says, "Our chickens don't make that sound."

"Really? What do your chickens say?" I'm stunned. It had
never occurred to me that chickens in different parts of the
world are imitated by humans differently.

Our chickens say, "Kara-kara-kara-kara."

"Really?" I say again. I sound stupid, even to myself.

"Yes," she says, as if everyone who is anyone knows this.

We are told that the school accountant is also a dentist, for
anyone who might need a dentist. She's the nicest woman in
the world. I trust her completely. I make an appointment to get

my teeth cleaned. She will drive me in her car. It's an excuse to leave the compound.

By the time of my appointment, I will have heard at the pool that another teacher, a recent graduate of Stanford, had been told by this same dentist during her visit that she had several cavities that would have to be filled. This young Stanford graduate had had her teeth checked by her dentist in California just before she came to El Salvador and knew she had no cavities.

Despite this disconcerting piece of information, I keep my appointment, partly because I want to see if she will tell me the same thing, that I have cavities I don't have, but mostly because I need to get out of the compound. Two weeks inside the walls is beginning to feel like being blindfolded. I have no idea where I am, no idea of what is beyond the walls.

At the end of her work day in the school accounting office, I meet the dentist and she drives us a short distance through leafy neighborhoods to her own modest home that has a dental chair and instruments in a room connected to the rest of the house. She begins and almost immediately tells me I have many cavities that need to be filled. I explain that I can't afford to have major dental work done in El Salvador and that I have Blue Cross insurance that will cover this back in Michigan.

I wonder why a woman, so plausible in other respects, would risk her reputation as a dentist and risk losing future clients by lying about cavities to someone who will almost certainly know differently. Perhaps it doesn't occur to her that Americans go to the dentist every six months. Perhaps she doesn't know that our Blue Cross insurance covers dental visits. But how could she have been working with Americans so long and not know these things? She must be desperate for money, is all I'm able to conclude. Perhaps her family, allegedly connected to the military, has fallen from favor with the powers that be or has had some other reversal of fortune.

Many of the Salvadoran teachers at the school sell things. I've heard that their wages are one-half to one-third what the Americans are paid and that they don't receive health insurance, pensions, or any other benefits. Several of the female teachers sell Avon. I don't know what the male teachers sell, but a female math teacher sells beautiful, expensive, handmade jewelry. One of the female second grade teachers sells soft cloth dolls made from hand-dyed indigo. I will buy one for my granddaughter for a Christmas present. They all seem to make money on the side, in addition to their jobs at the school.

While the woman works on my teeth she introduces me to her husband, her children, and her children's nanny, an older woman who was also her nanny as a child. "She is a member of the family. She is like my mother," the dentist explains. "In many ways she is my mother. I feel so blessed to have her with me." This nanny never had any children of her own. "My children," the dentist says, "are like her grandchildren."

The servants in El Salvador are given room and board, but not really paid a living wage. The relationship is complicated. The same servant families may have been with the same owner families for generations, and their identity is linked to the wealth and social standing of their owners. Sometimes maids will give birth to the children of the owners, so the families are linked by blood as well as proximity.

The friendly dentist, I learn, is also in charge of the school field trips offered to new teachers in the orientation period before school. There's a small fee, which I assume will go to her. Partly to compensate for the fact that I only want my teeth cleaned, nothing more, I sign up for the field trips. Two field trips are offered before school starts, one to the mountains and one to a lagoon, using the school's van for each one.

There's an afternoon tea at the American Embassy to which all the teachers and staff are invited. "There'll be good food," the worldly head of the English department informs us, "and free wine, if we're lucky." She has been to these American Embassy parties before in other countries. She seems to have taught all over the world. Her last teaching job was in Turkey.

The head of the English Department is the head because she has experience teaching overseas. It's hard to tell how old she is. She seems to be more than thirty and less than fifty. She is quick-moving, bird-like, impatient, aggressive, and single-minded. She is unmarried, with short brown hair, and glasses. She seems to know the ropes as far as international schools go but knows little about literature beyond the novels of Jane Austen.

She likes to organize things. She gets all the teachers in the English department to sort all the novels and textbooks that have accumulated over the years in the back rooms at the school. She is bossy, opinionated, and, as it will turn out, a serious alcoholic who can't remember her own opinions from one day to the next. I will learn to nod and agree with whatever she says and ultimately do things my own way. When she will tell me I should be doing this instead of that I'll apologize and say I must have misunderstood and that I'll make the correction, but then I never do. She herself can't remember what she'd told me to do so she never pursues it. But I don't know any of that when she encourages us all to go to the Embassy tea.

The American Embassy is close to our school and not nearly as posh as I had hoped. Yes, it's a big, mansion-like place with gardens. Little tea sandwiches are served by a discreet Salvadoran maid who walks around with them on a silver tray. But there is no wine. The American ambassador is an oddly taciturn, stodgy, heavy-set woman—like the tower in a chess set. She doesn't seem to speak. Her husband is almost like a wife. He's in the background, amiable and almost subservient. They are a strange couple. The afternoon tea is a lackluster affair.

The trip to the lagoon is arranged by one of the office secretaries. We go in two school vans. Other than the trip from the airport in the middle of the night, I have not seen any of the downtown parts of the city of San Salvador in the daylight.

In the streets are men in orange jumpsuits, some crippled or visibly deranged, begging with rectangular metal boxes. The boxes are locked and have a slot in the top for money. I think they must be licensed beggars.

At some intersections there are children, costumed and heavily made up as clowns, sometimes juggling, sometimes with an older female person who might be a mother or an older sister. They, too, collect fees but not in metal boxes. At some intersections women are selling the most beautifully decorated giant tins of olive oil. The explanation is that the Italians donated olive oil after the earthquake but it's unsuited to the Salvadoran style of cooking. Salvadorans are used to cooking with corn oil; they can heat that to a much higher temperature than they can olive oil. They deep fry a lot of food, and if they get the olive oil hot enough to do that, it burns.

We are traveling on a flat, sandy road. It feels like we are inland from the ocean by maybe a mile. There are palm trees and coconut trees. We pass shacks made of cardboard and palm fronds. In the front yards of the huts are dirty, aimless, naked children and dirty, idle, almost-naked men who stare at us. Their eyes are eerily empty. Women of all ages, sometimes topless, are working, tending to infants, washing clothes, and cooking over small fires. The women do not look at us. These are very small people, almost pygmies. The children have the chalky skin and protruding bellies of the severely malnourished.

It rains once. The rain comes right through the sunlight. The leaves on the trees glisten like miniature, reflective, green lakes.

Finally we arrive at a large, beautiful, sixties-style ranch home situated between the ocean and a lagoon. The man's wife is gone. When I ask one of the other female teachers where she is, she whispers that the school secretary is having an affair with the man who owns the home. She thinks the wife may be away for the afternoon, or possibly out of the country.

The school must be paying the man to host this field trip. There's an air of false and frightening friendliness coming from him. I find him terrifying. This is a man trying to be nice to tourists who seems like he was previously never nice to anyone. He appears to be an unemployed military guy whose well-placed friends are trying to keep him solvent.

Did it not cross anyone's mind that this field trip, as planned, might come across as creepy to sheltered Americans, unaccustomed to having thugs, smiling and being friendly for perhaps the first time in their lives, posing as tour guides? None of the new teachers have ever seen El Salvador. Many of us have never left the United States or Canada.

Some in the group have the shell-shocked expressions of people who've found themselves beyond the confines of civilization for the first time ever in their entire lives, like someone who's found the eye of an ox on his plate and is wondering how to eat it. Others look like college freshmen, dazed and overwhelmed, who can't wait to call home. Anyone more sophisticated than the members of our group had wisely decided not to sign up for this field trip.

I'm ushered onto a small rowboat and taken back to the shores of an ancient lagoon. The dark sand of the lagoon shore is scattered with pieces of what look like purple-black obsidian. There is a fish in the lagoon, we are told, a prehistoric fish, with the mouth of a crocodile. Back at the home the man's female servants have prepared hot dogs, potato chips and cake inside the house, while off the back porch the man's male servants throw coconuts to the compound's mangy dogs. The dogs fall on the woolly balls, the size of human heads, and tear them to shreds as if they haven't eaten in days.

On the next field trip, this one to the mountains, we travel out of the city in a different direction. This time we are all in one van. After about an hour we are traveling through an old town with a large plaza. Off to one side is a church that has been partially destroyed.

In the plaza are women selling corn they've roasted over charcoal. These women are tall and stately. They look like royalty, especially compared to the people staring at us from the thatched huts along the beach the week before, or even compared to the multitude of short, submissive workers at our school. They serve the roasted corn with ketchup and mayonnaise in a way that is ineffably dignified. One of my fellow teachers, a young American math teacher, says the corn is good, more like field corn than sweet corn. I like the familiar smoky smell of the roasting corn.

On the curvy mountain roads we are twice passed by huge, speeding Coca Cola trucks with two armed guards, one on each side, sitting inside the backs, in what look like bulletproof enclosures. Another armed guard sits in the passenger seat in the front. These mountains, once heavily forested with mahogany, are now eroded and barren.

We stop in a small mountain village. We are told the place is famous for shade-grown coffee. Someone asks where the coffee is grown. We won't be going there, we're told, because it's quite far and the roads are bad. There are only a few people in the village. We're told they're all cultivating coffee up on the steep slopes of the mountains.

There's an American program in the village to help people make sun-dried bricks. The young American, a Quaker, explains that houses made of sun-dried bricks are more earthquake resistant than houses made of other materials. This is an ancient, indigenous method of making bricks, and now the young man and his program are restoring the craft. The bricks are made with mud and straw. They are about eight inches square and five inches thick. They are laid out in rows in the sun, like square loaves of bread, to dry.

We visit a national park where I see an almost-dead tarantula. I wouldn't have known it was a tarantula but someone pointed it out to me. It's the size and shape of a baby turtle, about three inches across, with a furry back and hairy legs.

We come down out of the mountains to a small hotel by a stream, the border between Honduras and El Salvador. It's a trickle of water, about two feet across and we are encouraged to hop across it. "You are border-hopping," the dentist says, making a joke.

The oddest thing about the trip to the mountains is the wife of the military man in charge. She's an older woman with huge breasts, sallow skin, and dyed, brassy-blonde hair. She looks and acts like a prostitute. She wears tight, sexy clothes that reveal all of the flaws of aging. Her face is caked with makeup. She continually reapplies her purplish lipstick. As we pass by fields where peasants are working, she rolls down the window of the van and waves to the men, women, and children in the fields, smiling garishly and saying hello in a jolly, raucous way, a caricature of a royal princess passing through her royal lands.

Only one or two of the field workers appear to return her wave, and in such a desultory way it's hard to tell if they waved or not. If they did wave, it was an easy-to-miss flap of the hand, and so joyless, without a smile, as if they were afraid not to, with stiff faces and averted eyes.

At the end of the trip we are each given a glossy magazine, *El Salvador*, with many ads for beautiful hotels with swimming pools. The magazine is in gibberish English. Readers would be hard-pressed to tell you what they had read after they had read it.

The magazine opens with a sample of this writing, a message from a proud graduate of the school where I'm going to be teaching, a message from the current president of El Salvador, Francisco Flores:

"Without a doubt, tourism is a valuable tool for growing in the modern world. Isolation, fortunately, is impossible these days, and to such impossibility we owe a number of possibilities, most

of all when human beings know how to make the most and enjoy day by day, direct contact with an environment that cannot be limited by border.

Because we believe in this approach and its multiple displays, as a nation we are interested in becoming a delightful destination for our visitors, whom we hope to captivate for our proven hospitality, our natural scenery, and the typical cheerfulness we enjoy in the tropics.

Our recent past has allowed the Salvadorans to look at the future with more confidence in our vitality, enterprising spirit and understanding of the reality of the human being. That is why we value freedom with responsibility and place as a commitment to which we are always connected to."

The dentist instructs us to tell all our American friends and relatives about the wonderful tourist possibilities in El Salvador. It doesn't seem to occur to the people who have orchestrated the field trips that they have also told us never to leave the compound unless we are with them. Perhaps they are assuming that any foreign visitors to El Salvador will sign up for tours with their ex-military friends as guides.

The man at the gate and I begin, informally, speaking Spanish. "*Hermosa dias, Senor,*" I say and he responds, "*Buenos dias, Professora.*" We are all professors now. Professor is simply the Spanish word for teacher, but it has a different ring in El Salvador since teachers, because they are educated, are considered upper class.

I learn the gateman is married and has two children. He has a beautiful sister who, in the classic Cinderella story, was a maid for an American teacher at the school, and they fell in love and got married. This man's brother-in-law, the American teacher married to the gateman's beautiful sister, is now dying of cancer and the man's son, a scholarship student at the school, is about to graduate. The gateman is proud of this nephew. The youngster is an excellent student and will qualify for a scholarship to a school in the United States.

The gateman tells me he moonlights as a taxi driver. When he was younger and single, he lived in Los Angeles for five years and drove a taxi there. His taxi, like most of the taxis, is yellow but it's a hand-painted yellow, as if he'd painted it with house paint. You can see the brush strokes. It's a strange-looking taxi in other ways, too. Every part of it, like those dogs which are part dachshund and part collie and part eight other things, looks like it came from a different make of car. When I receive my second paycheck I hire him to take me to buy two fans and also some screens for the windows.

Seeing a small drugstore as he's driving, I ask him to stop. I need aspirin. The drugstore is run-down and sparsely stocked. They do have aspirin. As I'm paying, I see a set of brand new pots and pans for almost nothing. I buy them, even though I suspect they may be counterfeit and might deteriorate when I use them. They will turn out to be the best pots and pans I've ever had in my life. Fissler. Every time I use them I will wonder how they ended up on that drugstore counter.

I have heard from one of the other teachers that there's an artists' market in San Salvador where people sell handmade crafts. I ask the gateman to take me there on the way back to the *complejo* so I can see some of the things.

The market is next to a park with large trees. There are small paths between the booths, like any artists' market in California. But the goods are all cheap and ugly, badly made in a factory, not hand-crafted. The glue shows. There are paint drips. The images are clichés. The same images are repeated on everything. The clothing is not put together well. The material is cheap polyester and the seams are crooked and already pulling out. There is not a spark of creativity in a single item. It's a depressing artists' market. I never go back.

My maid tells me she will lose three days of work in the coming week because they have to shut off the water mains in the part of the city where her other clients live. The water mains throughout San Salvador are slowly being repaired after the damage caused the year before by the earthquake.

My maid is a pretty, plump woman, the fifty-one-year-old mother of four and grandmother of eight. Like many poor women in El Salvador, she seems never to have had a husband for long. The Latin male is itinerant even when married. The women have become accustomed, over many centuries, to the fact that their husbands have mistresses and father children randomly. My maid has shown me a photo of herself when she was young. She was very beautiful, short and shapely with incredible eyes. I had heard she had once been the girlfriend of one of the men who has children at my school.

She says she worked in the United States and sent money home while her mother raised her children. Those same children don't love and respect her, she says, because she went away. Even though she sent money home, her mother, the children's grandmother, the one who raised her children, is the one they feel is their real mother.

Now my maid, like her mother before her, is raising her daughters' children, while those daughters work in the United States and send money back to El Salvador. Her eighty-year-old mother is sick; my maid takes care of her. My maid's son, a construction worker who lives in San Salvador, has had an injury and can't work. My maid has many people to support. If a person loses three day's wages when they're already at bare minimum, then that's severe. I tell her she can help me clean my classroom for three days.

All the desks need to be wiped down with an antiseptic solution, Lysol or bleach. The windows need to be washed. The classroom is infested with mosquitoes. As we begin to work, one of the office staff comes by and says the school's janitors will do that. My maid can't help me.

This throws a monkey wrench into my plans, but I decide that as long as I have my maid with me, we should walk to the small store near the Princess Hotel and she can help me buy a needle and thread. After my experience trying to buy eggs with pantomime, I've been putting off buying a needle and thread. I can imagine trying to imitate a needle going in and out of a piece of cloth, but imagining this and then doing it and having it actually mean something to someone else—across a language barrier and a cultural barrier—are two different things.

I should have brought needle and thread with me but hadn't thought of it when I was back in Michigan packing to come to El Salvador. If I had thought of it, it still would have never occurred to me that a needle and thread would be difficult to buy because walking about the streets of San Salvador would be dangerous. Yes, I had known it was a violent country, but I hadn't known it was so violent that one couldn't go out, safely, and buy a needle and thread. My maid seems somewhat discomfited by my request that she go along with me to the store, but walks with me anyway, visibly uncomfortable for reasons I never learn.

After we walk to the store and return to my classroom, where I will be supervising the cleaning, I ask my maid to please go back and work in the apartment. I tell her I would like her to wash floors and do the laundry and ironing. I give her the needle and thread. If she has time could she please mend my blue blouse? I come home in the middle of the day for lunch and find her gone. I come back two hours later and she is still gone.

The second day she doesn't come at all. The guard at the gate comes to my apartment and tells me the maid called him and said she was sick and won't come until Saturday. I'm not sure what's going on. Was she really sick? Did she say she had no work when she did? Did she have to go to the other job anyway? Was her discomfort when we walked to the store due to her feeling that she was supposed to be at her other job and she was afraid someone might see her out walking with me? Did she have a family emergency and needed extra money and thought I might give it to her? Was her mother sick?

Saturday, mid-morning, about 11, she shows up with a granddaughter in tow. She tells me that she can only stay until noon. Both of them are all dressed up. She has dressed the little girl in a frilly dress and a baseball cap with fake blonde braids attached. I tell her the little girl looks cute. *"Muy lindo,"* I say. *"Muy bonito."*

I don't really need a maid, and with this incident discover that I don't like having one. I don't like the fact that the school more or less entered me into this relationship where one person, me, so clearly takes advantage of another.

Of course the usual argument is that she's better off with a job than without one. But it's still wrong not to pay someone a living wage. I pay her double, twenty dollars a day instead of ten dollars a day, but it doesn't help me to want her in my life. Having a maid you don't want is like dating someone you don't like; it's a situation of diminishing returns.

Not that it matters much, but my supplies of Mazola oil and laundry soap and Lestoil are going down faster than makes sense for one person living alone. It's not that I'm stingy, I'd give her the stuff in a heartbeat, but the idea that she's "gleaning" while I'm at work is just too weird for words. It's not on the up and up. It's desperate and it partakes of the weirdness of the entire country.

She doesn't steal the iodine, of which I use a fair amount to wash the vegetables. She doesn't believe it's healthy to wash vegetables in water that has iodine in it. I've been told to do this, so I do it. I myself have no idea if it's essential or not, or if the iodine has adverse effects.

Now she's cooking. She's making "Christians and Moors," a simple but delicious dish of white rice and black beans, cooked separately. The black beans are seasoned with garlic, cilantro, bacon, green pepper, onion and a little tomato paste. It smells good. I grade papers and simultaneously teach her grand-daughter a little English, first having her draw a picture of the word which I say in Spanish, something like *table*, letting her correct me and teach me the Spanish. Then I write the word in English on paper so she can copy it. I say it out loud, and she repeats it. The child is well-behaved and copies the letters onto the paper, five times for each word.

I say, *"Beuno! Bravo!"* each time the child completes a task. Meanwhile I'm aware that all of the scraps of cilantro, green pepper, and onion are going into a separate, small garbage bag. Later, as I'm falling asleep, I realize that wasn't garbage, but something she was going to use for her own supper.

Maids have to sign in and out of the *complejo*, the housing complex. They have to have their bags checked by the guard. If I give my maid anything I can't use—extra eggs, for example—I have to give her a note or walk her to the gate and explain. It's demeaning for all involved. She is strictly forbidden by the school from doing her laundry with mine, although I'm pretty sure she does it because she brings a change of clothes and of-ten seems to wear extra layers, even in the heat. If caught in the act by the school, or if one of the other maids becomes angry at her for some reason and decides to lie and say she saw my maid wash her clothes with mine, she would be fired. It's just a bad relationship in every respect: not honest, not caring, not fair, not something I want in my life.

I mull over the sly way she hinted that she needed extra work and then didn't show up for the time for which I'd paid her. What was going on in her mind? I'm also baffled by her relationship with the school itself. I feel like I was railroaded by the school into having a maid before I had time to think about it. Perhaps they just assumed that no one in his or her right mind would ever turn down the chance to have a maid for ten dollars a day.

For the first time, it occurs to me that my maid might be spying on me. Perhaps she's working for the school and getting paid by them, as well as working for me and getting paid by me; or perhaps reporting back to the school is one of the conditions for employment. I had heard from several sources that working in any capacity at the school where I teach is desirable work. It's safe, for one thing, at least inside the school grounds.

I don't want the administration to notice me, and therefore am not going to change anything. But I resolve that the next time my maid tells me she has a sudden loss of income, I will not offer to make it up for her.

I'm teaching Ninth Grade which has a curriculum similar to any in the states: *To Kill a Mockingbird, Romeo and Juliet,* vocabulary, grammar, spelling and composition. I tell my students to rent the movies of *To Kill a Mockingbird* and *Romeo and Juliet,* in English with Spanish subtitles, and to watch them over and over until they've learned the characters and the sequence of events. It will make it easier when we start to study these things in class. The students, we are told, have been studying English since kindergarten. Louisiana and I compare notes. "My students have a vocabulary of a hundred words," he says. He's given up on teaching *Gilgamesh,* at least for the time being.

As it always does in the first few weeks, the teaching requires all of my time and attention. The only person I have time even to say hello to is the young man from Louisiana teaching Tenth Grade English in the classroom next to me. We are the only two American teachers in the so-called chicken coops, the small, low-ceilinged classrooms. The walls are cheap, particle board partitions that don't go all the way to the ceiling. I can hear everything that goes on in the classrooms on either side of me.

The rooms are hot and swampy. We have air-conditioning but it's often not working.

The one lucky thing is that several dramatically beautiful toucans have come and camped out in the trees outside our windows. The toucans look like intellectuals, with big colorful beaks and sentient eyes. They make a soft whirring noise. One day a student tells me toucans are not commonly seen on the school grounds but are refugees, perhaps from the dislocations caused by the earthquake the year before.

The young man from Louisiana is an excellent teacher. He's handsome and charismatic. His students adore him. He can speak Spanish fluently. His students are fully engaged, but he can shut them down in an instant. They respect him. He'd told me he'd never taught before so that means he's a natural. I know this because the walls are so thin I can hear him. He uses Pictionary as a teaching tool. I wish I'd thought of it. My students, despite what I'd been told, speak almost no English.

I do have one Salvadoran student who is fluent in English and, more importantly, has an ability to understand and comment on what he's reading. When I mention this to his mother, a teacher in the elementary school, and say I could give him readings at a higher level so that eventually he could get a scholarship to a college in the United States, she seems alarmed. "He has many, many home duties," she says. "He has to take care of his sister. He cannot do that." The student who had been so engaged and delightful becomes as dull as all the others. After that, I never openly encourage him.

We are observed every day by the Dean of Students. She comes and stands outside in the intense heat, listening, with her arms crossed. She always wears high heels, so I can always hear her coming.

The sound of her high heels clicking on the tiles of the *passarella* as she approaches has become an ominous sound. At first it was unconsciously or subliminally ominous, but after a week, I'm conscious of a feeling of dread the minute I hear the sound of her high heels, "click-click, click-click," getting closer and closer.

There's a huge black moth in my classroom. If I link my thumbs and spread out my fingers, it's the size of both my hands together. The students tell me it's a bad omen, but when I show the Dean of Students she laughs and says, "Nonsense. A silly superstition, Salvadorans are very superstitious."

The teaching is all-consuming, and I have neither the time nor energy to leave the compound. I go to my classroom very early in the morning to prepare for the day, come back at sup-pertime and often go back again to my classroom in the eve-ning. It's the only place where I have a computer on which to create lesson plans and keep track of the usual things like at-tendance and completed assignments.

We study ten vocabulary words a day, Monday through Thursday, at the beginning of every hour: forty words a week. Every Monday I give them the list of words, and every Friday there's a test. We review the words at the beginning and again at the end of the hour. There is absolutely no reason these stu-dents can't learn five hundred words in a year.

Almost every day I have my students write a paragraph or two in their journal and then ask for volunteers to read out loud what they've written. "Reading, writing, speaking," is what the school emphasizes in their curriculum. The students' daily writing is a good way for me to begin to get to know their interests and their abilities. Only a few students attempt to write in English, and so for the rest we translate.

A girl writes about a walk in the country at the family's *fin-ca* or country house. She becomes hopelessly lost and cannot get back home. The reason? A torrential rain during the night had made a river where there hadn't been one before.

The families of my students have homes in San Salvador, usually in the neighborhood close to the school. Many families also have homes out in the country where they have horses, swimming pools, parties. They have lavish lifestyles. They ski in Switzerland. They drive Humvees. They have private planes. They have apartments in Paris.

These children have lots and lots of servants. The servants

work for almost nothing since there is little other work. The wealthy elite also hire other people—usually Americans: doctors, lawyers, teachers—who do not work so cheaply, but are infinitely replaceable. Educated workers have to be imported. There are Salvadoran teachers at the school, but there seem to be many more from The United States or Canada. The other teachers like me who teach at my school are called "the import staff," and there would seem to be an endless supply of us.

My students are not self-sufficient. If their hired help ever walked away, if they ever lost all their money, they wouldn't be able to dress themselves, much less boil an egg. Their maids do everything. I learn that sometimes my students hit their maids, or order them to be beaten.

My students are proud of not working. A very handsome, emotionally unstable, dim-witted, green-eyed, curly-haired blond Ninth Grade boy from one of the country's oldest banking families tells me proudly, "My father has never worked, Meese." The students pronounce "Miss" as "Meese," with a Spanish accent. To me it sounds like an ultra-plural. So that, if mice is the plural of mouse, then *meese* would mean many more mice than that. The sound itself is like a mouse's squeak and when many students are trying to get my attention it's as if the room is full of giant mice. I could imagine someone saying, "I knew the mice were coming into the house from the fields, but this is more than I ever imagined. Oh my goodness, Jennifer, look at all these *meese!*"

The elite Salvadoran males prefer their offspring to have light skin. To that end they have sought out American and European girls to marry. Many have succeeded in finding non-Salvadoran mates. However, it seems not to have occurred to them, or perhaps they don't care, or perhaps it was difficult to manage, whether or not the prospective bride is also intelligent. The ideal for these men, if they can afford it, the men with the most money and power, is some malleable female, preferably clothed in an expensive education, or at least designer couture, someone willing to pretend there's no dark side, someone to provide some semblance of civilization because a life of sheer brutality is difficult even for brutes.

One of my students, with an American mother and Salvadoran father, with a family name which is the same as that of a general who killed thirty thousand peasants, is known as "the only one who doesn't lie" in his Ninth Grade class.

A few students throughout the Ninth Grade seem to have American mothers. None of the students seem to have an American or European father. In almost all cases the Salvadoran men met their American wives while they were attending universities in the United States, during a time the girls were on spring break from college, vacationing in Florida, sunning themselves beside the hotel pools in Miami, or sunning themselves on the beaches in Fort Lauderdale. For a naïve American girl, or a very cynical one, marriage to a Salvadoran man from a family with lots of money, might seem like a path to a life of ease: a private plane, a big house, several gardeners, a chauffeur, a maid, a cook, a housekeeper, a nanny. What could possibly be wrong with this?

The boy who never lies, and who has an American mother, says to me, "You need to be more strict, Meese." He is sweet, earnest. He's a solid and serious young person, and likable. "We need to learn grammar."

I sense that this is coming from his father, not from him. I tell him that I am very strict and reassure him that he is learning grammar. "We diagram a sentence every day," I tell him. This is true but the "we" I'm using is the editorial "we." *I* diagram a sentence every day on the board and leave it there for the Dean of Students and anyone else to see as proof of my deep background in English. I had anticipated this demand for grammar and was ready for it. To the uninitiated, grammar seems concrete, whereas in fact grammar can be very abstruse. "Your grammar is excellent," I tell the boy. "You're bilingual because of your mother and you speak English beautifully.

Please let your parents know that we are learning grammar. We diagram sentences daily. Every vocabulary word has to be defined as a part of speech."

What I don't tell him is that all the vocabulary words are nouns since it's too hard for most people to make pictures of the other parts of speech. It doesn't occur to him that all the vocabulary words are nouns, nor does he know that learning the parts of speech is not all there is to grammar. Split infinitives, dangling participles, correlative conjunctions, mixed tenses and subject-verb agreement are so far beyond my students that I would not dare broach such abstractions. The weekly vocabulary test is to choose ten words out of the list of forty, make a picture of the word, and write a definition. They only have to get ten words right to get an A. They know on Monday the words on which they will be tested on Friday.

Therefore it's surprising one Friday when one of my best students, a tall girl with sallow skin and protruding green eyes, steals the test. I'm writing on the board, my back to the room, when the girl comes into the classroom early and—apparently thinking I'm not looking, have no peripheral vision, and will never notice—with impressive sleight of hand slides the vocabulary test off her desk into her other school papers, leaves a dummy test in its place and scurries out with the genuine article to share with her fellow students. This girl has perfected the debutante slouch and sullen expression to match. She's considered a great beauty in El Salvador because she does not look totally Indian and is not short.

I never point out to this girl that it isn't necessary to steal this test since students are always given the list of words, essentially given the test, on Monday. I don't want to embarrass her. Even an idiot should have been able to figure out that the test was flunk-proof since even the poorest student could find ten words out of forty that she knows.

Many of the vocabulary words are repeated from tests from all the previous weeks. Some of them are baby words such as cat, dog, and frog; others are cognates, such as palace and drama, words almost identical in both Spanish and English. I had designed the test specifically for them, and for me, so that I could pass every student and have the paperwork to justify it. I teach all the other required subjects, too, but the vocabulary tests are the only part of the curriculum that has a weekly test and a numerical score. Everything else—Shakespeare, composition, classroom participation—is graded with satisfactory or unsatisfactory and of course all my students are satisfactory. The only score that matters is vocabulary.

Altogether they have some unusual notions of learning. A young female student, when we are acting out scenes from *Romeo and Juliet*, tells me, "Meese, we need to learn the real Shakespeare."

I'm astonished and say, "This is the real Shakespeare. He wrote dramas."

"No, Meese," she says, "from the book."

I tap the cover of their textbook which is on my desk. "And it is from the book, your textbook right here."

She still looks dubious. She apparently thinks the real Shakespeare would be deadly dull and difficult, probably from a much larger, darker, heavier book, perhaps leather-bound and buckled.

One Monday several of my students are upset. I overhear some of them talking about how men with machine guns had come to an adjacent *finca* and killed several workers. They speak in Spanish. They don't know I can understand.

When something bad happens in the lives of my students, I become aware of it because they will be asking to go to the nurse's office. I always let them go. I've never taught anywhere where so many students needed to go to the nurse's office so often. One day during my planning period I stop at the nurse's office, pretending I have a headache. There is the school counselor, the female Salvadoran math teacher who sells jewelry, the pretty secretary from the main office who was having an affair with the man at the lagoon, and several students, male and female, all sitting around talking and taking aspirin and drinking purified water from the water cooler in tiny, pleated, ivory-colored paper cups.

My students often say, "Salvadorans are very lazy, Meese. They don't like to work." This is their explanation of the poverty in their country. This is their explanation for why their maids need to be beaten. This is their explanation for why the roads are so bad. It took me a while to understand that they do not see themselves as Salvadoran in the same way as the rest of the population. They are white, in their view, not actually indigenous. Somehow they imagine that they are European.

One day, standing in my classroom, looking out at a sea of Native American faces, I ask, "How many people in here have any Indian ancestry?"

No one raises a hand. "Meese," says a sweet little boy in the front row whose family owns a chain of grocery stores and who's simple-minded, perhaps from the accident with firecrackers that damaged part of his face, perhaps from birth. I've heard both reasons. "Meese," he says patiently and politely, in the tone of voice of someone explaining something so obvious it shouldn't need explaining, perhaps the way people have spoken to him, "we only count our ancestry on the Spanish side."

A large, plump, young man with an unusually big, round head, like a pumpkin (in fact he's called pumpkin-head, *cabeza de calabaza*, by the other students), writes about a ghost in the garden. He heard her wailing at night, he reads, and we translate for him. He saw her walking along the top of the wall.

She was wearing a white dress, the young man recalls. Later one of the gardeners said the ghost was a mother looking for her daughter, a beautiful young woman who had been tortured to death in the basement of the house. The young man's house at that time was the presidential palace, I learn from overhearing the other students in the class. This boy is very slow mentally. He's confused and saddened by what he had seen and unable to understand why the other students are trying to shush him.

"An apparition," I say, and write the word on the board, as if all we are doing in this class is vocabulary. "An appearance," I explain, "but one that is intangible." They have good references for examples of apparitions from the Catholic religion. I ask a student for the Spanish for apparition which I already know is *aparicion,* but I pretend I don't know so they can feel like they're helping. The student says the word. I repeat it and write it on the board. "For example," I say, "when the Angel of God appeared to Mary that was an apparition, or *l'aparicion.*"

I often come early to my classroom and leave late, so I see a lot of the janitor. He's a handsome man, but very short. He has to stand on a chair to clean the blackboard. He has quite a social life and is always on his cell phone. I wonder how he can afford a cell phone on his salary. Perhaps he lives at home and has no financial obligations. It will be weeks before I realize his cell phone is a fake one, after he forgets it in my classroom for a few minutes.

That day, when I pick up the cell phone to return it to him, I see it's a toy. Instead of taking it to him, I go and get him where he is in the next room and bring him back to get it. I don't want him to know that I know, and I never let on. Every day we smile, and go on about our respective chores, his of cleaning and mine of logging student work.

The other teachers had told me that the cheating by these students would be off the charts. The work the students would turn in, almost without exception, would be downloaded off the Internet. The head of the English Department has given all of the English teachers a list of websites so we can double-check the plagiarized papers. But I can't be bothered spending hours and hours verifying plagiarism and then confronting the student—and his or her parents—as the head of the English Department seems to suggest we should do.

I have my students do their writing in class. "Just do the

best you can," I say. "Your honest thoughts, that's what's important." I don't want an adversarial relationship with my students and their parents. And what about the students we don't catch? It just encourages them to engage in an endless game of cat and mouse.

I'm lucky I'm teaching English. The math teacher is not so lucky. He's a really nice, really smart guy from Connecticut who could have and should have gone to Harvard but wanted to pay down some of his student loans first. "If you'd studied for the test the first time," I hear him shout across the open concourse to a student who's complaining about re-taking a math test on a Saturday morning, "then you wouldn't have to take it a second time." Math, you can't fudge that. Either you know it or you don't.

With the exception of a Danish girl, the daughter of people working with USAID, whose work is perfect, and one Salvadoran boy—the one who could do more if his mother wasn't afraid—the writing the students produce is unreadable and so I don't. I don't read it. I solemnly collect the work, pretending it has great value, solemnly pretend to grade it and, continuing the charade, make a few corrections in the spelling and the grammar, and solemnly return it so they can add it to their portfolios.

Writing is about putting one's thoughts down on paper and one can't do that unless one has some. Suffocating the mind, like foot-binding, isn't reversible. The time for developing the ability to have thoughts is when people are children and everything's growing. If it's not allowed then, it's unlikely to happen later. My students are already too old. The part of the brain that should have acquired the wiring for thought has gone dark.

I work in a classroom next to an older Salvadoran man who is teaching history. Through the thin walls that don't go all the way to the ceiling, I can tell he is only teaching history from about the time the Spaniards arrived in 1500 to about the time they left in 1800. He doesn't mention all the massacres of the peasants since then by the *Catorce Grande*, the ruling oligarchs, *los ricos*. El Salvador is the only Latin American country where there is no indigenous dress. The reason, according to *Lonely Planet*, is that so many peasants have been taken out and shot that no one wants to look like one.

My cover is that I'm always working. I go to my classroom early and leave late. I seem to be the only one around at 7 A.M., other than the taller-than-average, well-dressed security guards. I like the quiet. After the security guards, there are the workers who come at 8 A.M.—short, dark, stooped men carrying tools. There is an endless supply of short, dark, stooped men in this country, laborers. They work like animals in the hot sun. They look old, even when they are young.

A security guard comes by my room and in broken English asks if I am always working. *Siempre trabahandron* is the Spanish. "Yes," I simper. I'm not going to tangle with these people. "*Si, senor, siempre.*"

Sometimes the kindergarten teacher stops by my classroom when she is on her way back to the housing compound, and then we walk together. She and her husband have two daughters in elementary school here. They came from New York State to have a family adventure and help their children learn about a larger world.

The kindergarten teacher had asked the school, back in early August when we were all supposed to submit requests for supplies, for a large dollhouse. Her plan had been to have her students learn the names of things by actually touching them. She has the high, chirping voice of a gerbil, the kind of voice kindergarten teachers often develop. Perhaps it's a good voice to use with her young charges. I want to tell her to talk in a normal voice, but always stop myself: that is her normal voice.

This day she comes and says, "Well, I have some good news and some bad news." She laughs. "The good news is that a big, beautiful dollhouse with all kinds of furniture arrived." She laughs again. "The bad news is that the Salvadoran head of the elementary school has put it behind a high, white picket fence with a large sign that reads, 'Do not touch,' in English and *'No tocar'* in Spanish."

Her husband is the computer teacher. He's a man with white-blonde eyelashes and hair to match. He always seems to be blinking in the light. He bought a car and outfitted it with a sophisticated global positioning system (GPS) he made himself. There are no printed road maps of El Salvador. They have invited me to join them on their journeys around the country, but it seems risky to me, after what the man from the State Department said about never leaving the school compound unless we were under armed guard, and so I demur, saying I have too much work.

This family has a maid who comes five days a week. The kindergarten teacher and her husband do not like to cook, clean, or do laundry. It was always an issue in their marriage. He complained that the house was dirty and she complained that he didn't help.

Together they make an excellent income and so can easily afford the two hundred dollars a month it costs to have a full-time maid. The kindergarten teacher says her maid steals from her—the same cooking oil, laundry soap and odds and ends that I find missing—but she doesn't care at all. Having a maid is such a good deal that the loss of a cup of soap here, a little Mazola oil there, is ridiculously unimportant.

The kindergarten teacher is making friends with some of the Salvadoran teachers in the elementary school, and one beautiful afternoon she asks if I'd like to go with her to a meeting of a group of evangelical missionaries. The Salvadoran elementary school teacher will drive.

I have not left the *complejo,* as our housing compound is called, since I've arrived except for: the two, strange field trips; three heavily guarded trips to the bank and the grocery store; my supper outing to the Princess Hotel with Louisiana; the egg-buying expedition; one little taxi adventure to get fans and screens; and the drab excursions to the American Embassy and the dentist. I feel suddenly like I've been a prisoner for weeks. I say that I would love to go.

It's a national holiday. There is no school. I've worked all day in my classroom on lesson plans. When the kindergarten teacher comes to get me to go to the supper meeting of evangelicals, the school janitors have just come to wheel my computer out on a hand truck so they can clean it. I mention to the kindergarten teacher that this is the second time the men have come to clean my computer and back home I never heard of that. I hadn't known that computers got dirty. She rolls her eyes and says, "They're checking your emails," then laughs. "Computers don't get dirty."

The kindergarten teacher tells me that one of the mothers of her students came in the day before, crying hysterically. She had been mugged at a stoplight. She told the kindergarten teacher that she wants to go to Los Angeles and start a cleaning business. When we drive through San Salvador—beyond the confines of our *complejo,* which is located in what I now realize is, relatively speaking, a very posh neighborhood—I see that the city is horrifyingly impoverished. People live in jerry-built, leaning homes made of scrap pieces of tin, car doors, cardboard, and plywood taken from shipping containers. The houses, the size of outhouses, are stacked on top of each other on the steep banks of a ravine above a little trickle of water.

The air is thick with smoke, and a smell like burning rubber, a stench of death, of sewage and of garbage. What *are* they burning down there? Several houses are wrapped with duct tape. The roofs are held down with rocks and garbage. I see part of a wringer washer on one roof, and what looks like a rusting motorcycle on another. I'm told that's where my maid lives—in one of those houses—and that the people must use the water in the ravine for bathing and cooking. The wealth of my students is obscene in comparison, but no more so than the wealth of people living in a Park Avenue high-rise in Manhattan, far above the homeless dying in the bowels of the city.

The kindergarten teacher is Jewish and I'm not of any religion. The house where the religious gathering is taking place is a traditional house. It's on a real street and it's on flat land, but it's dirty and crumbling. The walls and ceiling are made of plaster and lath, and in many places the lath is exposed. I'm told the home was damaged ten months earlier, during the big earthquake in January 2001.

The week before, the kindergarten teacher tells me, she went with members of this group to visit an orphanage. There were children there of all ages, covered with lice and with the swollen stomachs of the malnourished. She said it was unimaginably filthy and some of the babies, who were not only thin but sick, looked like they wouldn't last a week. Many were lying naked in their own feces. Even if such children survived, lack of protein for their brains and lack of love for their emotional development would not bode well for their future existence.

The food at the evangelical meeting is not really supper but small sandwiches, faux canapés, pink bologna on Wonder bread spread lavishly with yellow margarine, cut in triangles. Green Kool-Aid is available in a plastic milk jug. I understand from the rapidity with which the food is vanishing that it is considered delectable.

All the Salvadoran adults at this gathering are polite, almost too much so, like children on their best behavior in Sunday school. It's a long evening of Bingo where we're awarded small prizes, like toothpaste and shampoo. I win a three-inch-high troll doll, the kind with fluorescent pink hair that looks like it's been caught in an air vent. Its naked, flesh-colored, soft, plastic body has rolls of fat and the whole is clothed only in a tiny piece of gold lamé. The oddest thing about this troll doll is that it has small, rubber snakes wrapped around its neck, as if they are writhing. I remove the snakes and given them to two little boys who are running around. I give the troll doll to one of the little girls at the meeting.

Almost all of the students at my school used to be Catholic, one of my students had told me, but now they are becoming Jehovah's Witnesses, and Seventh Day Adventists, Mormons and many other kinds of evangelical religions. "We like it better," he says, "More modern." He says that his grandmother is still Catholic, and still goes to mass, but that the rest of the family has become Jehovah's Witnesses.

This transition, I deduce, although I don't dare ask directly, was related to the murder of Archbishop Romero, a conservative and compliant peasant bishop the ruling oligarchs had hand-picked to represent them. They, *los ricos*, were aghast when Romero had betrayed them by having the audacity to protest the murder of a priest who had spoken on behalf of the starving peasants.

They had never anticipated this and it was totally unacceptable. Romero was dispatched forthwith, and the disenchantment and disassociation from the Catholic Church quickly followed. I had seen the movies, *Romero*, and *Salvador*, back in the states in the 1980s, movies banned in El Salvador because they implicate some of the very people whose children I'm teaching. It must have been galling to such people to continue to be members of the Catholic Church, a church which had instantly become "the enemy" when one of its representatives had had the temerity to speak on behalf of the poor, *los povres*.

There are no wealthy people at the meeting, only poor people, some of whom seem to be waiting to get handouts. These are people who suffered during the earthquake and discovered that if they are willing to appear to be potential converts, they might get gifts of food and medical supplies. Maybe one of these missionary groups will rebuild their home. It is reason enough to be there.

One of the American evangelical leaders of the meeting asks

if I would like to volunteer in an orphanage. She's from Oklahoma and down here for two weeks as part of her church's missionary work. There are many orphans, she says, in dire need of care. Since I live in San Salvador, I could go every day or at least every weekend.

I'm fixing supper Friday evening when the young man from Louisiana shows up at my door with his pots and pans in a box and a big, down pillow on top of the pots and pans. "I want you to have these," he says, "and these." He pulls two wine glasses from the box and takes half a bottle of wine out from under his arm. "We'll have a toast." He tells me he's leaving on the midnight flight.

He says the Dean of Students told him that afternoon—she was waiting for him as he finished his last class—that he was fired because he'd been using Pictionary to teach vocabulary. He laughs, lifts his glass and says, "To Pictionary." He takes a big swallow of wine, draining his glass and refilling it. "The parents of my students are drug lords and gunrunners, human traffickers, and dealers in contraband. This is a country of criminals. The only ones who are making an honest living are the hit men."

He'll return to New Orleans, live with his sister, find work in construction, and go to law school in a year. I tell him I had thought the Dean of Students was monitoring me, not him. I had thought he was a perfect teacher.

After he leaves, I go out on my balcony and gaze over at the principal's home. The principal is a large, fleshy man from Arkansas. He's top-heavy, and sways, like those balloon figures at gas stations. At our weekly staff meetings he and the Dean of Students promulgate unpleasant untruths about our American director, a man who was previously the head of a small private school in the eastern part of the United States. It's clear to most of us that the principal is positioning himself to replace the director.

The principal's Salvadoran maid is out watering the flowers. She sees me on the balcony and I wave. She doesn't wave back. She is a girl from the mountains. She had been required to put her child in an orphanage in order to take this job. The principal's house has servants' quarters, but he had felt it would be awkward having his maid's child there with his own.

Saturday I overhear someone talking at the pool about how the young man from Louisiana had taken his students on a field trip the weekend before to the Museum of the Revolution at the Catholic University. No one seems to know that he is no longer at the school, and I don't tell anyone.

Sunday morning I wake up at 5 A.M. I have no one to talk to and I need to talk to someone. After I told my family and friends about my computer being "cleaned," they told me not to send emails from my classroom or call them from the phone in my apartment. Eventually I'll find a way to use the pay phones and Internet at various places around San Salvador, but right now I'm cut off from everyone.

That morning I decide to take all of my personal correspondence and hide it in my classroom in among the grammar worksheets. No one will ever look there. I make a conscious decision to start lying to my students. I will tell them every day how much I love El Salvador and how much I love them. Your country is so beautiful! You are all such wonderful people!

My oldest sister, a zoology professor in Minneapolis, has sent books on tropical birds to help with my appreciation of beauty and connection to nature. My second oldest sister, a zoology professor in Albany, has sent books I've asked for to help with teaching: *Shakespeare Set Free*, *Literature Circles* and *The Odes of Pablo Neruda*. The sweetness of this, as much as the books, is sustaining me.

My poet-friend Laurie Carroll took the story of the student who saw the apparition and wrote a poem about it. That someone could write a poem, an act of faith in the human spirit, sustains me, too. "This is for you," she wrote:

The first time I saw the red-haired girl,
she was on the roof of the kitchen house.

Half hidden in the dappled shade of the kapok tree,
she held her milk-white hands out
into a sun-beam,
as if warming them by a campfire.

A blood-red bird flew calling through the courtyard,
and when I turned back,
she was gone.

I saw her again one bright morning,
there, just outside the gate
standing by the woman who arrives at dawn
to sell oranges and lemons from a child's cradle,
and the blind beggar who will recite scripture
for one colon or two.

Her dress was crisp, and white,
like a schoolgirl's.
untouched by the red dust that settles here
on anything that is still for a moment.

She caught my eye, nodded,
and moved into the market crowd, seamlessly.
The blind man turned to watch her pass.

I asked the gardener about the red-haired girl.
Not the young one who listens to his CD player,
and whistles through his teeth as he trims the hedges.

But the old gardener, whose hands are brown and gnarled
as the roots of the fragile fruit trees
he has tended here since boyhood.

Ah, La Innocenta," he said, and crossed himself three times.
"She is one of the convent girls brought to this house by
* the soldiers."*
He leaned close to be sure I understood his Spanish,
"During the time of the Revolution."
He shook the dew from a blossom-laden bough,
"She often returns to be sure we do not forget her,
or the evil there can be in the world."

I saw the red-haired girl once more, at evening,
moving with the soft blue mist that swirls
through the young orchard
as the night stars begin to appear.

Her white dress shone
like hope
against the pearl gray sky.

It's not a poem I show to anyone. I tuck it away. I hide it. It's a little piece of privacy, a talisman, a memory of what it was like to live somewhere where people had thoughts and wrote poems without fear.

After a cup of coffee on my balcony, I decide to go to my classroom to work. I don't want to dwell on things I can't change. I'm here. They're paying me. I signed a contract. My house in Michigan is rented to the ex-priest who teaches religion at Lake Leelanau St. Mary's. I like the hummingbirds. I know how to teach English. I'll throw myself into my work, and that will keep me distracted and in forward motion. I cross the *passarella* in the dark.

It is very early Sunday. I have the feeling someone has been in my classroom. Later I will hear from another teacher that sometimes he has found a person sleeping in his classroom, a man who sneaks out like a ghost.

Mid-morning I realize I need to take a break. There is nowhere to go but back to my apartment. For the first time I decide to leave the school grounds on my own. The Princess Hotel, if I can remember the way the boy from Louisiana took me, is right across the street, if I go down the back way by the soccer field. I will get something to eat at the Sunday brunch I'd read about the time I ate supper there.

But I get lost, down past the school's soccer field. I end up in an area of trees and bushes where people are living. There are bright blue plastic tarps rigged from poles to create the semblance of rooms. There are buckets. There are fire pits. There are clothes drying on bushes. What do they do when it rains? The people who see me are embarrassed, as am I. I recognize the janitor who cleans my classroom, but we don't say hello. I beat a hasty retreat.

I head in another direction and recognize the church I'd seen the first time I'd walked out this way. I go in and see the same wizened old Indian woman who gives me the same penetrating look. I don't give her any money. I go up to the altar and kneel in prayer. Heaven only knows why, I'm not Catholic.

The Princess Hotel buffet has scrambled eggs, bacon, toast, tamales, orange juice, coffee, pastries; the usual. I take a little of everything. I smell a strange, non-food smell, like new carpet. I'm removing the corn husks from my tamale when I realize the husks are made of pale green plastic designed to look like corn husks. They've cooked the food in plastic? I take my tamale up to the table and say to the woman there: *plasteek, toxico. No es comida.*

She smiles. I try to explain that cooking the food in plastic is not healthy. She smiles. I smile. I go back and sit down. As I pick at my food, eating a few bites of toast, sipping some of the coffee and staring into the side garden, I'm thinking about the bland expression of the woman who sees nothing wrong with cooking things in plastic. She's a food person, isn't she turned off by the smell and taste of plastic? If they're cooking the tamales in plastic and serving them that way, what are they doing back in the kitchen that I can't see? I'm thinking about the maid putting scraps of onion, cilantro and pepper in a separate, extra bag, presumably for separate garbage. Did she think I wouldn't see her do this and wonder about it?

I look out the window at the beautiful roses by the swimming pool and think about the dentist telling a patient she had cavities when she didn't. Did the dentist think this would never be noticed? I'm thinking about the field trips with the tour guides who looked like psychopathic killers. Did the school officials imagine that such field trips were going to be pleasant and well received? This whole country is like *Through the Looking Glass*. There seems to be a total disconnect, or reversal, or conflation of the real and the unreal, the actual and the invented.

When I think "disconnect," that's when I have an epiphany about teaching my students. If the left hand doesn't know what the right hand is doing, then I can trick my students into learning. Most of my students seem to be fairly good at art. They don't see it as serious. They don't see it as threatening. They think of it as play.

I decide I will tell them we are going to study Greek gods and goddesses. It's not in the syllabus, but it could be. It's standard curriculum for Ninth Grade. They will each need to make a mask. I can find a place to buy surgical gauze and paint. They will write an "I am..." poem pretending they are a Greek god or goddess. This should be fun for them. Greek gods and goddesses are vain, amoral, cruel, and capricious. My students like to get stuff off the Internet. They like to cheat even when it's not necessary. I will warn them, "No cheating! In your own words, students, that's the important thing." They will then be pleased to do little plagiarized reports on the Greek god or goddess of their choice.

They are quite adept at figuring out from body language and signature details what someone's personality might be. They like costumes. So I will have them portray a "sad" walk or an "aggressive" walk. And what kind of clothes would that person wear? And what kind of body posture would that person have? They can pretend to be Zeus or the Cyclops, Circe or Medusa. They will learn, but they won't know they're learning. And neither will their parents.

When I go up to the front desk, I see copies of the Sunday *New York Times* for sale, printed off the Internet. It's very expensive, a dollar a page for twenty pages, eight-point font, a smeary gray mess, but worth it to me in that moment. I need some contact with the outside world. If I can periscope out, like someone in a submarine, I might be able to make it here.

As I pay, there is a man beside me, also waiting to pay his bill, an unusually tall, turbaned, slightly stooped Muslim man with ashy-gray skin and dark circles under his expressive eyes. I feel I recognize him, that I've seen his photo somewhere. I almost say something, almost say hello, but something in his manner tells me this wouldn't be appreciated.

On the way back to the school, I pass the church again. I see a dress store I hadn't noticed before across the street from the church. The store is small and the dresses in the window are compellingly attractive, especially one full-length yellow dress with seed pearls. The dresses look like designer originals. The clerk in the store seems nervous, as if she doesn't want me there. I look like what I am, a teacher, not a buyer of fancy dresses. All the dresses are in plastic covers. I wonder if she thinks I'll get the dresses dirty. I smile and leave.

Monday at the teachers' meeting we are told by the Dean of Students that the young man from Louisiana has left and will be replaced by a Salvadoran substitute teacher until a native speaker of English can be found as a permanent teacher. We are told that the young man who taught in the chicken coops "was not happy" at the school. We are also told that he was not suited to a career as a teacher. His classes disturbed the other classes because he couldn't control his students. He employed improper teaching techniques, such as using Pictionary to teach vocabulary. He had poor classroom management.

That night I have a weird and terrible dream. I dream there are six men dressed in dark clothes, seated in the bottom of a long, narrow boat, piloting it the wrong way, against the current, up a river at night with long oars, stealthily.

I wake up in my dimly lit apartment where only a little bit of light comes through the bathroom window from one of the lamps outside along the walkway. *Something bad is going to happen.*

I often hear gun shots at night and now, again, I hear them and wonder if that's what woke me. I think maybe the dream is about something happening in the street—a group of men, doing something that will hurt people.

I go out and smoke a cigarette on my balcony. The night is calm but misty. I can't see any stars or even the lights on the towers near the volcano—radio towers, my students tell me— that are usually there.

On Tuesday I'm teaching in my classroom when another American teacher comes by and says, "The Twin Towers have been bombed in New York City. Our country might be at war."

At noon I go to the library where the American teachers are watching the Twin Towers disintegrate on a blurry TV screen. As I'm exiting the library, one of my students, one of the ones who routinely goes shopping in Paris, says, "Now you know how it feels." She laughs hollowly. I pretend I don't hear her. Out in the corridor I replay what the student had said, and the way she'd said it. Did she really say that? Did she really laugh? She'd said it casually, somehow. She was a normal girl, not particularly mean, yet it was an inhumanly cruel and crazy thing to say. Because she said it without emotion, I'm guessing she's merely repeating something she heard her parents or other adults say.

It's the first time that I suspect there is great rage against America, even among the rich, like this child, who identify with us. I will come to understand that the poor here hate Americans because we are associated in their minds with the rich who do bad things in their country, and they are helpless to stop us. I will see that the rich hate us because they must collude with us; as well, they are jealous of our money and power and wish they had it. They pay a big price for their money and power, and believe—with some justification—that we don't pay. We never have to do any wet work, or even see it, and they do.

In the distance, outside the cafeteria, I see one of my Ninth Grade boys talking with one of the older women, a cafeteria worker. She is a pretty woman, popular with the students. He pantomimes jacking off. She laughs. She is old enough to be his mother, maybe even his grandmother. Is she laughing because she's afraid not to? Does she genuinely enjoy his salacious sense of humor?

I race back to the apartment and call my daughter in Connecticut. No answer. It's too early to call California. I return to school. Tuesday is the maid's day to come. I tell her something bad has happened in America and to answer the phone if my children call.

The Dean of Students visits all the classrooms of all the American teachers and tells us not to go to the library on our break to watch the news. We will have plenty of time to watch it once we return to our apartments. I am struck by how remote the Salvadoran staff has suddenly become, not cold exactly, just remote, as if they don't want to get involved, or as if they don't really care.

That afternoon when I get home, my maid says my children have all called. I call them back. My daughter, who is fluent in Spanish, and my son, who speaks enough, both describe the maid as "very sweet." My son says, "You're lucky, ma. You have a great maid."

The American teachers are stressed but quickly learn they have to get through the week as though nothing had happened. Wednesday morning at about 10:30 A.M. we are told that all teachers are to take their students, leave their classrooms, and meet in the Lower Field by the elementary school. I think it's the earthquake drill we'd been told to expect.

I ask the handsome, young Salvadoran history teacher in the room at the far end of the chicken coops, the only person still around, if I have to go to the earthquake drill. This is my planning period. I have no students in my room. He says, *"Si! Si! Pronto!"*

I reluctantly follow him down the hill to a large field I've never visited, a field about the size of three football fields, with an area of playground equipment and an area of huge rubber trees.

On the way through the parking lot by the school offices I notice dogs in cages and more armed guards than usual. So far that week we have had several seismic tremors, two days of torrential rains, and for the past two weeks there has been no water, again, in the city. Again I'd had to buy water in five-gallon jugs for bathing and drinking and pay to have it delivered and carried up the steps to my second-floor apartment. Seeing more than the usual number of men with guns and huge dogs in cages doesn't seem like that big a deal to me, not because it isn't, but because I'm a bit numb.

We stand in the hot sun for over two hours while dogs trained to sniff out bombs search the entire school. The Dean of Students speculates that it's an empty threat, but of course it has to be treated as a real threat. The students don't know any of this although several of them did figure out that it was a bomb threat because of the dogs: they've been through this before. The official word is that it's a "drill."

Keeping students occupied and tranquil for two hours is not easy anywhere, but in an open field in the heat it's almost impossible. That, plus the fact that it is lunchtime and they're hungry is a school day that I would not wish on anyone, teacher or student. All the maintenance people are out there, too. Altogether there are about seventeen hundred people in the field.

The students behave amazingly well, under the circumstances. But when they finally get to go back and eat, and have to continue waiting while the cafeteria is checked, yet again, and then the cafeteria runs out of food, they are pushed over the edge into a kind of hysteria.

The last hour of the day in the classroom, I simply read them a children's story about Eratosthenes, the Greek man who accurately measured the circumference of the earth two thousand years earlier. There are excellent illustrations. I read slowly. They calm down, as people usually do for a story.

I had hoped this would happen. I'm transporting them to another place and time. If it works for me, it'll work for them. I make my voice both soft and resonant. I want to hypnotize them into being calm. "You are feeling very calm," says the tone of my voice, "Your toes are relaxing."

Eratosthenes worked in the library at Alexandria where information was rolled up on immense scrolls like bolts of fabric. By working there long enough and by being very smart, he was able to put together enough information to determine the circumference of the earth. His measurements were only about two hundred miles off from the most recent satellite measurements.

He put together what he knew about the angle of the sun in Alexandria on June 21, what he knew about the angle of the sun at a city six hundred miles away from Alexandria on June 21, plus what he knew about the distance between the two cities, plus what he knew about the number of degrees in a circle (and a few other things came into this), and he came up with his measurements. I tell the students that what Eratosthenes did in order to measure the earth, is what we need to do to learn how to get along in the world. Two thousand years ago, measuring the circumference of the earth by putting together various pieces of information, was a mark of genius, but now they have to be the new geniuses, the ones who figure out how to do the same thing with social relations, globally.

The next morning I'm sitting in my classroom when one of my students, a pretty girl from a fabulously wealthy family—they have their own planes and their own landing strips—brings me a note. "My mother wanted you to have this," she says. I thank her and open it. Inside is a prediction from Nostradamus.

In the city of gold there will be a great thunder, two brothers (Twin Towers) torn apart by chaos. While the fortress (Pentagon) endures, the great leader will succumb. The third big war is when the city is burning. — Nostradamus 1654

That Friday night, after a hellish week, the male teachers start drinking the minute they get back to the *complejo*. The female teachers start eating and washing their clothes. Four teachers had been out sick that day, from stress I think. We all have friends and family in the States, but couldn't have gone there to help even if we'd quit our jobs. All the teachers, I have to assume, had as much difficulty getting through to people back home as I did. Also, since we were not allowed to discuss what was happening and our time was taken up with teaching, we had been "on hold" all week.

The men, as I said, were drinking, not at the pool as was their usual custom, but in little groups of two or three in their apartments. By this time the women were drinking, too. Some people took off immediately for Guatemala, just to get away, somewhere where no one could see them and they could unwind. Ordinarily on a Friday after school the younger teachers would have been hanging out at the pool, talking and swimming, and then going out for dinner. That's what they usually did, but not this Friday.

Monday the staff meeting for the American teachers is devoted to the horrors of 9/11 in New York and in Washington, D.C., and to the issue of "improper fraternizing" with students. One of the teachers, we are told by the principal, was seen by a parent drinking with students at the Princess Hotel. The principal doesn't mention that there is no drinking age in El Salvador and everyone drinks with everyone, everywhere, all the time.

After the principal's twenty-minute lecture on the dangers of fraternization, the Dean of Students approaches the lectern. She announces that "a certain immature teacher" had been "asked to leave the employ of the school," following a purported drinking incident. The teacher isn't named, nor is Pictionary mentioned.

We are scheduled to have parent-teacher meetings. I'm a bit worried about this. I had asked the very dignified and gracious Salvadoran female teacher of English if I could stop by her room and ask her about parent-teacher conferences and she had said I could. My students speak well of this teacher and the young woman who runs the writing lab, the one who went to a fancy women's college in the eastern United States, says this woman had been her favorite teacher when she'd had her for English in this high school five years prior.

This teacher is in her room every Saturday morning, as I'm in mine. But this morning her room is locked, even though I know she's there. I saw her go in. This will happen several more times. I knock on the door. I call her name. No answer. For whatever reason, she wants nothing to do with me.

I am forewarned by one of the older American teachers, the chemistry teacher who's been there a few years, not to be surprised if some of the parents come to the parent-teacher conferences trailing a small private army, and not to be surprised if some of the body guards are carrying assault rifles.

I have students who have missed several weeks of school.

Sometimes they say they were sick and bring a note from home. Sometimes they don't bring a note and say they were traveling with their parents. The girl who'd stolen the test told me, bragging, that she had gone shopping with her mother in Miami. The students always say they will make up the missing work, but then they don't. My school has more days off than any school I've ever worked in. They take all the Salvadoran holidays and all the American holidays and sometimes shut down for two or three days at a time for administrative business. I gave all high grades, all bogus. Now as the time for the parent-teacher conferences gets closer, I wonder if that was the wisest thing to do. What if I'm exposed?

When the afternoon of parent-teacher conferences arrives, I arrange all of the portfolios of all my students, class by class, to show to parents. No one comes. I wait and wait. After lunch I spy one of my students with someone who must be his mother and invite them into the room. She arrives with two large male bodyguards. She is very fat, very amiable, and after she merely glances at her son's folder is gone.

That evening it's the same thing. I wait and wait and no one comes. Finally a Salvadoran man shows up. He is small like my janitor. He is the father of one of my shyest students. Not a good student, but she does try to participate. She has an 'A' in the class, naturally.

This man is modest-seeming, well-dressed, articulate and cordial. He says he's a coffee grower and asks me if I like coffee. I say I'm addicted to coffee, but not a connoisseur. I tell him my favorite coffee was Peet's medium roast Columbian in San Francisco. He says he provides coffee to Peet's. "They have excellent coffee," I say. And he agrees. And that's the end of the parent-teacher conferences.

I suspect, although I can't verify it, that because I have given no grade lower than a B, it simply isn't worth anyone's while to come to a parent-teacher conference with me.

A tropical storm is like a northern blizzard. There is the same wild wind, perhaps blowing fifty miles an hour, but instead of blowing snow it's blowing rain. The sheer power of the storm is beautiful. It's blowing horizontally, into every crack and crevice, from the west, I think.

The thunder and lightning are terrifying. The power is out. I hear tree limbs cracking and breaking. Except for occasional flashes of lightning, the whole place is dark, dark, dark.

I go out on my balcony and, of all things, sing. I sing the old ballads my mom taught us on long car trips: *Annie Laurie* and *Go from My Window* and *Swing Low, Sweet Chariot*. I sing at the top of my lungs. I think the sound of the storm will drown out my singing. I'm sure no one can see me and if they hear me, they might not figure out it's me. I feel released. This storm provides the first privacy I've experienced since I got off the plane.

Towards daybreak, the storm seems to lessen. I see little groups of hummingbirds take flight from bush to bush, huddling in the dripping leaves. In Michigan our hummingbirds do not fly around in groups of three or four. Hummingbirds are not so abundant in Michigan. In El Salvador hummingbirds are considered a nuisance because there are so many of them. The sun doesn't really come up, but the sky lightens.

Friday, the day the kindergarten teacher usually stops by my room on her way back to the compound, I tell her I've had a bad feeling about the Dean of Students ever since the kid from Louisiana was fired. This day I mention that I don't think the Dean of Students can be the daughter of Margaret Bourke-White, just from the little I know about Bourke-White.

Margaret Bourke-White had gone into Buchenwald and photographed victims of the Nazis. She'd been outspoken about her hatred of fascism and her love of democracy. The Dean of Students at our school, so she has mentioned just in passing, is friends with Augustus Pinochet, the fascist Chilean dictator.

I tell the kindergarten teacher that I don't believe our Dean of Students had her PhD from the University of California in Los Angeles since, based on other things she'd told me, she would have been working in an international school in Saudi Arabia during the time she'd said she'd graduated. I find it hard to believe she lived next-door to *both* Desi Arnaz *and* Bill Cosby.

"You can look up Margaret Bourke-White on the Internet," the kindergarten teacher says. The kindergarten teacher is little and bouncy. She goes right over to my computer and clicks here and clicks there. "Margaret Bourke-White didn't have any children," she says after a few minutes.

"Well, maybe she had a child she gave up for adoption or something. Or maybe she adopted a child." Why would the Dean of Students claim that her mother was a famous, and famously childless, person since it could be so easily checked? Maybe she thought that the slight resemblance to the picture of Margaret Bourke-White in the big book of photos on the coffee table in the school library would be enough to convince people. Maybe she had started telling this fiction before the advent of the Internet. Maybe no one had ever questioned it. And what about those pearls? The pearls looked real.

"Do you think the pearls are real?"

The kindergarten teacher laughs, "The pearls are definitely real."

"Doesn't it bother you that she would lie about who her mother is? Doesn't it bother you she would lie about something that can be so easily checked?" I pause, because now I'm just realizing something, "If she is lying about something we can check out—and I guess we still don't know as there are some remote possibilities here, like maybe she's adopted, or illegitimate—I think that bothers me almost more than her lying. It's irrational, because we can find out the truth and then we'll know she's a liar. It's really, really crazy if she's lying about something we can check. It means everything is a show.

It looks like something, so therefore it is something. It's appearance, verisimilitude. It looks like a school, so it is a school. It looks like food, so it is food."

The little, bouncy kindergarten teacher is sitting cross-legged on my desk chair. It's a modern one, actually a typing chair, and she's swinging around, like a child. "I guess I just look the other way. I can compartmentalize." She says this with a kind of innocent delight, as though these were natural gifts, like being able to whistle two notes at once, or being double-jointed.

"But this isn't about being able to compartmentalize," I say. "I don't think that's what I'm trying to get at. This is about amoral lying versus crazy lying. If a person deceives other people to gain an advantage—perhaps in this case to elevate one's status by claiming a famous person as a parent, or they say they have a certificate of something or other when they don't and will be paid more money if they have the certificate—and if the lying can't be checked or would be difficult to check, that's dishonest and manipulative, but it isn't crazy. On the other hand, if a person in Dallas says it's snowing where they are, and you're on the phone with them, and all you need to do is check the weather report for Dallas—or call your other friend in Dallas to know, that goes beyond being manipulative. Don't you see?"

"I'm not like you, I guess," the kindergarten teacher says. "I don't like to think about things."

That Saturday I call the Traverse Area District Library back in Michigan and get my friendly reference librarian, Jim Cavanaugh, on the phone and ask him to do a little research. I tell him I'll call him again in a few days to see what he's found. When I do, he says there's no possibility that Margaret Bourke-White had had a child since she was infertile, according to all the information at his disposal; and also, as far as he can determine, she never adopted a child.

A week later the Dean of Students is practically running down the *passarella*, the long corridor between the chicken coops and the regular part of the school. She catches me just before I go into my classroom.

She starts talking out of the blue about how the record office of the school in California from which she'd received her PhD had been destroyed by fire and so she could never get the original copy of her degree but only a facsimile. For the first time I wonder if the school has placed video cameras and recording devices in our classrooms. How else would she suspect that I'd been checking up on her? Or had she finally deduced that the little anecdotes she'd shared were not adding up?

I am so sick I can't stand up. I've been vomiting for hours. I stagger out to the gate and get the man to call me a taxi. I ask him where I should go. "The Women's Hospital," he says, "is the best." Still reeling, I go in and register. They put me in a crowded room on a cot with no sheets.

Well, I think, this is the best hospital. Soon someone will come. I look around the room. I see that there's blood and feces on the floor and that it has been there a while. I stagger to my feet and leave the hospital. It is late afternoon. I have to get out of here and go before dark. I hail a cab and go back to the *complejo*. Better to be sick where it's clean, at least.

That weekend there's a fashion show in the school auditorium. The students have been getting ready for this for weeks. That night I hear firecrackers, not gun shots, into the wee hours. The next day, Sunday, I will learn that the parents of the students brought firecrackers to the fashion show. They let them off in the auditorium as well as outside it. They could have burned down the building. I learn that two years earlier an entire section of the city had been consumed in flames after an incident with firecrackers.

There are Halloween parties all over the *complejo*. The next two days we won't have school. There will be a five-day weekend because All Soul's Day comes right after Halloween. I'm exhausted from teaching and from the bout of stomach flu and so don't have the energy to do too much other than come home and rest.

I go to a Halloween party, briefly, just because I want to see the costumes. There is a young woman there, a blonde, six-foot-tall, big-boned, easy-going Californian, dressed as a scarecrow. She has the square shoulders of the two-quart glass Shetler's milk bottle back home.

She's a Salvadoran trophy nanny, a type, like Muammar Gaddafi's trophy Ukrainian nurse. She's about twenty, but disconcertingly immature, almost prepubescent. Originally hired when her employers were at their San Francisco home, she works for one of the wealthiest families at our school. We've all seen her, she's the kind of person who's hard to miss, accompanied by their armed guards, bringing the children in the morning and picking them up in the afternoon.

The question in the back of my mind every time I see them is, if her employers could have afforded to raise their children in a safe place like San Francisco, why would they bring them to El Salvador?

In March 2016 the Salvadoran writer Oscar Martinez will report in *The Nation* that a person is murdered every hour in El Salvador. I don't know how many people an hour were murdered in 2001 when I was there but I heard wisps of rumors, so presumably a lot. Students would come into the classroom and be visibly shaken and the whispers indicated that there'd been a killing, or might be a killing, or someone had been kidnapped, or someone had been shot at a stoplight.

The trophy nanny girl has her own apartment in the home of her employers. Naturally she misses her friends back in the Bay Area, and so her employers have encouraged her to attend the *complejo* parties so she can see other Americans. This girl has blackened her face with soot and sewn gingham patches onto her man-sized, farmer's coveralls. I ask her where she found a place to buy coveralls in El Salvador and she says she brought them with her, in preparation for Halloween. She is the largest Halloween scarecrow I have ever seen.

In El Salvador the Day of the Dead, or All Souls Day, is November 2. It's a national holiday. I had been lonely without the kid from Louisiana and so had sought out the girl he had been dating, a young Salvadoran woman who'd gone to a prestigious Ivy League school in the States and is in charge of the school's writing lab. She has been kind enough to invite me to go with her and her mother to visit her family's graves.

Everywhere, on every corner, there are for sale intricate skeletons made of sugar, and novena candles with pictures of the Mother of Murder on them. People are in a holiday mood. The culture of death here is popular with all sectors of the society. I'm vaguely thinking about Christ on the cross, God's only begotten son, human sacrifice for the final time in the Bible, Abraham and Isaac and the goat on the rock in the Old Testament, cannibalism carried out under the name of religion in Papua New Guinea, the ancient English song, *John Barleycorn Must Die*, vestiges of which are preserved in the innocent children's story about the gingerbread man who successfully runs away from everyone who wants to eat him, and at the same time, dazedly wondering why her mother is giving a smelly, stumbling, old drunk a little money to watch over her nice car while we go into the cemetery.

"If we don't give him money," the writing lab girl says, "he might wreck our car."

Her mother is petite and beautiful, with an expensive car.

The mood in the town is celebratory and it's that way at the cemetery, too. It's a large cemetery on hills. On every side people are walking, bringing flowers to tombs topped with houses that resemble Roman mansions from the days of Caesar and Nero. The houses on top of the graves are larger and better constructed than the slum houses we'd passed on the way. Someone could live in them, and maybe when it isn't All

Soul's Day, they do. It's the most crowded cemetery I've ever seen with tombs cantilevered every which way.

The girl says the jumble of graves is partly from the earthquake and partly because in El Salvador graves are put on top of other graves.

Later I will visit the club where the girl's family used to have a membership. The club is in a guarded area spread over several hilly and landscaped acres. Like many such clubs all over the world it's vaguely dowdy and down-at-the-heels with poor lighting and threadbare carpets and a musty smell from the pool area. I've encountered this before: it seems to be the affected genteel poverty of the extremely rich. Or maybe when they're altogether in a group, no one wants to be the first to pay their club dues. Whatever it is, penury or inverted snobbery, it never fails to mystify me. The girl seems to have fond memories of coming here, watching polo matches, playing tennis, swimming in the pool, and eating lunch with her friends. The girl and her mother seem nostalgic for an earlier, better time in El Salvador. When I do the math, the time they are sentimental about would have been a time of revolution and killing. But perhaps it hadn't touched them.

The girl and her mother don't much resemble each other. The mother is fine-boned and fair-skinned, innately elegant. She's wearing an understated sleeveless, brown pima cotton cardigan and tailored black silk pants with cuffs, silver leather shoes. She's wearing no jewelry. Whether or not everything she's wearing is extremely expensive, it looks that way. *She* looks expensive. She has straight, dark hair that she wears in a bun at the nape of her neck.

The girl is dark-skinned and stocky, with thick, black, curly hair. There is something aggressive in her bearing and her way of walking. She's wearing wrinkled, beige cargo pants, thick-soled tennis shoes and a sweatshirt with the logo of her alma mater back in the States. She's wearing a large watch. She is beautiful, too, but in an athletic way that is different from her mother's more fragile yet still steely way; perhaps she favors her father. Both of them speak flawless English.

Another Sunday I will meet the girl and her mother at their apartment near the school and drive with them to the botanical gardens. We will visit a big, new bookstore in the Zona Rosa, one with attractive design and multiple levels, like the Borders bookstore in Ann Arbor. The books on the shelves are mainly Bibles and related religious books, self-help books, cookbooks and biographies of Pinochet. There are lots of coffee table books with beautiful photographs, lots of calendars and cards. The girl and her mother seem very proud of this new bookstore. We are there only briefly.

After drinking delicious coffee in the bookstore, we drive to a Sunday brunch at the Sheraton. We drive past a mall the girl says has a big Simán store. She says the whole mall is air-conditioned. The Sheraton buffet is not an all-you-can-eat affair. There are several signs in Spanish and English—a large sign above the buffet table and also on metal stands at each end of the buffet table—saying people can't go back for seconds. When the girl does go back for seconds the manager stops her. She tells him, looking believably contrite, that she didn't know it wasn't okay.

"It was different before," the mother says, her voice trailing off. I look at her questioningly. Perhaps she will say that the brunch used to be an all-you-could-eat buffet if you were from the upper echelons of society, as she and her daughter are, and they would have never had to tolerate such effrontery from the hired help. But, no, she seems to be changing the subject. "We could walk around at 10 o'clock at night in El Centro [the three-block shopping area in the wealthy section of the city]," she says, "We could go out. No one had walls in front of their houses with concertina wire."

I had heard from the school counselor, a beautiful young woman who was genuinely kind to everyone, that San Salvador had not always been violent, and that even in the 1970s when she was growing up, the city had been generally peaceful. The name of the city means *Holy Savior* in English, she'd told me. It had been a lovely city with many parks and beautiful government buildings. Yes, there had been massacres of peasants from time to time out in the countryside. Things like that are unavoidable aspects of existence. But it had all happened out of sight of normal life. The educated people had always had more than the field hands, as in any society, the counselor had said, as in the United States and Europe, too, but it hadn't been a problem. "The poor ye shall always have with you," the counselor had said, quoting Jesus in the Bible.

From my reading back in Michigan I had learned that in the early 1900s, as El Salvador began to have more and more people, there was naturally less and less land to grow food, and more desertification and less and less water, and the water became more and more polluted and toxic. The poor, having no way to survive, had at this time started to stage various rebellions.

El Salvador is a small country. Once the basic resources of land and water were ruined, there simply wasn't enough good land and good water to go around. The only way the rich could maintain their comfortable standard of living was to use their money and guns to kill the peasants and thus intimidate the rest into working for starvation wages. A violent and dangerous society had never been what the rich had been trying to achieve, is what the gentle school counselor and the writing lab girl's upper-class mother seemed to be saying. It had happened in spite of them, not because of them.

The writing lab girl's elegant mother, sitting in the dining room of the Sheraton Hotel and musing about former times (while her daughter retreated from the breakfast smorgasbord where she was told she could not have seconds), wanted me to know that she and her well-educated daughter were good people, quality people. I nod sympathetically, not knowing what else to do.

From the Salvadoran man teaching Spanish down the hall from me, a dignified, short, stocky man who had been there forever, I learn that the teacher I'd replaced was a Salvadoran teacher of English. I learn from others that he had been an esteemed teacher but had left under strained circumstances.

This teacher had given a student a C and had been asked to leave the school. He was now teaching at another school in El Salvador. Under the guise of wanting to know how to teach English to Ninth Graders in El Salvador, I call and make an appointment to see him at his new school.

Like the Salvadoran teacher of Spanish in the room down the hall from me, this teacher, too, is short and stocky and dignified. I wonder if they're brothers but don't dare ask. He is called "Professor" by his students and treated with the utmost respect. He meets me at the end of his school day at a school only a few blocks from mine. The school is clean and well-tended, but compared to my school it's small and squalid.

I wonder if he will be sophisticated enough to know why I'm really there, so I go in slow. I begin with, "Ninth Graders are at such a wonderful point in their lives, the exciting transition from childhood to adulthood. What techniques have you found effective with this age group in this culture?"

He says it's important to engage them in something they like. I nod and take notes. He mentions in passing that the American teacher who'd been hit by the proverbial stray bullet had shown the Oliver Stone movie, *Salvador*, to his students. That's a warning, I think to myself.

Before I know it, he's telling me how angry he is that he was fired after thirty years of devoted service because he gave a student who had done no work at all, a C. The parents came in and asked him to change the grade. The teacher said if the student made up the assignments, which were few and not difficult, he would. The head of the school came and asked him to change the grade, and he argued that if he did that it would make all of the work done by his other students meaningless.

He received death threats. There were guns fired at his home. The school forced him to resign. He had to find another job quickly to support his family. He says he has friends and family in Los Angeles and has accepted a teaching job there for the next school year. He says his wife and children are already there.

"Thank you so much," I say as I gather up my notes and my book bag. "You have been very helpful. Perhaps you could leave now for Los Angeles, for the sake of your wife and children. There's a great demand for bilingual substitute teachers, they pay at least a hundred dollars a day. You would find plenty of work." I thank him for helping me better understand how to teach Ninth Graders in El Salvador, and we stand and say good-bye as the last of the students are leaving the school.

On the way home, I think I will visit the dress shop. I've been thinking about my students and their ability to understand design. They are naturally good at art. The masks they made were excellent.

But the dress shop is gone. I walk up and down the street, thinking maybe I'm confused. But there is the place across from the church, in the only place it could have been. There are the large flame trees between the sidewalk and the street. The building is gone, like the river the girl found one morning after the torrential rains and never saw again.

Friday, when I get my paycheck at noon, a heavy rain is falling. I decide to take a cab to the bank on my lunch hour. The bank is close enough to walk to, but even with an umbrella I would be sopping wet by the time I returned to the school.

There are always cabs waiting in front of the Princess Hotel, and I walk over and get one. It takes me a few minutes to realize that the man is not driving me to the bank. It appears that he is driving me out of the city. "*Por favor, Senor*," I say, and point back the other way. "*No es correcto. No banko aqui.*" He keeps driving. "*Stupido,*" I say, insulting him. "*Stupido.*"

I pull a pocket calculator from my purse and type in numbers. "*Padre mia*," I say. "Washington, D.C. *Presidente*." I point to the sky. "Photo. Satellite." I look at him and draw a finger across my throat and then point at him. I open my door. I'm ready to jump into the street.

Finally he pulls over, as if he's still unsure that he wants to do this. I'm out of the car and on the sidewalk before he pulls to a stop. I thrust ten dollars through the window. What if he isn't trying to rob me and I've made a terrible mistake?

I have no idea where I am. I go into the nearest office building, show my school identity badge, am approved by the guards, find someone who speaks English, and explain that I'm lost and need a taxi back to my school. The mere mention of the name of my school, plus the official name tag, is enough to have them all become polite and helpful.

All afternoon as I'm teaching, my mind keeps going back to the incident. He was not a man who seemed trustworthy. He had shifty eyes. As I stand before my students, I am two people, one going back over all the events with the cab driver, and one teaching. Was the driver truly confused and didn't know which bank to take me to?

Even though I'd shown him the piece of paper with the bank's logo, name and address, it's possible he couldn't read. Was he planning to kill me or just rob me? Surely he didn't believe that my father was President of the United States, but of course he couldn't be absolutely sure that I was lying. Shouldn't he have wanted to rob me *after* he took me to the bank? But he seemed too dull to think of that. His only thought was probably that foreigners had money. Perhaps my spoken Spanish was so bad he couldn't understand a word I was saying. He probably believed that I was sending a photo to a satellite. He probably didn't know that what I was supposedly keying information into, punching like crazy, rapid-fire, was nothing but a cheap pocket calculator. He'd looked frightened the minute I'd started.

If he'd been smarter he would have instantly realized that if, indeed, I was the daughter of the President of the United States, he was in a position to get good ransom money. But that would be a lot of trouble, too, and he wasn't planning anything big. He didn't have anyone helping him. Perhaps he was planning to drive me far out of my way, thinking I was a stranger in town, and then charge me for the extra miles. In the end my hunch is that he was a petty, part-time criminal who probably was planning to rob me, but not kill me.

This is the second bizarre encounter I've had in El Salvador with a taxi driver. The first one happened when I asked my driver to help me carry heavy bottles of water up to my apartment. He did, and when I tipped him he embraced me and kissed me full on the lips. He was unsavory and the kiss was more so. It wasn't something I could ever understand, and the second incident with the taxi driver who drove me out of the city is not something I can understand either. I need more information, and I'm never going to be able to get more information.

The kindergarten teacher asks if she can visit and if we can sit on my balcony and talk. I say I'd like that and ask if she would mind if I smoke a cigarette. She laughs and says, "If I can sit where the smoke doesn't blow on me." I get my pack of Marlboro Reds from the refrigerator. It's the same pack I'd bought back in August when I'd been in the Miami airport.

She tells me that a few weeks earlier her husband had begun to install a fountain in their backyard, like the fountain in the backyard of the principal, but that the school officials had stopped him. "He was perfectly capable of doing it right," she says. "He knows all about things like that." Her husband, before they were married, had built his own bicycle and ridden it across the United States. On the trip he'd worked odd jobs to earn money for food, slept in the open, and lived on almost nothing. He could fix the bicycle, or rebuild it, as required. He could even make parts for it.

She tells me about her family. She and her husband are estranged. He loves their children, but she had rejected him some years earlier, and since then they hadn't had sex although they did go on little outings as a family. She says he infuriates her because he makes her pay the two hundred dollars a month for the maid out of her earnings even though he makes more money. He tells her not to pay it, that he'll help with the housework, but since he has promised this before and never did it, she just continues to pay the maid, doesn't fight with him, but silently holds it against him. She says she will inherit millions when her father dies. She plans to divorce her husband, probably in a year or two when they return to the States, but for the time being tolerates what she has to tolerate in order to keep the peace.

She confides that she's bisexual and would like to have a relationship with me. I say that it's fine for her to be bisexual but I'm not. I hadn't been looking at her while she was speaking. I realized later when I thought about it that I was in the habit of never looking at the kindergarten teacher. Her eyes bothered me. They were flat, unchanging, like a duck's, like she wasn't thinking, and when I would look at her, the lack of expression in her eyes would confirm this and would make me squeamish.

On the balcony she goes on talking, with no change in her voice, and without my ever looking up, as if she had never indicated her interest in me.

She says she and her family have visited *Puerta del Diablo*, Devil's Doorway. It's a high rock from which the entire city of San Salvador can be seen. The story is that there's a cave there and a highwayman who had fallen in love with a beautiful girl had been chased by the girl's family and had escaped into the cave.

The kindergarten teacher says that on every step carved into the mountain, there's the name of a ballet dancer, a doctor, a university professor, a musician, a writer, a high school teacher who had been murdered during the revolution. Many of them had had their bodies dumped into the nearby ravine. Some had had their bodies dumped in the ocean. Some had been dumped at El Playon, a volcanic lava bed near San Salvador. "Let's take all the smartest, kindest, most talented people out and shoot them. That makes a lot of sense, right? My husband calls it unnatural selection. They're deliberately selecting for stupidity and violence." She laughs. "And it's working!"

The weekend before, she and her husband and children had gone to a resort in the mountains. They had hired some local peasants to take them out in a boat on a lake. It had been hot, and so the kindergarten teacher had taken off all her clothes but her underwear and jumped into the lake.

The kindergarten teacher is flat-chested and pear-shaped. She is short and thick-necked and thick-boned. Her arms, legs, neck and upper lip are covered with thick, black hair. She has male pattern baldness, she has told me, and it's as if all the hair that should have been on her head had decided to flourish instead on her legs, arms, and face.

"What did the men who were rowing the boat do?" I ask. "What was the expression on their faces?"

"Nothing," she says, "They just acted like it was normal."

I can't be cooped up any more in my classroom or in my apartment. Yes, of course, the streets are dangerous, but at some point a person has to live. On a street near the Princess Hotel, I had noticed a restaurant. I decide to go there. Why not? Live dangerously. I don't even care if they shoot me. If I spend another Saturday in my classroom making lesson plans, or another Sunday in my apartment ironing my clothes for the next week, I will go out of my mind.

I had learned in Richmond, California that early morning is a time there are few killers on the streets. They work at night, and by 8 A.M., they've gone home to sleep. They get tired, like anybody else.

I'm sitting in the little restaurant, wondering what to order when a girl who looks American comes in. She just has that American "let-us-be-up-and-doing-then-with-a-heart-for-any-fate," take-charge kind of walk, plus a sort of *naiveté*, too. She is brown-haired, somewhat over-weight, the way young college girls are with the weight they gain at first, "the freshman fifteen," or like someone on anti-depressants. She appears to be somewhat aggressive or at least sure of herself. "Hi," I say, "are you an American?"

She says, matter-of-factly, "Of course."

"Please sit with me," I say. "I was about to order, and I'll order—and pay—for you, too, if you'll help me figure out the menu."

She wants to pay for herself.

"Absolutely," I say, "I understand. But please join me." We both order something simple. She orders a pastry. I want the scrambled eggs and toast, *la platte. No carne.* She helps explain this to the waitress. We both want coffee with milk and want it immediately.

She says, "Did you know all the food in El Salvador comes from Mexico and Guatemala?"

I must look astonished.

"Yes, it's true. The elite families took all the communal land from the Indians to grow coffee and cotton. So now the peasants can't farm. A few might grow their own vegetables, if they can find a place to do it, but they can't grow enough to sell. They don't have land."

She tells me she's a Peace Corps volunteer from a village about fifty miles away and has just arrived by bus. She's from Wisconsin, is the only child of an elementary school teacher and a factory worker, is devoutly Christian, and joined the Peace Corps right out of college. I tell her that I'm from Michigan, have four sisters, two of whom are professors, with the other two being an artist and a businesswoman. I have three grown children with the youngest at Yale and the other two in the Bay Area of California. I teach English at the private school across the street, and this is my first time out alone.

When I tell her where I teach she says, "Those are the most evil people in the world. They only maintain homes here to come down and launder money. Anything that looks like a legitimate business is just a front for money laundering. There's so much contraband in this country. Half the trucks here are carrying illegal guns." My mind flashes on the heavily guarded Coca Cola trucks we'd seen in the mountains during our second field trip. What if they hadn't actually been carrying Coca Cola? She adds judgmentally, "You must make a lot of money."

I tell her exactly what my salary is. I also tell her that I have published two books of highly acclaimed essays with the University of Michigan Press, received a positive review from *The New York Times* and many, many other publications, worked for years as a writer for magazines, have received many writing awards and prizes and fellowships, have a current Michigan teaching certificate, a master's degree, fifteen years of teaching experience, and, if I'd been able to get a job in Michigan, would have earned more there. I tell her that my salary is adequate and the housing is, too, but that American-style education, where we encourage students to examine and question, is not something the school administrators want. I feel I have to restrict myself to teaching vocabulary. It's boring.

"Peace Corps volunteers don't get paid," she says bitterly. "My parents send me money or I wouldn't be able to stay here. But," she adds on a more positive note, "I'm learning Spanish." She says that for many young, well-educated volunteers, Peace Corps work is a prelude to government work, usually the foreign diplomatic corps. She doesn't plan to do that. She'll go back to Wisconsin and study microbiology.

"What about the *Catorce Grande*," I ask, "the fourteen families?"

"A myth," she says. The tone of her voice is smug, moralistic. She takes a sip of her coffee. "They're the Salvadoran mafia. They say they're coffee growers, but there isn't enough coffee in the entire world to support the way they live."

I look at her questioningly. "We have smart Peace Corps volunteers," she says. "They've gone to the best schools in the country. Harvard. Yale. Berkeley. They've studied political science." She lowers her voice so I can barely hear her over the restaurant music. "There may have been fourteen families at some point, but at least for the last century they've married anyone who wanted in on the action. We supported the wrong people here because we were afraid of communism. Now we've created a monster. We trained their military in Georgia. There's good evidence that we trained the people who murdered Archbishop Romero."

"Georgia?" For a minute I think she might mean, Georgia, in the Caucasus, but then it dawns on me that she probably doesn't. "Georgia? Do you mean in the United States? How do you know all this?"

She nods. "The School of the Americas in Fort Benning, Georgia," and here she slows down. "I know all this," she pauses for effect, "because I don't live in a walled compound."

Our food comes. She has a pretty pastry. My *platte* has sausage on it. The sausage has a sweet, putrid smell, like cat shit, and while I don't mind paying for it, I don't want it on my plate. I ask her to please explain this to the waitress and have her take the plate back and remove the sausage. We give my plate back to the waitress. The waitress is gone for what seems like a very long time. Finally, I go looking for her.

At last she returns with the *platte*. It still has the sausage on it. The Peace Corps girl says, "You can't get them to change."

"But you explained it to her," I say. "Your Spanish is good. I heard you. You explained that I would pay the same price, but I didn't want the meat. She understood. I know she did. She nodded her head. Anyway, how hard is it? '*No carne.*' I know she understood."

"I thought you couldn't speak Spanish," she says.

"Well, I can understand it better than I can speak it. I'm not supposed to speak Spanish with my students. It's easier if I just pretend I can't understand. I've been pretending so long, now I guess I think it's true."

"It's this culture," the girl says, gesturing toward the offending sausage. "They have been so oppressed for so long, everything is very rigid here. They are terrified to do anything against protocol. On some level she thinks someone might take her out and shoot her if she takes the sausage off the plate. She thinks she'll lose her job."

"It's hopeless, I guess." I stare at the putrid-smelling sausage. I wonder what kind of meat it is. Anything can be put into a sausage.

The girl reaches over and solves the problem. She takes the sausage off my plate, wraps it in her napkin. She says she'll give it to the starving man who's always waiting at her bus stop.

I almost tell her about my experience at the Princess Hotel, where the tamales were cooked in plastic corn husks, but don't. She probably can't afford to eat at the Princess Hotel. She's already indicated that she resents the vast amount of money she imagines I'm making—the tainted money working for the evil rich people—and she will think even less of me.

I tell her that I'd heard the rest of the country of El Salvador is extremely dangerous, that a representative from the State Department had come and told us not to travel in El Salvador and certainly not to travel alone.

"The State Department guys didn't tell the Peace Corps volunteers that," she snorts. "I go everywhere alone."

"Is it safe in your village?"

"People look out for you," she says. "My host family gave me two ceremonial swords."

I think she must be joking, but when I raise my head from taking a sip of coffee, it looks like she isn't.

She says she came into San Salvador to go to the Peace Corps office, which I learn is just up the street, and is also going to the Zona Rosa to get some small supplies. She says there's a bookstore there, not a good one as far as having good books, but it has great coffee and at least it's a bookstore. I don't tell her I have already been to this bookstore. I'm not sure why. Maybe it's because I found it disheartening, a fake bookstore, like the janitor's fake cell phone.

I say that when we leave, I will walk with her so that I can see where the Peace Corps office is and maybe visit it sometime. I tell her I might like to be in the Peace Corps and she says everything goes through their office in Washington, D.C. If I want to apply, I should write for the application forms.

In November the director of the school invites all the teachers to Thanksgiving dinner at his large, beautiful home in the compound. I'm waiting in my apartment for the writing lab girl who is going to go with me.

She shows up an hour early and says, "I'm not coming. They've put my father in prison in a small town near here. He stayed here and did all their dirty work for years during the revolution, when they were all safe in Miami. Now they're trying to get rid of him. There's been a riot in the prison. He thinks they started it so they could have an excuse to shoot him."

She's upset, but she's not crying. Her usually clear, dark skin looks muddy, and that's the only sign of her unhappiness. "I wanted you to know," she says. "I couldn't tell you on the phone. Your phone might be tapped. You shouldn't be seen talking to me. The school will fire me next. They've started saying I can't teach without a teaching certificate, but when they hired me they knew I didn't have a teaching certificate."

I know she will miss being part of the school because she had told me she loved it there. She was there for twelve years, half her life. She told me about a time she and her friends snuck into the school and met under the bleachers, against the school rules, and how much fun that was. I tell her I'm terribly sorry that this had to happen.

"Tell people I'm coming down with a cold," she says, "if they ask."

As I sit on the sofa after dinner in the director's house, exhausted, trying to pretend I don't know how to play Monopoly or Scrabble so I don't have to get down on the floor with the younger teachers, looking vaguely into the garden in the backyard, I find my mind drifting back to my students in the California prisons. In my replaying of those convicts filing into my classes and sitting there, and contrasting them to the powerful people who seem to be running things at this school and perhaps in the country, I feel a difference.

My prison and jail students, many of whom had committed horrible crimes, surprisingly seemed often to want to be caring and honest people, or at least they wanted me to think that they were. The criminality among the upper echelons in El Salvador, if my intuition is not playing tricks on me, is different. People seem to have no second thoughts. Even the writing lab girl and her mother, even when there's a reversal of fortune, seem not to question the basic tenets of the culture itself.

The writing lab girl was popular with the other teachers, but no one asks where she is, or even seems to notice that she's missing from the gathering.

Over the four-day Thanksgiving weekend, the computer teacher, the white-eye-lashed husband of the kindergarten teacher, tells me that we have a student in common who would like both of us to visit his mother in the hospital. This student knows the computer teacher has a car and will drive me. This boy is kind-hearted. He's an abysmal student but good at art and I let him make up his work with drawings. He's tall for his age and has a speech impediment.

I agree to go on Sunday afternoon. The boy's mother has cancer, the computer teacher says. The computer teacher speaks more Spanish than I do. He says the boy is doing well in his computer class but is worried about his grade in English. I explain that the boy has no need to worry. He has a B in my class.

The hospital is a small, solidly built place with lavish gardens outside, and inside an air of quiet refinement and good taste. I had no idea such a hospital existed in San Salvador. It is clean, like a hospital in the United States. The high-ceilinged rooms for patients are more like hotel suites. They include a sitting room, bedroom, and bathroom. There are nurses everywhere. They look competent and are nicely attired and have a sweet and intelligent air of dedication to their professional obligations. I write down the address. This is where I should come if I get sick.

The mother is pale and wan, as one might expect. She speaks very good English, but has tubes in her nose. My student adores his mother. He is solicitous of her every wish. He wants me to explain to her that he has a B in English. I do this and add that her son is a lovely person and is working to capacity in English.

Two weeks later the boy approaches me after class to see if I would be willing to visit his mother again. This time he says he would like me to visit them at their home. He will send a chauffeur for me. He arrives with the chauffeur. It's all a bit strange, since no other students have invited me to their homes. I assume the boy's trying to find people to visit his mother to cheer her. He can't still be worried about his grade.

The home is beautiful, understated, modest, and tasteful. There are extensive gardens. The mother is in a hospital bed in the living room. They have a small dog—a small, yapping dog. My student, suddenly with no speech impediment at all and in a very forceful, manly voice, tells the dog to be quiet.

My student says he raises doves and asks if I would like to see them. He has a back sun room or garden room where several exotic varieties of doves are. I'm surprised, I tell him, that he has such a passion for doves. He smiles shyly and says that, yes he likes all living things, even his silly dog.

He shows me his roses, too, carefully cultivated. I ask if he does the work and he says sometimes he does but that they also have gardeners.

We return to his mother in the living room. My student goes and prepares coffee for us. They must have let all the servants off for the afternoon. I sit next to his mother's hospital bed. She says, "I hate this country. I want to go to Costa Rica." Costa Rica is considered the Switzerland of Central America. They have no army, no violence, free elections, and the people can make a good living from tourism since the country is safe.

My student overhears his mother as he brings the coffee in—in white Wedgewood demitasse with gold trim—and says, "It's her medication. She loves this country, don't you, Mommy?" She seems not to hear.

"El Salvador is a beautiful country," I say, as if on cue. "I love the people of El Salvador—especially my wonderful students."

In the next few weeks I visit all the schools in El Salvador that might need an American teacher of English. Each school is more chaotic and disorganized than the last. Despite all their grand claims in their brochures, they are barely schools at all. They pay poorly, and there is no housing for the staff. When I visit, the American teachers are visibly miserable.

I also visit the so-called public schools in greater San Salvador. These schools are a bad joke. The teachers are paid only slightly more than my maid, and they have to teach a hundred students, or more, in filthy, crowded classrooms. The parents of the students have to pay. Most of the families in San Salvador, like that of my grandmotherly maid, can't begin to afford ten dollars a day, a day's wages, for school for their child or grandchild, even in the really bad schools that I saw in old, crumbling buildings. Parents will send one child, I was told, the one deemed most inclined to learn, and that one for only a few months at a time, only as they can afford it.

Oppressive poverty and lack of education hurt the poor.

But the doing of it, being the perpetrators of it, being the rich families behind the bad government, hurts the wealthy, too. They can't allow their children to learn the real history of their country. They can't allow them to know how they acquired their money. They can't allow them to learn how to analyze literature for fear they might learn how to analyze other things. My students deliberately, if unconsciously, make themselves unthinking.

Just based on what I can see in my students, their parents do not value work. They do not value integrity. They do not value thought. They value unearned privilege and unearned wealth.

People and groups of people with too much money and power undermine democracy all over the world. Excessive money and power—whether inherited wealth or money earned drilling for oil; whether it's power through caste, class, crime, or honest entrepreneurial or political genius; or all of the above— can't be kept in place without acceptance of unfairness.

One has to be able to be heartless enough to prevent poor children from receiving proper food, shelter, medical care, and education. Bad laws, no laws, militia, dissembling, cover-ups, secret punishments, and other enforcement would necessarily have to follow. Once you accept unfairness as the price of wealth and power, the only question is how much killing you are willing to do to keep it. In El Salvador, based on the civil war, disappearances, massacres, and men with guns everywhere, my guess is the amount of killing they are willing to do is unlimited.

I have never stopped thinking, not in El Salvador and not afterwards, of the kid from Louisiana who got fired. He knew too much. He was fluent in Spanish and young enough to hang out with his students. They liked him. They wanted to spend time with him in spite of their parents' warnings not to, in spite of their parents' fears, valid fears in this case, that their children would tell the young man things they didn't want him to know. Of course the school doesn't want the American and Canadian teachers to speak Spanish with the students; it would open the door to their secrets.

It's so obvious: the more bad things people do, whether it's as individuals, or families, or gangs, or governments, the more secrets they have to have, and the more they have to get rid of people who know things. What a horrible way to live.

The United States has terrible greed and materialism, terrible violence, way too many poor people, way too many black and brown poor people in prison, and, increasingly, way too many secrets. But, at least up to this point, in America we can talk about things, write about things, and try to make things better. El Salvador doesn't allow that: without the freedom to speak there can be no freedom of thought and without freedom of thought, everyone is thought-*less*, dumb, and nothing can change. The worse the government, the dumber the people.

America, if it wants to be like El Salvador, all it needs to do is: punish whistle blowers, make people afraid to talk, afraid to think; crowd the poor into underfunded schools in violent neighborhoods; close the libraries; punish women who've already been abandoned by the fathers of their children by making them raise these children, already declared unwanted by their male progenitors and the society generally, without enough food, shelter, daycare, or education. That way their children will be sure to know they're despised and when they grow up to be beggars and thieves, burdening the prison system and dragging down the society, the women will be sure to know that it's their own fault for making poor choices in the first place; make malnutrition acceptable; make the inevitable and irreversible brain damage from malnutrition acceptable; make dying of diseases caused by malnutrition acceptable; put a lot of people in prison; don't provide a living wage to people willing to work; let the rich live in armed compounds with security guards; make drugs available to everyone so they can deal with their harsh conditions; make it almost impossible to

keep families together; never call to account the corporate pol-
luters of the water, air, and soil; and, finally, destroy the natural
environment so no one has access to the solace of nature. It
won't take much longer to become a faux democracy like El
Salvador. But we'll have to keep doing what we're doing and
not thinking about it.

I think maybe it would be better for me to be volunteering in the Peace Corps. At least that way if I'm teaching, the
students wouldn't have to pay and some of them presumably
would actually want to learn. I want to be useful. I want to do
real teaching, not just vocabulary and pronunciation.

On a street near the Princess Hotel, I find the Peace Corps
office that the young volunteer had shown me. It's on a street
of large trees and fine houses. In the next block I see a man
who, after a moment or two, I realize is naked. I'm near-sight-
ed. At first I think he's covered in paint but then I realize he's
smeared with feces. He is lanky and tall for a Salvadoran. Is he
an American? He's waving at me frantically, as if he's in dis-
tress. His hair is long and uncombed. I suddenly see a small,
brass plaque with the words Peace Corps on it on a stone gate.

There's a hole in the wall, like in *The Secret Garden*, and I
call "hello" through this opening. An armed Salvadoran guard
in a bullet-proof vest eventually comes and looks out at me sus-
piciously. I explain that I'm a teacher from the nearby school,
an American, and want to visit the Peace Corps office. He acts
very leery of me. He goes back into the recesses of wherever
he came from and I wait. *Is everyone in this entire country completely nuts?*

After a few minutes, the man returns with another Salvadoran man, also armed and also wearing a bullet-proof vest.
Seemingly with great reluctance, they unlock the gate. Then,
almost before I know it, I'm in an ordinary beige office with
a red-headed, buff, middle-aged, gonzo, white-water-rafting
type American with a three-day beard. He's the director of

the Peace Corps in El Salvador. I tell him that I teach at the school around the corner, am interested in volunteering in the Peace Corps in El Salvador, but am concerned that my ability to speak Spanish is not up to Peace Corps standards. "Lie!" he says, startling me.

It strikes me as a very strange thing for a supervisor to say—not only because it is unseemly for someone in his position, but wouldn't someone know the minute I opened my mouth to say something in Spanish? But then I think that maybe he knows that my level of fluency in Spanish will never matter. It would never be important and it would never be checked. He's talking about filling out the forms, putting down whatever will look good on paper; the underlying assumption is that it will all start and end there.

I nod and smile and thank him for his time and—with my frightened, squirrelly, suspicious, gun-toting escorts—go back out the way I came in. I check for the crazy man up the street as I leave, but he's gone.

Lying, I realize as I walk back to my school, is what I'm trying to get away from.

It's almost Christmas. Every day I go to work alone and come home alone. In private schools in the United States, families often invite teachers to their homes during the holidays, especially those teachers from other countries who have no way to get home for the holidays; and even if they don't do that, they still make it a point to send cookies or small gifts. I'd been hoping for coffee. But there's nothing, not even a Christmas card.

In the classroom next to me where the young man from Louisiana had been, there's been a succession of Salvadoran substitute teachers who don't speak any English. I say hello. They say hello. But that's the end of it.

So I'm thrilled beyond reason when the parents of my female Danish student, people with the United States Aid for

International Development (USAID), invite me for dinner.

They make food that tastes like American food, something like roast beef and noodles, braised carrots, green beans, and chocolate cake. Their apartment is clean and well-lit. They are kind to me. I am grateful. They must have known, even before I did, that I might not be able to make it through the whole year and, for the sake of their very intelligent and sweet daughter, they want me to stay the course.

Over the Christmas break I go on vacation to Guatemala. On the bus out of El Salvador I travel with two second grade teachers from my school, one Canadian and one American. It's then I learn that the school has had me at the wrong pay grade all the time I've been teaching. They have not counted my experience or my master's degree. It's a short-fall of several thousand dollars.

When I return from my Christmas vacation and go in to speak to the American director of the school, he tells me to wait a few days to give him time to look into it. When I see him again he tells me that it was an oversight, that they can do nothing to correct it for this year, since the budget has already been allocated, but they will get me on the right pay grade for the second year.

The writing lab girl is gone. The Dean of Students tells us in a meeting that the school's budget was insufficient to cover the writing lab. The writing lab has been turned into a "Book Nook" where students can go in and read. They do go into the room; they like all the big, soft, yellow, bean bag chairs, but they do not read.

The Danish girl comes to me crying in the week after the Christmas break, saying her parents are sending her back to Denmark. Her parents are worried, she says, because she is only in Ninth Grade and has fallen in love with a Salvadoran boy. He's a senior, a scholarship student.

"I'm sorry," I say. "I think your parents are right. I'm sure your feelings are genuine and that his are, too. But you are both too young."

"I know," she says, sobbing.

I write to a friend, a woman who is also the editor and publisher of a student magazine in Leelanau County, and ask if my Salvadoran students can submit to her magazine. For a decade I had worked with students in Leelanau County through the Michigan Council for the Arts; my students had submitted there before. She says, "Yes," and that I don't have to pay any of the usual fees.

Using the "I am" poems for the study of Greek gods and goddesses and the "Where I'm from..." poems with their art work and their odes inspired by Pablo Neruda, I submit my students' work. Some of it is accepted and published. We are invited to the Authors Event back on the Leelanau Peninsula, to be held at the Old Art Building in Leland on the shores of Lake Michigan. I am terribly homesick. For about a day I have the fantasy of taking them all back to this celebration.

My friend sends me copies of the magazine. I display the magazine with my students' published work, along with their masks and other artwork, on big portable bulletin boards in the front lobby of the school. The idea is that the friends and families of my students will be able to see and appreciate their accomplishments. The magazine is for sale for ten dollars a copy, but no one buys a single one. In my previous experience in Michigan, published students had bought several copies for themselves, their families, and their friends. In El Salvador, no one does this. They have plenty of money, so it's not a question of money.

Not only do students not buy any copies of the magazine—I end up sending my friend a hundred dollars to cover the shipping and giving the magazines to the school library—but when the work is left out on display, someone, or several someones, comes and destroys it, slashing the masks with knives, covering the poems with obscenities and defacing everything with spray paint. It's alarming. I'm not able to decide if this has been done by other students who are jealous of my students and their published work, or if it was done by my own students, or maybe even some of their parents, maybe the same idiots who set off firecrackers in the gym during the fashion show, in a rage because I had tricked them into real expression.

My kindergarten teacher friend invites me to her house for Passover. She says she's going to have a traditional Seder. I've never been to one and thank her for the invitation.

She has arranged the table with flowers, plates, silverware, the bitter herbs, the candles. She has gone to a great deal of trouble, and it's very beautiful. At each place setting there is a portion of the script, a "reading," for each person typed out on a piece of expensive paper that's supposed to look like parchment. Her daughters go along with this. And her white-eye-lashed husband and I do, too.

But when it gets to the part about how God, on behalf of His chosen people, is going to smote and smite the Egyptians and send plagues of frogs, frogs that die and stink up the place; and cause a big drought so there isn't a single green thing growing anywhere; and God's going to kill all the Egyptians' first-born and the first-born of their maid-servants; and do an endless bunch of things all designed to strike terror into the hearts of the Egyptians and show them who's boss, all finally celebrated by symbolically dripping lambs' blood on the door posts and lintels of Jewish people to mark the beginning of Passover, and then roasting the lamb—no boiling allowed—with the legs and head together, and then celebrating Passover by eating the roast lamb—the kindergarten teacher's husband and I put down our scripts. We can't go on. If someone else, a rabbi maybe, had read the passage and we hadn't had to actually read it ourselves we might have been able to get through it.

But it's too much smoting and smiting and dripping of blood on lintels and doorposts and we don't feel right participating in it.

This is the voice of the Old Testament God, similar in cadences and ideas to the one Charles Manson heard in his head before he got his gang to stab pregnant Sharon Tate to death and kill some other people, too, and drip blood all over as a sign of power. The information in the Old Testament was first written down about five thousand years ago—on wet clay with sharp sticks—but the whole tone of it seems to be from an even earlier period in human evolution, perhaps from Paleolithic times.

In El Salvador, it's too close to home, too real.

It's the first time I've ever seen White Eyelashes look at his wife with compassion.

The kindergarten teacher is embarrassed and goes into the bedroom and cries. Her husband and I feel terrible, too, but we can't change our minds.

I look into their backyard where it's all torn up, the planned fountain project stopped before it was completed. Each is trying to find some way to stay sane. He wants to build something; that makes him feel better. She wants to go back to something she only vaguely remembers from Seders at her grandparents, some restoration of tradition, because that makes her feel more grounded.

We eat the food her maid has prepared, but we don't continue with the Seder. Following some polite conversation in their living room after the meal, I leave.

It's a beautiful sunny day. I cross the walkway to my own apartment, about two hundred feet, no more. The German girl, who lives in the apartment below me, the school's German teacher, is just coming home with her handsome, young, Salvadoran boyfriend. He's tall and muscular with lots of tattoos. I have seen them before, coming and going, but never on a leisurely sunny, Sunday afternoon.

We say, "*Buenos dias*," and "*Guten tag*," and "Hello," in all our various languages, all with full smiles.

I notice an open box of mechanic's tools, or what looks like mechanic's tools in a long, red metal box, on the back seat of his car. I ask the young man, "What do you do for your work?" I'm just making conversation.

His anger is instantaneous and terrifying. He seems to swell up to twice his normal size and says, "Why do you want to know?"

"Oh, just curious," I say in the same old-lady-making-conversation way. "I thought maybe you repaired cars for a living, maybe you're an auto mechanic."

"None of your FUCKING business," he says, loud enough for anyone with open windows to hear him. I think he might kill me with his bare hands right there by the camellia bush outside our small apartment building.

I go upstairs and vomit and vomit and vomit. It's then I know that at the end of the school year, if that day ever comes, I will go home and never return.

A week later, the German teacher goes out of her way to accidentally on purpose encounter me on the walkway. She tells me that her "fiancé" has gone to Germany. She says she will be joining him there at the end of the school year.

Just before Easter I have dengue fever. I cancel all my vacation plans. I spend three weeks recuperating on my balcony. I watch a pair of doves build a nest in the hanging basket. Doves are good parents. They carefully take turns sitting on the eggs, turning the eggs, and then feeding the little hatchlings.

In May I'm given my ticket to go back to Lake Leelanau for the summer. I tell everyone I hope they have a wonderful summer and I will see them again in August. I leave all of my pots and pans, clothing and bedding so they'll know I plan on coming back. I'd shipped all my personal papers from Guatemala months earlier.

In the San Salvador airport, we go through customs. Of all the teachers leaving on my flight, I'm the only one who has all her bags gone through, each item carefully removed, examined, and returned to the suitcase. It takes forever.

I don't breathe normally until the plane lands in Texas.

When I get home I write to the headmaster and say I've been "overtaken by circumstances" and will not be returning. He calls me. He's furious. He says I've broken my contract and he personally will make sure that I never get another teaching job at another international school. He says I owe the school three thousand dollars for the plane ticket. He says the school will sue me and I can expect to spend a small fortune in legal fees.

After the phone call I write again and say that, according to my review of my service to them, the amount I was underpaid by the school is several thousand dollars more than the amount of the plane ticket. I do not say that I can report the school to the consortium of international schools where his school has a membership. I don't need to write this in the letter since he surely knows that I can do this. Just in case, I document my position. I include a copy of my letter to him from April, a copy of the school's chart with the pay scale which I had solicited from another teacher, and his hand-written response to me saying they could not correct it for the current year but would do so for the second year.

I conclude the letter by writing that it was a wonderful experience to be part of such a wonderful school with such wonderful students and that I wish him, the school, my students and all the wonderful people in El Salvador every success for the future.

Small Coffins

The mournful roosters of Guatemala call out over the waters of Lake Atitlán in the foggy dawn. Their mournful cries echo off the dark, hat-shaped cones of the mournful volcanoes.

The roosters of Guatemala are mournful. My neighbor's roosters in Lake Leelanau say "Cock-a-doodle-do," like good little Mother Goose roosters, but the roosters of Guatemala sound like saxophone players, calling "Ah, one gone so long, where are you?" The call trails off like that of a train's whistle fading away in the vast ancient passes, and then repeats, at a slightly higher pitch, an invisible ribbon of sound, a lament of loss, "Ah, my only one, where are you?" a deep sorrow that stays in the bones like the cold of the dark mountain stones.

Lake Atitlán is a deep volcanic lake, considered by Aldous Huxley when he visited in 1834 to be the most beautiful lake in the world.

My Mayan tutor tells me there's a myth that you can swim to the bottom of the lake and from there out to the ocean. "But, if there's a passage," I ask, struggling to picture this, "wouldn't that drain the lake?"

He smiles the most charming smile, "It's a myth."

This is a land filled with myths.

Here in Guatemala the Indians still speak their native languages. I have come to San Pedro to study Spanish, but after the first day I decide I want to study the language everyone is speaking.

My school is a series of small rooms made of corn stalks for the walls and banana leaves for the roof with cinder paths between the classrooms. Each dirt-floored classroom is just big enough for two hand-made stools and a table which is a two-foot-square piece of plywood over a sawed-off barrel.

It's a beautiful school, sweet and simple, yet elegant, too, on the shores of Lake Atitlán with the purple volcanoes in the distance and red flowers in hanging baskets on the ephemeral walls, and red flowers in clay pots placed proudly on each side of the presumed doorway.

The director is an amazing man who never went to school but has somewhere along the way taught himself English. He's fluent in Spanish and also fluent in at least three native languages, one of them being Tz'utujil, which is what they all seem to speak together. He can read and write all these languages, and where and how he learned, with only a few days of real school here and there, is mind-boggling.

After two days I realize I don't want to learn any language, I just want to get to know people, but of course I can't very well say this to the monumentally formal and dignified director of the language school. His purpose as a person, and his integrity as a teacher, would be subverted by this.

The notion of self-directed learning, even with this self-made autodidact, hasn't yet reached Guatemala. The man wants me to learn what he is there to teach. And he wants to teach in the only way he knows, which is the way he learned for the few days he went to school: with repetition and response and the teacher in a position of authority and the student in a position of submission and rogation.

It doesn't occur to me immediately, but I realize slowly that I've signed up for two weeks at his language school as much for social connection and group protection as for learning a language. I need a break from having been confined to a classroom for the last five months, inside the grounds of a walled compound topped with broken glass and razor wire, where my computer was "cleaned" even though it didn't need to be, and where my every move seemed to be monitored. I need to unwind, literally.

I feel like I've been bound like a mummy in the fetal position in a windowless hole, my blood barely circulating for way too long. I need to move. My mind and my body need to roam freely. It's a normal urge.

I want to *know* languages, of course, anyone would. I'd be happy to know all of them everywhere; but I don't actually want to use my time and mental energy to painstakingly *learn* even one of them. So what I say is that I want to learn the language while walking around San Pedro. I don't think anyone is fooled, but they go along with it. I'm paying, after all, whether I learn a word of Tz'utujil or Spanish or not.

Every day, on my way home from school for lunch, I pass a terribly forlorn little girl selling a few peanuts. She has the saddest eyes of any child I've ever seen. She is dirty and her peanuts are even dirtier. One day, out of pity, I buy all of her peanuts, hoping that way I won't have to try not to see her mournful eyes, the next day or ever, beseeching me as I pass by her on the road. I plan to throw the peanuts away later, but then I become busy with other things and forget about them. That night, with what looks like an almost full moon outside, having eaten almost nothing all day, I wake up about 3 A.M. ravenously hungry.

I know all I have in my backpack is a little bottled water. Then I remember the peanuts. How dirty could they be? They're in shells. What I had thought was dirt, as I discover by smelling them and then eating them in the scant flinders of moonlight coming through the cracks in the walls of my room, is the natural charring from being roasted over an open fire. They are the most delicious peanuts I've ever eaten in my life. I never see the little girl again, and I look for her every day.

During the first two days of class the director is my teacher. I learn that he had been a peasant field worker who had been conscripted by a large, well-known American fruit company and then, along with many others, trucked to the coast to work on banana plantations. Vagrants had been rounded up, given a choice between jail and field work, then loaded into trucks and taken far from home. The workers had been given no place to sleep and the bare minimum to eat and he, like all of them, spent his meager daily wages on alcohol.

The work was hard, the days were long, the people were virtual prisoners of the fruit company, and so they needed to drink in order to be able to fall asleep at night and get up and work again the next day. Many of the workers became sick and died. But he was lucky, my director. He met a woman, fell in love, and she inspired him to stop drinking. Most of his children are now working in his school. He says a day doesn't go by that he doesn't crave alcohol but that he loves his family and resists the temptation.

Guatemala, like El Salvador, has a rich and ancient culture going back thousands of years, with accomplishments in math and astronomy that amaze scholars to this day. Like much of Latin America, it was a colony of Spain from about 1500 until about 1800. Peasants were routinely massacred, the heartlessness was unconscious, the exploitation was justified—on the rare occasions someone felt that it needed to be—with racist cant and religious tartuffery. Naturally the people lost a lot of their culture.

A series of military rulers and autocratic governments followed Spain's exit. The inequality was extreme. Finally in the 1950s elected leaders instituted programs to help the poor, including a program for public education and one for a more just distribution of land. These leaders were labeled communists by the United States, partly because of the American government's fear of Russia and Russia's connections to Cuba, and partly because the United States government was enmeshed with American corporations in Latin America.

Jacobo Arbenz Guzman, President of Guatemala in 1954, was ousted by a coup, backed by the Central Intelligence

Agency (CIA), a coup that was, according to Noam Chomsky in *Turning the Tide*, carried out in order to help the United Fruit Company stay in place. The United States government's hidden support of ruthless dictators, like Pinochet in Chile, was common all over Latin America. In Argentina in 1976, according to Graciela Mochkofsky writing in the *New Yorker* in March 2016 with information from recently declassified government documents, the United States secretly supported a brutal dictatorship. Latin America was a place where the United States government seemed to have no qualms about suspending the scruples professed at home. Clinton, and now Obama have apologized for our government's support of the carnage but it seems rather cynical and self-serving after the fact. Social chaos reigned in the aftermath of the ouster of Guzman in Guatemala, compounded by earthquakes, floods, fires, and disease. Guerilla warfare, assassinations, rigged elections, violence, and fraudulence of all kinds in business and trade, created the usual Stygian stew, the predictable Phlegethontic boiling up and boiling over that made for a miserable existence for all but the very wealthy who were, among other things, rich enough to leave the country until things improved.

Sporadic as well as full-fledged civil war raged in Guatemala up through the 1990s and it was awfully hard to tell just who was on what side, or what was really going on, much less what group was paying for it all. President Clinton went to Guatemala in 1999 and apologized, according to Elisabeth Malkin writing in *The New York Times* on May 16, 2013, on behalf of all of us. President Clinton said our country was sorry for the carnage during the civil war when women were raped, men were tortured, and children were allowed to starve to death in the mountains. American support for the violence of the Guatemalan security forces, Malkin quotes the president as saying, "was wrong."

There are fewer secrets now in the world. There's more transparency. Growing up in a small community in Michigan, we assumed that everyone knew everything, or would sooner or later. Someone will always see. Someone will always talk. But in cities, and in the larger world, one could be anonymous; secrets could be kept. Not everything was known. When the Nazis started shipping people to concentration camps, some people knew, but only a few; it took years for the world to find out, and then more years for people to believe that such a horrible thing was actually happening. Now things are less hidden, because with the Internet, there are eyes and ears everywhere, just like there always was in my little village of Lake Leelanau, and we're all better for it.

According to Scott Shane's December 9, 2014 report in *The New York Times,* the U.S. Senate's investigation of CIA history uncovered the information that the United States had a secret military presence in Latin America for years, including torture camps.

After the director finishes teaching me, he assigns his son to be my tutor. We walk to the post office to mail a letter. We pass a beautiful church with many people outside on blankets with little altars. Some are kneeling. Some are burning incense. I ask the young man what's going on and he explains that the people practice their own native religion outside the church and the Catholic religion inside. He says this church, like many churches in Guatemala, is built on top of an ancient, sacred site.

He takes me to see, somewhere nearby in the bowels of the city, a shaman who's selling artifacts. The shaman is a large, older man, shambling and affable, who looks like he had been very strong in his younger days. The shaman lives deep in the recesses of the town.

We have taken many, many, tiny alleyways to find this medicine man. I would have never found the man, nor would I ever be able to find my way back out of the maze, nor would I ever be able to find the man again, without my tutor. The shaman's home is small and dark, built into the hill so it feels like a cave.

I buy a small, clay talismanic fish from him. It seems the polite thing to do. My tutor assures me the talisman is ancient. As we are leaving, the wise man says in English, "Bring more tourists." He seems to have no idea that his little home is marvelously out of the way, impossible to find without a local guide such as my language teacher.

The next week the director's daughter is my tutor. Like her brother she is a lovely person. She's intelligent, kind, and has a sense of humor. She's willing to entertain my questions. She's tolerant of my not being able to walk as fast as she can.

Guatemalans in San Pedro can walk up a vertical grade on a jumble of rocks, really fast, and you have no idea how fast until you're walking with them. All over Guatemala, when you ride along those hairpin mountain turns in the chicken busses, you can see people far away up the steep slopes, tiny in the distance, walking zigzag up into the clouds.

We are walking to the next town along the cliffs above Lake Atitlán. We are taking a shaded mountain trail because, I will realize later, my tutor is afraid of my becoming more sunburned.

"Someone is watching us," I blurt out suddenly. I have no idea why I say this. It just pops out.

She glances around. Neither of us sees anything. We have assumed, without even thinking about it or discussing it, that we are the only ones on this mountain trail.

Just then a small, bright yellow snake raises his head from the leaves a few feet away and stares at us intently.

We stand very still. The snake then slithers back the way it had come, toward the cliff above the lake. We both laugh, the nervous laughter of relief. Ha-ha-ha.

"That must have been it," I say.

I want to know if that kind of snake is poisonous and she says she doesn't know but thinks maybe it is because of its bright color. Then she says, "This was the trail used by the revolutionaries during the civil war. They would come this way to go to the next town. The soldiers couldn't follow them unless they came on foot. The soldiers were lazy and didn't want to do that."

✝ I'm in a home-stay the school has arranged. It's a household where I learn the man's older brother had been killed during the civil war, and so he has inherited all the land. They had been on opposite sides. The man in my home-stay had been a policeman at the time his brother had been killed. His brother had been a revolutionary leader. I can't help wondering if the man in my house had killed his older brother to get the land. Perhaps I think this because his tone of voice when he talks to his wife and children is disrespectful and arrogant. His wife does all the work in and around the house and, as far as I can tell, also makes all the money.

She's a good cook and sells beans and tortillas from the back door of her home. She is Mexican, not Guatemalan, and looks like she may have once been quite beautiful. She also looks like she's older than her husband, but perhaps she looks older because she works so hard and the work has aged her. She has many ailments that seem psychosomatic to me and which she's always treating with expensive elixirs. Her illnesses seem to keep her husband in line. He is solicitous—only about the ailments—and, she tells me proudly, that he once even took her to a doctor in Guatemala City. Obviously if she dies, he will have to do all the work.

The man appears to go to the mountains every day with a mattock, a heavy stone hoe, to work in the corn, he says, but somehow he never seems to have been working. His clothes are too clean and, unlike his wife, he never looks tired. Perhaps he does go and work all day, but it doesn't seem that way. However, that night, when he comes home for supper, I ask him about the snake.

"*El serpente amarillo*," he says pontifically. "*Toxico. Peligroso.*" The yellow snake is a poisonous and dangerous one.

He says he kills such snakes with his mattock and swings it in pantomime.

I have the only bedroom in the house. I have no idea where everyone else sleeps when I'm there. There are several children. Perhaps they stay with friends or relatives. The woman of the household has an adult daughter who's visiting from Mexico and is apparently from an earlier marriage. This daughter is friends with the school director's daughter. She's in the house all day until late in the evening, but seems to sleep somewhere else as she's never there in the morning.

I think the man of the household might have a mistress somewhere and that possibly he stays with her, as he always leaves immediately after eating supper. The tension between him and his wife, when he leaves right after supper, is palpable. But I might be wrong. Maybe he's going to go drinking with his friends and he's spending all her hard-earned money; possibly that's the cause of the tension. It's hard to know. Wherever he goes, he doesn't come home until again the next evening at suppertime.

Their home is made of rough-sawn lumber, with cracks between the walls. It is possible to see through the cracks, but with difficulty, and probably not without being noticed trying to do so.

The doorway to my bedroom is two, large, dark, dirty, smoky-smelling serapes. In my windowless bedroom is a rough-sawn "bed" of raw wood built into the wall. The floors are swept and pounded dirt. There are no electric lights. In the daytime there's enough light coming through the cracks in the walls so that I can see to clean the room with soap and water. In the market I find copal, which smells like bergamot. I find sage and little, yellow, minty-smelling marigolds. I use these things to fumigate the room. I know that insects and stray animals usually don't like herbs and in any event the herbs make the room smell better.

In the morning, before anyone else is up, and before there

is any real sunlight, I go out to the "shower" in the yard. This is a simple affair, a bucket of cold water and a cup. I soap myself up and then rinse off in this little cabana that is constructed of corn stalks, a "room" after the manner of my language classrooms. The corn stalks for the room in the dirt yard are only vaguely there. I drape my towel over the "wall" on the street-side and hope no one else is awake or interested from the other directions.

My classes are in the morning, when it's cool. At noon I have lunch at my home-stay—a tortilla with beans—and then sleep in the heat of the day. I go out in the middle of the afternoon and walk around the town.

San Pedro is a town built on a series of concentric hills and thus is a series of natural mazes. It's easy to get lost. I know my way to the Internet, the only one in the town, where the keys are so grimy that I can't see the letters. The Internet is about a block up the hill from the boat dock where I will go when I return to Panajachel. I know how to walk back along the shore of Lake Atitlán, past the restaurant where the man from the Netherlands has all the books about Guatemalan history and lives with two Indian girls. They all sleep together in the loft.

The Dutchman is a big, pear-shaped, grossly unkempt, grossly overweight man who has the best collection of books about Guatemala of anywhere I've ever seen, including the major libraries and bookstores in America. Most of the books are in English and I read them all. There are a few in Spanish and one or two in Dutch and I can kind of make out what they're about so I read them while I'm eating, just to pick up the gist of things. I always stop there for a beer and *chili rellenos* and, of course, the books, in the late afternoon. At first I'd felt like I had to read the books there, on the premises, but after the first day he tells me I can borrow them. He says he knows I'm traveling and books are heavy, so he trusts me to return them.

Almost everything I know about the history of Guatemala I learn in those two weeks from the Dutchman's library, later corroborated by books I obtain back home through inter-library loan from the Traverse Area District Library in Michigan and by *The New York Times* online and of course the Internet generally; but during my visit to San Pedro those things weren't available. Discovering the Dutchman's trove of information, after a dearth of it in El Salvador, is like finding food during a famine. Google only started in 1998, just before I went to work in the prisons of California, and Wikipedia didn't start until 2001, just about the time I arrived in Guatemala. It was early days and information on the Internet was still sparse. The Dutchman's library was an information oasis.

In the evenings I would read in my room.

Back in Traverse City, before I'd accepted the teaching job in El Salvador, knowing there would be power outages, I'd gone to a camping store on Front Street, Back Country Outfitters, and purchased a strange little reading light, a flashlight really, that one wears like a miner's light on a headband.

Because I'd been told by traveling friends that it's much harder to stay warm in the tropics than it is to stay cool—for the simple reason that there's no central heating and that also there may be no stoves of any kind—I'd gone to Sears and bought three flannel nightgowns. Each was in a different pattern with audacious ruffles, like the ones my grandmother had worn when I'd shared a bedroom with her in the late 1940s. Three flannel gowns worn together, one on top of the other, with the warm air trapped between the layers, and the layers of ruffles along the bottom keeping out the cold air, I knew would be as warm and light-weight as down.

The added advantage is that the nightgowns could be switched out, so I would always have a clean layer next to my body. I hate to be dirty and smelly, as I suppose anyone does, but I really hate it. The combination of the outrageous nightgowns with the reading lamp, and the light shining from the headband (I'm just guessing because I didn't have a mirror) probably made me look like Keith Richards posing as a miner in grandmother drag.

I had not given this a single moment's thought until one evening my landlady sweetly, but totally out of the blue, decided to bring me a cup of hot chocolate. Hot chocolate in Guatemala is not made with milk, but with water. I think they must grate the chocolate into hot water because it never really melts and when you drink it you get little flakes of the chocolate caught in your teeth. It's not bad. Like almost everything, you get used to it.

She knocks on the wall next to the serape door, "*Chocolate Caliente.*"

I say, "*Si, por favor, venga,*" and she enters. I know I might look ridiculous. And I can instantly tell—by her carefully freezing every muscle in her face and holding this face in place—that "ridiculous" is exactly what she's thinking. I'm always amazed at how all human beings are able to perfectly pretend that everything is normal. It's a defining characteristic of our species. I could be one of the chickens in her yard for all she knows. She does not bat an eye.

A minute later I can hear her talking to her adult daughter in the other room. I do not need to be able to understand a word of either Tz'utujil or Spanish to pick up on the gasps of amazement and the muffled titters.

An hour later, another polite knock on the wall next to the serape doorway, and it's the daughter with another cup of *chocolate caliente.*

She also keeps a mask on her face of non-reaction. After she exits, there is total silence from the outer room but I can only imagine the rolling of the eyes and the raised eyebrows. For my part, I have secured two cups of hot chocolate in one evening.

One day I go for my walk as usual and everything is exactly the same, except for some strange reason I become lost. I cannot find the street to my home-stay. I leave the Dutchman's restaurant as I always do, walk the trail of volcanic cinders next to the lake, as always, go past the stable where the horses are, as I usually do, but I cannot find the street to my family.

I walk for hours. I pass the horse stable four times and think that if it comes down to it, I will stay there, since I know snakes don't like to be around the hooves of horses. I'm becoming exhausted and disoriented. The rough-hewn house of the hard-working Mexican lady and the sketchy man with the mattock is beginning to look more and more like "Home Sweet Home" as the sun gets lower and lower in the sky. Here, near the equator, the sun is gulped down into darkness in a matter of minutes. In Michigan we have hours before the sun actually sets. Here, it's daylight one minute and night the next.

I feel like I'm miles from the Dutchman's restaurant. I'm even more miles from the docks and the boats. It's getting dark. I'm feeling resigned to spending a night with the horses on the cindery shores of this volcanic lake when a small boy separates himself from a gang of ragamuffins and approaches me. He has the most beatific smile.

"*Perdido*," I say, which I hope means, "I am lost."

He takes me by the hand, his grimy wonderful little hand, and leads me to a knoll from which I can see my school and which I know is at the base of the street where I have my homestay. I had somehow gotten onto a path closer to the lake, parallel to my usual one, and almost identical. It looked the same but it wasn't: at a crucial turn the view of my school had been blocked by a clump of trees.

Perhaps he had been watching me all afternoon, wandering back and forth, and around the circular streets of the circular hills. Perhaps he is an angel. I give him all the money I have, which isn't much, but he refuses to take it. I press it on him and finally he smiles, shrugs, and gives the universal kid sign, for "Whatever, lady."

The morning I leave San Pedro I walk to the boat at 5 A.M. under a cold, gibbous moon. The night before at supper the woman of the household and her adult daughter had tried to talk the man of the household into walking with me to the boat. He had refused, rather rudely, but then wanted to know at what hour I was leaving. If he didn't want to escort me through the dark streets to the boat launch, why did he need to know what time I was leaving? What if he, or a friend of his, decided to rob me? I had never fully trusted this man. Politely I say I'll be leaving at 7 A.M., and perhaps if he changes his mind, he can join me, but I instantly know in my own mind that I will be up and gone a full two hours earlier.

I arrive at the shore at 6 A.M. and wait in the boathouse for the pilot and the other passengers. At 8 A.M., just as the sun is coming up, I get on the *barque* to Panajachel. Our pilot this morning is a hefty, runny-nosed, eight-year-old who has to suck the tube of gasoline to get the flow going to the motor. Of course he gets some in his mouth and has to spit this into the lake.

We are dangerously overloaded. The water of the lake washes over the sides of the boat all during the half-hour long ride to Panajachel. There are no life jackets. I find myself wondering if I could still swim a mile, as I had done frequently when I was a child, when I had swum across Little Glen Lake during the northern Michigan summers, from Gracie Dickinson's house to my own shore.

Panajachel at eight-thirty on a January morning is cold. I walk the length of the town before I find a truck stop on the outskirts near the highway where two women are selling hot coffee in tin soup cans. I buy a cup, perhaps made with water from the lake, but I think if it has been boiled it might be alright. A person needs coffee in the morning. I take the chance.

While I'm sitting on the curb drinking my coffee two, tiny, little girls come out of nowhere, selling scarves. I shake my head, "No." But they importune. I hold up six dollars, "*No mas*," I say, "*Solo que esta.*" I know the price of a scarf.

They look at each other, seem to have an "Ah-ha!" moment and then, eyes twinkling, pull a long, blue-green scarf from their bunch and, before I know it, have started to entwine it in my hair, chattering like little sparrows as they dance around me.

Guatemalans have an eye for color and these little girls, seeing my red hair, still hennaed from my time teaching in the San Francisco Jail, are having the time of their life. The scarf they pull out is green, blue, and turquoise, with tiny threads of black, purple and white so it shimmers like water. They have had some kind of epiphany, and apparently it concerns the color of my hair and the color of the scarf. Both of them, giggling madly, are doing something with the scarf and my tresses. I have no idea what.

When I look in a shop window an hour later I look like a Celtic queen. I know I look beautiful because of the way all the men are looking at me. During the next twenty-four hours it all begins to slowly fall apart, but for a day I'm transformed.

At 10 A.M. I meet the driver I had contracted with two weeks before to take me to Todos Santos. He is an excellent driver, a Mexican man with a family in Antigua. He had been the driver of the van that brought me from Antigua to Panajachel. I'd sat in front on that trip so I'd be less likely to be car sick, and had observed that he was careful, cautious, and very intelligent.

The driver's wife is a teacher, I'd learned during the drive. They had decided that she wouldn't go back into the classroom until their two daughters were in school. "*El amor de la madre es muy importante*," he'd said: the love of the mother is very important. "*El amore es siempre mas importante que dinero*," he'd added: love is always more important than money.

I had asked him during the trip if he had ever been a driver for one of the chicken busses, which regularly whizzed past us on mountain turns with no visibility. He'd said he had, "for two weeks." Why did he stop? "I didn't want to die," he'd said.

We'd both laughed. He'd explained that drivers were paid according to the number of runs, so naturally they drove too fast for conditions, otherwise they didn't make enough money.

The overloaded chicken busses, with people's belongings, including chickens and sometimes people on top of the busses, careen precariously. Once I saw a baby pig being held tightly in the arms of a tiny man, a man hanging on for dear life, and on whose face was an almost comically serious expression. But there is little that is comic about the chicken busses. They are notoriously dangerous and sometimes go off the sides of the mountains. You can see them down at the bottoms of the ravines.

The chicken bus that had brought me to Antigua had a man whose job it was to act as the side mirrors. He'd hung off the back of the bus, leaning far out to see what was coming, and sometimes ran alongside the bus to get better visibility, and then hopped back on. A Guatemalan Usain Bolt. Being bus mirrors: definitely a young man's job.

I had asked my excellent Mexican driver during the first trip to Panajachel from Antigua, where the smartest people in Guatemala were. He'd said, "In Todos Santos. The mountains. The conquistadores never got that far." He had agreed to take me there two weeks later, between Antigua-Panajachel runs.

Good as his word, he's there at the truck stop.

We slowly wind our way up into the mountains, through endless little towns. They look like towns in California's Sierra Nevada Mountains except that they are in Guatemala. The geography and the climate are similar but everything else is different.

Sometimes we see men in serapes lying by the side of the road. It's impossible to tell if they are asleep or dead.

In almost every small mountain town there's a funeral—sometimes three or four; often the funerals of children. We can tell by the size of the coffins.

Finally he deposits me at a hotel in Todos Santos where he seems to know the people. He says he'll be back in a week and I believe him. This hotel, like my home-stay in San Pedro, is constructed of rough-sawn lumber. They show me to a small, windowless room. There's a narrow bed attached to the wall, scarcely wider than a park bench but thankfully a little longer, made of rough-hewn lumber onto which I throw my sleeping bag.

There's a pump in the yard where I can get a bucket of water. There's a tin dishpan in my room. I can pour the water into the basin and, with a washcloth I've brought with me, can get most of the road dust off and wash my feet. It's sufficient. This hotel, like my home-stay and school in San Pedro, has no indoor plumbing.

In the morning, since I'm an early riser, I find the kitchen, where all the maids, perhaps half a dozen, are piled in a heap around the one wood stove in the place. They are young, barely more than children, clearly rural, and all have runny noses and a morose manner. I soon learn that they are required to cook and clean around the clock. No wonder they are all sick and sullen.

Todos Santos, like all of Guatemala, has beautiful textiles unique to that region. Every Guatemalan village has, for at least five thousand years, woven its own distinctive fabric out of wool or cotton. They were among the first people on earth to grow cotton and use it for cloth. The large pieces of dark woven navy wool of Todos Santos, with narrow bands of red, seem to pick up the purple of the mountains, the blue of the sky and the invisible deep red of the volcanic soil.

The fabrics in Guatemala are hand-woven, hand-dyed, very cheap, and incredibly beautiful. The colors scintillate and work off each other in a way that makes the colors in the cloth vibrate, throwing off tones that come as close as anything I've ever seen to the way colors in nature reverberate off each other. I want to buy almost everything I see, but simply have no way to transport even a single piece of this fabric wealth in my small duffle bag on casters.

In the rocky mountain meadows of Todos Santos, I see small, red poinsettias growing, a few inches from the ground, the height of a tulip or a trillium. I'd had no idea that poinsettias ever grew wild, or that they were ever less than a bit too large, verging on garish and overwhelming. The wild poinsettias are everywhere, small and beautiful and natural.

I am somewhat hampered in my search for the smartest by not knowing any of the native languages or even much Spanish beyond *por favor* and *gracias*. The native people in Todos Santos speak Mam, another indigenous language. I'm rapidly forgetting the little bit of Tz'utujil I knew. The truth is you cannot learn a language in two weeks. Understanding or speaking any language well enough to have meaningful conversations takes years.

I do find a young American photographer, however, and his father. They both speak Spanish much better than I do—helpful in walking around—and they are delightful. The photographer is freelancing for a travel magazine. The young photographer is, like the Dutchman in San Pedro, overweight and out of shape. What have we done to our young people that so many, other than the athletes, who are not the majority, look like they don't have the stamina to walk to the corner and back? We need more hours of recess in schools, more play-time generally, more safe parks, and less air pollution. We're ruining our children. His father is older, my age, elegant, in great shape, and remarried to someone other than the young photographer's mother.

We spend some time together walking up the mountains. I like the photographer. He is honest and has a likable reserve. At one point I see two young boys in bright red shirts digging a trench with a man in a bright blue shirt—all against the backdrop of bright blue skies, dark green meadows and vivid purple mountains, and say, "That's a good photograph."

He ignores me and I ignore the fact that he ignored me. When we have walked a little farther I say, "Why didn't you want to take that picture?"

"Todos Santos is where a Japanese photographer was killed by a mob," he says. "He was a pedophile and was taking pictures of young boys."

"Good call," I say. "Today is not a good day to die."

My faithful driver reappears on the designated morning and drives me back to Antigua. This time we have other passengers.

I stay again in the ancient hotel with the long corridors off a courtyard where there's a doorman, a silent dwarf, a hunchback, incredibly strong, who sleeps on a tiny, narrow platform with railings, above the door. He climbs down a ladder on the wall like a chimpanzee or a fireman when someone is at the door. Once down, he laboriously moves the thick heavy boards that prevent the massive, eighteen-foot-high, five-inch thick doors from being opened by anyone but him.

It's after 10 P.M. when we arrive at the hotel. I haven't eaten. So after depositing my things, I go to the fancy restaurant across the street and have the following: *ropa vieja*, "old clothes," a beef dish in a tomato sauce with olives, bacon, and spices; traditional black beans; a corn salsa with cactus, cilantro, onion and pimiento; saffron rice; a glass of wine; a slice of brown sugar cake with real, caramel-flavored whipped cream frosting and a dusting of ground Brazil nuts; and thick, dark coffee; all delicious, for the amazing price of twenty dollars. As I'm paying I see a sign on the counter that reads, "United States President, Bill Clinton, ate here." I wonder if President Clinton had eaten there when he visited Guatemala in 1999. I wonder if he had thought the roosters of Guatemala sounded like saxophone players.

A Walk in the Dunes

To understand and love the dunes, you have to love strange beauty. Not normal beauty, not popular beauty, not the kind where everyone agrees with you, but the reverse.

The dunes do not support life. Nothing grows there, or very little; the sand blows and smothers the things that do grow. In the Sleeping Bear Dunes you can't get water unless you want to drill at least five hundred feet down, or haul it from the lake.

In the heights above North Bar Lake there was a family of homesteaders, according to Ray Welch who came from a neighboring pioneer family, who did haul their water from the lake three hundred feet below to the top of the bluff. They didn't last long.

When I was growing up my friend Susy Schmidt and I would sometimes ride our horses up through Reverend Treat's farm south of Empire, and then out onto the bluffs. We didn't do this more than twice. It was slow going. The sand sucked at the horses' feet. We were afraid one of them was going to break a leg. We'd get off and walk them and then the sand would suck at our feet, too.

How does one learn to love something strange? The usual ways: proximity, dailyness, difficulties. The dunes are an ac-quired taste, a learned love, a developed aesthetic. One learns to understand the ways of something and, over time, that en-genders a relationship.

Anyone who has ever climbed to the top of the dunes from that place on M-109 where everyone always goes, where when you get to the top you can sense, and then see, Lake Michigan in the west, well, you want to go there. But the distances in the dunes are deceptive, it's farther to the lake than it looks, the sun is intense, and if you don't bring water, you'll wish you had.

Most of the people who've grown up around the dunes have walked to the lake across the top, but I've never met anyone who's done this more than a few times. It's hard to walk in soft sand. If you're like me, you walk to have that rhythm of walking, so you can daydream and let your mind unravel. But you don't get that rhythm in the dunes. You get good views, and that's sometimes worth it, but it's not a walk you choose to take very often; the rhythm is wrong.

When we were little in the 1950s, my mother used to take us and our cousins— eight kids —to the dune climb at the end of the day. "Show me how many times you can run up and down!" she would incite us. "I'll bet you can't do it twenty times! Oh, you *can*, can you? Well, you show me, and keep track on this piece of paper." She had official-looking slips of paper and tiny pencils on which we could tally our prodigious achievements. "Maybe you will prove me wrong!!! I can't believe you have enough energy to run up and down twenty times!!! My goodness, how could you ever do it?"

She had a stack of magazines—*Newsweek, Saturday Review, Life, Harper's, The Atlantic* and she would sit in the station wagon, the kind with wood panels on the side, and read, only being interrupted from time to time to feign total delight and surprise and wonderment every time we chalked up another run up the dunes. Then she'd let us all swim in Glen Lake. Some of us would already be asleep as we pulled into the driveway. We were soon in bed, and she could look forward to another blessed hour or two of peace before she also retired for the night.

The dunes aren't what they seem. When I was running the scenic drive in the dunes for my father, we routinely had people try to drive on the dunes, and we'd have to haul them out with the tractor. We had signs everywhere, "Don't drive on the dunes," but people said they hadn't seen the signs and they probably hadn't. A lot of people can't be bothered with signs.

Back in the mid-1970s a lady called from *Esquire* magazine in New York and said she wanted to come do a fashion shoot in the dunes and asked if I could I give her permission to use our roads. When they arrived she took one look at the dunes and asked if she could hire me as a scout. I had no idea what that might entail but quickly said that my standard fee was five hundred dollars. I felt like a bandit until I learned that the previous manager had received ten times that amount.

My sister Ann and I once went on a winter picnic out on Sleeping Bear Point. We chose a spot at the very tip, so close to South Manitou, it felt like we could swim there. It was a nice day and a nice walk from our house. A few years later the whole point fell into the water. The currents in the Manitou Passage, like the dunes themselves, are strange.

You think you know everything about something. How much could there be to know about a big pile of sand? Then you realize you don't know anything at all. It teaches you humility. It teaches you not to make assumptions. I like it when that happens. It makes me feel young.

From my mother's house above Sleeping Bear Bay, we can see the northern expanse of the dunes for about six months of the year. From November to April when the leaves are off, we can contemplate that languid golden-pink length of sand, looking so soft and inviting, especially when the sun rises and when it sets. The dunes have an abstract and inscrutable beauty; when the light changes, it changes everything.

To see the dunes is to see and viscerally connect with primal forces: earth, air, fire, water. To see the dunes is to be challenged to imagine the ions of one's substance in constant relationship to everything else. To see the dunes is to find the ground of one's being, the ground of one's believing that there is something greater than one's self. Every grain of sand was once part of a rock. The wind and water shift over and over again, and evolve new formations, just as we do, and so we never tire of contemplating the shifting patterns, the changing light, of allowing ourselves to be rocked back to our primal beginnings, and renewed.

ASIA

Buddha's Brides
on the Thai-Burma Border

I'm not the first to see the cobra. Or, maybe I am, but I don't know what I'm seeing. Through the dirty bus windows my eyes momentarily sense movement and vaguely, in the brown leaves, a pattern that is not leaves.

It isn't until I feel the bus tilt and see that several people have come to my side of the bus to peer out, their pupils shattered like black diamonds, both giddy and scared, faces glistening with sweaty excitement, like people at a Muay Thai kick-boxing show on TV in the home of my Thai host teacher, that I begin to comprehend that something momentous is happening.

Then I see it, a photo in *National Geographic* only real: Mata Hari in a cowl, the flat, black eyes, tiny as sunflower seeds, without expression, the tongue flashing like a slender dark flame. Cobras are creatures so far back in our evolution they pre-date not only conscience, but consciousness. To see a cobra—legless, armless; just a face, at the top of a sinew rising from the earth—is to look back down the ladder of endless time into the dark, bottomless depths of the void.

There are holes in the wooden floor of the ancient bus. I wonder for a minute if the cobra's cousin will come up through one of the apertures. The bus is moving slowly, grinding its way up the mountain. I keep my eyes peeled for a brown slither.

I'm going to Mae Hong Son on the Thai-Burma border to teach in a camp for Burmese refugees. My niece has been doing research in the camps for her Master's in Education. She says some of the smartest people she's ever met, both refugees and volunteer instructors, are there. The stories of escape, recapture, torture, hiding in the forest, injury or death of a friend or family member along the way, betrayal, daily survival on roots and insects, constant hunger, are legion.

Worldwide there are about a million Burmese refugees, about one hundred and fifty thousand in the camps. My niece is advocating for an international degree for all refugees worldwide based on a standardized test, a degree that would be approved by the United Nations. This would allow the camp educations of more than sixty million refugees all over the world to be validated, giving them a chance for better jobs once they find a country to accept them.

Currently, because all refugees are non-citizens or illegal aliens, any education they have received is not considered legitimate. Some in the camps arrive with educations—doctors, engineers, professors—others are street smart. They all take classes in the camps while they wait for visas to other countries. Some have been taking classes for thirty years.

Burma has some of the same tribes along the northern border as Thailand, nomadic peoples who share the same languages and who have crossed back and forth for millennia. The presence of the migratory peoples has made the trafficking in illegal substances all along the borders easy and inevitable.

For the last hundred and fifty years Thailand has been generally more modern and prosperous than Burma, in part because when Burma was ruled by Britain it was drained of its wealth. Burma also bore the brunt of the Japanese occupation during World War II. Although there was a brief popular uprising after the war, for the last fifty years Burma has been ruled by a military dictatorship so harsh and benighted that many Burmese have fled the country. Those who remain are either in jail, under house arrest, part of the military junta, criminals, or subsistence farmers.

My niece had told me that the Burmese she was seeing in the border camps were often from the same tribes as the Northern Thai and looked the same, but unlike the Thai, the Burmese seemed to have a tradition of reverence for literature. Good

BAMBOO TRAVEL PILLOW
Luxuriously soft and cool!

SALE!

WHY PAY SHIPPING SEE COUPON

ONLY $~~24~~ **$19** STOCK NO. 11-71977-0

Enjoy a comfy nap in the car or plane with this soothing neck pillow. It's made from dense memory foam to support your head and neck while you doze, doing away with the constant head movement that jerks you awake. The zippered removable cover is made from soft, breathable bamboo and polyester for cool comfort. Spot clean. Plastic snap button keeps it in place. Polyurethane foam fill. About 13"L x 12"W x 4"H. Imported.

K24580_R2

SEAT BELT COMFORT PAD
Reduces friction and irritation!

ONLY $~~5~~ **$3** STOCK NO. 12-13677-6

Put the comfort back into car travel with this fluffy seat belt pad! It covers those digging, irritating straps with a soft, plush fabric that feels heavenly against your skin. Fits easily over standard shoulder belts, fastening snugly in place with its hook-and-loop closure. Also ideal for straps of handbags, luggage and sports bags, it takes the pressure off your shoulder when carrying heavy loads. A must for those with sensitive skin! Washable polyester. About 7" x 9¼" overall; imported.

K04310_R54

SALE!

WHY PAY SHIPPING SEE COUPON

Great for luggage straps!

government and prosperity made Burma one of the most literate countries in Asia from the 1500s through the time of British colonialism. The British were in Burma from 1824 to 1948. George Orwell, the British writer and author of *Animal Farm*, was there as an imperial policeman from 1922 to 1927. Today it's the English literature of the nineteenth century, writers from the time of Charles Dickens and Thomas Hardy, with which the educated Burmese are most familiar.

Thailand, unlike Burma and many adjacent Asian countries, has never been colonized. This is partly because during the heyday of colonialism in the 1800s the French and British wanted to have a neutral area from which to rule their nearby colonies, and also partly because Thai rulers, due to their country's geographical position as a cross-over land, had accumulated considerable experience and collective expertise when it came to avoiding being taken over by other countries. The French had Laos, Cambodia, and Vietnam. The British had Burma, which they would lose to Japan in World War II. The British and French wanted to colonize Thailand, then called Siam, and of course so did other major players such as the Dutch, the Chinese, the Germans, and the Japanese.

Thai rulers fought for their country in every way they could: they used their army; they negotiated; they prevented railroads from being built in order to prevent the movement of foreign troops into and within their country; they gave away small chunks of land; they paid out sums of money; and in general did whatever the situation seemed to demand, all in order to keep out foreign powers. The Thai leaders made accommodations as needed, with things like The Treaty of Amity and Commerce in 1826 with the British and various deals with the French, to prevent colonization. Thai people are justifiably proud of having never been colonized.

The more southerly part of Thailand, according to some linguists and archeologists, is populated by ancient peoples who appear, based on language, to have come from China and also, based on some cultural symbols and artifacts, to have come from Malaysia as well. During World War II European countries and the United States were all in and out of Thailand, with the United States finally holding sway. We established military bases there during the Vietnam War, purportedly to protect Thailand from the communist revolutions in neighboring countries.

Thailand has become a tourist destination, especially the southern coasts where the beaches and islands offer snorkeling, deep-sea diving, boating, sun-bathing, and stays at gorgeous, clean, and inexpensive hotels. Picture: bamboo cabanas—white curtains blowing gently in the breeze—and discreet servants somewhere in the background. It was this coastline that was so hard hit by the tsunami in 2004. More than eight thousand people died or were horribly injured on the coast of Thailand, many at Khao Lak, including a much loved granddaughter of my longtime friend, Grace Glynn of Traverse City, Michigan. The tsunami of 2004 killed a quarter of a million people in Indonesia and Asia.

Thailand, for ten thousand years, has been a place people had to get across to get to other places. Rulers and business people became skilled at maintaining autonomy by avoiding confrontation, orchestrating backroom deals, and making public displays of friendship. Over the centuries a culture of surface gentleness, behind the scenes ruthlessness, underlying secrecy, and institutionalized censorship has evolved.

Burma and Thailand have conquered each other several times over hundreds of years, mostly in skirmishes but sometimes with wholesale takeovers of the seats of power such as Pagan (now called Bagan) in Burma and Ayutthaya in Thailand. Most recently, in the early 1800s, the Thai had the major city of Chiang Mai (La Na) in the north returned by Burma; and the Burmese got back Tenasserim, in the south from Thailand.

Both countries originally had indigenous, stone-age populations which were overrun and usurped by—and intermingled with—invaders from Mongolia, India, China, Persia, Europe, and, in more recent times, America. Both Thailand and Burma were introduced to Buddhism many centuries ago, with Burma's Buddhism coming a little more from Tibet and Thailand's coming a little more from India. In both places Buddhist religious observances are often a thin layer on top of a much deeper animism or folk culture.

I'm using my Peace Corps sanctioned trip to go and teach in the Burmese refugee camps, partly because I've heard so much about them from my niece that I want to go and see for myself, but also because I need a break from my Thai host teacher, the one who has me living in her house. This absence has been officially approved in writing by the Peace Corps office in Bangkok. The rule book stated that I was permitted to do special teaching projects in places other than my assigned site during school vacations.

The two rural schools to which I've been assigned by the Peace Corps are closed for spring break. For weeks now, no longer teaching the classes of a woman I shall call Mrs. Tahcheroo, I've been alone with her in her home, or alone with her in her car. Her life consists of eating pastry, playing video games, watching kick-boxing on TV, visiting temples with her cousin to beat gongs and put gold leaf on the Buddha and pray for money, having sleazy loan sharks visit her home at all hours, and going to doctors in Bangkok or Chiang Mai.

My host teacher is a very pretty woman, always impeccably groomed, and her home is an expensive re-make of a traditional Thai teak home with the giant teak trunks holding up the second and third floors, multiple staircases and balconies, all with elaborately carved decorations. Inside the house is a kind of filth that would be hard for anyone to imagine. She says she can't find anyone to help her clean, but a more likely explanation is that it would be a monumental task, or perhaps, because she's deeply in debt, people have learned that she can't pay them.

This house is infested with what I'd at first thought were rats but are a kind of Asian shrew, *suncus mucinus*. They communicate by echolocation, making strange, deep, rumbling sounds like a rock thrown into a barrel, that help them find their way in the walls. In India they're called chuchundra, a word that approximates the sound they make. In China they're called money shrews, because the sound of their nails clicking along the insides of walls sounds like jingling coins. It's the sounds at night in the walls that unnerve me. They live on insects and there's an endless supply of insects in my host teacher's home.

Raw sewage runs from a broken pipe in the bathroom, under a flimsy wall and across the kitchen floor to a ditch in front of the house. Insects and flies swarm around this steady stream of funk. Mrs. Tahcheroo doesn't cook. She buys food in plastic bags from a food vendor who comes around twice a day. She doesn't usually finish this food and so leaves it in a bowl on a table, or, still in the plastic bag, hung from a nail on the wall. The decaying food attracts flies, roaches, and vermin. The stench of rotting meat makes the place smell like a charnel house. There are creatures creeping and crawling, slithering and sliding, all over her house. The largest cockroaches I've ever seen in my life live in her bathroom. One morning one dropped from the ceiling onto my head.

Mr. Tahcheroo, a dissipated man with a thin Salvador Dali moustache and a sunken chest, comes home late at night and falls asleep downstairs on a bare wooden bed. Twice he's had car wrecks, or as Mrs. Tahcheroo puts it, has "got terrible with my car," and the car had to be towed home secretly in the dark by her brother, a man I've never met. There are two children in this family, one a high school student and one a college student, but they are never around. They have been raised by relatives for years because, according to Mrs. Tahcheroo, she has had three bouts of meningitis and her health is fragile.

In the morning, when I make coffee while Mrs. Tahcheroo is still sleeping upstairs, I also make it for Mr. Tahcheroo since my activity in the kitchen invariably wakens him from his wooden couch. This wooden bed has a wooden pillow. I had thought this bed and pillow would make sleeping difficult, but when everyone was gone one day, I tried it and it was surprisingly comfortable. A wooden bed is exactly right for the tropics because it's not too hot. When I bring Mr. Tahcheroo the steaming hot cup of Nescafe with lots of sugar, the way he likes it, he smells like formaldehyde, like death.

My Thai host teacher tells me she's related to the royal family. This is not as far-fetched as it might seem. King Chulalongkorn, the King's grandfather, had a harem, and all the kings before him did, too. Thailand is a small country. They could all be royalty. The King of Thailand, Bhumibol, my Thai host teacher had announced proudly one afternoon when we were attending one of the many village cremations, had sent the fire for her mother's funeral three years earlier. It was her mother who had cooked and cleaned and managed the house while my Thai host teacher was employed in the village school near the temple.

But Mrs. Tahcheroo has seldom taught for any extended period of time, according to some of the other teachers at her school. Her principal, a thick-necked Thai farmer, had been teaching her classes most of the time until I came. It's unclear if he did this because my Thai host teacher is royalty and he is not, or if she was on sick leave so often he simply became accustomed to teaching in her stead. I don't understand the Thai language well enough to scope out nuances and have no one to ask.

Mrs. Tahcheroo's older sister teaches in the prestigious palace school in Bangkok, "The Princess School," Mrs. Tahcheroo tells me proudly. Her brother, the mayor of a nearby village, a man I have yet to meet although he seems to be always in the wings, is an important man. "Everyone is afraid of my brother," my Thai host teacher often says. She'd said this during the school's flag-raising ceremony the first day I'd arrived and when I'd asked her why everyone was afraid of her brother, she'd shrugged and flounced away.

My Thai host teacher is the only member of her family to live in the family's ancestral rural village which is what qualified her to be assigned a Peace Corps volunteer. Placing volunteers in remote, rural villages was the current Peace Corps mission in Thailand.

The Peace Corps had told us during training that if the Thai teacher left the classroom, then, with a smile and implacable sweetness, we should leave with them, saying, "By do why," or, "I'm coming, too." Literally, "We go together." Thai teachers taking advantage of the Peace Corps program by dumping their teaching load on the eager, unsuspecting volunteers, was a well-known scenario.

The problem of keeping the Thai teachers in their rural classrooms, especially since the poverty and low station of the rural student population confers negative status on the teachers, is a big one. To keep track of their teachers' comings and goings the schools had traditionally had huge, three-foot-square, leather-bound "log-in books" which every teacher was supposed to sign when they arrived and when they left; but all they did was come, sign in, and leave, returning hours later to sign out.

The schools were now transitioning to very expensive electronic "fingerprint scans" like the kind we see in spy movies, at the CIA headquarters in Langley, Virginia. These are digital scans, similar to the ones done by police with ink, but biometric. One holds one's finger up to the camera and it copies and records one's unique fingerprint. As might have been predicted, the teachers were doing with the scans what they'd done with the log-in books: they were coming, scanning, leaving, returning, and scanning "out" at the end of the day. Fingerprint scans would be absurd in any small, rural school anywhere in the world, but are especially so in rural Thailand.

Some of the absenteeism, and just plain lollygagging, was understandable. Some of these women were expected to maintain their homes and their families, as they had traditionally done, but now had teaching jobs in addition. Some had household help, but many didn't. One woman was not only taking care of her husband and two children, but her aging mother. Her mother was incontinent and unable to leave the bed. This teacher had to go home every few hours to help her mother with all the things one needs to do for someone incapacitated. Even if the female teachers didn't have this kind of burden, they still had many home duties. They worked long hours every day. They couldn't reasonably be expected to put the same energy into teaching that they did into taking care of their families. Their families came first.

There's something else to consider, something an American wouldn't necessarily think of right away. In a country with so much censorship, where information was difficult to get, couldn't be verified, and might even be dangerous, why bother to know anything?

The rural schools were built in the 1960s, most of the money allegedly being U.S. dollars that came into the country in exchange for our country being allowed to have American soldiers there during the Vietnam War. The schools I work in seem not to have been touched since. I teach in schools with holes in the floors, holes in the roofs, and holes in the walls. The squat toilets are a sluice of poop so that one has to avoid glissading into the stew of feces. Once I dropped my cell phone in the squat toilet. It would have been inconceivable to try to retrieve it.

In two of the classrooms we had to put the large teachers' desks over the holes in the floor so I wouldn't fall into them while teaching. The Thai teachers, being more agile and adept than I was in this—as in everything—were able to avoid the holes in the schoolroom floors. To this day I marvel at their balance, poise, and physical acuity. As for the silly fingerprint scans, since everyone in a tiny place knows what everyone's doing every minute, you don't need fingerprint scans or, for that matter, even the giant log-in books. What were they thinking? This is a question I always wanted to ask, but never had the temerity to do so.

Buddhism is the unofficial state religion in Thailand. It's taught in the schools. It's practiced by ninety percent of the people. Buddhism as practiced in Thailand, views women as naturally inferior to men. Although in other countries there are Buddhist nuns, this is not the case in Thailand. Thai women, according to Kevin Bales in his 1999 book, *Disposable People: New Slavery in the Global Economy*, are viewed as "impure, carnal, and corrupting." In addition, the culture views the fact of birth, particularly for girls, as incurring an eternal debt to parents.

Fathers can and do sell their daughters, a few as young as six, to the brothels. It was explained to me that they sometimes need to do this to pay their debts and keep their farms. They can sell their wives, too. A Thai woman, who came to speak at a presentation on human trafficking at a Peace Corps conference in Bangkok, had been sold to a brothel by her husband and her mother-in-law.

Thai men can and do have more than one wife. Some of the men who lived around me, even poor men, often had two wives. Some had several. Most women seem to tolerate this but some don't. Thailand has the largest number of reattachment surgeries of anywhere in the world.

Poor, rural children are often raised by grandparents while the children's mothers work in the cities. Many of the mothers work in brothels in Bangkok and Pattaya, dutifully sending the money home. If the woman is beautiful enough or lucky enough to snare an American husband while engaged as a sex worker, then the man's money, the marriage "proceeds" as it were, are considered as belonging to the extended family back in the village. This discovery is always a shock to the unsuspecting soldier, sailor, welder, pipe fitter, businessman, or tourist.

The royal family in Bangkok began to recognize the importance of educating females at the end of the 1800s, but this did not become widespread beyond the palace. The first teacher training program for females opened in Bankgok in 1913, but it affected only the most privileged women.

Thailand traditionally has been a rigidly stratified society, starting with the royal family and the Buddhist monks at the top, descending through merchants and military, to the poor peasants, field workers, indentured servants, and slaves at the bottom. Women have the status of the men to whom they're attached.

Slavery didn't officially end in Thailand until 1912 but forms of it exist to this day in terms of the debt of gratitude a woman owes her family, expressed as a debt of money, or labor in lieu of money. A person may owe their families, a lender, or an employer. Family members can be relegated to lower positions within the family, following random reversals of fortune such as death of parents or injury, anything which causes a change in economic circumstances.

This was brought home to me one day when I visited a highly respected Thai teacher, a woman who had held a prominent position for decades at a prestigious private school in the largest town of the province. I liked this woman and enjoyed her company. She had befriended me, shared her teaching materials with me, and wanted to come visit me at my home in Michigan. She was reasonably well-to-do, at least middle class and, like an American teacher, had a decent pension and had invested wisely. She liked to travel and had been to America twice, but never to Northern Michigan. I was looking forward to having her visit me someday.

We were sipping tea, as was our custom, and chatting in her home where she lived with two other sisters, down near the big river in the town. We had been served tea by a woman I'd never met before. She never introduced this woman, a silent person with an ineffable air of sadness, and when the woman left the room, I asked who she was. My acquaintance explained that the woman was her sister.

She explained that this sister, born into her family when there were too many mouths to feed before the Second World War, had been sent as a child to live with an aunt and uncle out in the country. Now this sister, an aging woman, had returned to the family fold, having nowhere else to go. "We didn't like her then, and we don't like her now," this teacher said, laughing, as if she was saying something humorous, something she had said many times before. She and her other family members had all apparently made a tacit agreement to treat this blood relative, a sister, as an underling.

Many middle-aged Thai women out in the rural provinces, even women from wealthy families in these rural places, have elderly mothers who'd never attended school and were essentially illiterate. Consequently these daughters, some of whom became teachers when the government began to facilitate their training, never imagined themselves actually working in the rural schools. In their minds, schools, especially rural schools, were not for females and certainly were not for females of their high station. If the government hadn't mandated it, they wouldn't be there.

For two thousand years Thai boys from poor families, usually farm workers, were educated at the Buddhist temples and their sisters stayed home and cooked and cleaned. In the 1960s the government instituted a policy of compulsory education for all children, including females, up through sixth grade.

Suddenly peasant girls were allowed to go to school, but there were no teachers for them.

The Thai government's solution to the dearth of teachers was to take thousands of young women from rich families and give them fast-track teaching degrees and establish them in the village schools. The female teachers of English I worked with were always from the country's most elite families, always beautifully attired, and usually drove incredibly expensive new vehicles.

The poor, rural schools in Thailand in the outlying areas, as I experienced them—and as a mentor teacher I would ultimately work in five of them—are more like summer camps or day care centers. This was borne out by the experiences of other Peace Corps volunteers there as well. I taught in two rural schools on a regular basis the first year; during the second year three other schools were added, and I worked in those too. The closer the school was to the province's large metropolitan center, the stronger the school was academically; the farther out it was in the Thai countryside, the weaker it was.

Some teachers did arrive at the schools on time and stay until the close of school; some even stayed in their classrooms. But the schools seemed to be more of a gathering place, a social center, rather than a place for actual instruction. Teachers were always sitting around on the porches, vaguely there but not doing much. They often needed to leave for "meetings" and on such occasions their students would always be left unattended in the classrooms.

The female teachers were pleasant toward me—I never worked with any male teachers—but almost all of them would say, as a preemptive disclaimer for why they weren't actually teaching, that the children were not interested in learning. They never had lesson plans. They didn't seem to prepare for their classes. If they had a workbook, which was not a given, they followed along, totally by rote. It seemed to me that the workbooks were only for show as they seemed to produce them only when I was there. The workbooks looked unused—no cracks on the spine; no wear on the pages—and also seemed unfamiliar to the teacher.

There were usually one or two male teachers in each school, in addition to the male directors of the schools. I found the male teachers to be more invested in teaching than the female teachers. Perhaps the history of educating males in Thailand, whether in city schools or in the temples, made them more comfortable with the idea of education.

The male teachers looked at pornography on the computers in the school libraries. Their students were in the same library. This was not a hidden activity. The male teachers and the heads of the schools sometimes went to so-called meetings in Laos where it was understood they visited brothels. Brothels were an acceptable part of life. They were a poor man's harem. The director of one of my schools, married to one of the school's teachers, a beautiful and sickly woman, would often show up at the end of the day, in his cups, with his clothes all disheveled. One of my co-teachers explained that he'd been having "many relax."

The director of a large school, where my Filipino friends taught in the main town of the province, took a beautiful high school girl as his mistress. This was regarded as permissible by everyone, including the girl's parents, since the man had agreed to send the girl to college. Americans have the naïve notion that only foreigners visit the brothels, but anyone who has been in Thailand for more than a week or two, knows that a very large number of the male visitors to bordellos are Thai.

During a trip to an education meeting in Chiang Rai, the male teachers sitting in the front of the van with one of my directors (not the director who was a Thai farmer) who was driving, watched a video of naked female dancers on the TV on the dashboard while the female teachers sitting in the back of the van, myself included, politely tried not to notice by chatting with each other in such a way that we were turned away from the front of the van, or, in my case, by mostly pretending to sleep.

The schools had a routine for daily activities: salute to the flag; prayers; children go to their classroom; the teacher might write something on the board for them to do or pass out a worksheet or turn on the educational TV; the teacher might or might not stay in the room; this goes on until lunch time with breaks for recess. Religious and culture instruction in all public schools are mandated by the government; such instruction may be conducted by monks or by the head of the school. The head of the school has usually spent some time as a novitiate in a monastery. Religious holidays are important, and preparation for them—with decorations and dances and food—can take weeks and will involve the whole community.

It amazes the American Peace Corps volunteers in the teaching program that the Thai children, even the tiniest and youngest, are able to stay in their classrooms unsupervised, without a teacher, and without destroying everything in sight and getting into fist fights and tussles with each other. They don't, for the most part, although I'm not sure why. They are gentle children, in my experience.

The reason that Thai children are mild-mannered may be that, except in unusual cases, they are brought up without corporal punishment. I think the lack of aggression may result from the way they are treated in their families, their extended families, and in their communities. If a small child in Thailand does something he or she shouldn't, the parents or supervising adults just smile and redirect. Whatever the reason, the children can be, and are, left alone in their classrooms for endless time. They move around, naturally, they're children. But they don't destroy things.

Despite the Peace Corps' excellent advice to leave the classroom whenever the Thai teacher leaves in order to insure that the teacher stays in the classroom and co-teaches, as per agreement, it makes no sense for me to leave the sweet, eager-for-learning Thai children since the alternative would be to accompany my Thai host teacher and her cousin on their endless rounds of pastry-eating, temple-going, and massage-getting, all the while politely listening to their rationalizations about how the poor children of Thai rice farmers are not worthy of their time. Only the children of the poor farmers attend the rural schools. The children of the rich, like those of my Thai host teacher and her cousin, attend expensive private schools in the larger towns.

Mrs. Tahcheroo, as part of the agreement with the Peace Corps, was supposed to help me find my own lodgings, but the places she'd seen fit to show me—a broken corn crib in a field complete with cows and cow patties; an infirmary where some of the inmates were so wasted it looked like they were dying of AIDS; and, the *coup de grâce*, a dilapidated house in another village where inside the house, on the floor of the bedroom, next to a mattress, there were bowls of decaying rice and dead flowers brought for "mother" who, as it turned out, had died some months before but, as it was explained to me, had a spirit that was not ready to depart—made it clear that she wasn't going to let me or my rent money out of her sight.

Surreptitiously, when I wasn't teaching, I had ridden my bicycle around the village, looking for housing, telling people I could pay five thousand baht, the amount I was giving Mrs. Tahcheroo for rent, food, and transportation. I was willing to pay all of this for housing if I could move. Places in the village usually rented for one thousand baht a month. Five thousand baht was what a Thai teacher was typically paid in a month, and yet everyone told me they knew of no spaces for rent. I had no way of knowing if this was true or not, but I felt strange about it.

As the bus wends its way through the mountains of the Golden Triangle, my mind goes back to my niece Sidonie's visit to my Peace Corps site a few weeks earlier. She had wanted to get away from the refugee camps for a few days and had wanted to see me before she left Thailand and returned to her university in the Netherlands.

My niece was still very young, in her mid-twenties; but she was, and is, worldly. She had been studying international diplomacy and had already worked and studied in Africa, Asia, Latin America, and Europe. Sidonie didn't know how to speak Thai any better than I did, but she had been more places in the world. It wasn't just that she knew how to take trains, planes, and busses. She had a broader frame of reference than I did for all kinds of people and all kinds of cultures.

Sitting in my Thai host teacher's old-style teak house, a house that was new despite its traditional look, Sidonie had complimented Mrs. Tahcheroo on her home. Without being asked, Mrs. Tahcheroo pointed out the burn marks on the giant tree trunks holding up the second floor. She volunteered the information that the trees had been "rescued" from hill tribes who had been going to use the trees for fuel.

I could instantly tell, because Sidonie did not make eye contact with me, that she thought this was a lie. People don't cut down a giant tree for firewood. It's too much work. They use down or dead wood or cut small trees. The colossal trunks of the trees, with their zigzag surface burn marks, looked like they'd been deliberately scorched with an acetylene torch, an unconvincing attempt to make the trees look as if they had been burned.

Illegal logging has removed most of the big trees in Thailand in the last fifty years. The illegal logging was known to everyone, but nothing was done about it. The same thing was happening in Laos and Cambodia. *The New York Times* reported in February 2016 that the Prime Minister of Cambodia, Hun Sen, had authorized the military to target smugglers with rockets to warn them away from illegal timber cutting.

All over Thailand the illegal logging had been going on for so long, there were no longer any large trees to hold the water in the soil. In a place where the news is censored, the only way one knows of these things is through word of mouth, or by visibly witnessing the end result.

Erosion had naturally followed the clear-cutting, and of course the erosion has been followed by desertification. The water in my Thai host teacher's village was treated sewage. I had a skin rash that I thought was from the chemicals in the water.

I was a *farang*, a foreigner, and my Thai host teacher got points for parading me around in the village. I felt like a pet ocelot with a string around my neck. Now, with my niece's arrival, Mrs. Tahcheroo had two *farangs*, one of whom was stunningly tall, blonde, and beautiful.

But my niece was having none of it. When she heard Mrs. Tahcheroo say, "You cannot leave the village unless you go with me," she'd laughed out loud.

"My dear Mrs. Tahcheroo," Sidonie had said in a sweet and loving way, still laughing, "*None* of these people *ever* leave the village?"

Mrs. Tahcheroo looked alarmed and affronted. She was not prepared for my worldly, good-natured Dutch niece. "THERE IS NO TRANSPORATION!" she'd screamed. Her surprise that someone had disagreed with her was total. The transformation was like computer-generated special effects. Her beauty vanished and in its place was the face of a creature. It looked like her eyes were on stalks. Her neck seemed to get longer. Her skin seemed to turn pale green. Her mouth changed to a small black hole. She looked like a star-nosed mole I saw once coming out into the daylight, really grotesque. "YOU WILL NOT BE SAFE!"

My niece had just laughed again in the same warm, kindhearted way. She appeared to be almost twice the height of my Thai host teacher. To my surprise, Mrs. Tahcheroo had laughed with her.

Twenty minutes later Sidonie and I had a ride in the back of a *songthaew*, a pickup truck with two benches on either side of the bed of the truck and a canopy over the top. We learned that a *songthaew* came through the village four times a day. As we rode past the rice paddies and through the small villages, I asked Sidonie what she thought about the site the Peace Corps had chosen for me, especially the placement with Mrs. Tahcheroo. We were the only riders in the back of the *songthaew* and could speak without fear of being overheard.

My niece said that the visits of the loan sharks to the home in the middle of the day, even while she was there, indicated serious financial problems in the family. She thought my Thai host teacher's husband was on something in addition to alcohol. She had been totally repulsed by the way the brother-in-law had looked at her during dinner at the restaurant the first night she'd arrived, after we'd picked her up from the bus station, undressing her with his eyes. She didn't like the way the brother-in-law had laughed and called his wife a "fat cow" in English in front of everyone. She had not believed for a minute that the huge teak timbers holding up the house had been rescued from hill tribes. She did not believe that Mrs. Tahcheroo had survived three bouts of meningitis.

"She's a spoiled rich girl in a terrible marriage," my niece said. "She won't be happy until she has you teaching all of her classes, tutoring all of her friends in your spare time while she's collecting hefty fees for the tutoring. She wants you staying in her home and being there to display to the loan sharks. She wants you cooking and cleaning. She wants you attending every funeral and social function so she can parade you around and get status points for having an American at her disposal. She wants you paying her five times the going rate in rent because, and she'll make sure you believe this, the only other place for you to live is a corn crib. They're dishonest people. I didn't like the brother-in-law. I don't even want to try to imagine what he does for a living. Everything about him made my skin crawl."

What should I do?

My young niece wasn't sure. She said she didn't have a lot of respect for the Peace Corps. She'd seen Peace Corps volunteers all over the world, not doing much more than hanging out in the bars. Yes, of course, she'd heard there were some wonderful volunteers. But she was talking about what she'd encountered in her travels. She'd heard, as everyone had, that the Peace Corps had been a front for the CIA in the 1980s. Even if it was no longer a front for the CIA, the Peace Corps was seen by some of the more cynical in the international community as little more than window dressing for the nefarious machinations of the government of the United States or, if not that, then as a data-gathering operation. My niece knew about the quarterly reports we were all supposed to file and which were sent to Washington, D.C.

I told Sidonie that not filing our quarterly reports could get us thrown out of the Peace Corps instantly, from everything I'd learned, but not showing up to our teaching assignments was viewed as a minor matter. I had heard of volunteers in Thailand, especially those who weren't teachers and who were involved in something vaguely called community building and outreach, volunteers who seemed to spend two years doing little more than riding their bikes around. The whole focus of the outreach program was something called "intentional relationship building" which, as far as I could tell, was socializing with the purpose of gathering information. Was it spying? Not precisely, but it wasn't honest somehow, not to me. It was a form of trading on friendship.

My niece said that, as a Canadian, she hadn't been subjected to the brainwashing about the glory and goodness of the United States, something that people who'd grown up in Michigan, for example, might have taken in almost unconsciously over a lifetime. She'd heard, as we all had, about the high incidence of rape of female Peace Corps volunteers all over the world. She thought it was a poorly run organization and, while many of the volunteers were amazing people, the support provided for those volunteers by the United States government was minimal, or at least it had that reputation among the international, non-governmental organizations (NGOs) where she had friends and colleagues.

I had already told Sidonie that the word among the volunteers was that, Peace Corps disclaimers to the contrary and an entire section in the manual about the procedures for mediating issues at site with Thai host teachers or schools, volunteers with problems of any kind were sent home posthaste.

We are seated near the open back so we can look out. In the distance on both sides of the road are rice paddies. We can see women with wicker baskets doing something. They are far in the distance. Possibly they are planting rice or maybe catching frogs, stooping in the shallow waters.

It is Songkran, the Water Festival, the hottest time of the year where people ritually throw water on each other. It's a gentle and fun festival and Sidonie and I are not going to be deterred from enjoying it in the nearby town. She has brought two squirt guns, one for each of us. "It's not like you're a refugee with no papers," she says, putting things in perspective. "I know you feel like you've been sold into slavery but she doesn't own you, even if she thinks she does. The worst thing that can happen to you is that you'll decide to go home. I know you don't want to leave Thailand. You'll figure it out." She shoots me a knowing smile. "And you'll have fun doing it."

Now as my rickety bus rises higher through the mists into the sacred northern mountains of the Golden Triangle, switchback after switchback, it's getting colder and colder. It had never occurred to me that I might be cold in Thailand, but now I'm curled into a tight ball, trying to stay warm with my large cotton purse, a purse almost the size of a laundry bag. I had worn a long Thai skirt and long-sleeved blouse, usually more than warm enough, but now I'm feeling the mountain cold.

In the seat across the aisle from me is a young man with his hand wrapped in a bloody cloth, his girlfriend next to him. Two of his fingers have been cut off. He is wisely holding his hand above his heart. Red lines are streaking up his arm, a sign of infection. How much blood has he lost? I have no iodine, no bandages, no antibiotic, no aspirin, and no way to help him. The young man's eyes are glazed with pain. He's smiling wanly. Buddhism teaches acceptance and resignation in the face of life's pain and suffering.

I learn from the girlfriend that the young man's boss had punished him for protecting her from the boss's advances. The girlfriend, clearly paralyzed with fear and worry, is perhaps praying he doesn't die, as I, too, am praying.

Instinctively knowing that if I can sleep, it'll lower my body temperature and I'll feel less cold, I try to trick myself into dozing. I cover my head with my purse to keep more heat in my body.

Through the loose weave of my large embroidered purse, draped over my head and eyes, I can dimly see the young man a few feet away. Who had attacked him and what could he do about it?

There's no rule of law in Thailand, not really.

There's a sweet and pleasant surface in Thailand. It's always "sa-wa-dee-ka" (hello), and "mai-pen-rai" (no problem), and "sanuk" (fun) everywhere you go. But underneath a smooth surface, there is something else. Guns, drugs, people, human organs, trees, endangered species, and gems are trafficked through Thailand to other countries with the police and politicians all getting a cut. Secrecy and strict censorship mean there's little news of this on TV or in periodicals. Some who've lived in Thailand a long time, like British mystery writer and attorney John Burdett, provide believable, and what would appear to be informed, fictionalized depictions of the Thai underworld.

Sex tourism is huge in Thailand. It became one of the country's biggest sources of income during the Vietnam War. American soldiers carried the news back to their buddies in the service and ever since, Thailand, especially Bangkok and Pattaya, has been a popular place. Most American men, my own son included, will say that Thailand is one of the most beautiful places in the world and that the Thai women are gorgeous, and leave it there. People on vacation for two weeks in a tropical paradise don't want to think about human trafficking and who can blame them? The beauty of Thailand and the beauty of the women are both indisputable. Foreign male tourists will insist they love Thailand, not because of the massage parlors and other offerings, but because the people, being Buddhists, are so gentle.

But AIDS is also rampant in Thailand. Globally almost two million children a year, according to the United Nations Children's Emergency Fund (UNICEF), are sold into the sex trade but figures for the exact numbers in Thailand, as with anything illegal, are hard to pin down. In my village one day I saw my neighbor crying on her porch and when I asked why, she said that her uncle had just died. He was an alcoholic and had fallen into the rice paddy and drowned; this I knew. She couldn't bring herself to attend his funeral because years before he had sold his daughter, her cousin and her childhood playmate, to a brothel in Pattaya. On a back street of my small village there were several huge new mansions built by American men who had married the Thai women they'd met in the brothels. Some women sell themselves, too, as a choice; the work in the fields is poorly paid.

Thailand has bizarre crimes. A severed head was found hanging from a bridge in Bangkok. The police deemed it suicide. How a man managed to cut off his own head and lived to hang it from a bridge was a question in the minds of only the Americans and other foreigners. The Thai police, always the laughing stock in the ex-pat community, felt compelled, after all the jokes about this, to do an investigation and send out detectives. One of their detectives found a book of matches, the kind of stereotypical clue that might be in an old Agatha Christie mystery, on the bridge. The book of matches had on it the name of the man's hotel. With this evidence, completely unconnected to how the man cut off his own head in the first place, let alone how he managed to then hang it from a bridge over the Chao Phraya River in the center of Bangkok, the police again determined that the man's death had been a suicide.

In 2009 the American actor David Carradine was found dead in a closet in a hotel room in Bangkok, supposedly, according to the Thai police, a death from auto-erotic asphyxiation. However he died, Bangkok is the kind of place where there are frequent rumors of bizarre things like that but these things only make international headlines when the person is famous, like Carradine.

The very strange 1967 disappearance of American silk entrepreneur, Jim Thompson has still not been solved. He just vanished when he was on vacation with Thai friends at a posh retreat in the Cameron Highlands, just over the border in Malaysia, surrounded by all kinds of people. Coincidentally, or not, Thompson's sister was murdered in America at the same time, a crime also still unsolved. By the time mysterious events have evolved into the kind of peculiar newspaper stories you find in a country where the news is censored, there are so many layers and contradictions and counter-stories, that one's never able to know what really happened.

Thomas Fuller, a correspondent for *The New York Times*, covered Asia from Thailand for ten years, leaving Bangkok in February 2016. "My decade here has been one of intense ambivalence," he wrote in a farewell piece. "I was enchanted by people's warmth, congeniality and politeness.... But I despaired at the venality of the elites and despaired at the corruption."

Now that Thailand's King Bhumibol Adulyadej is aging and in failing health, people are worried about who might replace him and the chaos that might occur after he dies. Repression has been stepped up by those in power. The Thai film maker Apichatpong Weerasethakul in the *New York Review of Books* in March 2016 was reported as saying that Thailand has recently gone "from less democracy to no democracy" and that he will no longer make his films in his native country. Weerasethakul's subtly political film, *Cemetery of Splendor*, was well received at the New York Film Festival in the fall of 2015.

The cult of the king and the promotion of Thailand as a young democracy came, in no small way, from the United States government. In the 1960s, according to Paul Handley in his book, *The King Never Smiles*, the U.S. Information Service "had virtually taken over public relations for the Thai government...[promoting] an anticommunist, pro-monarchy theme."

The campaign was successful, I think. People in America, like my friend Grace Glynn, believed what they'd read about Thailand, or heard from friends and relatives who'd gone there on vacation: Thailand is a country of gentle people where even the king is a Buddhist. Thai people *are* gentle and the king *is* a Buddhist. But where did the king get all his money? And how did his brother die? These are questions that in Thailand could get you killed. The *lèse-majesté* in Thailand is something the west hasn't seen for a thousand years. *Time* magazine reported in December 2015 that a man was facing forty years in prison for saying something negative about the king's dog.

Most of the photos of the king, found in every Thai home, were printed by our government. The U.S. public relations folks, in an overzealous early phase, had multicolored soap bars distributed around the Thai countryside, with every new layer of color, according to Handley, "exhorting the bathers to love the king, follow Buddhism, and fight communism."

In 2009 King Bhumibol Adulyadej, who started out with almost no political power and little money in the 1950s, was listed by *Forbes* as the richest royal in the world, worth a mind-boggling thirty billion. His great wealth, Thais believe, is a testament to his great spiritual worth. King Bhumibol, whose photo is everywhere, thanks to the successful U.S. government public relations blitz, is believed to be a bodhisattva, not just royal, but holy, directly connected to God. He can imprison anyone who is suspected of having the temerity to defame him or anyone who disparages a member of the royal family.

In Bangkok once, during a heat wave, I went to an air-conditioned theater and watched *Beverly Hills Chihuahua* three times. As is required, I stood each time they showed a picture of the king on the screen and played the Thai royal anthem. I stood, exactly like everyone else in the theater, with a reverent expression on my face and my hand over my heart.

I didn't know what happened to people who didn't stand, but I didn't want to find out.

In the middle of a forest, the bus is flagged down by Thai soldiers in camouflage. They are so young they look like teenagers. They are smiling, shy, almost girlish. They get on the bus and begin randomly asking for identity papers. I hear the word "Myanmar," the other name for Burma, and guess they are looking for Burmese illegal aliens; but it doesn't seem as if they want to find any.

The Burmese cross the border, hide in the mountains and make their way on foot to Chiang Mai or Bangkok. They try to make themselves invisible so they can work illegally, often taking the most menial jobs in enterprises that are already illegitimate.

The refugees as a rule don't have money for busses and anyway this bus is heading *toward* Burma, not away from it. Of all the people on the bus, I look the least like a Burmese refugee. I'm old, white, female, and look like the kind of person who would have all her papers in order. The soldiers check a few harmless-looking Thai people, randomly asking for papers, and then, putting on a show of seriousness, three of them stop and ask for my identity papers. It might take three of them to handle such a dangerous passenger. I am the only white woman on the bus, and one of two elderly riders. The other elderly rider is a Thai man. "Do I *look* like a Burmese refugee?" I want to ask them as they rouse me from my slumber, but I don't. It would be silly. I meekly hand them my papers which, continuing the charade, they sternly scrutinize, even though it seems highly unlikely that they can read English.

The soldiers move off down the steps and the bus continues its climb. Soon we are coming down the other side and the switchbacks are becoming more elongated. Gradually the land flattens out. The air becomes warmer and then, at last, we are again in tropical torpor. A small boy had vomited all over everything when we'd gotten on the bus back in Chiang Mai and now the smell is overpowering in the heat.

I tuck my head into my arm to avoid the smell of the little boy's vomit and my mind goes back to the day before. I'd been packing to leave my Thai host teacher's home. She had been watching me, companionably, like a sister or a friend, and had confided she wanted to be best friends.

Her brother, that discreet man I'd yet to meet, had brought her some ant egg soup and left it on the counter, so recently it was still warm, and she invited me to share it with her. It was a seasonal delicacy, I knew, and her offering it was a generous gesture. I said I'd like to try a little, that I had heard it was delicious. I said I wanted to be best friends, too. I said I loved Thailand. I said I loved her village. I said it was fun to tutor her because she was such wonderful company.

The ant eggs, she'd said, pointing out the large, white ones the size of gourmet jelly beans floating in the clear broth, a broth flecked with green onions and hot red peppers, were pure fat and smooth and creamy. They have a slightly nutty taste, like Macadamia nuts, with the texture of cream cheese.

The soup is beautiful. I had seen men in loin cloths going through the fields getting the ant nests out of trees with what looked like butterfly nets.

We were sitting upstairs in front of a fan and practicing English. On weekends since I'd arrived in her village, I'd also been tutoring three of her well-to-do friends. We convened in the home of one of Mrs. Tahcheroo's prestigious relatives in the nearby municipality. The ladies, nimble as gymnasts, would sit cross-legged on the cool, pale green tile floor for hours, while I being not nimble, and American, would be consigned, like a gargoyle, to an antique, ornately carved, mahogany chair.

They all were slated to take a national English test and if they scored high enough, could win a free, all-expense-paid, six-week trip to Australia. So desperate and so befuddled was the Thai government by the low quality of their English language teachers in the rural schools that they had resorted to blatant bribery to get them to improve. Things like the free trip enticement, and the finger print scan surveillance, spoke volumes about the Thai government's mindset.

After a few times tutoring my Thai host teacher and her friends, I'd thought it was hopeless. It just wasn't working. Despite college degrees, in reality they barely had even a fourth grade education. They each had an infinitesimally small information base and, largely because of censorship, had no precedent for ever sharing information. I couldn't use prior knowledge to engage them, a standard teacher's ploy, since they were in a state of blissful ignorance concerning just about everything. They didn't read books. They had no curiosity about anything. They lived in a country where all real news is blocked. They had no idea of the larger world. They wanted to spend their time eating pastries and gossiping.

Only by accident did I hit on how to get them to learn. I taught them tricks. Having obtained a copy of the multiple choice test from a previous year, I showed them that on a multiple choice test, where they were asked to choose the one best answer out of five, they could immediately eliminate two that were clearly not right. Then it was down to three, and of those, one would be less right than the other two. Once it was down to two, they only had to choose the one most likely. Even if they chose randomly, they still had a fifty percent chance of getting the right answer. Of course they said they wanted to learn about grammar because that seemed important-sounding and professional, and of course I lied and I said I would teach them all about English grammar, knowing that it would never help them pass the test. I also knew that as soon as I agreed to do it, they would forget all about it. Grammar was not something they actually wanted. It was only something to say they wanted.

I was relentlessly cheerful and encouraging, heaping praise on them at every turn. My plan was that they should all pass the test, especially my Thai host teacher. I'd already decided that if she managed to pass, I would move the minute she was out of the country. I'd found a place with the help of a friend.

Just as I'd done in El Salvador, I was slowly and luckily able to create local connections with people I could trust. What I would tell the Peace Corps, after it was a *fait accompli,* is that the water had gone out in my village. It was true, but I didn't want to tell them prematurely and be in the midst of moving and have to fend off any objections or interference from Mrs. Tahcheroo. If at all possible, I wanted her on another continent when the time came for me to move. I didn't trust what she would say to the Peace Corps. I didn't trust anything about her.

I didn't tell Mrs. Tahcheroo and her friends as I was teaching them, because they would've never understood and would've been put off, but I was going to teach them, not English, but how to take a test. I told them that most of the test would be vocabulary and if they could memorize at least one thousand nouns and their meanings, they would stand a better chance of passing. I made a vocabulary game by having them toss a pretty ball around. Whoever caught the ball could draw a word from a pretty basket, and if they knew the word and the meaning, they would get a point. The winner with the most points would receive a special prize: nail polish, or a hair ornament, or a mystery prize. I paid for these things and was more than happy to do so since it seemed to encourage their interest in learning. They played the game with squeals of delight and after that we all got on famously.

Now my Thai host teacher was enjoying her soup while I quizzed her on vocabulary. Through the open window I could see into the large, square, empty upstairs room of the house next door. Less than eighteen inches separated the two houses. Every day I would see there a beautiful old woman in traditional Thai dress sitting on the clean, bare wooden floor staring into space. When I would go to the window and wave and smile, she would respond. I had seen her for weeks, sitting in there all alone. She was very thin and I wondered how she got her food. Now she pretended not to see us and got up and left the room, going to a part of the house where we could not see her. "Who is that woman?" I asked.

"My cousin," Mrs. Tahcheroo said. "When she was a child, her father and mother died and she and her brother became our servants. We saved their lives."

I wondered what would happen to the woman now that she was old, but was afraid to ask.

Mae Hong Son is pink and gold and blue-green, or at least the people in the parade are. When I arrive, a ceremonial procession is in full swing, complete with elephants, Thai-style marching bands, and young boys dressed to look like girls being carried on the strong shoulders of male friends or relatives. The boys are the brides for Buddha, I learn, novitiates for the monastery, some of whom will become monks. They are wearing shiny satin and sequined outfits in pastel shades of pink, blue-green, and gold. The boys are heavily made up, with rouge, lipstick, mascara, and thick, pinkish pancake make-up. They look dazed.

Theravāda Buddhism is the religion practiced by most Thai people. There are a few thousand Muslims in the south of Thailand. There's a sprinkling of Chinese Christians throughout the country. There are a few other religions, too, such as Sikh and Hindu and some Christian sects. Religions other than Buddhism are tolerated but not encouraged. The Thai government restricts the number of registered missionaries and makes Buddhism a required part of the curriculum in all the public schools. I have heard that Buddhism is also taught in private schools, even the Christian ones.

I manage to wend my way along the crowded sidewalks. I'm looking for some place to buy a Coke and some salty crackers. I feel dizzy and nauseous. I will need to find my lodgings, the happy-all-the-time-guest-house, but first I need to get my electrolytes back in order. The high mountains, the cobra, the wounded man, the rough ride, the bad smell from the child being sick to his stomach, have all taken their toll.

In the front yard of a temple, now deserted because of the parade, I find a bench and some shade. In a while I will locate the guest house and then will try to find the NGO. It will be closed. Today is Sunday. But I will need to know where it is in order to be there by eight the next morning.

There are many kinds of Buddhism. In India, Nepal, Tibet, China, Sri Lanka and a hundred other places, even America, there are various versions. Depending on the place and the people, it's always a little different. Here there's an elaborate gold stupa, a conical structure which will have a relic of the Buddha inside—an anklebone, a finger, even excrement.

This stupa is ornate but I've also seen stupas that look like those sand and water creations we make at the beach, dribbled mud in rings, one after the other until you can go no higher.

This temple has a naga, or snake, large as a log, draped up the steps to the temple. A real naga was recently found somewhere in Indonesia, so they must have existed here, too, at one time.

The main precepts of Buddhism, according to Anna Leonowens, author of the book about the Siamese court which became the basis for *The King and I* movie, are: don't kill, lie, steal, become intoxicated, take another man's wife or concubine, don't indulge in anger and gossip, don't covet a neighbor's things, and don't wish anyone else misfortune. These are recorded in many, many other places but not as succinctly and not as specifically about only Thailand, called Siam, when Leonowens was the royal governess in the court of King Mongkut from 1862 to 1867.

The King and I, the movie as well as the book it's based on, is banned in Thailand. This is not because Leonowens' story is fabricated, in my opinion, but because it isn't. Leonowens, following the death of her husband, took a position as governess for the king's various wives and concubines and also for his eighty-two children born of those associations. These wives, concubines, and children were treated by the king, according to Leonowens, with varying degrees of kindness, fairness, cruelty, and capriciousness.

Just as the U.S. government's public relations experts whitewashed Bhumibol's reputation in order to gain a foothold in Thailand, they appear to have tarred Leonowens' reputation, perhaps for the same reason, in order to appease their Thai cohorts. Her perceptions were probably not shared by the royal court, especially these many years later. The unvarnished views of an English governess concerning Thai royalty were not what the royal family wanted Thai citizens or western visitors to learn about them.

All that notwithstanding, and allowing for Leonowens' Christian bias and the fact that the book was written almost one hundred and fifty years ago in an ornate style, I found her reasonably clear-eyed, tolerant, and truthful about what she was experiencing. She had little reason to lie, as far I can determine. That her book is banned in Thailand should not surprise anyone since only flattering depictions of Thai royalty are legal in Thailand.

Things Leonowens described from the 1860s were not inconsistent with what I was seeing in the present, especially when it came to ideas about social hierarchy, natural inequality, rote learning in education, and the treatment of women as lesser beings and sexual objects. Leonowens was an educated woman, had almost six years in the country, spoke the language fluently, lived on the palace grounds, was not a tourist, and didn't confuse the Buddhism she saw in Thailand with Buddhism in other places.

Like almost all religions and philosophies that have lasted thousands of years and have large followings, Buddhism boils down to something like, "Try to be nice." Initially Buddhism in India was a heresy against the Hindu Brahmanism. Buddha said that everything is insubstantial and in the ever-changing world no one can say "this is me" whereas Hindus believed in an eternal, blissful self. In practice, from what I've seen in Thailand, the rich care about money and the poor care about eating, a more basic version of the same thing.

"Hi, how are you?" in Thai, is "*Gin cow*?" literally, "Have you eaten rice today?" Rich and poor, they go to the temples to pray for survival: food, shelter, safety, good health, love, luck, and money.

People have beautifully ornate spirit houses in their backyards. These are small houses about the size of a mailbox. They look like little temples. They're on posts and about the height of mailboxes. The man near my school, a handsome man who raises fighting cocks, always puts grains of rice and small coins in his spirit house the day before a big fight. Cock fights are not illegal but gambling on them is. Gambling is done anyway, as far as I can tell, and no one intervenes.

A neighbor on the other side of the street from the cockfights is a policeman, but I never saw the policeman come and intervene to prevent the gambling. The gambling was not a hidden activity. It drew large crowds of rowdy, inebriated, excited men flashing wads of cash. The policeman seemed to be conveniently never around when the cock fights took place. Thai people say that the cock fights are better treatment of the birds than America's way of treating laying hens in laying factories. At least their chickens can move, they say. They have a point.

Depictions of the Buddha in Thailand show a guy who could be a girl, so androgynous that like some of the Thai lady boys, the *Gatoy*, you can't tell if they're male or female. I have seen statues of the earliest Buddhas in Thailand, many centuries old. Those early Buddhas were fat and jolly, middle-aged and masculine. That's not the modern version.

One of the things I like best about the people in Thailand is their enlightened attitude toward gender preference. They determined long ago, perhaps with the advent of Buddhism, perhaps before, that a gay male is a woman's spirit reincarnated in a man's body. It starts early. When a young boy tries on his mother's dress, for example, the male toddler is then raised as a girl, a *Gatoy*. The Thai people adore these young boy-girls and teach them to dance, sing, wear make-up, and perform as girlish entertainers from an early age. With females who take on male qualities, the approval is less pronounced, but the Thais seem to accept that a male spirit could be born into a female body, as well as the reverse. The acceptance is a good thing. However, I'm not so sure that other people deciding that a boy is a girl when he's only two is so great. It should be up to the individual, not other people. What if the kid is just trying on his mother's dress for the heck of it? However, in terms of walking around somewhere, I like the fact that the Thai people are comfortable with men being homosexual. It's definitely preferable to the hatred and killing of gays in some parts of the world.

I think about my own brush with being transgendered, my good luck really in having been raised as a boy for the first ten years of my life. My parents were undoubtedly responding to their lack of being able to have a son. Their sense of terrible loss over the sons who had died at birth through some congenital defect must have been nearly unbearable for them. So, instinctively, without thought, they made me the designated boy. This was more commonly done then, I've learned since, not an entirely unheard of phenomenon.

When the division of labor was somewhat gender-based, this was done partly so the work could be accomplished. In Afghanistan if there's a family of all girls, one of them is often chosen to play a male role. These girls are called *bacha posh*. Someone needs to go to the market, after all, and girls are not allowed out of the house. Most of the *bacha posh* do not remain boys, partly because young women, when they reach puberty, can be sold. In the mountains of Albania, the *burrneshas*, similarly chosen girls who were made to be boys, until a generation ago were encouraged to become celibate so they could be the head of the household when there were no men for the role. In my case, my father needed a boy, it was thought, to help carry on his lumbering business. It must have made sense at the time.

It was unusual in America, probably even in the 1940s, to make a daughter a son, but the result was that I had unlimited freedom, not just in what I could do but in what I was permitted to think. My sisters had to do the indoor chores and I had to do the outdoor chores. I had the job of taking care of the horses and, as long as I was outside doing that, was not responsible for dusting knick-knacks inside the house. I could read in the barn while they were cleaning. I could play with the kids who lived half a mile away in the lumber camp, off limits for my sisters.

Was I a boy or a tomboy? Hard to tell. They blurred the lines to make it more socially acceptable, or possibly reversible, but the result of being the designated boy was that I got to spend a lot of time with my father, learning from him, emulating him, trying to be him, in the way that children do. I learned to read early and so, until we moved north to Empire when I was in Third Grade, instead of going to school, many days I went with him to cut trees. After we moved north, when I no longer went with my father to the woods, no one at home told me I couldn't play in the ice caves alone, or go swimming alone. I still played with the kids who lived at the mill, as I had when I'd been accompanying my father to the lumber camp. I could leave the house whenever I wanted, alone.

When puberty hit and it was clear the boy plan probably wasn't going to work long-term, I'd still had all those years of unlimited freedom behind me, time modeling myself after my father because it was with him that I spent most of my time, time which had formed my way of seeing the world, my way of living in the world. I hadn't, in fact, been raised as a girl. It's something for which I'll always be grateful. I think it may have given me more joy and courage in living than I might have had otherwise.

This courtyard in Mae Hong Son is filled with bouquets of marigolds; the incense is still burning.

On the way to my guest house, following my Internet directions, I pass the Salween Restaurant. It's closed, but it opens at 6 A.M. I will eat there in the morning. My guest house, pronounced "geh how" by the Thai, is a rustic place. My room is a simple cement one with a mattress on the floor. It's reasonably clean. It's good enough. I cover the mattress with black plastic garbage bags and a sheet I've brought with me. I fall fast asleep. I wake up in the light of a full moon. It is 5 A.M. and I've slept more than twelve hours.

The Salween Restaurant is run by a former Burmese refugee from the Karen tribe who was taught by her English boyfriend how to make bread. The bread tastes exactly like my mother's homemade bread from the 1950s. It's perfect. The place is spotlessly clean, a Godsend. I hadn't known how homesick I was or what a difference familiar food could make to my outlook until I had fresh bread with butter in a place that didn't reek of sewage, in a place without rats, cockroaches, or clouds of houseflies.

Finally, I begin to feel like my old self. I look at my teaching materials, children's beautifully illustrated books of fairy tales: *The Three Billy Goats Gruff, Hansel and Gretel, Rapunzel, Cinderella,* and *The Three Little Pigs.*

We will adapt the stories to their lives, adding their own details as I draw them out. I've brought materials to make impromptu costumes: tape, wire, glue, scissors, a stapler, crayons, paper, and cloth. I've learned improvisation and acting are freeing for students. I have character names on signs with strings that they can hang around their necks. Which stories we use will depend upon the students and how much time we have.

Later in the camps, high up in the mountains, beyond the mists of the valley, it will slowly dawn on me that all the stories are stories of escape, fitting for the refugees and fitting for me. For the next two weeks, as we work through the stories, I will realize that the value of stories, plays, and poems is that stories allow people to get the tangled mass of emotions in their minds out where they can look at them and deal with them.

The students are, as my niece had said, brilliant. They range in age from six to sixty, but with the flexible format of the dramas, we can incorporate all of them. All speak Thai, Burmese, and English more or less fluently. Some recent arrivals speak mostly their own tribal language. Some of my students act as translators. Burma has over one hundred ethnic groups and at least that many languages. One of my students speaks seven languages and several dialects, fluently.

At some point during *The Three Billy Goats Gruff* I'm inspired to say to my students, "Didn't I see a rope bridge over a chasm? About two miles from here? Couldn't we have the troll under the bridge there? Why don't we go there to act this out?"

My class seems nonplussed and then worried. I say, "Can everyone walk two miles?"

Finally the gentle, elderly physical education teacher from Rangoon says, "Everyone but you, teacher."

Of course, I'm too old for their steep trails and too white for their bright sunlight, but I forget that when I'm teaching.

The look on their faces had been, first, that I'd completely lost touch with reality; and, second, alarm, as they began to realize that if they couldn't dissuade me from this crazy plan, at some point they'd be carrying my dead weight on a litter up and down over jungle tree roots for two miles through the mountains in the tropical heat.

On the way back to Mrs. Tahcheroo's home and the village to which I'd been assigned by the Peace Corps, I go back a different way, down the west side of Thailand, through Mae Sot on the Moei River. My niece is no longer in Thailand, but Mae Sot had been my niece's home base when she'd been interviewing people in the camps for her master's thesis. There are NGOs from all over the world.

The bus enters Mae Sot and passes a vast area that looks like a garbage dump. There are many stray dogs wandering the far side of this area, over near a scrubby-looking forest. Next to the road are small children digging through the rubble. Perhaps they are orphans or refugees or simply very poor children. Someone on the bus tells me you can buy a child in Mae Sot for two dollars.

Down the street from my guest house is an Italian restaurant started by an Italian doctor who had worked in the camps and had grown so homesick for Italian food that she opened a restaurant and taught Thai people how to cook the food. Across the street from my lodgings is a minimal Indian restaurant, a table and stove under a bamboo awning. The lentil dahl is excellent, made with coconut milk and red lentils. I watch as the woman expertly chops radishes, red onion, carrots, jalapenos, tomatoes, garlic, and cilantro to the size of peas, adds a little salt and a squeeze of lemon, for a fresh vegetable *raita*, a kind of Indian salsa. She grates cucumber into homemade yogurt for another *raita*, adding ground cumin. She slices a ripe mango, drips some honey over the slices, and serves it with yogurt. Yogurt seems to be keeping me healthy in Thailand. I consume it whenever I can.

In the center of town is a giant building, a gem market: pearls, sapphires, emeralds, rubies, jade. Many burly men with AK-47s guard the merchandise. The proceeds go to the military government in Burma where the rulers have recently built for themselves a huge, walled, unbelievably expensive, air-conditioned city in the center of a tropical jungle. Outside the walls of this air-conditioned jungle city, people are starving, according to the refugees I'd been teaching in Mae Hong Son. All over Burma people are starving. The United States has an embargo on gems from Burma because of Burma's abuse of human rights, but Thailand freely buys from Burma, and American jewelers freely buy from the Thai merchants.

Down near the Moei River is a vast tented market which must extend for a mile in either direction. Seeking to get out of the midday sun I wander among the stalls, vaguely looking for hand cream and finally purchase a small tin of it in the murky light under the awnings. The man selling it looks at me and does a full-on double-take. Thai and Burmese people are polite and do not stare, but he's clearly so struck by something about me that he can't help himself.

When I get back to my guest house and take the pretty little tin out of my bag, I see that in full light, and not the light under the tent, what I'd thought was hand cream is skin whitener. The man must have thought, looking at me, *Wow, I guess this stuff really works.*

I give it to the maid. She laughs when I tell her the story.

Mrs. Tahcheroo wins the trip to Australia. I congratulate her on her hard work. I give her a handmade "Congratulations" card. All my hours of tutoring her have paid off. She's no sooner on the plane than I move to a village ten miles away, a mile or two from the outskirts of Phrae, the province's main twenty-thousand-person metropolis.

Luckily I had found some friends to help me move my things; otherwise it might have been difficult.

When I was in El Salvador, one of the first things I did after the kid from Louisiana was sent packing, was find someone I could trust, someone I could pay, someone who could drive me to the border. I never needed it, but knowing there was someone who could have done this if there had been an emergency was important to my peace of mind. One can't survive without friends, but they have to be trustworthy. In Thailand, as I'd done everywhere I've ever lived, I found people I could trust, people who could make me laugh, people I could make laugh, people just like the people in Lake Leelanau: honest, kind and wise. I have not written about any of these people. I would have liked to because they were incredible people, but I have wanted to protect their privacy and, in some cases, their safety.

The new village is a little ethnic enclave. They are Laotian people and came from Laos centuries earlier when Thailand was a wilderness. This new village is rural, as required by Peace Corps. A chance encounter with a former Peace Corps volunteer from the 1960s during the forty-fifth year celebration in Bangkok at our swearing-in ceremony back in March, a man who knew people in my province, had given me the contacts I'd needed to find another place to live.

When we'd met and talked at the big ceremony in Bangkok, this man had given me the names of a few "friends of friends of friends" who would help me make arrangements to move, if it came to that. I didn't go into detail. I just let him know that I might need to change my situation. He had been sympathetic, amused, and hadn't needed or wanted any explanation concerning what I thought I should do or why. He had understood perfectly.

When the time comes, with the help of my friends, I transport my few belongings to the new place. Then I get on the bus to Bangkok for a Peace Corps conference. I had told my Thai host teacher about the conference before she left. Her husband knows that I'll be away for a while at a meeting in Krungthep, the other name for Bangkok. He doesn't seem to notice when I leave.

"The water went out in my village," I tell my Peace Corps supervisor when I see her in the Peace Corps offices in Bangkok. I had read their poorly written manual cover to cover, and several times. No water in the village was a sanctioned reason for changing the original site assigned by the Peace Corps. I show them the skin rash that I think is from the chemicals in the treated sewage that now constitutes the village water.

The Peace Corps occupies a former mansion on a street of diplomatic residences. It's in a walled garden with a half-circle drive. Huge SUVs with diplomatic license plates are parked in the yard. The mansion is three stories high and it's air-conditioned. There's a special place for the medical staff and a lounge for Peace Corps volunteers. The mansion has high ceilings and wooden wainscoting. It has an elegant staircase. It's near the palace, on one of the best streets in Bangkok.

It's true that the water has gone out in my village. The Peace Corps could verify this if they wished. But they don't, as far as I know, perhaps because I also tell them that Mrs. Tahcheroo is out of the country. I praise Mrs. Tahcheroo to my Peace Corps supervisors in the teaching sector, telling them about how she has won, because of her hard work, an all-expense-paid trip to Australia.

The best advice I ever received about the Peace Corps was from a man who was a former director and who talked to me when he visited the Leelanau Historical Society one summer in the 1980s. He said, "The Peace Corps doesn't want any problems with the host country. They're there to make friends. Keep your head down and your mouth shut. Don't make waves."

I tell the Peace Corps office that Mrs. Tacheroo had studied diligently with me for all those weeks, and did beautifully on the national English test. Naturally I'm very proud of her. She will have a chance to practice her new English skills in Australia, will participate in a cultural exchange with her Australian host family, and will study with people at the university there. She won't return until just before the Peace Corps visits our site in two months.

Coincidentally, the Thai government's supervisor of the Peace Corps volunteers in my province is also out of the country. This woman charges fees to take Thai teachers on educational trips, and at this time is on a trip to Singapore. She won't be back for a few weeks. Mrs. Tahcheroo had been on several of these trips, paying more than it would ever cost to simply go to Singapore, or Switzerland, or Manila. Her doing so had put her name at the top of the list to get a Peace Corps volunteer.

Although I let the Peace Corps higher-ups know that I've only moved temporarily to a place where there's potable water, as an emergency precaution, I tell them I would like to make this move permanent.

Technically, if they wish to see it that way, I've broken a rule by moving from my assigned site without prior approval and they can send me home. However, they can also choose to believe that I'm in transit and seeking approval for the move.

I serve out my full twenty-seven months in Thailand. Just before I'm getting ready to go back to Northern Michigan at the end of my service, I find a moment to ask one of my Thai co-teachers why Mrs. Tahcheroo's director had tolerated her as a teacher in his school and why he had been willing to teach all of her classes, something that had always puzzled me because he seemed like a no-nonsense, stand-up kind of guy. We are in a school van, going to work with one of the hill tribes. I think I know enough Thai by this time that I can trust myself to ask this delicate question without saying something else by mistake. I think this teacher knows me well enough, after twenty-seven months, that I can ask her.

She hesitates and ducks her head, and with a little smile, finally says, *"Khea klaw phi chay knxng thex."* Thai is a tonal language and the tones make this statement a ripple of sound, that goes up and down and up again, like someone artfully shaking crumbs out of a long white tablecloth after a banquet. It takes me a minute to put it altogether. When I realize she's said, "Perhaps he's afraid of her brother," it makes no sense to me. Mrs. Tahcheroo's director is a big strong guy, at least by Thai standards, and he doesn't seem to be lacking in courage. It doesn't seem reasonable that there would be someone so much physically stronger that he would be afraid.

"Afraid," I repeat, mystified, "afraid of what?"

My Thai co-teacher takes one hand from the steering wheel and draws it across her throat.

We drive in silence then for a while.

Sometimes I think about Thailand. I remember the lanterns in the sky at New Year's, the little spirit boats with candles that they put into the rivers at Loi Krathong, the lovely evening festivals where families and neighbors come together, the music, the singing, the strange instruments. I remember the soft mornings with the orange-clad novice monks coming through the streets with their brass bowls, the ladies selling soup with noodles and fresh vegetables in the outdoor restaurant next to my school at noon, the young boys catching frogs late in the afternoons out in the rice paddies, and the people dancing at night in the back yards with the music playing, moving slowly in the Thai way with their hands like birds.

Two Old Men of Chiang Mai

This is the story of two old men who live in *Chiang Mai* in northern Thailand. One drives a traditional Thai *songthaew*, a pickup truck converted to a share-taxi. The other is the owner of the all-day-American-breakfast restaurant. Both are near *Tah Pai* Gate, the gate near the center of the ancient part of the town. This is the place where goods used to come up from the river.

Thanong Tha Pai is the main thoroughfare from the *Ping* River to the town's old gate. The *Ping* River itself was the main way to get to *Chiang Mai* for untold centuries. *Thanong* means road, *Tha* means pier and *Pai* means where you park your raft. The street is still a straight shot from the river to the gate.

To give you some context, picture first the old, crumbling, flowerpot-clay, soft red brick city wall surrounded by a forty-foot-wide moat filled with dirty water. Most of the seven-hundred-year-old wall is returning to earth except for places where it's being restored or has miraculously survived.

Chiang Mai means "new walled city" and it was "new" seven hundred years ago when the city of *Lamphun*, now little more than a bus stop on the outskirts of *Chiang Mai*, was the cultural center of Northern Thailand.

Chiang Mai was always a place of trade and the wall was put up to protect merchants from marauding bands of thieves. Donkey caravans of Chinese-Muslim businessmen, guarded by experienced fighters, would wend their way down out of northern Asia bringing spices, gold, opium, silk, and tea to a place a few blocks back from *Tah Pai* Gate and a stone's throw from the present-day Night Market. Artisans and craftsmen followed the caravans, seeking work and safety. Some stayed to build the myriad golden temples after Buddha passed this way, which he did, either literally or figuratively, take your pick, a few hundred years ago.

Chiang Mai was originally peopled by the northern *Tai Yuan*, according to several sources, a group some believe was originally from China. Also, at different times in the last one thousand years the city has been in the hands of the Burmese, the Laotians, and the Chinese. Muslim traders have been in and out of *Chiang Mai* for centuries. In this mix are the *Shan, Mon, Hmong, Lawa, Karen* and other nomadic tribes. Many of these tribal people still walk the streets wearing jingles on their hats and selling wooden frogs that make a sound, "*Gop, gop.*" All of these groups, and a few more besides, have probably intermarried a zillion different ways over the years.

The hand-loomed and hand-embroidered fabrics and clothing for sale all over *Chiang Mai* are of extremely high quality in both workmanship and the use of color. Each tribe has something a little different to offer in the way of weavings. It's a challenge to resist buying a sample of everything. I have a coat I bought on the street in *Chiang Mai*, all hand-woven and hand-embroidered. It's soft and warm and light. It's wearing out but I still wear it because of the beautiful colors and knowing all the hours someone spent making it.

The hill tribe people look remarkably like Native Americans from Michigan, or Arizona, or Canada, or Peru. Who knows where we all come from? Or where we all wandered off to over the last sixty thousand years or so? Did we all really come, after a fashion, from the shores of Lake Victoria in Africa? Hard to believe, such a long time ago, such vast distances. Who can really take it all in and make sense of it? Most of us, and I'm speaking for myself here, can't remember where we were last week, or imagine much beyond walking to the corner an hour from now to get a bottle of milk, much less think about the past and future ramifications of a genetic odyssey across the globe.

An article in *Scientific American* in July 2008 told how the DNA of everyone can now be traced through mitochondria. With a little more time and a little more effort, scientists are going to be able to determine the paths of migration around the globe. In another fifty years or so, maybe someone will be able to figure out how a bag I have from Lake Atitlán in the mountains of Guatemala has a pattern that textile experts in *Chiang Mai* identify as *Karen*.

Chiang Mai has probably changed more in the last one hundred years than it did in the previous ten thousand. Relatively recently, in 1921, the railroad came to the north and twelve years later *Chiang Mai* became a province of Thailand.

THE SONGTHAEW DRIVER

Let's start with the *songthaew* driver first. He was born in *Chiang Rai* in 1935, about a hundred miles north and east, and came to *Chiang Mai* by train "before there was a road from *Chiang Rai*" and walked the three or four kilometers from the train station to *Phra Singh* Temple. He was fourteen years old then, he says, "but look big."

Now he is a seventy-year-old man who is much larger than most Thai men. He has a full head of thick, white hair and an unlined face marked only by the remnants of teenage acne scars. A good smile. He has a broad, rangy frame and invariably wears a freshly washed and pressed shirt every day to drive his *songthaew*.

"Name *Gao*," he says, "old language, *Lanna* language." His son helped him change the name to *Apichai*, which is the standard Thai language and, he says, means the same thing as *Gao*. Thirty years ago, according to the *Lonely Planet,* the northern dialect or *Lanna* language was considered backward and was gradually replaced by standard Thai by those who wanted to be more upscale and modern, and fit more comfortably into the general culture of Thailand.

"My father, farmer. In small village. *Ban Nong Hauw*. No cars. All people walking. No motorcycle. Little bit, bicycle, one/two." *Gao* is talking in his *songthaew*, parked across the street from J.J.'s all-day-American-breakfast restaurant, where he usually parks it.

It's too early for customers who want to go to the elephant park and so he tells me about Thailand seventy years ago, in his village in the Province of *Chiang Rai*. "Radio. Don't have. Head of village have, big one, but not use everyday. No electricity. Use battery. No gas, no oil. Use 'kee-yah'—insect go to making inside tree, yellow, for lamp. Nobody know how, ha-ha, ask old man like me.

"Mother dead. I helping father go to looking buffalo. Buffalo make the rice, early morning. Middle day, very hot. Then again four o'clock, buffalo making rice in field. I not stay with father. New wife. Many people there. No food. Mother's sister dead, too. I learn in temple. I can read, I can write *Lanna* language, Thai language. Before, don't have Thailand. We are *Lanna* country."

La Na, also spelled *Lanna*, which means "land of a million rice paddies," is the old name for Northern Thailand. The land leading up to the northern mountains is flat and extremely fertile. Several rivers provide abundant water. Thai people were growing rice ten thousand years ago, according to recent archeological findings, when my people were most likely still trying to bring down a woolly mammoth and praying for the glaciers to melt, and even the always up-and-coming Chinese were only eating millet.

"Come *Chiang Mai*. Learn now *Pali* language from India. Other boys not come because have father, have mother." The temples in Thailand still host orphan boys. On the streets in April you see dozens of boys dressed in orange. On my bus to *Chiang Mai* there were several of these boys. Many, so I've been told, are without parents. They are beginning their novitiates.

Homeless girls are not so lucky and they must become ser-vants, or worse. *Chiang Mai* is a magnet for some of the world's most unsavory and unscrupulous men. At night it's a common sight to see scrofulous and sagging males, many of my own race, roaming the streets hoping for a last chance, at a price.

"Only learn, no work. Sanskrit. Study Buddhism. Every morning we walk out the temple, carry the bowl. Eat two times a day. Eat rice. Maybe once a week have meat. I stay. Five years." Buddhism began about two thousand five hundred years ago in India, after the birth of the Buddha. An early form of Bud-dhism probably came to Thailand sometime in the next one thousand years. Theravāda Buddhism, the state religion of Thailand, came from India six hundred years ago, according to some estimates. The sacred texts were in the *Pali* language of India. Some texts were also in Sanskrit, a related language.

There are many old and beautiful *Wats*, also called temples, in *Chiang Mai*. Once one is inside these ancient golden tem-ples, the history of the ages is palpable, like an invisible golden seine, a fine mist that settles over one, carrying one back and back to the brink of some other time, some other incarna-tion, to the very edges of timelessness. Thailand's never been bombed. *Wat Phra Singh* and many other temples are much the same as they have been for hundreds of years.

"When I nineteen, I out from the monk. I go to teacher in country, *Ban Hoi Soi*. I first teacher, because before, not like now. Don't have." The head of education for the province gave *Gao* a teaching certificate based on his three hundred hours of teaching monks in the *Wat*. It was not a great job in terms of money, but it was dignified work. "I stay, [with] head of vil-lage, but drinking whiskey, old style. I don't like. I say I want to go stay in temple. I not married yet, I take care of temple. My salary, one month eighty *baht*. After that, about seven or eight year, ha-ha, my salary get four hundred and twenty *baht*."

Gao never succumbed to the blandishments of whiskey or smoking, not in his first job with the whiskey-drinking village head man and not later as he helped American soldiers have a good time in Bangkok. This is something that, if you think about it, must have required considerably fancy diplomatic footwork, not to mention self-discipline.

Gao is frugal, too, bringing his lunch from home, eating it in his beautiful, shiny, red, newer-model *songthaew*. These *songthaews* are seen all over Thailand and Laos. They function as share taxis for Thai people and, in a large city like *Chiang Mai*, for foreign tourists, too. *Gao's songthaew* is one of the nicest and he keeps it in excellent shape.

Between customers, *Gao* cleans and polishes his *songthaew* so that when he takes people on elephant tours and to visit the temples in the mountains around *Chiang Mai*, he can do so in style. He does not need money, he says, but does not like to sit at home and watch television. His wife packs his lunch every day, "take from home, no spend money." And she must be the one who irons his crisply starched bright white shirts, much as she must have when he was a young bachelor-teacher in her village.

He drives me to the flower market. We pass people in tattered clothes huddled together on the street corner. They look gray, dispirited, heads down, shoulders slumped, like animals waiting for slaughter. "Burma people," *Gao* says. "You want clean house. Work garden. Can do. Very cheap." They are here illegally and, just like the Mexicans and Salvadorans in San Francisco, wait on the corner, trying to be visible and invisible at the same time, hoping to be unnoticed by police but there to be seen by anybody who will hire them. Day laborers. Burmese refugees. Along the highway, from the windows of the air-conditioned busses I've taken to *Chiang Mai* or Bangkok, I have seen Burmese refugees, sometimes even old women, doing the heaviest kind of road work, dressed in rags, working in the rocks without shoes.

Gao was a teacher in his wife's village until he was twenty-six, then he went to work for one of the biggest timber companies in *Chiang Mai*. His job was that of estimating board feet of standing timber and grading the cut lumber. I understand this line of work because it was what my father did as a young man in northern Michigan. Very few can do it, or want to.

It's highly skilled work and, although the pay is good, it requires long days alone, in all kinds of weather, in often very rough terrain. It also requires exceptional math ability and a sterling reputation for honesty. It's easy to fudge the figures and even easier for people to imagine that you have, and those who are found out, at least in northern Michigan, and I'm guessing *Chiang Mai* is no different, might have an "accident" in the woods. "I use abacus. Chinese. I can do. Monk in temple teach me. I make fifteen hundred *baht* in the woods [for one month]. I good man. Honest. No corruption. No stain. You understand?"

For the first time I notice inky Chinese characters tattooed on the inside of *Gao's* forearms and I ask what they might signify. "If you like to know from me," he confides, "long time, oh, ha-ha. Work in forest, ten years." This is an answer so inscrutable that I don't know how to reasonably pursue it and, for once, fall silent, busying myself with my notebook and a slew of papers which have quite suddenly slipped off my lap and onto the floor.

It's an awkward moment in the small cab of his pick-up truck. Later I will learn from a Thai friend that when *Gao* talked about "no stain" he was probably talking about the widespread illegal logging, and saying that he had had no part in it. It would have made sense that, forty-five years earlier, he had indentured himself to a Chinese lumbering company, most likely because he had debts to pay off. His time of indenture was probably tattooed on the inside of his wrist. It was called debt servitude, slavery in all but name, and it was a common practice. Slavery did not officially end in Thailand until 1912 and versions of it continued for a long time after that. Aspects of it can still be found. The Associated Press ran photos in February 2016 of fishermen from Burma, Cambodia and In-

donesia, being released after having been enslaved on the coast
of Thailand.

Gao is the only person I have ever known to have an actual
laugh like the cartoon comic book rendering of laughter on
paper as "ha-ha." And this "ha-ha" is delivered in a flat fashion
that makes it even more like that paper laughter. It is a marvel
of irony, he seems to be saying with this "ha-ha," that he could
have lived in such different worlds. Now a tank of gas for his
songthaew costs a million times more than an entire leaf house
ever did, especially considering that leaf houses cost nothing,
and no one even lives in leaf houses anymore. How can it be,
he seems to ask with that laugh, that he can have a memory of
a time when the droppings of insects lit the lamps of the village
houses? And now maybe there are only a dozen people in all
of Thailand who might remember those insects, or the word,
kee-yah? How can that be?

Gao learned English, his fifth language, from the American
soldiers during the Vietnam War. "I take care." He was a soldier
in the Thai army at the time and his supervisor assigned him to
the American base "because I not have problem with people."
Gao could, and did, get along anywhere. His English, considering that he is self-taught, is extensive. Many Thai people who
learned English in school cannot understand English on the
telephone, but *Gao* can. "First time I stay in gate. 'Hello. Morning.' Like friendship looking." He made friends, not enemies.

When his military service with the Thai army was over, a
captain in the American army, "Mygoodfriendrobert," which
he says all run together as if it were one word, "Mygoodfriendrobert," asked him to go with him to Bangkok. *Gao* goes, and
makes himself useful, "Carry the bag, walking along him."

I ask *Gao* what Robert's last name was. He pauses for a frac-
tion of a second and then says, "Not know." Interestingly, he
doesn't say he doesn't remember.

Almost certainly, another Thai friend tells me, *Gao* was
acting as a bodyguard for the American soldier. *Gao's* size,

strength, intelligence, fluency in English, sober habits, ability to exercise sound judgment and navigate new and difficult situations with aplomb, would have made him an excellent one. Was the American dealing in contraband? Maybe. But probably no one needs that kind of help for weeks and weeks in order to eat lunch or go to a brothel. Americans generally carry their own bags and usually only to and from the train or the hotel, not as something they always have with them. And what was in the bag that was so questionable or heavy that the American couldn't carry it himself?

Gao helped Robert navigate Bangkok and, after some time, when Robert was ready to leave Bangkok, he asked Gao what he could do to help him in return. "Mygoodfriendrobert," he says, and repeats, "Mygoodfriendrobert, he asks, 'What you do after, *Gao?*' *Gao* my name, means glass, broken glass, *Lanna* language. My son change, *Apichai*, mean same thing." He tells Robert he wants to have a farm. "[If] I have farm. I [can] get married with my wife. I know her from when I teach in her village, but not marry, because I don't have money too much."

Robert gave him seventy-five thousand baht or about three thousand dollars. "I buy land. Marry normally, monk come to pray in new home. Before her home make by leaf of tree. Change to cement. Because my wife, I find her when I teacher. She help me clean my clothes and plan, like that." They had two sons, one drowned as a child and the second is a businessman. They have two granddaughters. *Gao's* children were born in the clinic "by the doctor by the river" and that doctor's son, J.J., now has the all-day-American-breakfast restaurant across the street. "My good friend," *Gao* says.

THE RESTAURANT OWNER

I had been taken to J.J.'s spotlessly clean all-day-American-breakfast some time earlier by my wonderful niece, Sidonie. She had already been in Thailand for several months. Sometime in 2007 or 2008 she began to do research there for her Master's in Education from the University of Amsterdam. She knew her way around the entire country by the time I met her in *Chiang Mai*.

I was so relieved to find homemade yogurt and whole grain pancakes that I didn't stop to wonder where the modest, soft-spoken Thai owner of the restaurant had learned how to make this food or to speak such impeccable English. On a return trip, I asked him to tell me his story.

I learned his name was *Anandh* and that he had been educated in New Zealand and Switzerland, which is where he learned how to speak English, and which is also where he became familiar with such breakfast foods as yogurt and whole grain pancakes. He learned how to make the food when he opened his restaurant in 1986. His father was one of the first doctors in *Chiang Mai*, and wealthy, which is how he could afford to send *Anandh* to the best schools in the world, an opportunity the father himself had not had as a young man. *Anandh's* father was a self-made man who had run away from his Chinese businessman father in Bangkok to study at the Presbyterian Mission School. So that, in a roundabout way, is the story of the pancakes and the perfect English.

Anandh's worldly ways to the contrary, he was born in *Chiang Mai* when all the food still came into town by raft and bullock cart. He grew up in an old-style Thai wooden house with many verandas on the banks of the *Ping* River. His parents ran a clinic and a maternity laying-in hospital next door.

"My father was a workaholic. He saw two hundred patients a day." *Anandh's* mother was a nurse who helped his father in the clinic and "she just went along with him." He and his three brothers were cared for by a bevy of servants. His parents had little time for their children and when *Anandh* went to school in New Zealand as a teenager, lonely and scared, he didn't get letters from home. *Anandh* nonetheless survived the classically cruel power struggles of a boys' English-style prep school in

New Zealand and later, when in college in Switzerland, he also weathered a series of wealthy European roommates with whom he had little in common. "All the Chinese people in *Chiang Mai*," *Anandh* says, continuing his story, "came to my father because he was the only Chinese doctor."

He says that the Chinese people generally, like his father, were known for being able to work very hard and make money. Many Chinese people in Thailand are involved in business. Thai people, on the other hand are known for making excellent food and loving music. The Thai had an easier life and more leisure time than the Chinese, so it would seem. There were fewer people in Thailand and they were able to hunt and forage for food and seldom needed to work. Far out in the country, where there are still a few huge trees along some remote rivers, people live in the trees in something like American-style tree houses. The houses, so I've been told, are cool and comfortable and safe from wild animals. Some people have suggested that the traditional Thai house, held up by tree trunks, with people living on the second and third floors, is a style that evolved from those ancient tree houses. The old-style Thai houses, built before air conditioning, are elegant and, indeed, surprising cool.

People from the countryside would come to the clinic, *Anandh* says, and they would pay with "rice, peacocks, even, once, a bear."

What *Anandh* remembers about the *Chiang Mai* of his childhood are the sounds of the brass bells on the bullock carts as they rolled into town early in the morning for the market; that, and the mist rising from the river. The river was clean then. He and his three brothers swam in it. When *Anandh* was growing up, the city had only three automobiles, one of which belonged to his father. There were still animal fat lights in many houses and, although there was electricity, it was fitful, limited when it was there, and often out for days. *Anandh*, like *Gao*, remembers a world before radios, or at least a world before radios were a fixture of everyday life.

The *Ping* River outside the front door was like a road, *Anandh* says, and rafts carrying goods to market traveled down the river and past his house. Logs from the forests were tied together and transported to the mills. He can remember men with cant hooks leaping across the cut trees to break up the log jams and get them moving on the waterway. "There was a bamboo footbridge over the river."

People come in and out, ordering homemade yogurt, freshly squeezed orange juice, hash brown potatoes, homemade bread toast, grilled ham, French toast, bacon and eggs, croissants, sandwiches to take on picnics. "I could walk the dirt road from our house [by the river] to *Tah Pai* Gate in ten minutes," he says as he gets up to help customers.

He points to the dark, old-style, three-story, teak Thai house across the street from his restaurant and says, "When I was a boy, that was a rich man's house." The dwelling looks forlorn somehow, almost lost among larger, more modern buildings. It looks unlived in.

The bullock carts, the kind *Anandh* remembers from his childhood, had a pair of horned bulls pulling them and "the wheels were as high as a man and wooden. The pace was slow." There were elephants, too, from time to time but "most of the elephants worked in the forest" outside of town.

Anandh has a refined and practiced way of carrying on a conversation: sensitive to nuance, aware of subtle humor, quick to respond, remembering details, never losing track of the interwoven threads. He has a stocky build. His face is like that of the moon in my old Mother Goose book: twinkling almost closed eyes, a line drawing nose, a good-natured smile that verges on laughter. "The bullock carts carried rice and other goods into town early in the morning. There would be one lantern on the cart, the sound of the bells. The mist. Sometimes you could feel a chill."

The newspapers report that the price of a barrel of oil will be two hundred dollars by the end of 2008. Warren Buffet says the economy is terrible. George Soros says it's the worst he's ever seen it. If Israel bombs Iran it could precipitate a Third World War. Right now Thailand, in early 2008, like America and everywhere, is suffering from what some say is artificially high energy costs and the related high costs of food.

Burmese refugees, on the verge of starving, are pouring over the border into Thailand. And they are the lucky ones: the ones snared by human traffickers or caught and returned to Burma have desperate lives, if they live.

Anandh says he came home one summer from college in Switzerland in the early 1960s and *Chiang Mai* had changed. American soldiers from the Vietnam War were everywhere. The quiet town of families eating supper and celebrating *Loi Krathang* and going to bed early had become a place of beer and brothels or "Turkish Baths" as *Anandh* says they were called. As a young man he and his friends found it strange, and exciting, too.

A Dutch couple comes in and *Anandh* is up again, and I'm reminded of my niece, Sidonie, a citizen of the world, with passports from three countries: the Netherlands, Canada and the United States. She speaks five languages: Dutch, French, English, Spanish, and Swahili. Her formal birth name means 'star going towards happiness' and is from the Inuit language. Her parents were working on a film together and living among the Inuit in Northern Canada when she was born. She is tall, proud, like Boudicca, the Iceni female warrior who led her people against the Romans two thousand years ago. Her hair is a beautiful strawberry blond, long and curly, waves and waves of beautiful gold and red, like a flag unfurling.

My mind goes back to how my niece and I had been walking back from the Night Market several months earlier. We had passed a fat, aging American on the sidewalk, just as he was saying to his not-beautiful, working lady-of-the-evening,

"I thought I just gave you two hundred *baht*." My niece and I didn't comment on this, then or later. The look on my niece's face had been, "There, but for the grace of God, go I," and I pretty much knew what she was thinking: *We must be strong, we must carry on*, like the line from the Eric Clapton song.

My niece had taught the children of prostitutes in an orphanage in Guatemala when she ware barely out of high school. She got lice there and had to shave her head. Then she worked in Ghana, training teachers who did not show up for her trainings or who, when they did show up, talked while she was talking, as if she wasn't there. She got malaria in Africa and still gets it. Malaria, a lifelong disease, stays in the blood. In Ghana sometimes the students would sit all day under a tree waiting for teachers who never came. When the teachers did come in, they would often complain that the students were not capable of learning. The teachers in Ghana, like the teachers in Thailand, were paid very little. My niece still travels the world and is still working in global education, although now in a supervisory role.

We wanted a beer after the heat of the Night Market and so stopped at one of those bars that are more on the sidewalk than not, tiny chairs and tables spilling into the street. "*Sxng Heineken*," I'd said, holding up two fingers. *Sxng* is the Thai word for two. Two Heinekens in large green bottles appeared on the little lace-covered coffee table in front of us.

Just as we each took a draught the man next to us was saying to his fellow traveler, "Here's a place where you can get a beer and a blow job, one price." Without a word my niece and I rose as one and soon were on the street again, walking quickly, only to find the waitress running after us: in our haste to leave, we had forgotten to pay.

"*Newsweek* I think, maybe it was *Newsweek*, I forget, did an article about how maybe, early *Homo sapiens*, protohumans, mated with cave men back in the dawn of time, maybe Neanderthals, maybe Cro-Magnon," I said after we paid, "but there's no evidence." She'd laughed, as I'd hoped she would. "There's your evidence," she'd said, "the world's oldest profession."

Now my niece is getting married in the Netherlands but having her engagement party in Toronto, after seeing my branch of her extended family in Michigan. We used to think only rich people lived like this, but now everyone does. My sisters and I never imagined our children traveling all over the globe. We never imagined the Internet.

When Bill Gates and his friends were in high school out in Seattle, and playing around with making computers, people imagined that computers would be the size of the Sheraton Hotel and be used to spy on Russians, if we even knew about computers which we mostly didn't. We only knew about Russians. They were bad. Russians were bad. Americans were good, naturally. We had drills in school where we were taught to hide under our desks if the Russians bombed us. I never thought about this at the time or even later and neither did anyone else, but if the Russians bombed us, hiding under our little wooden desks was probably the last place we should be.

A recent issue of *The Economist* says the next bull market will come about because of technological advances in energy. There's infinite capacity in wind and solar energy and, like the Internet, it won't have to cost very much. Someone will figure it out. Some new Bill Gates or Copernicus is out there pondering it at this very moment. Next thing we know, the money people who gamble on such things can make a bundle, the way they did with the Internet and fiber-optics and the Model-T. The same kind of human being who can figure out how to light a lamp with insect offal, can figure out, twenty thousand years on, how to light our lamps with energy from the sun. Thank goodness someone's working on it.

Anandh now lives outside of town in a family complex. His grandson often comes to work with him and *Anandh* sits with him, talking, helping with homework between customers. I read the *International Herald Tribune* and the *Bangkok Post*. The telegraph office in Bangkok, opened a hundred years earlier, is closing. The trains in Thailand have all had to be taken off the rails and cleaned because of an infestation of body lice.

Anandh's father was Chinese, from Bangkok. And his mother was half-Thai and half-Chinese from the hills above *Chiang Mai*. His father was Christian, his mother was Buddhist. *Anandh's* father's father had also run away from home in southern China, *Suo Tao*, and come to Bangkok. "My grandfather, whom I never met, came from the poorest part of China. They had nothing. And Thailand was so rich. Maybe not rich, but things were plentiful."

And what of your mother?

Anandh's man-in-the-moon eyes twinkle, the way I've learned they do when he's about to say something surprising, "Her father was an opium dealer." When I've had time to sort this, he says, "His wife, my mother's mother, died in childbirth, so my grandfather took the baby and rode on horseback up into the mountains and left my mother with a man and his wife who wanted children but could not have them." Being an opium dealer was legal then and very dangerous.

"My grandfather traveled with a dozen gunmen to protect him." His eyes twinkle again. "The best gunmen in Thailand at that time came from Phrae." Anandh knows I live in a little rural village near the city of Phrae, "And very cheap, too," he says, "A hundred dollars [to kill a man]."

Many weeks later, when I share this story with my Thai friends back in my village, the husband of one of them says, "If I lose my job at the ministry, I can be a gunman for Katie." He thinks this is a great joke. He pantomimes being a gunman like in the American Wild West, pulling six shooters from holsters at each side, defending me, guns blazing.

And so what was the grandfather like?

"Charming," *Anandh* says. "My grandfather had many women, all up and down the mountains, in every village. He was charming." Later, when the grandfather was kidnapped, *Anandh*'s mother sold all her gold jewelry to ransom him.

Rambo 4 is playing at the *Chiang Mai* Cinema and in the heat of the afternoon I sit in an air-conditioned theater and watch Sylvester Stallone rescue missionaries who've been captured by Burmese soldiers. The missionaries, in my view, are not appealing people, not worth rescuing, or wouldn't be for me. Sylvester Stallone looks strange, like he's had a lot of Botox treatments. The movie was filmed in the mountain jungles outside *Chiang Mai* which is the most interesting thing about it.

That night there's a *takraw* match in the square at *Tha Pai* Gate. *Takraw* is a traditional Thai game played with a small wicker ball, very light-weight, about the size of a tennis ball. The game resembles Hacky Sack, that small cloth ball filled with pellets that kids kick with their feet. Only the feet, head, and elbows can be used in *takraw*; no hands. Several teams of small-boned, lithe young men try to get the *takraw* wicker ball through a hoop about twenty feet in the air. Above that is the moon. An old woman sits on the sidewalk with a paper cup in front of her, her hands permanently placed in a *wai*, the Buddhist gesture of prayer, supplication, and greeting.

European and American tourists, carrying purchases from the Night Market, cross the plaza. Young Thai parents with small children wander the square much as they might in San Francisco or Copenhagen. Hill tribe ladies hawk their wares, silver bracelets and wooden frogs.

The hard thing about living anywhere, I decide, and traveling in general, is that one can never live long enough or see enough of the world to fully understand the long arc of the universe and make any sense of it. Little bits are all we get, and it's never enough to see the big picture.

Enoch "Knuck" Harris

I wanted to have African American relatives long before I learned that, through marriage, I did. It just made sense to me that with the Stocking family in America for almost four hundred years that sometime, somewhere, somehow, we had married people who were black.

In 2016 we on the northwest coast of Northern Michigan, on the streets of Traverse City, and in some of the tourist spots, are just beginning to see dark-skinned people. Sometimes these visitors are recent immigrants from India, Africa, Indonesia, Japan, Korea, the Middle East, Latin America, and other places around the world. More often they are African Americans whose ancestry can be traced to the founding of the republic in the early 1600s.

Many African Americans have ancestors who were in America at least a century before some of those with European ancestry. Some Americans with English or European ancestry are excessively proud of having been in America long enough to qualify for membership in the famously exclusive and racist Daughters of the American Revolution (DAR). The irony is that the tenure of these race-proud Europeans on the continent, those who claim primacy of place, is often eclipsed by that of most African Americans who were here usually a century or more earlier.

Dark-skinned people from everywhere are coming to live, work, go to school, or just to enjoy the beaches for a few days like the other thousands of summer tourists. It's a trend that will increase with time. By 2050, according to census predictions, fifty percent of the population in our country will be people of color. People of European ancestry, white people like me, will become at that time, officially, a minority.

I was born in 1945 and grew up on the northwest coast of Michigan. I never saw a single African American until my mother took the three oldest of her five daughters, ranging in age from four to twelve, shopping in Grand Rapids. There I saw for the first time men, women, and children with very dark brown, sometimes almost black, skin.

I was little, with few words, and remember my mother's instantaneous, "Hush!" and the rough jerk on my arm when I asked, "Who are the chocolate people?" I can still feel the roughness as she pulled me aside and got down to my level and looked me in the face and said in a stern whisper, "They are people, just like us. We aren't rude. We don't talk about other people. We don't stare."

She was right, of course, on all counts, but I still didn't know who the chocolate people were. They were not Native Americans. I had grown up knowing Indians. They worked in my father's lumber camp, and although they had fairly dark skin, as did my own father and his mother, some of the people I saw on the streets of Grand Rapids were darker and their features did not look like those of the Indians where I lived. It would be years before I found out who they were or thought about them again.

If we're living in the present moment, as most of us do, and not thinking too much about all the events in previous times, it usually doesn't occur to those of us who live here now, that people didn't used to have cell phones or cars, much less that this part of northern Michigan wasn't always populated by people of European ancestry.

In reality there were several black families, usually intermarried with Native Americans, in the Detroit area as far back as the early 1600s. There were others, scattered among the Indian tribes, all across the country. A classic book on this subject, *Black Indians* by William Katz, has photo documentation of African American fur traders, entrepreneurs and scouts, mixed-race men usually, whose parents had married into various tribes.

Samuel de Champlain, a Frenchman who explored the Great Lakes in the 1600s, traveled with a free-black translator, Mathieu da Costa, who knew many languages: French, Portuguese, Dutch, English, and several versions of the Algonquin language. It boggles the mind to try to imagine where he came from originally, or how he learned all those languages, especially those of the Native Americans. A good guess might be that he had become a sailor at a young age, free-black or slave, and that his gift for languages, acquired over the years, a skill very much needed by explorers, allowed him as a young adult to name his own price. Some people have an aptitude for language acquisition. I have met them in Guatemala, Romania and Thailand and heard about them in other places, a Sherpa for example in Nepal who spoke seven languages fluently. But these people are rare.

My father was racist; my mother was not. When I decided my sophomore year at the University of Michigan to live in cooperative housing, inexpensive, communal housing that had been set up by the university in the 1930s during the Great Depression to help students be able to afford to stay in school, my father took one look at the dilapidated former mansion on Lawrence Street and said, "I hope you know how to tie your sheets together and hang them off the balcony so you can escape when there's a fire." Later, back home in Leelanau County my father described the housing to my family, and then said to me, "Well, at least you won't have N—ers sleeping in your bed," which coming from him, dark as he was, especially compared to my mother, was a bit bewildering.

My father was a backwoods kind of guy. He didn't read much. He didn't keep up with current events. He didn't know about the civil rights movement. He'd never heard of the Reverend Dr. Martin Luther King, Jr. He'd been in the Civilian Conservation Corps (CCC) when it had been segregated, as was the armed forces, as government policy. Most people follow the example set by the leaders in their government.

During my father's lifetime President Woodrow Wilson had made a concerted effort to remove black people from civil service jobs, such as those in the post office, and keep them away from any kind of work with the federal government. State voting restrictions, legal in many southern states, kept most black people there from going to the polls up through the 1960s. But it wasn't just the south that was racist. The popular 1915 silent movie, *Birth of a Nation,* which showed a triumphant Ku Klux Klan had been sanctioned and enjoyed by almost everyone who wasn't black.

My father had been taught some wrong things about black people and didn't know it because almost everyone he knew had been taught the same wrong things. He didn't know a single black person and had only ever seen very few. He was expressing commonly held views, views promulgated by many leaders in his nation's government, and therefore he had never thought about those views, which is what people do.

My mother had instantly hushed him with, "Pat!" when he said the "n" word.

My mother read books. She taught literature. She studied. She listened to the news. She knew that Eleanor Roosevelt had resigned from the DAR because they wouldn't let black singer Marian Anderson perform at the DAR Constitution Hall.

My mother would propose a course in African American literature at the Traverse City Central High School when she was teaching there throughout the 1960s and '70s. She wanted to teach the works of Langston Hughes, James Baldwin, Sojourner Truth, Frederick Douglass, Maya Angelou, and many others. My mother was referred to as "a scholar" by her colleagues. She was in charge of all the honors classes: mythology, great books, Shakespeare. She knew there were some ancient, famous thinkers and writers who were black: Aesop, Eratosthenes, St. Augustine, Alexander Pushkin, and Alexander Dumas were considered to be black. In some quarters the blackness of these men is disputed because Aesop, Eratosthenes, and St. Augustine were also Greek or Roman citizens and St. Augustine was from the North African Berber tribe on his mother's side and might be considered as Arabic, most depictions of their faces indicate someone with dark skin and African features. Pushkin was reportedly part-Russian and part-black and Dumas was allegedly part-French and part-black.

My mother was a staunch Republican. She was anti-union and never joined the teachers' union at her school. Nonetheless, she was an advocate of inclusion.

The principal of my mother's Traverse City High School, Art Schubert, a pinkish-white man, a popular administrator and a former football coach, as many school administrators were in those days, had developed a remarkably porcine appearance by late middle age. In response to my mother's proposed course in African American literature, a response which showcased his typical short-sightedness, deep ignorance of anything but sports, abysmal lack of knowledge of a larger historical perspective, absence of any background in scholarship in any area whatsoever, inability to foresee and prevent the dissension caused by injustice in schools and in society, and a dearth of awareness of civil rights, said, "But, Eleanor, we don't have any black people in Traverse City."

The Traverse City schools at that time had a known but unwritten policy of never hiring anyone Jewish. They had no African Americans working in the schools in any capacity, even as janitors. If they had any gay employees, they didn't know it. They didn't think of their hiring practices or choices in curriculum as discriminatory, unfair, hateful or being in any way a path to the misunderstanding and possible violence that comes from exclusionary practices. If they thought about it at all, which they probably didn't, they would have thought this was simply the way the world was supposed to be. They were blissfully ignorant and, like Art Schubert, blissfully ignorant of their own bigotry. They were detached from reality. They were insulated and isolated in their institution. They saw no reason to change.

My mother, always self-assured and somewhat amused by her superiors, had responded, "We will, Art."

Art Schubert, bless his heart, had the final say. He turned down the proposed course. Art Schubert had been right in a way: Northern Michigan had no African American residents in the 1960s or '70s. It would take another fifty years. And so, my mother, who saw it coming and wanted to prepare her students, had been right, too.

In Michigan, as soon as the last treaty with the Native Americans was signed in 1855, the state began to give away land to non-Indian people willing to stay five years and put up a dwelling. They did this to encourage the remaining Indians to move on, and to officially secure the lands the government had claimed by treaty. At this time African American homesteaders began to come into Michigan along with all the other immigrants. Everyone wanted the free land. Probably no one, other than the Native Americans, gave a moment's thought to some of the violent and dishonest ways all that land had been acquired.

In the early years in America there were no laws affirming slavery. In the thirteen colonies there were no laws against miscegenation, mixed-race unions, until the late 1700s. If you think about it, when Anthony fell in love with Cleopatra, a woman who certainly looked African in sculptures, no one seemed to be focused on her skin color. Royal lineage was important two thousand years ago but, even in the Bible, skin color doesn't often seem to be mentioned. There were many slaves, white *and* black, two thousand years ago. Associating skin color with slavery is a relatively recent development that had to do with the boom in sugar and cotton in America. In America the Fugitive Slave Act, legally requiring the return of human "property," wasn't passed until 1793. The Civil War would follow sixty years later. The aftermath of that war would reverberate through the culture, and is still reverberating.

In the 1900s ideas about white supremacy and a master race, and the concomitant anti-miscegenation beliefs, ideas derived in part from the German philosopher, Friedrich Nietzsche, then twisted and further distorted as they were blended with biologist Charles Darwin's ideas about survival of the fittest, were carried to crazy extremes by Hitler. Ideas about white supremacy gave rise in the United States to racist and Neo-Nazi groups such as the Ku Klux Klan, John Birch Society, White Citizens' Council, Christian Identity, White Aryan Resistance, and the United White Knights, a special Texas version of the Ku Klux Klan. Many clubs, such as the Knights of Columbus, the Daughters of the Eastern Star, the Rainbow Girls and a whole host of fraternities and sororities did not accept black members.

Sometimes, given our country's fraught history regarding race, we forget that not all black people had ever been slaves or that, conversely, many white people had once been routinely enslaved. Before machines, the whole point of war, in many instances, was to get slaves: nobody wanted to do all that heavy, manual labor. In Greece, Rome, Jerusalem, basically everywhere, there were slaves two thousand years ago and they were not necessarily black. In Russia, until the peasants rebelled in 1917, the peasants were slaves and they were white. Many white people in the United States were indentured servants, little better than slaves. Ben Franklin had been indentured to his brother, had run away and was never prosecuted for it. Andrew Johnson, seventeenth president of the United States, had been a runaway indentured servant with a ten dollar bounty for his arrest and return.

This country, for most of the first two centuries, was an all-bets-are-off free-for-all. Both white and black pioneers were married to indigenous peoples. Thomas Jefferson had advocated marriage between white pioneers and Native Americans, something noted in Robert Bieder's excellent book, *Science Encounters the Indian.* It was happening anyway, and marriage was cheaper than war. Lena Horne, the singer, was all three races and so were uncounted others.

Tiya Miles is an author, a Harvard graduate, a MacArthur award winner, and a professor of African American Studies at the University of Michigan. She has written and co-authored several wonderful and well-researched books about the phenomenon of mixed race ancestry in America, including *Ties that Bind,* a book about a part-Cherokee family in the southern part of the United States.

One prominent Connecticut family of Indian, white, and black people, was able to document with photos and birth and death records, their family's long history in North America. Their book, by descendants Alene Jackson Smith and Adeline Jackson Tucker is, *Live, Labor, Love: the History of a Northern Family,* (1700-1900).

When my mother lay dying in the late spring of 1995, in a hospital bed in the living room of her house on the hill above Sleeping Bear Bay, I was asked to be writer-in-residence for two weeks through the artists-in-the-schools program of the Michigan Council for the Arts (MCA). This program would soon have its funding drastically cut as the automakers began to move offshore and take all the jobs and tax funds with them, but at that time the MCA was still an economically viable program. The head office had written to me telling me that my services as a writer had been requested at a small, public, elementary school in Bridgman, Michigan, down near the Michigan-Illinois border.

I didn't want to go. I thought my mother might die while I was gone, but she had insisted: go make a difference for the better, she had said, and whether she was there or not when I got back, it wouldn't matter. Help kids, was her idea. Do what you can to make the world a better place and everything else would take care of itself.

Just before I left for southern Michigan, a man I knew at the Soil Conservation Service (SCS) office in Lake Leelanau, a division of the United States Department of Agriculture (USDA), told me when I went to pick up my seedling trees at the end of April, that something interesting had come across his desk recently: an African American farmer in Joliet, Illinois, who raised ostriches and his last name was Stocking. Raising ostriches sounded just like the kind of entrepreneurial scheme my father might have been intrigued by. What if we were related?

Stocking is an unusual name. It's not a name anyone would assume. In fact several Stocking relatives in the past have changed the name to the following: Stock, Stockton, Stokes, Stocken, and Stockenton. Makes sense. I was often teased about my last name and called, "Christmas Stocking," or more crudely, asked if I would like to have something put inside my Christmas stocking. You don't need to be a genius to figure out how to make fun of such a name. I thought it might be interesting to try to find the Joliet ostrich farmer over the weekend during the two weeks I'd be working downstate.

There isn't much to do in your "off" time when you are a writer-in-residence somewhere. I ate. I slept. I prepared for my classes. I walked the beach. I tried not to think about my dying mother. I visited Carl Sandburg's summer home over on the shores of Lake Michigan. It was a wonderful, rambling cottage, now a national historic home. I went and heard William Styron Jr. in a cavernous high school auditorium in Dowagiac. Styron, author of *Sophie's Choice*, and many other excellent books, was being sponsored by the Dogwood Club in Dowagiac. He spoke about his travails with clinical depression. Dowagiac is a Potawatomi word, so I'd learned from my youngest daughter's Native American father; he had said it means "where the geese walk backwards." Wikipedia says it means "fishing [near home] water." Perhaps it means a little bit of both. His father had come from there, near Pipestone. Pipestone, I was told by my daughter's father, was where his Ottawa and Potawatomi relatives got the stone for their tobacco pipes.

I went to hear Maya Angelou speak at a dinner gathering of the Economic Club of Southwestern Michigan near Benton Harbor. It wasn't cheap but someone at the school had given me their ticket. As we ate dinner and waited for Ms. Angelou, an elderly gentleman at my table said to his wife, "I didn't think they let people like her [Angelou] in here." I looked around. He seemed to be right. It was an all-white crowd.

His wife responded, "They aren't letting her *in* here, dear. She's just giving a performance."

Angelou spoke, sang, and recited poetry in her eloquent, deep, alto, resonant cadences. Anyone listening to her would have wanted to find their African American relatives, assuming they had any.

The black farmer in Joliet had agreed to meet me at a restaurant in Joliet and also to show me his ostrich farm. In the restaurant he tells me that when he first saw my name come across his caller ID, he'd thought I was one of his ex-wives trying to contact him. The restaurant is an odd place. People are coming in and out with scraps of paper that they give to someone at the till, messages of some kind.

The black farmer is very dark, very short, bandy-legged, a wheeler dealer with a huge SUV. After we have coffee, he tells me to follow his SUV out to his ostrich farm. His ostrich farm is not much of a farm. It's a fenced paddock, about half the size of a city lot, with a shed. Ostriches are giant birds, tall as a man, or taller. Mr. Stocking tells me that if an ostrich kicks a person in the head, that person is pretty much a goner. He says the price of ostrich meat, once high, is now too low for the farm to be profitable. Around the outside of the paddock are three, huge, new, presumably expensive cabin cruisers.

Mr. Stocking says he has business to conduct during the afternoon, but will meet me back at his home at 6 p.m. He gives me driving directions. I have nothing to do in Joliet, but decide that I should follow this to its conclusion. We've barely spoken and I know nothing about him.

I find Mr. Stocking's home in a middle class subdivision that seems to be mostly African American. I wait and wait on the street. The sun is setting when a group of teenagers comes down the sidewalk on the other side of the street half a block behind me. One of them rips the antennae off a car and starts whipping it at another one of the young men. I slowly pull forward and drive to the end of the street and then, going the maximum legal speed, drive out of the subdivision and back to Bridgman. The next day I call my son and tell him it was a very strange encounter. I'd thought the restaurant might be a front for the numbers racket and the ostrich farm might be a front for shipping contraband in the cabin cruisers.

My son laughs and laughs and laughs. He instantly puts himself in the ostrich farmer's place. "This man's thinking—he's thinking you are out of your frickin' mind. He's thinking, 'The only way we could be related is if some of *her* people, *owned* some of *my* people.'" It was one of those things that, afterwards, all you can say to yourself is, well, that was embarrassing.

In 2009 I came home from the Peace Corps in Thailand and took a job as a ranger at the Sleeping Bear Dunes National Lakeshore. Peace Corps volunteers have a year's time after their service in which they can be hired by the federal government without being vetted with the usual, time-consuming process.

The woman who hired me had been in the Peace Corps in Costa Rica. We hit it off immediately.

I was waiting for Workers' Compensation to approve the repair of my anterior cruciate ligament (ACL) in my knee. I'd torn it during the second year of my service in Thailand. After months of physical therapy, the doctors at the hospital in Bangkok recommended that it be surgically repaired. The Peace Corps didn't want to repair it there, on their dime, although what they said was that I'd receive better care in the United States. In fact Thailand has excellent surgeons. Thailand is known all over the globe as a medical tourism destination. The Peace Corps wanted to avoid paying.

I had already signed a two-year contract for an English teaching job back at an International High School in Chiang Mai, my favorite city in northern Thailand. It would pay sixty thousand dollars a year, lodging, travel between Thailand and Michigan at the beginning and end of my contract, and one round-trip ticket mid-way through for a trip back home. It was good money anywhere, but in Thailand it meant that I could live comfortably and also save enough to put new siding on my home in Lake Leelanau. It would mean real teaching with a real income. I loved Chiang Mai and was looking forward to living there.

The National Park Service (NPS) job was a bit of *déjà vu*. I had run the Pierce Stocking Scenic Drive for my father from 1974 to 1976, thirty-five years earlier, before it became part of the national park. Now I was sixty-four, closer to sixty-five. I had not been back to the dunes in all that time.

My father's land had been taken over by the federal government through the right of eminent domain, a traumatic event that had been followed by a protracted and nerve-wracking, ten-year, legal battle in the federal courts. My father had died the day after he'd received his settlement. My stepmother would immediately cash the check and leave for Sun City Arizona, never to be seen again, their home burning to the ground on the day she drove away from Michigan. Going back to the dunes reminded me of all of that}

But a job is a job. I'm thinking that if Workers' Compensation doesn't approve the surgery soon enough, then I can stay and work for the park instead of going back to Thailand. I would like being outside. I would like being in my own home again after years of traveling. If I don't go back to Thailand, I'm thinking, and instead stay in Leelanau County and work for the NPS, I'll get a cat and a dog.

I don't tell anyone at the NPS that I have to wear a knee brace under my uniform. I'd had to fill out a form attesting to the fact that I'm fit; and I am. My physical therapist advised me not to mention the knee brace. He told me to go into the ladies room and put it on whenever I had to be out hiking on rough terrain. And that's what I do.

The first week, my supervisor, the former Peace Corps volunteer, asks what informational programs I'd like to do. I say that I have no idea and ask what my choices are. She suggests that I do programs on my father and his scenic drive.

I politely demur, telling her that I think this might be too personal. What I really think is that it would be in incredibly bad taste. I'm stupefied that she could even suggest it. It would look like self-aggrandizement, on my part, even if it wasn't. Also, if I wrote up a program on my father and the scenic drive, once I left the park service, they could alter whatever I'd done, but still claim that I had provided the information. I didn't want to pre-authenticate something that might be changed or expanded in a way that made me or my family uncomfortable. I didn't want to appear to be the kind of self-serving person who was promoting my family by promoting my father's legacy.

This supervisor is not happy with me from that moment on. It finally occurs to me that she had hired me with the sole purpose of having me do programs on my father. All the other rangers are young, either just out of college or still in college. There are a couple of older rangers but they are still a decade or two younger than I am and they were hired when they *were* young.

I have to be the oldest ranger anyone there has ever hired. For the first time my supervisor realizes she has hired someone sixty-four, someone who appears to have trouble walking fast up hills or on uneven ground, and someone who has inexplicably refused to develop programs on her father, Pierce Stocking. It had apparently never entered her mind that I would reject this perfectly wonderful idea. Her entire attitude toward me changes.

My supervisor, now curt and rude instead of smiling and collegial, shows me several huge filing cabinets. She tells me to find something in the voluminous files on which I could do programs. In the meantime, she has hired an assistant from some other park. This new assistant goes everywhere with a clipboard. At every turn, she begins to find fault with me according to some checklist she has: that I had misidentified a basswood tree as a poplar tree; that my uniform shirt is too baggy; that my Smokey the Bear hat needs to be worn lower on my forehead.

During the initial two-week orientation and training period, I perused the files in the cabinet as instructed. After a few days I go to my supervisor, the one who had been in the Peace Corps, and tell her I'd like to do a program on the African American pioneers who had lived within the area of the Sleeping Bear Dunes National Lakeshore. I had heard from one of my father's workers, an old man named Ray Welch who came from one of the early pioneer families in the Empire area, that a family of black pioneers had lived near him on Welch Road above Glen Lake. I'd believed him; he was the soul of veracity. But I hadn't been too interested in black pioneers one way or the other at the time. Now in the NPS archives I see their photographs with names.

The next person I see is the assistant with the clipboard.

She wants to see the photos of African American pioneers. I show her the children outside the Aral School at Otter Creek in the national park. I show her the children at the Springdale School on Welch Road near Glen Lake in the national park. I show her the children at the Brotherton School on Voice Road near Empire in the national park.

The national park offices in Empire, called "Fort Empire" by local people because of its fort-like architecture, has a high-ceilinged front area for visitors, and then a warren of low-ceilinged offices in the back: one side for rangers who do outdoor programs with park visitors, and the other side for the superintendent and her office staff. There are back doors, front doors, and a connecting door from the ranger side, through a closet, into the lecture and slide show room. One can cross through the usually dark, cavernous and vacant amphitheater to where there's another door to the office side.

This assistant is young and short. Her personality is a peculiar combination of officious and dithering. She has close-cropped brown hair and wears large, funny-looking glasses. She takes herself and everything else way too seriously. With her clipboard and, in a flurry of activity, she goes out one door and comes back through another, ranger side to administration side, and back around again. She is choosing to cross through the empty amphitheater and then, apparently going out an office door over on the administration side and then into the parking lot, perhaps to avoid going through the throng of visitors, she comes around again through the back door into the place where the rangers work. Her movements are like those of a wind-up toy. She pauses in front of me, then seems to remember something and takes off again, all discombobulated, to make the same circuit all over again.

She stops in front of me for the second time, a few minutes later, and says, rapid-fire, "The African American pioneers within the confines of the Sleeping Bear Dunes National Lakeshore did not make significant contributions." Then she leaves again. I'm thinking, *What? What did the white pioneers do that was so significant? Running from sheriffs' posses, vicious dogs, and bounty hunters isn't significant? Surviving not being allowed to read and write isn't significant? Surviving the continuous breakup of families and separation from loved ones isn't significant? Surviving slavery long enough to escape isn't significant? Carving an existence out of the frozen wilderness isn't significant? How does she even know what the black pioneers did? Pioneer life was difficult for everyone and must have been even more so for escaped slaves.*

She comes back through again, for the third time now, in a total tizzy, huffing and puffing on her little track, stops in front of me and, never looking up from her clipboard, announces, "You will do shipwrecks."

And that's what I did, all summer long. One night at the various venues around the national park, there were several of us rangers, all doing presentations on shipwrecks on the Great Lakes.

⅄ Michigan, an anti-slavery state, had integrated schools from the beginning. In Lansing, in the state capitol's history archives, there are photos of Michigan's one-room public schools. In some of the photos, some of the students are visibly African American. In museums in Leelanau and Benzie Counties there are also photos of African American pioneers and their children.

Census figures reveal that some black Leelanau pioneers were farmers, like the Levi Johnson family on Welch Road above Glen Lake, and the Boston family in Cleveland Township near School Lake. Some, like the Skinner and Hall families in the Empire area, were loggers. There were African American families in the Benzonia and Frankfort areas with the last names of Davis, Batey, Dorey, White, Hays, Ward, and Richardson. Photos in the Benzie Area Historical Society archives indicate some of these families may have been of mixed race. This was certainly true of the Joe Davis family over in Benzonia, and in that family it's been documented.

Some of these African American families were from Canada and New York State, indicating they might have been manumitted, that is, officially released from slavery with the documents to prove it. They could have managed this by buying their freedom or, more rarely, being released through the largesse of their owners. Some list their birthplaces as southern states which might indicate they had come up by way of the Underground Railroad.

There were several abolitionists in northern Michigan and this may have made it seem like a place of refuge for runaway slaves. Reverend George Smith, a missionary in Northport, and Morgan Bates, one of the founders of the only newspaper in the north, the *Grand Traverse Herald*, were both staunch abolitionists.

The Benzonia Academy was founded in 1891 by an anti-slavery group from Oberlin, Ohio. Some of these founders had been active in the Underground Railroad down in Ohio. Nat Brandt, formerly an editor at *The New York Times* and managing editor at *American Heritage* has written a book, *The Town that Started the Civil War*, about Oberlin and the refusal of white citizens there to give up black fugitive slaves. The Benzonia Academy building, now the Mills Community House, still stands. Part of it houses the public library. In 1974 when I returned from New York City, I worked as a freelance writer for the weekly *Benzie Herald-Examiner* and covered meetings which were sometimes held in that building.

Bruce Catton, Pulitzer Prize-winning author and historian, was the son of the headmaster of the Benzonia Academy. He lived in what is now the public library before he went off to Oberlin College in 1921. Born in 1899 in Michigan, Catton is known nationally for his books about the Civil War. In Michigan, Catton is best known for his books about his home state. His careful research and lively writing style have made him one of Michigan's best writers. In his bicentennial history of Michigan, Catton wrote about the African American Morgan family in East Jordan, founders of the town brickyard. When Mary Morgan died in 1951 at the age of 107, the entire town of Boyne City shut down for her funeral.

Black families were in the area of the Sleeping Bear Dunes National Lakeshore from the late 1800s through the early 1900s. Black children with the last names of Skinner, Hall, Johnson, and Boston were in some of the photos from the Aral, Brotherton, School Lake, and Springdale schools in the area now part of the Sleeping Bear Dunes National Lakeshore (SBDNL). Aral was the name of the lumber boom town at Otter Creek on Lake Michigan. Aral now is nonexistent except for the name. The mill, the town, the one-room school, and the boardwalk are gone.

The Brotherton School was on Voice Road near Empire. Photos show black students there. Voice Road was named for Edward Voice, the accountant at the Empire Lumber Company two miles away, one of the largest lumber companies on Lake Michigan. Voice, a son-in-law of the abolitionist Reverend George Smith in Northport, was one of the most prominent members of the community.

The School Lake one-room schoolhouse was in Cleveland Township on the northern edge of the park. The Springdale School was on Welch Road near Glen Lake. All of these schools were within the boundaries of the national park. A photo of one of the Skinner men sitting on top of a pile of logs shows him looking confident, even jaunty. He's wearing a large fur coat with an incongruous white ermine fur collar.

"African-American pioneers on the West Michigan logging-lumber frontier," according to the Historical Society of Michigan (HSM) spring 2010 issue, "participated in, and became able contributors to, the economic and civic life of that frontier." Gretchen Paprocki, the author of the report, writes that one European traveler staying at a primitive lodge on the

Muskegon River where the pillows and bedding were made of marsh hay, was awakened in the night by ten men who took the other five beds. "In the morning we found they were all Negro lumber rafters."

The Negro lumber rafters in Paprocki's HSM article may or may not have been manumitted. They would have had skills so hard to find and so necessary to the lumber industry that, as with Da Costa's skills as a translator when he traveled with Champlain, no one was going to ask any questions. The rafters risked being kidnapped and sold back into slavery, whether free or not, but by traveling in a group there was less risk of that.

In the fall of 2009 Ken Burns aired his televised documentary about national parks on the Public Broadcasting Station (PBS). It was noted in the film, although not made an issue, that there were few African American visitors to national parks and not very many African American rangers. There was one, Shelton Johnson, a black ranger in Yosemite. He did programs on the Buffalo Soldiers, the handful of black soldiers in the 1800s who were allowed to join the U.S. military where their assignment was to kill Indians.

That same autumn, I had knee surgery. Workers' Compensation took so long to approve the surgery that I was forced to break my contract with the school in Thailand. I stayed in Michigan. I had some time and so I wrote to the regional head of the National Park Service in Omaha, Nebraska, and suggested that the Sleeping Bear Dunes National Lakeshore do programs on the African American pioneers who had lived in the area of the park. It took a while, but I finally received an answer.

Ernest Quintana, Director of the NPS Midwest Region, had been in touch with the local park administration and he wrote a letter which I have kept. In his letter Quintana stated that the NPS had decided that since the African American pioneers had made "no significant contributions" to the culture and history of the area around the Sleeping Bear Dunes that, unless such contributions "came to light," the park couldn't justify creating any programs about them.

When I returned to Leelanau County in 2013, following another tour in the Peace Corps, this time in Romania, I again wrote to the heads of the National Park Service in Omaha and Washington, D.C., and also to the Secretary of the Interior and reminded them, once again, that it would be nice if the Sleeping Bear Dunes National Lakeshore would include the African American pioneers in their annual pioneer festival.

By this time the National Park Service had as part of its five-year plan, the mission of including programs on African American history, wherever relevant in the nation, in their public presentations. Mike Reynolds had replaced Ernest Quintana in Omaha as director of the NPS Midwest Region. I sent him a copy of a Sleeping Bear Dunes National Lakeshore newspaper insert that advertised all the wonderful sights of the park and asked, "Where are the brown or black faces in your various photos?"

Reynolds wrote back and pointed out that, if I looked very carefully, I could see a small portion of the back of someone's lower leg, a person standing with their back to the camera at the NPS store in Glen Haven. Reynolds wanted me to know that this glimpse of the person's leg, possibly a brown leg, indicated that the leg had in fact belonged to a person with brown skin. I can't be sure looking at the photo if this was simply someone with a tan, or not, but of course take Reynolds' word for it. And, Reynolds implied, therefore the NPS was being inclusive. The dead-serious tone of this letter was a marvel. I kept the letter to remind myself of how hard it must be to be a bureaucrat.

One evening in the summer of 2013 I was invited to dinner in Glen Arbor to meet the young relative of Frederick Law Olmsted. This Olmsted relative and I talked about my father's design of his scenic drive and Olmsted's design of Central Park. We spoke of the importance of having public parks and access to nature for all people in a democracy, especially the poorest and most disenfranchised who would never on their own be able to buy a cabin in the woods or even take their children fishing.

We were amused by the coincidence of how our Stocking and Olmsted forebears had originally been from Hartford, Connecticut. We also talked about Olmsted's little-known journey through the south prior to the Civil War and his reporting from there for the *New-York Tribune* on the condition of slaves and southern life. In one article he wrote about a woman being hung for the murder of her child. Before being hung the woman confessed and said that her owner was the father of the child and the child had been treated so cruelly by her mistress that she had killed the child to save it further suffering. Olmsted's reporting was remarkable for his details and his unemotional style.

When I wrote to the various heads of the park asking them to do programs on the black pioneers, I included carefully researched articles I'd written on the African American pioneers in the area of the Sleeping Bear Dunes National Lakeshore. I had written informational articles about the Levi Johnson family and their homestead on Welch Road [above Glen Lake], the African American children in various schools, [including the schools at Aral on Otter Creek, on Voice Road near Empire, and in the Springdale School on Welch Road]. I included reprints of my articles from the *Traverse City Record-Eagle* and the *Glen Arbor Sun*.

I gave a lecture at the Empire Museum, a building across from NPS headquarters, in October 2013 on the history of black pioneers in the area. Still, to the best of my knowledge, as of 2016, the Sleeping Bear Dunes National Lakeshore has not recognized the historical presence of African American pioneers within their boundaries in any park informational programs, photo displays, or written material.

Yes, my father was a knee-jerk racist, as were many supposedly white people who were born in 1908 or before. But it's a little more complicated than that. He struggled to find ways to connect to other people, and the color of their skin was the least of it. He was, like Henry Thoreau or John Muir, a man who loved nature, and could relate to nature better than he could relate to anything else.

Like Thoreau and Muir, my father spent almost all his waking hours outside. I didn't go to school until third grade and went with him to the woods instead. What my father cared about was the necessity for all people everywhere to have access to nature. He thought access to nature was as vital as food, water, and shelter. He would have wanted access to nature for all people: children, old people, men and women of every kind of ethnic or racial background. If people could see and appreciate what they saw from the top of the dunes, the panoramic beauty of water, sky, and islands, maybe they would have that in common. He designed his scenic drive so that parents with infants, people in wheelchairs, and old people with walkers, could still see the dunes. He could miraculously connect to other human beings with his park; sadly, that was about the only way he could connect to them.

Nature to my father was a deep source of spiritual peace and renewal, like church is for some people. He would have felt that to deny any human being access to nature, or to discourage them in any way from having access to nature would be wrong. He would have felt that to make anyone for any reason feel less than welcome to visit and appreciate the beautiful spots in nature would be unethical. He understood the power of nature to heal and inspire, and based on his own relationship with nature, he understood access to it as a birthright. He knew that human beings are instinctively drawn to nature, and feel connected to it, at a deep and preconscious level. He knew that being outside can teach us about overcoming difficulty, about how to live. He knew that nature gives meaning to life because of the beauty and the mystery inherent in all aspects.

If there were programs on the African American pioneers in the Sleeping Bear Dunes National Lakeshore, as there are programs, many of them, on the white pioneers, that would show honor and respect to those black pioneers and to the children of African American visitors to the park. It would be a gesture of courtesy and welcome.

It's particularly important that children learn to love and take care of the land. This not only benefits the children, but it benefits the country as a whole. The more people there are who love the land the better for all of us. All people in this country need to be able to love this land, because then they will want to protect it. People love what they understand. People love what they take care of. We need all the young people in America, no matter what the color of their skin, to learn how to love the land by taking care of it, enjoying it as a playground, and experiencing it as a place of beauty and spiritual renewal. If that doesn't happen, we're all in trouble.

August is when the vast and varied Stocking family gathers at the brick house above Sleeping Bear Bay. These are the offspring of my father, Leelanau lumberman Pierce Stocking, the man for whom the Pierce Stocking Scenic Drive is named. The people who gather there on the hill every summer are also the offspring of my mother, the consummate English teacher. My mother's family, the Lee side, came in the late 1800s from Scotland. That's the tall, red-headed side of the family.

One August a few years ago, during "the gathering of the clan," as we have come to call it, I went with my Canadian niece, Nora, and her artist-father, Mitch, to Otter Creek on Lake Michigan. This is where the little town of Aral, a lumbering site with a general store and a school, was built in 1870. Aral, named for the Aral Mountains in Eastern Europe, faded quickly after the timber was all cut and today there are only memories of it.

Mitch's mother and my mother had been teachers together in the Traverse City Public Schools. It was through that connection that Mitch and my sister met. Although the marriage didn't last, Nora's father is still a member of the family. Mitch is gay and he's out. He's also a good guy, has a wonderful art gallery in the Bay Area in California, is a talented artist, an excellent teacher, and is great company.

Mitch and I are the same age. We both grew up in northern Michigan and graduated from the University of Michigan. In the years we have known each other, Michigan's Leelanau Peninsula has changed. Chef Mario Batali, in *Esquire* in 2009, described Leelanau County as one of the world's best places to live. Thanks to filmmaker Michael Moore, nearby Traverse City now has a summer Film Festival and a winter Comedy Festival. John and Bonnie Raines, longtime summer residents on the Leelanau Peninsula, announced in 2015 that they had stolen papers from an FBI office in Pennsylvania in the 1970s; they were compared to Edward Snowden by *Philadelphia Magazine*. During his sabbatical year from Temple University when he was young, John Raines drove the school bus for the Glen Lake Community School where my children attended. Where Mitch and I grew up, is no longer a rural backwater.

This particular day at the beach, Nora's father astonished us all by revealing that his brother, a very successful businessman who had recently become fascinated by genealogy, had discovered that a male ancestor on their mother's side was part black. Enoch "Knuck" Harris had been listed as "mulatto" on the first property transaction in Michigan, and was recorded as "white" on the next one.

Harris, born in Virginia in 1784, had been educated in a Quaker area of Pennsylvania and had come into Ohio as a young man with five thousand dollars, an extraordinary sum at that time. According to an article published in 2012 in the *Ohio Genealogical Society Quarterly*, there were hinted connections to James Madison and Benjamin Franklin. Whose child was he? How did he come into all that money? No one knows. He was mulatto, illegitimate, rich, educated, and had secret origins. He was Nora's great-great-great-grandfather.

You have to picture my niece's family. A teacher married to an artist, with two beautiful daughters and living in an elegant, oak-paneled home in a Canadian university town, this family looks like the people in a Jane Austen novel. Due to their Canadian accent, they sort of talk like that, too. They're not just seemingly white, but seemingly upper crust.

Tall, dark-haired, with blue eyes and fair skin, Nora looks like a young Sigourney Weaver. She has an hourglass figure and a raucous sense of humor. Her daughters are as beautiful as she is, only much taller with legs that never stop. Nora's husband, Cyrus, looks like a six-foot-six, gray-eyed, dark-haired Brad Pitt. My niece's father, Mitch, the one with distant and mysterious black ancestors on his mother's side of the family, looks like George Clooney.

When I had to do a show-and-tell about my family during language class while serving in the Peace Corps in Romania, this branch of the family, being the last people I'd seen before I'd gone abroad, were the only people for whom I had photos. One of my fellow volunteers said, "These people all look like movie stars." It's true, they do.

The rest of the Stockings do not. We are horsey-looking, with long necks and receding chins and veins that stick out (in the men) and a tendency to arthritis in old age (in the women). We are homely in that English-y way, that is a mark of distinction in its own right, but will never get us romantic leading-lady or leading-man roles on stage, at least not in America, where the preference in good looks is for smaller noses and more regular features.

Sometime after Mitch's astonishing revelation at the beach, I decided to get a DNA test. I wanted to be black or Native American, even just a little. I didn't like thinking of the bad things, things like slavery and genocide, that had been done by the group whose skin color I shared. Skin color is just one of hundreds of characteristics. I knew that. Maybe somewhere in the DNA was something that would, if not exonerate me, at least give me some wiggle room. But, no, the results were that I was mostly Scandinavian with a touch of Eastern European.

I know those Viking raiders got around, so lots of people might be part-Scandinavian. What I still can't figure out is how the spawn of Viking raiders recognized each other, every time, on the continent of North America over a four-hundred-year time span. I'm not sure I could tell the difference between a Scotsman, an Irishman, an Englishman, or a Dane; and maybe there isn't any. My Canadian niece says she's heard a person needs to not just do a cheek swab for the free test, but use real blood and pay real money to get accurate DNA results. If the first DNA test results I'd received were accurate, it would seem to mean that my father's dark skin was probably the result of his spending so much time outside; nothing more and nothing less.

Anthropologists tell us that fifty to sixty thousand years ago we were all black and very likely living on the shores of Lake Victoria in East Africa or someplace like that. We got whiter and whiter as we migrated north.

Red-haired, blue-eyed people, like a lot of my relatives, are a recent mutation, perhaps one that helped us process vitamin D from the sun in places where there isn't much sun. In these times, with the sun getting hotter, it's good for people with no melanin at all in their skin to marry people who have it. That means our survival instincts are intact.

One morning in late fall this past year, on a day that was particularly warm and sunny, I took my puppy, Happy, down to Otter Creek in the Sleeping Bear Dunes National Lakeshore. There was no one there that day where Aral used to be. There was nothing but the vast, unruffled blue waters of Lake Michigan, and my dog playing in the water lapping the shore.

Happy is a beautiful creature. She's cheerful and social, like a Golden Retriever. She does the herding dog's zig-zag running, like a Collie. And she has luxuriant, soft fur, like a Samoyed. My grandchildren, some of whom are of mixed race, just like Happy, love her. They had played with her at Otter Creek back in August when the whole family gathered for a grand family wedding.

The sound of water lapping the shore is soothing. It's timeless. It makes me feel connected to all the water encircling the earth, and to the mystery of that connection. Do dogs know that this is wonderful? I think they do. Or maybe I like to think that they do. Such joy in the splashing. It's contagious.

My mind goes back to the previous summer's wedding on my mother's hill above Sleeping Bear Bay. How young the young people were. The children and grandchildren running here there and everywhere. Another beautiful niece, and her intended. The boughs of evergreens and flowers making an arch through which one could see the lake.

The familiar lines from *Corinthians* woven into their vows: "Love is patient, love is kind. It does not envy, it does not boast, it is not proud. It does not dishonor others, it is not self-seeking, it is not easily angered, it keeps no record of wrongs. Love does not delight in evil but rejoices with the truth. It always protects, always trusts, always hopes, always perseveres."

The people at the August wedding, just like the people one now sees at weddings all over America, were from every part of the globe. They were of every shape, size, age, sexual preference, gender, and color. We looked like the Coca Cola ad, "I'd like to teach the world to sing..." and why not? If Coca Cola can be available to everyone everywhere, why can't everyone everywhere come here and be accepted? It makes perfect sense, if you think about it.

Robert Houdek, a Just Man

He died the week before Good Friday, a time when Northern Michigan always seems deserted: schools closed, restaurants empty, no cars on the roads, everyone away. That day toward the end of March, when I heard he'd died, the whole county seemed suddenly too large, echoing. A good man was gone.

Robert Houdek, at fifty-three, was still young. Until the end, when his illness caused pain, he was a naturally joyful man. Before I went into the Peace Corps in 2006, Bob was still helping me with the odd jobs a farmer could do, keeping a lawn mower going, and cutting dead trees. Sometimes his wife Vicki and sons Bradley and Joseph, would come, too, the world's sweetest family, so they could be together and make the work go faster. I often thought of them while I was in Thailand.

Bob never wanted to take money for helping, and he didn't like to cut down a healthy tree. One year I had a big pine infested with insects. "I can hear them in there, *chewing*," he said, holding his clenched hands like mouths next to his own mouth, making teeth of the fingers and imitating their sound, "Swesh, swesh." He was a man wholly without guile: honest, open-hearted, with that intuitive intelligence of people who are in tune with nature. He wanted to help people not because he needed money, or even because he had time, but because he was kind. Bob loved his family and often spoke of them. Once he planned a rare camping trip with them and was as excited as a kid, talking about where they would go and how they would keep their food cold.

The people in the church sit quietly. We are not separate beings, we are different strands of the same being. Father Janowski announces that the funeral procession is taking longer because they are carrying Bob up past his farm where he grew his delicious organic acorn squash and pumpkins. The original Houdeks came from Czechoslovakia to the Leelanau Peninsula in 1875. I picture the ranging hills, the ice still in North Lake Leelanau, the soft spring sky and the clouds, the sunlight and shadow. It's Holy Week, unseasonably warm, the kind of day every breeze carries the breath of the lake.

Now they have arrived, beautiful Vicki and her two hand-some sons, and the whole extended Houdek family, filling several pews. Now we are singing a hymn. Now Joseph Houdek is reading from *The Book of Wisdom*, "But the just man, though he die early, shall be at rest. Understanding is the hoary crown for men, and an unsullied life, the attainment of old age. He who pleased God was loved. "

Leaving the church, as happens among those who have suf-fered a loss together, we want to look after and protect each other, because we felt that he, in his own inimitable way, had always looked after and protected us. He was always kind and we want to be, too. Now he is more present than ever.

EUROPE

Something Else Week

It had crossed my mind I might run into difficulty when I'd suggested my students host an open house for their parents during the aptly named "Something Else Week" that was coming up in April at my Romanian school. My students had liked the idea.

The Peace Corps had told us everything was supposed to be initiated from the grass roots and so by mutual agreement my beautiful Romanian partner-teacher had stood up at the conference in the fancy hotel in Sinaia and suggested the idea. She was a credible person with flawless English. She was tall and pale and well-dressed. She even looked English. The head of the Peace Corps education program came up to me afterwards and told me what a wonderful concept my counterpart had presented.

Romania, east of the Danube, is a back-of-beyond kind of place, with a reputation exactly like that of America's Wild West, although since it's in relationship to the rest of Europe, it would have to be the Wild East.

Eighteen hundred years ago the Roman conquerors were already mostly done with Craiova, the industrial Romanian city to which I'd been assigned, and had moved on to Britain. Remnants of Emperor Trajan's arch bridge are still visible in the Danube near Craiova. This was the world's longest and finest bridge at the time and it would remain so for a thousand years. It had been designed by the Greek architect Apollodorus from Damascus. The bridge was destroyed when the Romans left. They didn't want the barbarians following them home. Hadrian, an emperor who came after Trajan, found Appolodorus annoying for some reason and had him executed.

I mention this because it's an indication of the harshness of life even for the rich and famous. Random killings were not confined to the battlefields.

War was pretty much a constant in the area around the Carpathian Mountains, an area now known as Romania, starting in about 2,000 B.C. when horses were first domesticated. The first warring tribes on horseback came sweeping out of the east, terrifying the local people. Initially the farmers had thought the horses and men had been, literally, horse-men: one body, like the mythic centaurs. Soon they would figure it out and obtain their own horses.

Romania has had one of the most turbulent histories of all of Europe. Wedged between the Turks and Mongols in the east, and the Slavs and Huns in the west, it was constantly overrun. The Romans were there taking the gold out of the country for almost two centuries. Romania only broke free of the Ottoman Empire in 1877. The Hapsburgs took over, then the Russians. One of the Romanians I met on the train said he'd lived in the same place all his life and it'd been three different countries with three different languages. During World War II, Romania, which only a few years earlier had been a group of principalities just beginning to think about becoming a country, was first on the side of the Nazis, then the Allies. When Stalin, Churchhill and Roosevelt redrew the boundaries yet again, Romania wasn't invited to the table.

King Michael, the tail end of royalty in Romania after WWII, a great-great grandson of Queen Victoria and cousin to England's Queen Elizabeth II, was thirty-four when the country was given by the Allies to the Soviets after the Second World War. He was at a New Year's party in Sinaia at the time. There's a photo of him driving down the steps in Sinaia, taking the shortest route to get him back to Bucharest to one of his other castles. Instantly, this quick-thinking scion of Romanian royalty loaded up several train cars with as much of the country's artwork and gold as he could get his hands on and, of course, his fancy automobiles, and left.

King Michael liked cars and liked to drive them fast and as a rambunctious teen had heedlessly struck and killed an innocent person on a bicycle, a crime for which he was never prosecuted. Before and after he married he openly visited prostitutes in the streets of Bucharest, calling them into his car while his chauffeur waited. These things were well known because they were done publicly. Media accounts, now online with many sources, were repressed in Romania at the time. The strangest thing about King Michael wasn't his nefarious escapades, blatant greed, or egregious self-dealing, since these were fairly typical of a spoiled royal, but that he is revered by many in Romania to this day. Sitting next to a math professor at a fancy dinner in the home of a former boyar, or nobleman, I was amazed to hear this educated, charming, well-to-do Romanian bemoaning the loss of this fatuous former king. Staring into my bowl of *ciorbă*, the sour soup for which Romanian cooking is justly esteemed, I wondered silently to myself if the professor and I had read the same history books.

Sometimes out the window of the train from Sinaia back to Craiova I'll see a shepherd with his sheep, a few goats and a herding dog. I ask the woman across from me why there are usually a few goats with the sheep and she says, "Goats are smarter than sheep. You can get them to go where you want and then the sheep will follow."

The Carpathian Mountains gradually transition to the plains. There's no part of the Romanian countryside that isn't beautiful and the things the people make are beautiful, too. The clay urns and handmade rakes Romanian people use, the embroidered shirts and sheepskin capes the shepherds wear are lovely, and they're the same as they have been for thousands of years. The people are close to each other and close to the land. Borders changed and languages changed, but life in the fields stayed much the same.

The hay meadows in the foothills of the Carpathians are often still mowed by hand. The fields have fifty kinds of indigenous grasses, according to a 2013 article in the *National Geographic*, varieties that no longer exist on America's prairies and scarcely anywhere else because of chemical fertilizers and pesticides, and the people who work the land can name them all.

Forty-thousand-year-old human remains, the oldest in Europe, according to *Reuters* in 2015, have been discovered in a cave in Romania. The Romanian religious scholar Mircea Eliade, a professor for many years at the University of Chicago, has written about the funeral food, *colivă*, still used in Romania and made from an ancient sacred grain that goes back to a time before history in the fertile plains of the Danube. Eliade believed the sacred in human existence was eternal and universal. He thought western civilization missed something with its insistent focus on Greek mythology and the Bible. I've eaten *colivă*. It tastes a bit like barley and it's gray, the color of cremains.

The Danube wends her way from a small spring in the Black Forest eastward and south across eighteen hundred miles of Europe, about a third of that along the southern border of Romania. It flows south to *Constanța*. The river is gray-blue, viscous, like engine oil. It's wide and peaceful. When there's no wind the slow-moving waters reflect the clouds. I can imagine being on a barge out in the river, staring at the stars in the night sky, listening to a dog bark somewhere in the distance, thinking some day I'll learn the constellations.

The majestic Danube, like rivers all over the world, like all the rivers in America, is lined with factories. The factories dump their waste into the rivers. In 2000 a retaining wall in a gold mine broke in Baia Mare in northern Romania, according to the BBC and many other news sources, and flooded the Someș River and eventually the Danube, with cyanide. Thousands of fish died. The Danube Delta, home to more migrating birds than anywhere on earth, is visited by birders from all over the world. The birds, like the fish they eat, are increasingly at risk from the toxins in the river.

The Danube Delta, "where the Danube flows into the Black Sea," the poet Ovid wrote in A.D. 8 (*Ovid's Poetry of Exile*, David R. Slavitt translation, Johns Hopkins University Press), is where Caesar Augustus had exiled him to Tomis, a Roman military outpost. Tomis, a Greek name left over from when the Greeks rather than the Romans were a dominant power, is now called Constanţa. Clearly Ovid said or did something that displeased Caesar but we never learn what. From his poor hut in Tomis, Ovid writes to his wife, telling her how he can hear the sounds of fighting from his window where "around me cruel Sauromatians vie with Bessi and Getae."

In this place, Ovid writes, "The farmer plows in armor, if he plows at all, looking from left to right over his shoulder" for marauders. Ovid writes that the local tribes practiced human sacrifice, "which makes some kind of sense, since meat is scarce." From his prison hovel he says he can see poor captives, "women mostly," those "the raiders' whims have chosen as slaves" being led away "into exile, bound, weeping, gazing behind as they're dragged out to the empty steppes for a last burning glimpse of their lives' ruin."

Ovid instructs his young third wife to fine-tune the altars back home in order to persuade the gods, Venus and Jupiter and all the rest, any god at all, to intercede on his behalf. But "Augustus Caesar," he admits, is "the ultimate deity." He tells his wife to "go from house to house, let them know how I suffer," to try to find a time to talk to Caesar's wife, but to "pick a lucky day" and "go to a temple first to kindle a fire on some holy altar" which is not much, "but it's all we have."

Eight years before Ovid's exile, Christ was killed by Pontius Pilate. Pilate, charged with keeping order, was probably acting in accordance with what he thought were the wishes of the rulers back in Rome where Tiberius Ceasar was the leader. It was two thousand and some years ago, early days in the realm of communications and media. The kinds of ideas and events that inspire changes in the way people see the world took hundreds of years to transpire when Ovid was alive. Christianity wouldn't cross the Mediterranean, replace the Roman gods and set up shop in the Papacy for several more centuries. Still, something must have been in the air in Tomis when Ovid was there. The old gods, Nemesis and Minerva, as Ovid uses their names, are almost metaphors, not quite real any more. The candles on the home altar which he tells his wife to keep lit day and night are more about ritual and reassurance than an actual solution.

Christianity won't arrive on the shores of the Black Sea for almost another three hundred years, not until the reign of Constantine the Great. Constantine, the warrior who would conquer Byzantium (now Istanbul) and have it named after him, was born in eastern Europe in 272 A.D., the son of a Roman general and a camp follower named Helena. The illegitimate Constantine will set Christianity in motion. Constantine's military father will flee from the uncivilized area east of the Danube as soon as he can, returning to Rome and marrying a noble woman of his own class. His brilliant and lucky son will stay behind with his mother, the intrepid Helena. Constantine will survive fierce battles and treacherous internecine politics, and ultimately go on to rule the world as Constantine the Great.

Constantine would rule first as a non-Christian and then, after his mother Helena's conversion in Palestine and after he himself reportedly sees a life-changing vision of Jesus during a battle, as a Christian. He will make Byzantium on the Bosporus "the Rome of the East" and elevate the Christians. But Constantine, who grew up in a time when Christians were routinely tortured and executed, was in a transitional period and he knew it. He cleverly covered all bets, building a temple to Aphrodite one minute and a church for Christ in another.

I'm jolted from my daydreaming by a woman who's eating a raw garlic condiment in the seat next to me. The smell of the raw garlic and the smell of the overflowing toilets are mingling, making my eyes water. She must have boarded at the last station and I hadn't noticed her. She is eating chopped garlic with club soda from a small dish, spooning it onto fresh bread. She's a beautiful woman. Most Romanians are naturally good-looking. I think it's because they eat right. No Twinkies or Kool-Aid here. Like the Thai, they prefer real food, and like the Thai, they have glowing good health. Their eyes are clear. Their skin has good color. Their bones look strong. Their posture is good. As far as I'm concerned, after a moment's thought, my seatmate can eat all the raw garlic she wants.

I smile and say, "*Buna*," or hello.

"*Salut*," she says. This is another word for hello. *Buna* and *salut* are used interchangeably. People are friendly on the trains. I had five years of Latin in high school and this has made my language acquisition easier here. The Romanian language has been called "living Latin" because it's so close to the ancient kind used by Caesar. I'm not good at it because I don't make time to study, but I can usually understand it and read it. If you ever learn a language, it will come back eventually.

I'm worried about the Open House idea that I have now foolishly become yoked to, but only slightly worried. I think it's going to be alright since the *Altfel* Week, literally "Something Else" Week, is totally new for everyone, being something the Romanian Ministry of Education has just invented. The Ministry is requiring everyone to submit ideas. My Romanian teacher-partner, having always aspired to be more professionally connected to the Ministry of Education, had been enthusiastic. It will look great on paper and it will have her name on it.

All the Ministry expects is that educators "do something different" so we have wide latitude. In Sinaia the Peace Corps had praised my Romanian counterpart for having had such a wonderful idea and she had stood and beamed and bowed before the entire gathering. Everything had been perfect in Sinaia. This is the mountain resort town called "the pearl of the Carpathians" with its beautiful old train station, extensive parks, ancient monastery, and king's castle. Sanaia is a fairytale village in a snow-globe.

Once back in my school in Craiova, however, even though I talk up the idea every chance I get, it's pretty clear that my Romanian language skills aren't up to the challenge of selling people on the prospect of "putting on a show" for parents. My director is in Bucharest. She will be there, except for rare visits to the school, until school gets out in June. Her father is in a Bucharest hospital. In Romania the custom is for family members to oversee the treatment of their loved ones. They need to provide clean linens and food. Constant gratuities to all the nurses and doctors are *de rigueur*.

The Romanian teacher assigned to me by the Peace Corps seems to have no recollection of what she'd said in Sinaia. I corner her in the crowded teacher's lounge one day and ask loudly, so everyone can hear, "What about the *Altfel* Week Open House for the Ministry of Education?" She acts like she can't understand. She gets up from her chair and says she must leave immediately for the train station. She's going to an important meeting with the Ministry in Bucharest.

The Russian communists have been gone from Romania since 1989, but the bureaucracies they established are still the places with which people want to be associated. The Ministry of Education people who visit our school drive nice cars, wear nice clothes, and eat in nice restaurants. They seem to have money and they seem to be free to come and go as they please. They seem to spend a lot of time at meetings in the country's capital, Bucharest. Bucharest is clearly where most sensible people would like to be, not in a run-down public school in a big, dirty, polluted, industrial city like Craiova.

Craiova, a city of three hundred thousand has seen better days. Its parks and town center, museums and once-fine mansions, suggest a time of leisure and refinement. It was in Craiova that the sculptor Brâncuşi (pronounced Bran-koosh), world famous for *The Kiss* and *Prometheus* and many other sculptures, was discovered in about 1890 when he was an illiterate peasant boy working as a servant. One day he made a violin out of scrap from the refuse piles in the alley, according to local lore, and a wealthy boyar, a nobleman, saw his talent and sent him to art school.

The Russians came in after the end of World War II and in 1948 set up an education system that was based on rote learning and repetition, but at least there was an education system: rote learning is better than none. An estimated four and a half million illiterate peasant children were brought in from the fields, along with their families. Often whole villages were relocated to cities. The parents were put to work in factories and the children were sent to school.

The Romanian dogs followed the farmers into the cities, so I was told, and that's why there were so many stray dogs everywhere. Romanians like dogs and are opposed to euthanizing them. A scruffy sheepdog in Bucharest had adopted the Peace Corps office and was so sweet and smart that he was given food and a doghouse outside the gate. A noble German shepherd took on the job of protecting the peasant museum and presumably he, too, was given food and shelter.

Under the Russians the teachers had to be in their classrooms when assigned, or they didn't get paid. They had an inspector who came around and checked on them. They still have such an inspector from the Ministry of Education. The teachers know when she's coming, they prepare a class for her benefit, get their excellent rating and the next day and the next and the next, do little or nothing, as usual, if they show up at all.

Now in the Romanian schools, since the Americans and their money and ideas have come into the country, there's more of a *laissez-faire* system. The teachers don't have much sense of anything other than that the rigid authoritarian system they had known under the Russians is now gone. They see this new way of doing things as an excuse to go easy on their students, and, of course, themselves. During my first visit to my school, I had seen the halls filled with broken furniture. The students had broken all this furniture, I later learned. Left alone in their classrooms for endless time, and having nothing better to do, they destroy things.

One can sense the American thinking behind "Something Else Week" as if someone had said, "Do something else for a change! Be creative!" But it's hard to be creative. Even if you happen to be a naturally creative person, if ordered to be creative, the mind goes blank. Most of the teachers, like most of the students, seem to see *Altfel* Week as a reason to leave early for vacation. If they actually planned to stay through the week, their idea of something creative was a field trip to a resort in the mountains.

The director of my Craiova school is a jolly woman, a chain smoker, reputedly good at math. Both her father, now almost eighty and seriously ill, and mother, who died a couple of years earlier, had been math professors under the Russians.

Smoking is not allowed on school grounds, but it's allowed in my director's office. She says she's under so much stress, she cannot quit. She's good with computers and is always online. In the fall when I saw more of her, she shopped online and several times a week dresses and shoes were delivered to her office. "It lifts so much my spirits," she explained to me as she received a package one afternoon when I was in her office, "and I need that," adding, "because my father is sick." Perhaps the clothes weren't delivered to her apartment because she didn't want her father, who lived with her, to see how many sets of new clothes she was buying.

"You are my friend," she said every time she saw me. This was nonsense. And I'm sure she knew that it was nonsense, and also knew that I knew that it was nonsense. Even in Romania you don't assign your "friend" five hundred students with no teaching materials.

I'd asked people on the trains and in the busses if five hundred students was a normal teaching load, and they'd all said, to a person, that it wasn't. My director could ask the wealthy parents of my students for funds for materials, and she probably already has, but those funds, presumably somewhere in her purview, were obviously never going to be used to help the students in my classroom.

Whenever my director said, '*You're my friend*,' I always flashed the "peace" sign in response, holding up two fingers, the classic rabbit ears. I couldn't bring myself to verbally say to her that she was my friend, too. What would that mean, after all? That I accept this fiction as truth? That anyone who takes advantage of me is my friend?

At the start of school, I'd asked her repeatedly about teaching materials and she'd effectively ignored me. However, one day I came into my classroom and there was a man installing a giant TV on a shelf in one corner. My director said one of the parents had given her the TV. It was never hooked up. After several weeks I went to her and asked to have it removed. It was a small room and I kept bumping my head on the TV shelf.

My director had an assistant, another teacher who also smoked and they were often together in my director's office since it was the one place in the school where smoking was allowed. After the TV was removed from my room, her assistant, also an English teacher, brought me a tattered copy of George Elliot's *The Mill on the Floss* and said I could use it to teach English. It was her book from university, she said, but I could keep it. I found these gestures, with the TV and the book, touching but also mystifying.

My director looked like the troll doll, minus the rubber serpents writhing around the neck, someone had given me years before at a gathering of evangelicals in San Salvador. She dyed her short hair white-blonde and shaped it into peaks in the newest fashion. Her taste in clothing tended toward clingy, skimpy gold lamé polyester tops, short skirts, snake-pattern tights and red, faux-leather go-go boots, as if she were thirty years younger and many pounds lighter. She was a giant woman, large of frame and easily three hundred pounds. Enormous and, I think, probably very strong.

She's an excellent cook. During my first week at the school she made me stuffed cabbage rolls that were the best I've ever eaten: simple, subtle, and delicious.

Whenever I go into her office, she tells me about her boyfriend. She likes to talk about him. He sleeps in his barn with his animals. She shows me his photo every time I see her. He's handsome, in the Romanian way, with great bones like the Romanian sculptor, Brâncuşi. She tells me that sometimes the two of them will get into her new, red car and drive somewhere for days, on a whim, to relax together. "I need that," she says. "And he understands me so well."

I can't help but like some things about my director. She loves life. It's an attractive quality. One day she invites me into her office to watch a *Ted Talk* on her computer monitor. Sir Ken Robinson is talking about creativity and education. I have already viewed it, but out of politeness don't tell her. When Robinson tells the story of the little girl drawing a picture of God and her teacher says, "But no one knows what God looks like," and the little girl answers, not lifting her head from her paper, "They will in a minute," my director laughs so uproariously and so genuinely the sound stays with me for days, like glorious sunshine.

One day in February, on a day she's not in Bucharest, I go into my director's office and ask her if there's any way we can fix up the small, mostly empty back shed behind the school for the *Altfel* Week Open house. She offers me chocolates from one of the many big boxes of chocolates in her office, as she always does. I have never before or since seen so much chocolate;

and it is good chocolate, really good. The parents send these gifts. This is considered one of the best schools in Craiova and I've been told there's a long waiting list.

My director says she's in the midst of an interview with prospective parents when I approach her; she excuses herself to take them on a tour of the school. She has to deal with me, but she doesn't want to. This has happened before. It's a routine.

When she leaves I see a formal gift bag on her desk. It's a large, decorative bag and the open side is facing me so I can see that inside there's a toy truck, and a lot of money. The money is held together with grimy rubber bands. She must have forgotten it, in her haste to escape from my importuning her, and didn't put it away before she left. Bribes in Romania are never mentioned. The money simply appears, often along with an ordinary gift, and, if not spurned, then the deal is done.

I leave my chair near her desk and go sit at the big conference table on the other side of the room near the window and the coffee pot. I get a cup of coffee so it will look like I have moved my seat to get coffee.

Romanians love their families. They love their friends. But I'm an American, an interloper, like the Mongols, the Tartars, the Greeks, the Turks, the Romans, the Austrians, the Slavs, and the Russians, in the country before us.

There's a giant American aluminum fabricating plant near Cluj. There's a Ford factory on the outskirts of Craiova. All the Romanians I meet around town, the ones who help me with my computer, or who help me make photocopies, or the man who put a table together for me, the lady who mends my clothes in her street-side shop, the man who repairs my shoes in a little room in my apartment building, are intelligent and capable.

Although the people at my school never show any interest in my work with the students, the people at the computer and copy shops have been intrigued and supportive. They often help me free of charge. I asked the owner of the computer and photocopying store I went to most often, one on a side street in the center of town, why he wouldn't let me pay him. He said, "We don't charge unless we sell a piece of equipment." But, I had countered, they had helped me endlessly with computer problems. He said he had looked up the Peace Corps on Google and knew I wasn't getting paid. He said, "You're helping our children. We see how hard you're working." His child didn't go to my school, so he was helping me just because, and they were all amazing with computers. I'm guessing that those Romanians hired by foreign companies are excellent workers.

The American and other foreign capitalists came in to fill the vacuum when the Russians left. They offer low wages, but it's so much more than the Russians paid, that Romanians are thrilled to get the jobs. "They come, they go. We stay," is what the Romanians say about the successive waves of foreigners.

My first inclinations about this beautiful land with its over-lapping, sometimes peaceful and sometimes warring, ethnic groups came into my life back in Grand Rapids, Michigan in the winter of 1992 when I was conducting an 8 A.M. writing workshop in a large, city high school. In a group of twenty-five students all sitting around a long table, I asked them to do some free writing for five minutes as a warm-up, starting at the beginning of a day or a journey and just writing "and then, and then" and so on as fast as they could, without thinking. It could be about their journey to school that morning or a vacation they took with their families. It could be almost anything. They would then read these out loud. As long as they were writing, that was all that mattered. No judgments would be passed. It was my way to get them to put the pencil on the paper and learn to keep it moving.

The students wrote, as they always do, some complaining that they couldn't think of anything and finding it slow going and others rapidly transcribing as if from a personal muse. Finally everyone had something to read. One after the other, as is always done, they read their work. The writing was more or less mundane, as it usually is, but people were becoming comfortable in the group, which was the point.

Midway down the line, when her turn came, a shy, dark-haired girl began to read from her paper, keeping her head down. We listened, as we had to the first dozen people, prepared to be bored and trying not to show it, polite. But slowly, the group's reaction shifted as the girl's descriptions of mountain trails, running from killers, campfires in the mouths of caves, the sun rising, the sharing of roasted meat, the small cousin who broke his leg and had to be carried, the leeks and potatoes they found when they were starving, the moon on a cold night, take us right out of that chalk-odor classroom with its fluorescent lights and into the world she was creating for us. When she was done, we were transformed, speechless. She had changed us.

"You've done something remarkable," I told her when I found my voice. "Do you see how we are all enthralled?" Then I asked her how she had been able to write like that. I had come into the room knowing the students were Midwestern, sheltered, barely awake, literally and figuratively. When she finally raised her head, we saw that she was beautiful. Who was this child?

Before we knew it, she had opened her backpack and spread photos out on the table. "I carry them with me," she said. "It's all I have of my family."

Everyone had been lost to her, she said, communication cut off, perhaps they were dead, she didn't know, but she had survived and had been sent to live with a family in Grand Rapids, Michigan. That was the first I knew of the people in the Balkans. They had all been getting along fine, she said, all the different ethnic groups, until they weren't. And then neighbor was killing neighbor.

Elie Weisel, the author of *Night*, a book about his time in a Nazi concentration camp, had described something similar in his village in Romania. First everything was peaceful and the Jewish people were part of the community. Then, almost overnight, certainly within a few months, everything changed.

Albert Einstein fell in love with a woman from east of the Danube. He badly wanted to marry her, but his parents objected because the young woman was from a famously uncivilized part of the world. This woman, Mileva Marić, was a student with him in Switzerland, a brilliant mathematician who helped him do the equations for his theory of relativity. They loved to study together and drink coffee together and make love together. "Love is not a sin," Mileva wrote in one of her notebooks. She returned to her home in the Balkans, gave birth and left their infant daughter. In an eight hundred and eighty-two page biography of Albert Einstein, biographer Albrecht Fölsing writes on page one hundred and fourteen, "The fate of Albert Einstein's first child is totally unknown." After the love letters between Albert Einstein and Mileva Marić were published in 2000, there have been many books about this mystery and many theories about what happened to this first child. Possibly there existed another Einstein, with a different name and different gender but a similarly unusual mind, out there in the world. Although the couple eventually married and had two sons, the marriage never seemed to recover from the breach of trust and grief caused by the abandonment of that first child.

My director returns from taking parents on a tour of the school. She says she has forgotten why I'm there. I'd expected this. With my back turned, I hear her quietly slide the bag of money into a desk drawer, as if it contains something alive, a baby rabbit or a sleeping viper. Knowing this moment would come, I had already occupied myself with straightening up around the coffee pot, facing away from her.

When I turn back around and remind her of why I'm there, she says there's no money in the school budget to fix up the back shed for the *Altfel* Week Open House. The janitors are much too busy. It would require hiring extra help. Actually the janitors are not busy at all. I was cleaning my own classroom until I started paying one of them to do it. But you can't blame them. They get paid even less than the teachers. They are poor peasants, struggling to survive on so little it defies imagination as to how they do it.

I don't expect any help from the Romanian education staff in the Peace Corps office in Bucharest in terms of navigating the politics of my school. The United States is scheduled to close down the Peace Corps in Romania in a year, in the summer of 2013. The capable forty-year-old Romanian woman in charge of Peace Corps education programs in Bucharest is on maternity leave. She'll return to her post before the United States pulls out, but unfortunately not soon enough to help with my situation.

Two previous Peace Corps volunteers had bailed on this site, one after the school had been in session two months and one before school ever started, I'd learned after I'd been there a few months. The first, like me, didn't know she'd be teaching five hundred students. The second figured it out during the site visit and left the Peace Corps immediately, reportedly for a job in Japan.

Initially the Peace Corps had sent me to a beautiful, remote village in the northern mountains. During my site visit back in June the mountains had been covered with wild flowers. A gorgeous stream cascaded through the rocky landscape. The Greek Orthodox Church there was painted in glorious detail. But I'd been housed in the skeleton of a hotel, abandoned in 2008 when it was still under construction, all wrapped in scaffolding. Tattered pieces of dirty, transparent plastic blew from the ramparts, making a sad, ragged sound. In some places there were unfinished stairs and missing walls. I was all alone there. The only part of the hotel finished before the 2008 crash had been the bar. Loud and drunken parties below my room at the bottom of the stairs didn't end until the wee hours of the

morning. The food at the bar was badly made and outrageous-
ly expensive. The nearest town was two hours away by bus. The
middle-aged woman who owned the bar came through from
time to time. I was told she lived in a walled compound somewhere nearby. She was very pretty and sexy until she opened
her mouth. She had black teeth.

My Romanian host teacher at this mountain site, the only
daughter of a wealthy lumberman, had assigned me all of her
classes. The school was picturesque, unpainted inside and out,
heated with beautiful porcelain wood stoves, and there was a
yard full of flowers. The children were lovely as they always are,
but my host teacher had me walk the two miles to the school
along a lonely mountain road traversed by large logging trucks,
even though she drove the same road in her car.

When I returned to the Peace Corps training session back
in Târgoviște, I discussed the visit to the proposed permanent
placement with some volunteers who were finishing up their
service and were about to leave the country. They had been
brought in specially to train the new group. I told them what
a weird place I'd thought it was. They told me that a young
volunteer from their group, with the same host teacher, had
begged to be removed from that site, had become dangerously
depressed, and was ultimately medically evacuated to a hospital
back in the United States. Since I was a veteran of a previous
Peace Corps tour in Thailand, we speculated that the director
in Bucharest, new to her post and inexperienced, had perhaps
imagined that she could assign me to this dicey site, off-hand-
edly called the suicide site by one of the Peace Corps volunteers
from that earlier group, and thereby establish the fact that the
site was perfectly fine but that the previous volunteer had not
been up to the challenge. When I came back with a negative report, having known none of the back story, I was suddenly not
popular with this young Peace Corps Country Director. She
smiled, but like Brutus. And for my part, I was starting to question everything seen and unseen in the Peace Corps.

In the Peace Corps office in Bucharest, there were no water filters like those they'd insisted we install in our Communist-era apartments which, rumor had it, were plumbed with lead pipes. The water in my apartment building in Craiova came out different colors on different days. Sometimes the water would be shut off for a week. Sometimes the water had a sulfur smell. Sometimes it smelled like sewage. Other times like moth balls. The Peace Corps office could have attached water filters to their faucets, too, just as easily as we did, in fact more easily, and saved the American taxpayers some money. Instead they had two, big, expensive water coolers, the kind we were told not to buy because they would be beyond the means of a volunteer trying to make ends meet on the meager Peace Corps stipend.

When two Peace Corps staffers, the doctor and the safety and security person, had come for their official site visit to check out my apartment, I had, in the usual gesture of Romanian hospitality, offered them each a glass of water from the tap to which the prescribed Peace Corps water filter was affixed. In unison, with the smoothness of a well-rehearsed duet, they had hoisted their Peace Corps issue water bottles and said they had brought their own. It was at that moment that I decided to take the water filter back to Michigan to see if it was adequate. Could I trust my government? Amidst all the beautiful snow-white clouds of high-sounding rhetoric about our noble and good America in the Peace Corps literature, what about the black-ops site rumored to be where the United States has conducted torture at a place near the Otopeni Airport outside of Bucharest?

I feel like I'm trying to keep some kind of moral center and sense of reality, meanwhile trying to function inside overlapping corrupt institutions. The Peace Corps is a good thing; but if it's a Trojan horse, that's a bad thing. Being given a water filter is a good thing; unless it's a placebo, in which case that's a bad thing.

The Peace Corps had recently shut down their program

in Kazakhstan for "operational considerations" but the back channel story was that five female volunteers had been raped in one year. But would they have shut it down if Congress hadn't just passed a bill to protect Peace Corps volunteers from sexual assault? And would Congress have done that if it hadn't been for ABC's 20/20 program on the considerable number of female volunteers who'd been raped over the years and, worse, treated as if it had been their fault?

My Romanian supervisor in the Peace Corps education division in Bucharest, a stand-in for the more seasoned and forthright woman on maternity leave, is an attractive young woman who had studied to be an elementary school teacher in Romania but had never taught for long, if at all. She'd repeatedly said during training, to the private skepticism of some of the volunteers because it was so ridiculously overdone, "How I so love the little ones," her shoulders shaking in a frisson of joy. One of the volunteers could imitate her perfectly, to the delight of all of us. When I'd told this young woman in September that I'd been assigned five hundred students, not the fifty students the school claimed, and that I was expected to teach without having been supplied with any materials, any textbooks, or any books of any kind, she'd said nothing.

When I'd told her that one of the Romanian teachers of English, when I'd asked how anyone could do this for two years, had said, "You can teach fruits and vegetables," she'd also said nothing. Then she cancelled her scheduled visit to my school, this woman who so loved the little ones, claiming ill health. When we rescheduled, she cancelled again because of bad weather in Bucharest. Two weeks later she said she couldn't reschedule until spring since the weather was sure to be bad all winter.

At that point I took matters into my own hands. I convinced my director to give me two hundred and fifty students the first semester and two hundred and fifty the second. I silently speculated that my director got more and better fees if she could promise parents that their child would have a Native Speaker in their English class.

Native Speaker is the catch phrase. I hear it everywhere I turn. During a long car ride up into the mountains of Hunedoara for a week-long school retreat before school started, the man driving me, the father of one of the youngsters who would be one of my students, said he hoped I would make school fun. Meanwhile, I am trying not to hum out loud the lyrics to the Dr. Seuss song, "Fahoo fores, dahoo dores," improvising, "Fahoo fores, dahoo dores, we are going to Hunedoares." I'm in my language-learning mode, where I try to find connections to things I know so I can try to remember things I don't know. It's called mnemonics or something like that.

My driver is a lovely person. He works for Ford in Craiova. He is big and strong, like most Romanians; at the Easter break it will be his son who will help me day after day with the *Altfel* Week Open House. But none of that has transpired yet as we traverse the mountain roads to Hunedoara, crossing and re-crossing the Olt River. This man tells me that the school had a Native Speaker, a young British man, a few years earlier, a college boy visiting Romania for two months during his gap year (the year one takes off in Britain before returning for the last year of school). The young man had been a wonderful Native Speaker, according to my driver, and he had taught fruits and vegetables and it had been fun. This was their only experience with a Native Speaker and they could imagine something like that again. I pictured this young man playing soccer with the students after school. I pictured the young Brit, very fit, having students run relay races with teams named for fruits and vegetables.

Why, I wondered, other than money or just not thinking it through, would my director assign me five hundred students, all the students in the school from all of the Fourth Grades through all of the Eighth Grades? I decided she hadn't thought about it.

"You don't want to kill the goose that lays the golden egg," I say to her when I see her in passing, smiling and winking broadly and flashing the "peace" sign. Fairy tales are our common language. She knows them all and so do I.

As the time draws near for the *Altfel* Week Open House, it's looking more and more like I might be the only one doing it. The cookies and cakes from the *bunicas*, the Romanian grandmothers I've heard so much about but have never seen, are solicited but never appear. The student writing, which I'd tried to get from the school's four Romanian teachers of English, the student artwork from the one Romanian art teacher, never really materialized. A few pieces, afterthoughts, emerged and I think the teachers were ashamed. It was poor work. I didn't want to embarrass them, so I stopped asking.

Romanian teachers are already so underpaid, it's a joke. They are resourceful people, and so have devised a way to survive in spite of not being paid enough to survive. What they do is use their government teaching position as a way to recruit students to tutor outside of school. The teachers are not required to be in the school unless they are scheduled to teach a class. So they come to the school, scout for private students, the ones they plan to tutor in their homes and who will actually pay them, step into their classrooms from time to time so they can say they did, fill out all the necessary paperwork for the Ministry of Education as needed, spend some time in the teachers' lounge socializing and snacking, and then go home to tutor their private students, the ones they've recruited from among their assigned students. Everyone knows this. It's not a secret. But it's never discussed.

Robert Kaplan, the prolific American author of many books on foreign affairs, visited and wrote about Romania in the 1970s when it was still under communism. Kaplan has a new book, *In Europe's Shadow*, published in 2016. In it he quotes the Countess R.G. Waldeck who wrote in the 1940s,

"'Throughout Rumania's [sic] history the country had survived because of clever pliancy ... The Rumanians possess to the highest degree the capacity of receiving the blows of destiny while relaxed.'" Kaplan extrapolates that "The Romanians, in Waldeck's intimation, were no so much fatalists as wise in the ways of history: in which, because there was no end to the process of permutation, there was always the possibility for adaptation and for finding new angles in order to survive." Kaplan's and Waldeck's observations seem generally true to me based on my experiences teaching there.

In my Romanian school there was an expression, voiced often, "*Ei pretend sa ne plateasca se ne prefacem la locul de munca.*" The translation is basically, "They pretend to pay us, and we pretend to work." They would say this with a slight lift of one shoulder, a little shrug and a sideways smile, and that's the closest anyone comes to letting on that it's all a sham.

My director is supposed to teach one class a day in Fifth Grade math, but I learn that in the five years she's been director, she never has. The students sit in there and wait and, of course, being bored, break furniture. One of the reasons I'm a popular teacher, and that the furniture in my room is intact, is that I show up.

As I'm waiting and hoping for some action on the *Altfel* Week idea, I'm recalling a summer in 1969 when I was a Head Start teacher in Ann Arbor, all of us cute and sweet little co-eds who'd been recommended by the University of Michigan's Education School. Head Start was new then, having started in 1965 as a summer program for poor children, and I think it was still mainly a summer program in 1969. One of my fellow teachers, the cutest and sweetest and littlest, in fact, suggests to an overweight, always tired, old-before-her-time, African American single mother of ten small children that her offspring might enjoy making chocolate chip cookies with her some afternoon after she comes home from her double shift as a nurse's assistant and before she makes them supper. The co-ed, talking to the woman but referring to her in the third person as "mom" as if she were out of the room, explains that if "mom" baked cookies with her children, then the children would be acquiring the math skills used while measuring the ingredients during this fun family project. Thus, the co-ed patiently explained to this mother of ten, "mom" would be helping to prepare her offspring for school and her children would score better on school tests.

Since I lived then in the African American community in Ann Arbor, on Felch Street west of Main Street, literally on the other side of the railroad tracks, I was privy to the story of this suggestion that made the rounds in churches and corner grocery stores. It was greeted, as one might expect, with hoots of laughter and rambunctious knee-slapping. I could only imagine that my fellow teachers in Romania, many of whom had taken on extra tutoring and other side jobs in order to make up the income they'd lost when their already extremely low wages had been cut twenty-five percent by the Romanian Ministry of Education because of the 2008 economic crisis, probably feel much the same way about the gala Open House for parents suggested by the way-too-idealistic Peace Corps volunteer. They must see it as a huge amount of unpaid work, on top of the huge amount of unpaid work they are already doing. This *Altfel* Week nonsense was yet more stupidity from the Ministry of Education, the source of all their travails.

Not that it matters much. I have five hundred students and they've all been doing good work. I have about two decent, displayable pieces from each student, poems and essays and short stories, a thousand more or less. I have a photograph of each child to go with their work. I had asked the kids who finished first to illustrate their writing while they waited for their classmates to complete the assignment. I have plenty of illustrations to go with writing. But where am I going to display it?

I'm shown a dark, cluttered storage room, up a cluttered staircase in a back building. One of my students said he thought it used to be a horse shed. It has a loft area that's being used to store broken furniture. It would need a lot of work before it could become a display space: cleaning, painting, even lights. There's a floorboard missing in one spot. Some of the steps seem like they're rotting away. And that's only what I can see.

There's also the possibility of using my own classroom but it's a tiny, hot, top-floor, corner room, previously so hot it was only used to store janitorial supplies. I can barely fit twenty-five students into it, much less their parents. Then there's the little matter of the three flights of stairs, sixty-seven steps, to get to my room, a daunting prospect for some. I would have to start with big yellow arrows at the front gate, and a student standing by each arrow, to even get the parents up there.

I'm not going to hold the Open House in Parcul Pushkin across the street from the school. Several people had suggested this and I'd thought of it myself, but as beautiful as the park is, the benches and buildings and even the children's swings are covered with racist graffiti against the gypsies. The people in Craiova seem to feel they are on solid ground in their prejudices since gypsies are considered a nuisance all over Europe and have a reputation, rightly or wrongly, for cheating and stealing. France and Italy have provided some gypsies with free, one-way tickets back to Romania, something Romanians find galling.

Another name for gypsies is Roma and people outside of Romania assume the term means that the gypsies are from Romania, which infuriates Romanians who insist this is a terrible misnomer. The rampant and internationally renowned corruption in Romania doesn't help this confusion over who is and who isn't a Roma or a Romanian. In my school in Craiova everyone I work with down to the last person, no matter how gentle or educated, loudly proclaims their hatred of gypsies and boasts of it. It seems to be a way for them to say, "We are not them," but in fact one cannot tell the difference between the ethnic groups here, at least not by their physical appearance, which is maybe why they feel they have to declare it.

The gypsies arrived in the Balkans 1500 years earlier, most people agree, as the slaves some conqueror had picked up somewhere in India or the Hindu Kush; or perhaps they were Untouchables who had come of their own accord. When British writer Donald Hall visited Romania in the 1930s he spoke with a "princess" in a castle outside of Bucharest who said that her husband's family, nobles for six hundred years, had had three hundred tzigani or gypsy slaves, liberated in 1846, which gives some credence to the slavery idea.

But I'd heard different theories. Maybe there had been several different migrations of the gypsies, maybe from India, maybe from other places, too. From the third story window of a large building in the center of Craiova, I could see gypsies cooking in the alley. However they had come, they have never been completely accepted. They have kept their own language and their own customs and live in separate sections of towns and villages.

In Craiova the gypsies find haphazard shelter in and among the abandoned train cars on the outskirts of the city. They live in unimaginable squalor along the sides of the train tracks near large cities. Craiova has a large gypsy population. I have seen no gypsy musicians, although I've heard there used to be some in Craiova. I have seen the children and women begging in the streets. I've seen a few old men selling wooden spoons and dishes at the side of the road.

Many gypsies, like the Jews, had been exterminated during World War II. I haven't met a single person of Jewish descent, or at least none who admitted it, although the fancy hotel in Sinaia where the Peace Corps had held a conference was owned by Israelis. The hotel had hosted an international convocation of Jewish rabbis that overlapped with our Peace Corps training conference. It's known, although not talked about, that many Jewish people had not only been deported and all their belongings stolen but that one group, according to several sources, including Romanian author Virgil Gherghiu, had been literally butchered in Bucharest at a meat-packing plant. The gypsies, too, had been deported, but many have returned, having nowhere else to go.

My school in Craiova, where I've been assigned by the Peace Corps, has no gypsy students. I'd heard that the Ministry of Education required that two spaces in every classroom be available for gypsy children. One day I'd asked my director why there appeared to be no gypsy children among my five hundred students. She'd responded, "None have ever applied."

A sign on the wall of the public restrooms in Parcul Pushkin across from the school reads, "*Mort a la tzigane*." *Tzigane* (pronounced *Siz-gah-nee*) is another word for gypsy. One did not need to be fluent in Romanian to know that the sign read, "Death to the gypsies."

Once I'd ridden with a gypsy taxi driver in Bucharest and he'd said the gypsies had been better treated under the Russians since at least then they could send their children to school. Leslie Hawke, mother of the actor Ethan Hawke, had come to Romania as a Peace Corps volunteer in 2000. Sent to the north, she'd stayed after her Peace Corps service and founded an organization to help gypsy children attend school.

No one, as far as I can tell, not even the gypsy cab driver, thinks life was better under the Russians when, according to everyone, every third person was paid to spy on their friends, their neighbors, and their families. The *International Herald Tribune* (a publication of *The New York Times*), in December 2006 reported that the graft and corruption which had become entrenched in Romania under communism, remained because so many of the people who'd worked in government under the Russians were still in positions of power. The Romanian newspapers were always reporting the suicide of a government official, a suicide which might actually have been an assassination, or reporting that a government whistle blower had to move his family to another country because of threats and intimidation.

One always had to be prepared for suspicious surcharges at

the government-run post offices and train stations. I never understood the cause. Once when I had to exchange a train ticket and was charged twice as much as the original, I asked a Romanian friend to go back to the train station with me and ask about it. My money was refunded. In the post office I always paid whatever extra fees they charged since it would have been too time-consuming to do anything else. I didn't encounter this kind of thing in regular stores, perhaps because my repeat business was volitional.

The administrators at my school, like so many, as I'd heard from both Romanians and fellow Peace Corps volunteers, regularly took "fees" for placing students and so naturally catered to the wealthy. The word on the street was that the school had once had a good reputation but since the infiltration of the Romanian mafia, who paid to have their children there and where teachers were frightened and understandably loath to give poor grades, the school had lost some of its previous luster.

I never see the parents of my students. They don't visit my classroom. However one sleety December evening when I was leaving the school about 7 P.M. after staying longer than usual, I'd had to walk by their waiting vehicles, including two or three Humvees and Mercedes, all with their motors running. The adults seemed to be dressed in different shades of brown and black leather, like the Joe Namath recliners and leather sofas in the little Lake Leelanau furniture store where I'd worked in the summer of 1988. They were standing smoking on the sidewalk. I was clearly an elderly female teacher who had been teaching their children all day, emerging from the school doorway with a satchel of books over one shoulder and heavy bags of books and papers in each hand. No one looked at me. No one greeted me. Did they imagine I was their servant? Were they the new, self-designated boyars? None of them moved to let me pass down the sidewalk and it would have been very easy for them to do so. I had to go into the muddy and snow-filled street to get around them. I had to walk out in the wet snow in the road all the way to the end of the block, trying to avoid being hit by their vehicles as they wheeled in and out of slippery parking spots on the narrow, dimly lit street.

There's only one realistic choice. The Open House is going to have to take place in the front yard of the school where parents coming to pick up their children won't be able to miss it. But how crazy and aggressive and way too earnest and in-your-face is that? Well, totally.

After a few minutes of reflection I think the smartest thing I can do is admit defeat and cancel the whole thing. None of the school's English teachers, the four I've been assigned to work with by the Peace Corps, seem to have any time to work on it. The students have never done anything like this before. I've never had a single parent, much less a *bunica*, visit my classroom during the whole time I've been teaching. Whenever I mention the *Altfel* Week Open House in class, which is pretty often, the kids look down at their desks and finally someone will say, "I'm not going to be here that week."

The student population of the school, even three weeks before *Altfel* Week, has thinned out alarmingly. Some students are clearly leaving early for a nice long Easter vacation with their families. Is there going to be anyone left?

Two weeks before the event I learn the Small Project Assistance (SPA) grant, funded through the auspices of the United States Agency for International Development (USAID) specifically to host *Altfel* Week projects, has been approved. My very first thought is that I should turn down the money.

In my head, I'm writing the letter. "Dear SPA officials..." But I hate to turn down money. I weigh the pros and cons and ultimately it's my Calvinist-banker-horse-trader-rum-runner DNA that holds sway. This is not the visible DNA, the free-spirit-poet, I know-you'll-still-love-me-in-the-morning, anything-for-a-windmill-Don-Quixote, join-the-Peace-Corps DNA. This is the hard-drive DNA that goes back before

Calvin to mastodons and before that to some swamp where my ancestors crawled onto the land. It's only a little money, five hundred dollars is a little money, but it *is* money. I feel I will have to go through with it.

For the next two weeks I spend hours putting my students' writing with their photos, the photos I had taken of each student to prove to the Peace Corps office that I had been assigned five hundred students, not fifty as my jolly director and ambitious counterpart had told them, the same jolly director and ambitious counterpart who the Peace Corps, in consideration of their silence on the matter, apparently chose to believe about the numbers of students.

As I sit there I remind myself of all the things I like about Romania. I love the scenes from the train windows. Even though the trains themselves are like rolling porta-potties, from the train I can see the land and the people. I love the shepherds herding sheep. I love the way the entire family works the harvest, from the oldest to the youngest. The Russians, someone told me on the train, took all the mechanized farm equipment when they left so you see people, like figures in a Brueghel painting, out with hand sickles and handmade rakes, doing the harvest. I love the peasant museum in Craiova with its stone hearth and low, handmade wooden stools and the shelf in the chimney for the kitchen spirits. I love the brilliant colors in the woven wool rugs and wall hangings. I love how they use so much red. I love the Easter eggs decorated in intricate patterns. I love the noble Carpathian Mountains and the majestic Danube. I love the history of this place that has been invaded and conquered so many times by so many different groups and the way the Romanian people have survived. I love the resilience of the Romanian people.

I put the students' writing and illustrations in plastic protector sleeves in the event it rains on the day of the Open House. I cut crepe paper streamers, deliberately doing the work in front of everyone, on the front steps of the school if it's sunny, and inside in the lobby if it's raining. The parents might come out of curiosity, if nothing else.

My director is in Bucharest with her father. The few times I've seen her in the school, it looked like she'd been crying. Someone said the director's boyfriend had broken up with her. But she could have been upset because her father was dying as well. The last time I had seen her she had told me that she was going to go to the Black Sea resort where she had always gone every Easter. "If I only do one thing," she had said, "I am going to do that. I deserve it."

The parents or their retainers ask, "*Che Fachette?*" or "What are you doing?" as they come into the school to pick up the children. Some of the parents can afford household help, even chauffeurs. Sometimes grandparents come to collect the children. Whether parents or servants or grandparents, whoever comes through the door, it's clear they think I'm nuts.

And I answer blithely, "*Oo La La*! *Altfel* Open House! *Trey Aprillie.*"

I always like saying "*aprillie*" because it makes me feel like Chaucer saying, "*Wan that aprillie...than longen folke to goon on pilgrimages.*" I'm longing to goon on a pilgrimage myself, a long one.

This whole *Altfel* Open House thing is shaping up to be a big mistake. It's going to be a horrible disaster. I'm going to do all this work, day after day, and when April 3 arrives I'm going to be sitting there alone, in the rain, with my crepe paper streamers. April, where I am in Romania, is like April in Michigan. Craiova is on the forty-fifth parallel, just like the Leelanau Peninsula. April can be balmy or snowy. One never knows with April. It can be a capricious time of year.

I had generated the writing with my usual tricks: turning cartwheels and somersaults on the lawn, chasing my tail and emitting high-pitched yips of joy. Saying, "Bravo!" And, "Way to go!" And, "Good job!" And, "I love what you're doing." And, "Wow! You're all doing such incredible work!"

I learned long ago that all anyone needs is a little encouragement and they'll do great things. Children don't know they can't write novels. I'm really a cheerleader not a teacher. But I did all this, at least the cartwheels and somersaults, metaphorically, not physically.

If this crazy Open House idea is ever going to happen, I'm going to have to get physical and go up a ladder and hang crepe paper. I'm going to have to rake the litter out of the grass in the front yard. Once I was young and worked every conceivable job, from picking strawberries to cleaning barns to hefting heavy trays while waitressing, but I haven't picked strawberries since I was twelve, haven't been up a ladder since I tore my ACL tendon in Thailand four years earlier in 2008, haven't done any serious raking since I first left my home in Michigan in 1999, and have steered clear of hefting and hauling for years.

So, like Madame Defarge sitting with her knitting during the French Revolution in Dickens' *A Tale of Two Cities*, I just keep sorting kids' writing, repeating in my mind little clichéd phrases of self-encouragement: there is no success without failure; the safest thing is to take a risk; stay calm and carry on; there is work to be done in the dark before the dawn; no guts, no glory; you have to stand for something or fall for everything.

But what does any of this stand *for*? I have a little time to think, sitting there sorting kids' writing for endless hours, getting it ready for presentation, pretty much like working in a Chinese laundry. After days and days, I realize it all comes down to democracy: all of this stands for democracy.

You can't have a democracy without thoughts and feelings and that's what the kids' writing is all about. It hadn't happened overnight. It had been a slow process. First there was no writing at all. "But I have no ideas, teacher."

No ideas, teacher, was followed, as it always is, by bad writing, take-me-out-and-shoot-me bad writing, produced by people whose only exposure to writing was essays on the furniture in the Romanian Royal Palace. "You have to write badly before you can write well," American author Eudora Welty famously said. And it's true, without bad writing there'd be no writing at all. Like learning the violin, one has to wait and have faith through a lot of wrong notes.

Finally, there were little glimmers, like the daffodils in front of me trying to poke their way through the frozen ground of the school yard. And at last, finally, I see real thoughts and real feelings, from every kid.

If I display their writing I'm saying it's important. I'm saying they're important. With that thought, I know I'm going to string up their writing if it's the last thing I ever do in my life. The worst thing that can happen is that I'll make an utter fool of myself and that's nothing new. I'm very good at that. It's far and away my best talent.

My mind goes back to a day three months earlier when I'd been in my Margaret Thatcher mode with my second set of two hundred and fifty students. They were all looking at me in a slightly shell-shocked way after I'd given my usual speech demanding that in my classroom they participate fully, be kind to each other, not bad-mouth gypsies or anyone else, express their thoughts and feelings, and not be tardy.

"This is an American classroom," I say emphatically, "and we do things the American way." This was utter nonsense since I had no more idea about what an American classroom might be than they did. "And," I go on, clarifying, "I'm not doing things the American way because I'm trying to change you; I'm doing things the American way because it's the only way I know."

This had never occurred to them and in fact, had never occurred to me until I heard myself saying it. Substitute "my way" for "the American way" and you'll have something closer to the truth. And, naturally, being an adult, I was trying to change them which, naturally, being kids, they knew.

In retrospect I think what I meant was that I expected them

to have feelings, to have thoughts based on those feelings. I just couldn't help myself from anticipating that from them. And maybe that's true because I'm an American, but I hadn't been conscious of it until I was in their school in Romania.

They did it. And the more they did it, the more they liked it. And the more they liked it, the better they got at it. And here in their writing is the proof. It would be a kind of crime not to recognize their efforts.

When I begin to rake the yard, three hefty, female janitors show up and do it for me. When I begin to weed the flower beds, they come out with the proper tools and do this a million times better than I would have ever been able to do it. Some-one shows up with flats of pansies and these are planted in the freshly tilled ground.

When I ask for a ladder and begin to string up writing and crepe paper streamers, my students appear out of nowhere and begin to do this, too. A sturdy little fifth grade boy, thrilled by the attention from the sixth, seventh, and eighth grade girls, comes early in the morning and stays until late in the after-noon, carting boxes of writing around, climbing the ladder, and blowing up balloons. He's amazingly strong but more than that, he's cheerful, sweet, and has great stamina. His older fe-male schoolmates know exactly what to do. They smile and flatter him and say what a terrific guy he is to help them with all the heavier work. And he could not be happier.

Things are starting to look beautiful and clean and shiny and fresh. There are lines and lines of writing hung up like lit-tle baby clothes. We run out of places to hang writing and have to set up tables in the hall. The place looks like a hillbilly yard sale: More inside!!

The kids, by the day of the Open House, have simply taken over not only all the physical work but the selection of writing to display, the hanging of the homemade banner, the welcome sign on the white board, basically everything. At one point I say to one of the girls, "Thank you so much for doing all of this. I never expected all of you to come every day and help."

She says, somewhat nonplussed, "*This* is what we like to do." And I think slyly to myself: next year I'll entice them to write by telling them we're going to display it at an Open House with crepe paper streamers. I have coffee, tea, sugar, and hot water but no cookies. But cookies miraculously appear.

Most of my students are the only child in their families. Everyone had learned a terrible lesson under Romanian President Nicolae Ceaușescu (pronounced Chow-chess-cu), assassinated in 1989. Ceaușescu, wanting to increase the number of Romanians, had outlawed birth control. This was a country at the time with empty shelves in the grocery stores. One teacher told me of standing and looking through a dirty store window at a few paltry oranges one day near Christmas and crying because she could not afford them for her children. This was a country with dire poverty. The predictable result of making birth control against the law, predictable by everyone but Ceaușescu, was many unwanted children. Those unfortunate children languished in state orphanages. Scholars from all over the world came and studied the Romanian orphans. *The New York Times* in 2007 and the journal *Science* in the same year documented the stunted mental growth. The orphans displayed the "failure to thrive" syndrome of children who were seldom picked up or held by another human being. Many died; others, with irreparable neurological damage, lived out miserable lives.

"I am loved," my students often said. They knew it. They felt it. Their parents made sure of it.

If it had rained, the *Altfel* Open House might have been the disaster I'd been picturing in those first few days as I sat there sorting student writing.

But the weather is perfect: not too hot, not too cold, sunny and glorious. Blue skies. Parents come. Lots of them. It's the last afternoon of school before Easter vacation. Everyone's in a good mood.

For almost six hours, from 1 P.M. when school is over for the younger students until 7 P.M., when the last class is over for the older students, the parents visit the open air art and writing exhibit.

A parent who has a daughter in one of my classes, a man who used to be a journalist, calls his contacts in the media and reporters come from the newspapers and the TV stations. The *Altfel* Open House with the children's art and writing would be on the national news that evening in Bucharest. One of my fellow Peace Corps volunteers would put the TV program up on YouTube.

At the end of that day, I know nothing matters but the kids and how they feel about themselves and what they've accomplished. And the kids are thrilled. No one can deny it. It's worth it, for that day, for that time, for those kids. So, yes, "Let's put on a show!" You never know who might come.

Istanbul, the Gateway to Asia

Who would have thought that Istanbul would remind me so much of where I'd grown up on the northwest coast of Michigan above Sleeping Bear Bay? Everywhere I turn there's a vista of turquoise water. There's a pinkish tinge to the light, that I've never seen anywhere except on the Leelanau Peninsula. If I don't stop and think for a minute and remember where I am, the straits of the Bosporus and the waters around the Golden Horn could almost be the waters of Lake Michigan between the Manitou Passage and Pyramid Point.

What brings me to Turkey is that one day in the market in Romania I saw some strange fruit and bought some just to try. I had no idea what they were. We don't have them in Michigan. The sign said, "*Smochine de Turcia*." I understood it to say, "Figs from Turkey." They did not look particularly appetizing. They were purplish-greenish, almost black, pear-shaped, but much smaller, about the size of a quail egg and soft to the touch, like human flesh, almost too much so.

Figs are delicious if they are ripe and fresh. They are mostly ruby-colored inside, with a core of golden seeds, a thin layer of chartreuse after the ruby color and then the thin, purple skin. If they are cut through, they look like layers of a tourmaline, an edible one.

After the figs were no longer in season, I would sometimes think about *Turcia*, Turkey, so close to Romania. Istanbul straddles the gateway between Europe and Asia. Istanbul was formerly Constantinople, and before that Byzantium, and before that the city of Troy. A modern tunnel under the Bosporus has unearthed ancient ships, according to an article in the August 2015 issue of *The New Yorker*. Amateur German archaeologist Heinrich Schliemann wanted this kind of excavation back in the 1800s when he sought to prove that Homer was a real writer and that Troy had been more than a myth. Near here on the shores of the Aegean is where the Trojan War was fought, so legend has it, where the great warrior Achilles was finally dragged into battle, despite his mother's trick of dressing him in girl's clothing.

Five thousand years ago Troy, now Istanbul, was just a fishing village, like Leland on the shores of Lake Michigan in the late 1940s. I was a toddler when I first went to Leland with my father. He was exploring ways to ship his lumber down to Chicago. The area around the Leland Harbor then was a collection of unpainted shacks on the shore, everything permeated with the smell of smoked fish, and that's how Troy must have been in the early days.

And so that's how, eating a fig and imagining ancient Troy, you know the way one thing always leads to another, there came to be a December morning when I registered in the Sultan's Inn on a little, narrow and steep cobbled street above the blue-green straits of the Bosporus. I'm in the old part of the city, a district called Sultanahmet, near what had been the Sultan's Palace.

I hastily put my few things in the room, eager to go out and walk. It's overcast but there is color everywhere. Woven goods in brilliant patterns fill the windows of the stores and spill out onto the sidewalk. A faint aroma of cinnamon and nutmeg lingers in the air. The facades of buildings are intricately pieced with different kinds of wood or tile. I'm in the middle part of the slope of a hill and heading up, block after block of little turning streets.

Everywhere I turn I can see the minarets of the mosques above the city and through slender places between the buildings, little glimpses of the blue waters surrounding the peninsula. If I went out in a boat I could traverse the straits of the Bosporus which connects the Sea of Marmara to the Black Sea. Heading in the other direction, I could get onto the isthmus of the Dardanelles and from there go to the Aegean and from there to the Mediterranean.

Picture connecting waterways shaped like an hour-glass: one fat sea, the Aegean, leading west to the Mediterranean; and the other fat end, the Sea of Marmara, leading east to the Black Sea; with Istanbul at the narrow waist. Europe and Asia almost touch here, the most natural place in the world for a great city, whether huge and modern, as Istanbul is today, or the ancient collection of fishing huts in legendary Troy.

The straits of the Bosporus separate the Gallipoli Peninsula in Europe from the Anatolia Peninsula in Asia. The Bosporus is a naturally occurring waterway between the Sea of Marmara leading to the Black Sea and then west to the Danube on the west side of the Black Sea.

It is confusing to talk about but it's not confusing to look at. It becomes very clear once you're there. I think the reason it's confusing to talk about is that naturally occurring narrow waterways connecting large bodies of water are unusual in the world. One does not see them often and they are therefore hard to picture.

On the opposite side of the Sea of Marmara, the straits of the Dardanelles—much smaller than the Bosporus—connect the Sea of Marmara to the Aegean and then to the Mediterranean. The Dardanelles are only about forty miles long and two miles across. George Gordon, Lord Byron, swam across it in 1810.

In ancient times all these interconnecting bodies of water were easily crossed by boat. The city has been under siege numerous times in its ten thousand year history and the residents, presumably, like the people in the British Isles, became good fighters because of this. Naturally the name changed with different conquerors.

Istanbul is a lively place. Imagine the Muppets, dressed in Turkish kaftans and turbans, dancing across the hills surrounding the waterways, singing, "It's Istanbul, not Constantinople... Why did Constantinople get the works? That's nobody's business but the Turks."

The Russians came through once, according to an account I heard in Romania, and managed to put greased logs on top of the water, thus avoiding the large chain under the water that prevented ships from entering, and their vessels slid into the city. Whoever was in charge at that time, responded by burning the Russian ships with a kind of tarry stuff called Greek Fire. There were pagans, Christians, Muslims, Jews, Buddhists, Mongols, Russians, Chinese, Arabs, Indonesians, Romans, Greeks, Europeans, a veritable multitude of ethnic peoples in and out of Istanbul since Troy was a fishing village, and the city today retains that multicultural atmosphere, an acceptance and expectation of differences.

I'm the kind of traveler who's happy without maps and guided tours. So the first day, I climb to the top of one of the hills so I can get a better view of the water. It had been raining lightly when I left the hotel but now, almost to the top, it's raining harder. I see signs for something called, "The Grand Bazaar," and head in the direction of the arrows.

Before I crest the top of the hill, I buy an umbrella. I'm now thoroughly drenched and cold, and thinking I should get out of the rain and maybe have a cup of coffee. Seeing a little café with pastries in a window at street level, I descend a short flight of stairs into a coffee shop.

I'm on Christmas vacation from the Peace Corps in Romania. It's the off-season and the hotel was cheap. The weather in Istanbul in December is like Michigan's in September. Yes, there's rain, but when the sun comes out it's glorious. And there are flower stalls everywhere and flowers blooming. I promise myself I will buy roses and put them in my room and that will be my Christmas tree. I'll go in mid-afternoon to that upstairs restaurant with a view and watch the boats and that will be my Christmas dinner.

For the moment, I've escaped the rain. I'm shaking out my umbrella and ordering coffee. The coffee is the Turkish style, very strong, in a delicate little demitasse. I will need cream and sugar. When I finally lift my head from my umbrella and my feet, preparing to pay in Turkish lira, I notice that all the other customers are men and they are pointedly looking away from me. I feel like I've stepped into the men's bathroom by mistake. Is this a café for men only? Do women not go out to places like this? Do women not drink tea or coffee? I forget about cream and sugar. I hastily sip my thick, bitter coffee, and gently place the miniscule cup back on the counter. I pay, somewhat awkwardly as the Turkish lira are still new to me, and leave, all the while not looking at anyone.

I'm about to cross the street and enter under a golden awning marked "Grand Bazaar" when a man approaches and asks, "Are you from England? I want to offer you tea with my friend." I tell him I'm from America and I'm on my way to the Grand Bazaar. He says, "But your feet are wet." He points to my muddy, wooly, brown socks inside my muddy, old, red, canvas Ecco sandals. "Stop for a few minutes and have tea in my friend's shop."

He says his friend is a merchant with rooms of beautiful carpets. I'm a little leery of being led into some pirate's den, but decide it's not that kind of thing. I quickly explain that I'm a Peace Corps volunteer. I hold out my empty hands and turn them over, in a gesture of "No money, folks," and tell the man he should save his cup of tea for someone able to purchase something. But he says he's just offering a cup of tea because it's cold and wet outside.

The tea is excellent and the man's shop is sumptuously elegant, as well as well-lit and warm and dry so, once thus refreshed, I cross the street to the Grand Bazaar which is also mostly warm and dry, a maze of shops. I am more lost than not. "Oh, beautiful lady, I'm falling in love with you, buy my scarves," calls out the merchant. He's one of the bolder ones, but many are aggressive. They stand in their little shops all day trying to sell things and become quite hardened to the ups and downs of making a living. I buy three beautiful scarves for my three beautiful children, Christmas presents from another land. I'll send the scarves from Istanbul if I can figure out how.

I finally wend my way out onto a street as the winter afternoon, still raining, is darkening. I make my way back down the hill toward my hotel. I stop on the way in a small, street-side, open-air restaurant I'd seen that morning. I select three different kinds of eggplant from their buffet. They make eggplant so many different ways and I want to try as many as I reasonably can so I can learn how to cook them. One thing they do, and they are doing it as I eat and have seemingly been doing it all day, is they grill the eggplants over charcoal on an outdoor grill. It brings out the slightly meaty or nutty flavor of the eggplant, almost like veal or cashews, in a way that oven-baking simply doesn't.

I've walked for hours that day so in my tiny, high, top-floor room in my three-story ancient hotel, after a hot shower, I fall asleep instantly in a bed with clean, sparkling white, rough cotton sheets. There are fancy hotels on my street, places I could have spent five hundred dollars a night, but mine isn't one of them.

At 7 A.M., I find the breakfast room. It's clean, but spartan. Other than the coffee, all the food is cold: cucumbers, ham, cheese, bread, yogurt and fruit. My hotel is clean and safe and I'm grateful.

Four Romanians, two couples, are in the breakfast room with me. I know this from their language. The women and the men all have surgical stitches on their faces. At first I think they've been in a drunken brawl but one of the women, perhaps seeing me look away, explains that they've had cosmetic surgery. They have come to Turkey expressly for that, the men, too. I'm guessing they're all in their thirties or their forties at the most. They are ordinary looking people and not less so because of whatever it was they had done to themselves. They all seem happy and excited with the thrill of looking, as they imagine, like movie stars.

The next day, after I'm invited for tea several more times, I learn that the man who had found me in the street the first day was literally, "a finder." The carpet merchants send out their most gregarious friend to look for likely tourists to bring back for a cup of tea and, of course, a sales pitch. I learn that the man selling umbrellas isn't just selling umbrellas: he has a cousin with a carpet shop. The sixth time I'm accosted, very near the doorway of the man's shop, I go in and sit on a hassock and, looking up, say to the dignified-looking older man standing in the shop, and the younger man who has followed me back in, perhaps his son, the person who had approached me in the street, "No tea, thank you, I have a question." And when they are both looking down to where I'm seated, I say, "Do I look rich?"

They look somewhat taken aback and finally the son says, "Yes."

"Okay," I say. "Now, tell me the truth here, since I'm not rich and I'm not wearing expensive clothes and I don't think I look rich, do I look rich to you because I'm old? Because I'm blonde? Because I speak English? Because why, gentlemen?" I figure if they are going out every day and looking for people to bring to the shop, they must know what they're looking for.

"Truth," I say.

They exchange glances, and then the younger man rises to the occasion, like a reluctant schoolboy. We all know the kind, the diffident student who always seems to know the answer but seldom volunteers, perhaps because he does know and doesn't want others to feel jealous, or perhaps because he knows and has nothing to prove, or perhaps because he's naturally reserved. He says stiffly, almost in a monotone, "You are self-confident, proud. You are high-spirited. You are brave to walk alone. You are curious. You are taking in everything. You have a mind of your own. You appear to be an intelligent woman of quality. You are dressed in a way that is understated. You move with assurance. You walk as if you have an army, a very large one, outside the gate. You are not afraid to make eye contact. You wouldn't be that way if you did not have a strong family behind you and financial security of long-standing." He could have been sizing up a race horse in the paddock at a public auction.

"And I'm old and blonde and speak English."

They laugh.

And what I don't say is that the crash of 2008 hurt their business. And they have a shop full of expensive carpets, like all the other carpet sellers, and they have no one to buy them. And they're desperate.

"You have beautiful carpets," I tell them. "I would buy one if I could." I pause and add, reciprocating the son's sweet flattery, "I would buy them all, if I could."

They smile and offer me tea again, and this time I accept.

I love to walk. Istanbul, in my experience of it, is a beautiful city. People are friendly and helpful. One doesn't see the pitiful multitudes of homeless people that one sees in New York City and Washington, D.C. and Los Angeles and Philadelphia and Chicago, those people sleeping in piles of rags in the dirtiest and most dangerous corners of our cities, or on pieces of cardboard on subway grates, old people down on their luck, veterans from the wars in Vietnam or Iraq or Afghanistan, teenagers kicked out of their homes, or escaping from foster care. American cities used to be clean and safe like Istanbul, but it's been so long I've forgotten what it's like.

The Istanbul tram is easy to use because there are written directions in English and the stops are frequent; if one misses a stop, which I did once or twice, one can get off and walk back. There are policemen, seemingly everywhere, seemingly discreet and polite; they look as if they are there only to help. There are kiosks with information. It's raining off and on, but there are so many places to get out of the weather, little cafes and bookstores and museums, that it's not a problem.

If you don't want to be accosted in the street, don't make eye contact. This is true in any city but it's especially true in Istanbul. They interpret eye contact as an invitation. I make eye contact because I instinctively want to read people's eyes to have a better understanding of my surroundings. If they approach me, that's even more information. I'm unusual, I admit it.

Without ever leaving the safe and heavily trafficked tourist area of the hills around Sultanahmet Square, there's so much to see. There's the beautiful museum that used to be a church and then was a mosque, Hagia Sophia, meaning Holy Wisdom, with a vast dome visible from almost everywhere, dating back fifteen centuries to Roman times. There's the five-hundred-year-old Blue Mosque with the intricate blue tiles like something from M.C. Escher. There are several art museums, a pudding shop with the most delicious rice pudding I've ever eaten (and have never been able to duplicate despite numerous attempts), and down the hill, next to the park with six-hundred-year-old trees, an archeology museum with stunningly ancient artifacts.

I'm not fascinated by the ten-thousand-year-old tombs. They are merely big and old and not interesting, at least not to me. I am taken by the four-thousand-year-old Sumerian tablets. Who were the Sumerians and where did they disappear to? Who were these ingenious people who could create the epic of Gilgamesh? I like the cuneiform. I like the little, sharp, wedge-shaped marks made long ago by capable hands in wet clay. I like the love poem written by a priestess:

> *Bridegroom, dear to my heart*
> *Goodly is your beauty, honeysweet*
> *You have captivated me.*
> *Let me stand trembling before you*
> *I would be taken to the bedchamber ...*
>
> *Bridegroom, you have taken your pleasure of me*
> *Tell my mother, she will give you delicacies ...*

This is the only love poem I've ever read where the woman's mother is so involved. I find that strange, hard to imagine, and therefore delightful.

Not far from the rug shop where they gave me tea, slightly down the hill, is the Topkapı Palace. I learn from reading their little brochure that six hundred years ahead of Europe, Istanbul had public libraries. The harem, my guidebook says, means "family quarters." The Sultan produced many sons with the ladies in the harem, perhaps the place where we can imagine the expression "an heir and a spare" first occurred, but then this was taken to extremes. To avoid the power struggles among heirs, it was the law that all male offspring, except the next designated Sultan, would be strangled when the time came. The sons all knew what was in store for them. It was part of the deal. One little boy said, "Could I finish my figs, and then be strangled?"

One of the harem wives, Roxelana, a lovely girl who had been kidnapped somewhere in Eastern Europe, first won the heart of Suleiman the Magnificent and then encouraged him to kill his sons by other women. Roxelana, the daughter of a

Coptic priest, according to one source, is claimed by several countries in the Balkans, and with borders that changed so often over all those years, years now lost in the cascades of time, any claim is plausible. Concubines were not allowed to become wives under the usual rules, but Roxelana somehow persuaded the Sultan to marry her. Suleiman had a son, Mustafa, by an earlier wife. Mustafa, a favorite of Suleiman and the entire palace, a young man praised by everyone for his wisdom, was ordered by his father to be strangled to death in his presence, by the eunuchs who had raised Mustafa, presumably so Mustafa's father could know his beloved son was truly dead.

Suleiman wrote many love poems to Roxelana, "my wealth, my moonlight, my most sincere friend, my very existence, my one and only love." But what of Roxelana's love for him? How could you love someone who had kidnapped you? It must have been that Roxelana learned how to feign love, perhaps even fooling herself, so that she could facilitate the survival of her sons. Suleiman and Roxelana's son, Sultan Selim II, known as "the sot" and known for debauchery, precipitated the decline of the Ottoman Empire.

The efficiency that made the palace a model of fairness and order (except for the harem part and the strangling part, which they don't do anymore), means that even today everything in Istanbul works. I mail my three beautiful scarves, separate packages to separate places, from the post office and the process is quick, easy, and inexpensive. The people working there are polite and efficient. The atmosphere everywhere in the city is similarly civilized, competent, and genteel.

Turkish men seem honest to me in their business dealings. Many times I would walk into a shop and no one would be there. They seemed to trust the shoppers not to walk off with the merchandise. Sometimes the men would be across the street having tea and they would see me enter and then come over, but in no rush. It's the off-season so that explains some of it, but the trust and camaraderie remind me of my tiny north-

ern Michigan crossroads town of Glen Arbor when I was growing up, not what you'd expect in a city of fifteen million.

Let me give an example of the basic fairness I felt with the
story of my meal in the elegant restaurant above the Bosporus.
This restaurant is right up the street from my hotel and had
been recommended by the young man at the desk. I don't usually eat in fancy places but it's Christmas, and short of going out
on a boat which would cost a lot more and also looked like it
would be cold, I didn't know of any better way to see the water.

Perhaps it's because it's mid-afternoon and the regular cook
isn't there. Perhaps it's because their business is suffering, but
the food isn't great. I drink my tea and eat a little pita bread
with hummus. I don't care for the lamb and eggplant dish. The
creamed spinach isn't fresh. The chocolate cake is stale. My
server asks how I like the food and I answer honestly, "Disap-
pointing," adding however, as I gesture toward the long row of
windows above the water, that I love the panoramic view and
seeing the boats, and especially how beautiful it is just as the
sun is getting low in the sky. He refuses to let me pay. It isn't a
lot, about fifteen dollars. I leave the money as a tip.

The next day I go across the city to where I've read there's
a great bookstore, Robinson Crusoe Books, on *Istiklal Cadessi*
or Independence Avenue. According to several sources, this is a
part of the city where there was a large Jewish community and
where the Europeans generally lived. The neighborhood used
to be called *Galata*, meaning, according to the Greeks, the
place of the milkman because it was where shepherds watched
their flocks. It was also calla *Pera*, from the old Greek (*Peran
en Sykais*, literally the fig field on the other side). What I like
about Istanbul is all the layers of history going back thousands
of years, all the way back to Constantinople and Byzantium
and even to legendary Troy.

Robinson Crusoe Books is where I will make my biggest
financial transaction. I am standing outside its dark wood and
glass front at 8:30 A.M., long before they open. It's a beautiful

sunny day and there are flowers blooming everywhere. It's early, so even though there are people in the streets, it isn't crowded yet. I go for breakfast and come back and browse the shelves for a long time.

When I discover I don't have enough money unless I pay in all the different currencies I'd willy-nilly acquired—the lei, the euro, the lira, the pound, the dollar—the man is kind enough to figure all the different exchange rates, first in his head, which he does so quickly I'm amazed, then with a calculator, writing it on paper for my benefit. It takes a few minutes, but I'm the only one there except for the usual quorum of Turkish guys leisurely sitting around drinking tea and talking. By this time I've come to expect that I may be the only woman in a room full of men sitting and talking and that such a group is apt to be a fixture of any shop in Istanbul. It doesn't bother me now, as it had the first day. I like the feeling that Istanbul is a place where people freely seek each other out and freely talk together.

By afternoon it's raining again, a cold rain, and I'm back on the other side of the city in the old area around the ancient palace. When you have enough books, you don't mind the rain. I make my way to my hotel. I pile the pillows high behind my back and begin skimming and sifting through vast tomes about ancient Persia. One of the best books is by Ogier de Busbecq, the sixteenth century ambassador to the Ottoman Empire from Flanders.

Busbecq describes the city of Constantinople as "created by nature to be the capitol of the world." Constantinople, which had been Byzantium for a thousand years, became Constantinople in 330 A.D. with Constantine's conquest. It would remain Constantinople until 1453, just a hundred years before Busbecq arrived. It officially became Istanbul in 1930. Perhaps the Turks, largely Muslim, didn't want their capital to be named for a ruler who'd converted to Christianity. Istanbul, according to Wikipedia, is Greek for *is-stan-polis*, to-the-city, and so isn't named for anyone.

Busbecq admired the fact that a shepherd or a slave could be promoted to the highest office in the government. He was amazed by some of the advancements in animal husbandry that he saw in Istanbul. Horses could live decades longer in Turkey than they did in Flanders since they were better fed and not beaten. He saw partridges being herded like sheep. When the partridges were first hatched they were put inside the shirts of young boys where they were kept warm and also fed saliva from the mouths of their caretakers. Turkish farmers were many centuries ahead of Konrad Lorenz in their understanding of imprinting. Special care rendered the partridges tame enough to be called with a whistle.

Busbecq is lively and genuine and wants to know about everything from tulips to turtles, from the politics of the harem to the turbans of the soldiers. He was the illegitimate son (legitimized in adulthood) of a Flemish nobleman and a lady at court. Busbecq was given a fabulous education. He spoke several languages and was, from all accounts, an excellent diplomat.

British historian Philip Mansel, in the introduction to the wonderful Eland 2001 edition of Busbecq's *Turkish Letters*, says that Busbecq's ambassadorship was "in part façade, masking the activities in Constantinople of a secret network of Hapsburg spies...possibly unknown to himself [Busbecq]." That the Hapsburg spies would have been unknown to Busbecq seems highly unlikely. Busbecq, in my understanding of the man based on my reading of his work, was not only extremely knowing but savvy enough to pretend otherwise. He grew up among the royals in Flanders and described the life at court as "the seat of envy and throne of bad faith." Busbecq was in Turkey for ten years and it seems it would have been difficult, if not impossible, to not be aware of any Hapsburg spies; his survival would have depended on both his knowing and his pretending not to know.

Busbecq was especially taken with the merit system in Turkey, where anyone of ability could advance, as opposed to Europe's system of conferring rank based on birth. Of course his own situation, where he had grown up in the palace and was on intimate terms with everyone, yet was still unable to be given full rights, would have given him a special appreciation for the merit system. The role of merit in Turkish public life, and Busbecq's writing about it, would have marked his views in Europe at the time as radical.

Busbecq writes, "On the Ottoman side are the resources of a mighty empire. Strength unimpaired, experience and practice in fighting, a veteran soldiery, habituation to victory, endurance of toil, unity, order, discipline, frugality and watchfulness. On our side is public poverty and private luxury, impaired strength, broken spirit, lack of endurance and training..." Only in the family of the Sultan does birth confer rank, other than that "no single man owed his dignity to anything but his personal merits and bravery."

Perhaps Busbecq's beginnings as an illegitimate person forever clouded his marriage prospects. Although often throughout his life he appears to have accepted assignments from various royals for the guardianship and care of their children, he seems never to have had the circumstances or the will to marry and have children of his own. Perhaps, after witnessing the passion of his parents, he was aware of the pitfalls of romance. Perhaps even a legitimized bastard had no real future. Perhaps like me, in order to keep loneliness at bay, from a very early age he grew accustomed to distracting himself by being interested in the world around him, and that became his life. A person without a partner, over time, learns to partner with the world.

Busbecq worked for the Hapsburgs, both directly and indirectly. The Hapsburgs were a vast family, an entity unto themselves, a bureaucracy. They were embedded in the royal houses from the British Isles to the Urals—whether Spanish, German, French, or English. They seemed to be in positions of power which they had engineered with political marriages all across Europe. It was not a very clever plan, but it worked for a long time: with an amazing persistence but decided lack of imagination, the Hapsburgs married cousins to cousins all over the place for four hundred years until they became hopelessly inbred, too crippled to walk, and too stupid to rule.

"As for the Hapsburgs, who with a little magnanimity might have become the saviors or at least the champions of Europe," sniffs Belgian historian Henri Pirenne in his *History of Europe*, still one of the most concise histories ever written, "they never managed to rise above the level of a greedy, hesitating policy... [and were] incapable of understanding" the Turkish invasions of Eastern Europe except as "an opportunity of appropriating the crowns of Bohemia and Hungary," waiting until those countries had been weakened by fighting off the Ottoman Empire, defending, as it were, Europe. Then the Hapsburgs moved in to add those places to their dynasty, always first and foremost serving the Hapsburg dynastic drive and little else.

Busbecq was the Austrian ambassador to Turkey when he was in his early thirties and served various members of the vast and powerful Austrian Hapsburgs until the end of his life. When he was seventy years old, the Hapsburgs allowed him to return to Flanders. Only a few days out, going from France to the Netherlands, Busbecq's traveling party was allegedly attacked by highway men. Busbecq died from his wounds.

All over Turkey Busbecq was impressed by the sense of community service in the culture. On a highway outside of Istanbul Busbecq found a place where villagers had provided water to travelers by creating a log sluice from a spring in the hills to a cistern by the road. In Turkey, according to Busbecq, selflessness and public service of all kinds were esteemed. Yes, in war they were fierce, he allowed, as everyone usually is, but in their everyday lives they were highly civilized. In Istanbul when Busbecq was there in the sixteenth century, there were soup kitchens for the poor. He reported that community members spontaneously took care of stray dogs and cats.

Turks are fond of cats, Busbecq notes, something I had observed even in my brief time: every store had a cosseted, resident feline. Turks regard cats as clean and intelligent, and so take care of them very well. Busbecq said they did not like dogs, regarding them as not clean and not intelligent; however, Busbecq reported, if there was a stray dog with puppies, they would make sure she had a warm, safe place for herself and her puppies, and would bring her bowls of food on the street.

Busbecq was housed by the Sultan in a three-story wooden house on a narrow side street near the palace, a house perhaps similar in many ways, despite the intervening four centuries, to my old hotel. From his upper story windows Busbecq could see slaves being herded into the city. Turkish soldiers fought so hard in part because the spoils of war, including slaves, were theirs. If they were lucky enough to survive the fighting, they could become rich. Busbecq was horrified by the slavery but did report that there were rules regarding slavery that were more humane than in many places in Europe. In Turkey, according to the laws at the time, a slave who had outlived his or her usefulness as a worker had to be supported until death.

As the ambassador from Flanders, Busbecq was part-prisoner, part-guest. He was monitored, as Peace Corps volunteers and other people generally are when they're working in foreign countries. In Romania, Thailand, and El Salvador I felt I was definitely under scrutiny at all times. People seemed polite on the surface, but underneath, it was as if they weren't sure whether to take advantage of me, throw me out, or become friends. I can relate to Busbecq's sense of curiosity about his hosts, and his diffidence toward them as well.

There is much to admire about Istanbul in all its incarnations: the beautiful parks, the soup kitchens for the poor, the public libraries, the excellent trolley. No, for me it would be about—and I'm speaking as a woman here—being able to read. Maybe I could have survived in the harem; I've always been a pushover for the guy who offers to go kill the tiger in the village while I stay home. And I like figs. You could eat a lot of figs before you were replaced by a younger woman. But to whom would I talk? Even today in Turkey only twenty percent of the women are literate. Would I have to do a reversal of Achilles, and dress like a man and go sit and have tea, if I wanted to talk about the economy?

We all die sometime, so it's about how good a life you can have until they come for you. But for me it would be, "Could I finish my book and then be strangled?" But since women weren't allowed to read, it wouldn't have even been a question.

I like figs, but not as much as books, so I think I'd have to pass on the harem. I would have been an unlikely candidate to become the Sultan's "one and only." I would have probably been one of those tiresome women who always wants to talk about the relationship. He'd be just getting back from some military campaign, ready for a little rest and recreation, and I'd be starting in again, talking about how I couldn't trust him, basically since the kidnapping. I'd probably be one of those sold again, to another buyer, into hard labor somewhere like Transylvania, far from the beautiful turquoise waters and the pink-tinged light surrounding the golden peninsula.

Amsterdam

Even with a cold, sleety rain blowing in off the North Sea, I'm sad to be leaving Amsterdam, not just because I love Sidonie, my niece, and she lives here, but because Amsterdam is one of the most joyful places in the world to be. I'm happy here. Other people are happy here.

You only need to walk down the street to feel it. On an overcast winter day with intermittent rain, the buskers in the center of town are playing great music while all around them people are laughing and talking and strolling with their families. The expressions on people's faces reflect the kindness, honesty, and intelligence of people who are reasonably safe, warm, well-fed, and well-educated. They smile and nod hello. You'd think the sun was out.

There are hot French fries for sale in paper cones. There are those cookies my mother always had in the cupboard that we called windmill cookies and the Dutch call *speclulaas*, pronounced *spake-close*. The cookies are rolled flat, about the size of a playing card. The top side depicts a horse, a bear, a house, or a ship. In Amsterdam on the day I walk through the city center with my niece, I see almost everything on these cookies except, ironically, the windmills that are on the version sold in America. The cookies used to be sold only at Christmas, Sidonie tells, me but are now sold all year. They are being baked as we pass. The cold, damp air is filled with the delicious aroma of nutmeg, clove, cardamom, and ginger.

There are steaming cups of hot coffee to go with the cookies.

There are food stalls all through the center of the town. At one point there seems to be an entire block of food markets, or perhaps a giant restaurant. It's like the multiple kitchens under a royal castle, with huge, befogging kettles of soup, savory roasting meats, fresh fish, lobster and other seafood that can be prepared as you wait, bright-colored vegetables in an amazing variety, all kinds of salads, and a luxurious array of desserts.

The city's flower market is located at the Singel Canal, a two-block long stretch, or longer, with an incredible variety of beautiful flowers: roses, amaryllis, chrysanthemums, Gerbera daisies, baby's breath, lupines, calla lilies and fragrant hyacinths, tuberoses, narcissus and jasmine. Beyond the flower market itself, there are flower stalls on almost every corner.

My niece explains that the Dutch like to have fresh flowers in their homes and places of work year-round, even or especially in winter. This is the country that went crazy for tulips five hundred years earlier and today has a two-million-square-meter flower auction warehouse in Aalsmeer just thirty minutes from Amsterdam. Lest you think the Dutch are extravagant, they aren't. They are modest in their tastes. They do not put on airs, just the reverse. The well-to-do use public transportation. In the Netherlands, among even those who can afford it, unnecessary or ostentatious purchases are considered in bad taste. Sidonie says the Dutch simply like flowers and consider flowers a normal and necessary part of everyday life. Flowers are not an extravagance.

Amsterdam is rainy and cloudy two-hundred-and-fourteen days a year, but it's not a depressing place, just the reverse. From asking directions, to buying a book, to sitting down on the tram, there's only openness and respect in the people you meet. There are one-hundred-and-seventy-eight different ethnic groups in Amsterdam, more than London or Manhattan.

Russell Shorto, author of *Amsterdam—A History of the World's Most Liberal City*, hypothesized that the culture of tolerance developed because Amsterdam has been a major world trading center for at least five hundred years. You can't successfully conduct business with folks and also be telling them how to dress, when to eat, where to worship, and what to think.

The Vermeer painting that I think of when I think of Amsterdam is the man with the globe, *The Astronomer,* from 1668, where an intelligent young man is looking earnestly at the whole world, curious about it. There's only the light from a window so we know there's no electricity. He's dressed in heavy layers of clothing, so we understand there's little heat. This was four hundred and fifty years ago, but it's a prescient or prophetic painting, modern in its sensibility. The intellectuals of Amsterdam, maybe because of the ships coming and going from everywhere, already understood that they needed to do things in the context of a larger world.

It's a well-known fact that the Dutch are the tallest people on the planet. You might think this is simple genetics, but it's not: the Dutch were the same height as everyone else a hundred years ago. In fact, it was Americans who were the tallest a hundred years ago but now, according to ABC News, we are the shortest people in the industrialized world. Sidonie is five-feet-ten-inches and her husband is six-foot-eight. Sidonie grew up in Canada where she was taller than other Canadian young ladies and always had trouble getting clothes that fit; now in the Netherlands, she says, she's average: there are lots of clothes in her size.

People in the Netherlands started to get taller about the same time they established a liberal democracy in the 1850s, according to J. W. Drukker, a professor of economic history at the University of Groningen. Prior to that, the Dutch got rich off their colonies but the money stayed in the hands of the wealthy few. In the middle of the nineteenth century, however, the rule of law, individual civil liberties, health care, and free education were guaranteed to every citizen.

The Dutch are taller and better educated and healthier than we are because they have better government. "If Joe is taller than Jack, it's probably because his parents are taller," according to science writer Burkhard Bilger in an article called *The Height Gap* in the *New Yorker* in 2004. "But if the average Norwegian is taller than the average Nigerian it's because Norwegians live healthier lives." According to Bilger we achieve our stature in three spurts: in infancy; between the ages of six and eight; and in adolescence. Remove any one of fifty essential nutrients and the body and mind stop growing. Bilger says that iodine deficiency alone can knock off fifteen I.Q. points. Americans started to get shorter in the 1950s, about the same time the greater height of the Dutch was becoming unmistakable.

The Netherlands have free post-natal and prenatal care and it's available to everybody, equally. My niece had a home health care nurse visit her while she was pregnant and after the baby was born. She had six weeks leave from her job. She, and everyone else in the Netherlands, is eligible for reduced work hours, without losing their jobs or their income in order to be allowed to spend time with their children during the years the children are small.

Taking care of children is one of the nation's top priorities. In the Netherlands they have a capitalist economy, but they use the money to create social programs that provide education, housing, food, and health services so that their citizens are not limited in their ability to provide adequately for their children. The Netherlands has minimal income disparity between rich and poor and has one of the highest standards of living in the world.

The Dutch aren't perfect. They were involved in the Atlantic slave trade up through the early 1800s, but they outlawed it fifty years ahead of the United States. South Africa, settled by the Dutch and British, had one of the most racist governments in the world until Nelson Mandela, after enduring twenty-seven years in prison, became president in 1994. The Dutch had Indonesian and African colonies for centuries; they liberated them in the mid-1900s. The Netherlands doesn't have an unblemished present either. The influx of immigrants from Morocco and Turkey has created a backlash against Muslims that you hear voiced by otherwise tolerant and educated Dutch citizens.

The one issue on which my niece and I disagree, politely but absolutely, is about *Zwarte Piet*, or Black Pete, the mythic servant of the Dutch Santa, *Sinterklaas*. Santa Claus arrives in the Netherlands by steamship in mid-November accompanied by several Black Petes. Together they pass out treats to children. Children in the Netherlands dress in black face in the holiday parades, don shiny, black, plastic, cheap, frizzy wigs, garish gold earrings, and large, wax lips. According to several sources, including Matthew McKnight writing in a December 2014 *New Yorker*, Black Pete brings not only treats but punishment sticks for bad children, and it's for the latter that he's historically most famous. Sidonie said that although she personally does not favor the tradition, "people love Black Pete," as a fantasy figure and she has never seen him bring punishments.

A letter from the United Nations High Commission on Human Rights in 2013, asking the Dutch to discontinue this "living trace of slavery" because Black Pete perpetuates an image of people of African descent as second-class citizens, was met with public protests. A court ruling in Amsterdam to prohibit parades with Black Pete was overturned by one of the country's higher courts in 2014.

But I think the Dutch fondness for Black Pete is a simple blind spot, more about a failure of good taste than an indication of a culture of racism. Your average young, African American male would probably rather be arrested in the Netherlands than in New York, would choose to be black in Amsterdam before Ferguson, Missouri. The Dutch generally, when it comes to race, religion, age, income, and gender, are a tolerant people, and have a reputation for being so that goes way back. English poet Andrew Marvell, observing Amsterdam in the 1600s, writes, "Take Christian-Pagan-Jew…[Amsterdam is] where [every] strange opinion finds credit and exchange."

By the time Marvell visited Amsterdam it had been a trading center for hundreds of years, a place where people found it expedient not to quibble about a client's religion or customs.

When the country was under the rule of the Holy Roman Empire in the 1500s, the Dutch were ordered to execute heretics and burn books. They mostly said they would, and then they mostly didn't. Always thinking ahead, they knew they might have to transact business with some of these so-called heretics, or the friends or relatives of the heretics, at some point in the future. There was also the very real possibility, the way things can change depending on who's in power, that the heretics might not always be considered heretics. It was unwise to make future enemies.

Shorto has a wonderful anecdote about a Dutch mayor who promised the Holy Roman Emperor that he would punish Protestants. The mayor rounded up eight people who'd attended a Lutheran service. Instead of having the people burned at the stake, boiled in oil, tarred and feathered, hung by their toes and so on, as was done elsewhere during the Inquisition, he ordered the sheriff to make the heretical Lutherans, all holding candles, march in a parade of a few blocks.

When I was going to school in the northwest Michigan lakeshore town of Glen Arbor in the 1950s—population under a hundred—we studied what we all called Holland. We knew it was also called the Netherlands, but out of habit or a preference for the shorter word, we called it Holland. Everyone did. My niece says this is not correct. She says I was taught wrong. Holland refers to two separate provinces, one in the north and one in the south, both of which are in a country called the Netherlands. The two Holland provinces are the equivalent of two of our states, so it would be like calling the entire United States, Michigan, for example, or Florida. So now I say the Netherlands when I refer to the country as a whole. And I say it the Dutch way which is Nader, like Ralph Nader, and Lance, like Lance Armstrong, so it's NA-der-Lance, with the emphasis on the first syllable and a lot of "z" at the end, as if you're Zorro with a light sword.

In Glen Arbor we learned that the Dutch were known for windmills, wooden shoes, and tulips. Those things are true. But what we were not taught, in addition to the proper term for the country, is that Netherlanders figured out, long before most people, that a rising tide lifts all boats, that everyone is better off when everyone is better off, and that a culture of basic fairness engenders a humane and intelligent people.

There are bicycles everywhere in Amsterdam. One-third of the people commute on bicycles. Sidonie has two cheap bikes, one at her home in Amsterdam and one at her work place in The Hague. Other people in Amsterdam can rent a city bike, a system where they buy a code for the lock, and leave the bike for the next person, who also has a code. My niece says that when Amsterdam started a program of free bikes, a lot of bikes ended up in the canals. Then they fine-tuned the project, adding the coded locks among other things. There are bike lanes and bike racks everywhere. There are streams of people on bikes all over the city.

The Dutch are famously practical. They have legalized soft drugs, like marijuana and alcohol, but restrict the use to certain areas; and the same with prostitution. This way they can control the negative aspects for health and safety and they avoid the creation of an underground market which is harder to see, harder to control, and more dangerous. They were the first country, in 2001, to legalize same-sex marriages.

A new program in the Netherlands is one where alcoholics are given jobs where part of their pay is in beer. According to *The New York Times*, December 4, 2013, the new program isn't about getting alcoholics to stop drinking, but about giving them something to do, "other than sitting in the park and drinking themselves to death."

One of the reasons my sister Keylaira fell in love with Sidonie's Dutch-born father is that he was practical, polite, and unflappable. When they were first together and working on a documentary together up at Frobisher Bay in the Canadian Arctic, the film crew was having lunch, sitting on the floor inside an igloo with several other people around a piece of frozen meat in the center, a kind of Inuit-style sushi, each person slicing off a thin piece with an ax. As I heard about this back in Michigan at a family gathering, I wondered if that had been socially awkward and asked the prospective brother-in-law, "What did you say?" My sister's future husband answered, "I said, 'Please pass the ax.'" You could fall in love with a person like that, and my sister did.

Six thousand years ago the population along the North Sea was sparse. The area was tundra, barely thawed. Three thousand years ago people in that part of the Netherlands were living in long, low, windowless houses made of thatch. You couldn't stand up in them. They were like thatched pup tents. There was a stone hearth at one end and people crawled in through a hole in the other end.

So how did the Dutch get from houses that looked like thatched pup tents on the tundra, to the prosperity and enlightenment of the present? There are several answers. Partly it's that Holland is miniscule. It's the size of Maryland, one-fifth the size of Michigan. They talk to each other because they can, and because they have to; they occupy such a small space, they can scarcely avoid it. As a tiny country with a small army, they were sensibly always more inclined toward making money through business than through war.

Farming was always difficult because of the flooding. Netherlands means, literally, low lands. They had great natural harbors, however, at Rotterdam and Amsterdam. As soon as they discovered boats and shipping and educated themselves about navigating on the ocean, they became a center for foreign trade.

The Dutch tend to be egalitarian, according to Shorto, because they have a history of working together, going back hundreds of years, as they worked together to reclaim land from the sea. It wasn't something one person could do alone. The land they reclaimed was owned by individuals and towns, not by feudal lords. Shorto theorizes that the Netherlands was never part of the feudal system entrenched in the rest of Europe, and so they developed democracy long before the rest of the continent.

The printing press was invented three hundred miles from Amsterdam in Strasburg, Germany, in the middle of the fifteenth century by Johannes Guttenberg. According to James Burke, author of *The Day the Universe Changed*, a printing press began operating in the Netherlands about the same time.

In the early seventeenth century, the heyday of Shakespeare in England, protestants, dissenters, renegades, debtors, people down on their luck, people wanted by the law—immigrants of all kinds—began crossing over to the Netherlands. It only took a day from Ipswich to Rotterdam. The idea was to ship out from Dutch ports to America. The English immigrants often had to stay in the Netherlands for years, however, trying to work and save enough money to leave, before they got on a ship to New York (then called New Amsterdam) far across the Atlantic. While they tarried in the Netherlands, they naturally absorbed some of the culture.

Professor H. de la Fontaine Verwey, referenced by Shorto on page one hundred and seventy-nine of his Amsterdam book, claimed there were many publishers and bookstores in the Netherlands at this time. (Both my niece, Sidonie, and my proofreader questioned the number Shorto gave, which is why I have not given the specific numbers and have supplied Shorto's page number.) The English pilgrims waiting to travel to America, and the Dutch already living in the Netherlands, according to Shorto, were all reading. To this day, whenever there's a problem, the Dutch think about it, read about it, talk about it, and do something about it.

This is how smart the Dutch are: they were the first to reclaim land from the sea, but now they're also the first to return it. They are to date the only country in the world to have taken precautions against global warming. The salt marshes and mud flats are crucial for preventing flooding along the edges of the North Sea. The Dutch didn't know this at first, but now they do, and so despite having a pressing need for land, they are letting it revert back. The Dutch try new things, they give it some thought, they collaborate, and if something isn't working, they change.

Because rising sea levels caused by global warming would be so disastrous for the Dutch, they have been hard at work trying to think of ways to combat this. They use bicycles as a way to cut down on carbon emissions. They do research. A retired geochemist in Utrecht, Olaf Schuiling, according to *The New York Times* November 9, 2014, believes olivine, a mineral that removes carbon dioxide from the atmosphere, can be used on roads and playgrounds and would slow the rise in global temperatures. Dr. Schuiling says, "Let the earth help save the earth."

The path to tolerance and reasonableness in this population appears to have been a gradual process. A few hundred years ago when other countries were trying to deal with the Spanish Inquisition, the Dutch started encouraging immigrants and refugees, including Jewish bankers and merchants from Portugal and English Dissenters from the King, to come to The Netherlands. Just like America's policy of encouraging immigration, they got the best and the brightest.

We often forget that the Dutch were in the New World before the English. New Amsterdam wouldn't become New York until the British invaded in 1665. Harlem and Brooklyn and a hundred more places were named by the Dutch. Coney Island derives from the Dutch and was first called *Konijne-neiland*, Rabbit Island. Broadway was originally *de Brede Weg.* The Dutch system of laws and protection of individual rights, the humanism that was formulated by the religious scholars Spinoza and Erasmus, among others, became part of the culture in America, too. That's one of the reasons the Netherlands today feels so comfortable to an American: a lot of what the Dutch brought to the New World became the foundation for our own democracy. The English Dissenters from the King, some of whom were my ancestors, came to The Netherlands in the early 1600s precisely because it was so liberal. They wanted to escape the repression in England and find a safe place to work where they could earn enough money to set sail for the New World.

The United States and the Netherlands, according to Drukker, Shorto, and others, were similar in values until the early 1900s, at which time they diverged. Where America made democracy and capitalism synonymous and allowed the big corporations and banks to get bigger and bigger, to the point that their power corrupted the political process, the Dutch were more sensible and when the economy started getting off-track and people were suffering, they rerouted.

The Dutch economy burgeoned in the early 1900s and, as might be expected, "factories got larger, competition increased, owners slashed wages and lengthened work days," according to Shorto, and that's when Dutch society fell apart. "Parents were forced to send children to work; girls became prostitutes; boys stole." All this in turn brought in socialist parties that offered the promise of a better life.

That's the point at which the Dutch took a different path from the Americans. The Dutch incorporated socialist principles into their democratic governance in the early 1900s. After the Second World War and the moral collapse, they did so again, according to Shorto, who writes, "In effect, the Dutch asked themselves: 'Who are we, what do we want to become, and how can we use this crisis to arrange our society to advance our goals?'"

Shorto's theory about why the Dutch took a different tack is that, "Where in neighboring countries society in the dim past had broken down into nobility and peasants, the Dutch with their...need to battle against the sea...had an ingrained group ethic." Maybe, but America didn't have a history of peasants and nobility, and we certainly knew how to do community barn-raisings and community harvesting and threshing in the early days, and yet, at least at the present time, we seem determined to let corporations become the new nobility while the rest of us—working for eight dollars an hour when that's the cost of lunch, a used book, or a good pair of socks; poor wages that won't support a person much less a family—feel ourselves regressing, slipping and sliding, inevitably back to some sort of medieval serfdom.

Other than my niece and her family, the only person of Dutch extraction I've ever known is my neighbor in Lake Leelanau, Anneke Wegman. Her father had immigrated to Canada after the Second World War and she had come from there to Michigan. Her mother's family had been in Haarlem, about thirty miles from Amsterdam, and had lived in a home above their seed and bulb warehouse on a canal. The family had been there for four hundred years when the Nazis came to Haarlem and blew up the home, the warehouse, and the bridge. "It was in a strategic location," Anneke told me, without emotion since she probably had been over this many times before, "so they dynamited it."

Haarlem was historically a wealthy trading center for at least a thousand years. It's still wealthy. There are some huge mansions in a forested area close to the North Sea. In the fog and rain and blue-gray Vermeer light, my niece's husband points out the thatched roofs on some of these large, gabled homes and says that's the latest fashion, that thatched roofs have become very desirable. Thatched roofs are expensive because few people know how to do it. Thatched roofs fell from favor because they are a fire hazard. They have only recently come back into vogue because people find there is a quaint charm in a thatched roof.

Thatched roofs have to be routinely maintained and also have to be replaced every thirty years or so. Sidonie's husband said his grandfather on his mother's side had been a thatcher, a highly skilled trade. It went out of style, as things do, but now there's a revival. My niece's husband joked that if he had learned how to be a thatcher from his grandfather, he might today be one of the wealthier craftsmen in Haarlem.

The North Sea has a wild and gray look, fierce and dangerous, like Lake Superior. Between the town of Haarlem and the North Sea, there are low dunes. It feels like Michigan. The wind is blowing. Not hard, just in that constant way that you get near a large body of water, especially in the winter.

The morning I leave Amsterdam I get up at 4 A.M. and move quietly so as to not disturb my already sleep-deprived hosts and their new baby. Later Sidonie will tell me she woke up and watched me from the window, just as I was leaving. She waved, but I never looked up because I was waiting for the taxi, looking into the street.

In the dark and rain, I trundle my small, old, stained, sturdy, brown duffle bag on brass casters across the small bridge over the canal and to the curb. A duck in the canal is happily floating on the slight current. Ducks like fog and rain.

There are a few people out at this hour, coming home from parties. There's a man on his bicycle, peddling madly, perhaps on his way to work. Just before I get into the taxi I say hello to a family out for a bike ride: a mother, a father, two small children, all on their bicycles; clearly it's a recreational outing. At four in the morning? Yes, but only in the Netherlands.

My 400-year-old English Ancestors

I don't know if you've reached the place in your life yet where you want to find your ancestors. It seems to be something that comes with age. Maybe you don't care. I didn't care for years. But the truth is that all Americans, I'm speaking as one here, came from somewhere else. Native Americans were always here, but what about the rest of us? Sooner or later we start trying to trace the trail back.

When I was a fractious teen at Glen Lake High School, my parents decided I should spend my senior year in Buffalo with my oldest sister, a biology professor at Canisius College. In September, before Ann and I drove out across Canada, my father told me that if I got a chance, I should go to the Buffalo Public Library and see if they had the book, *The Stockings in America*. There'd be a big library there in Buffalo, and he thought they might have it. He'd heard about the book from his grandfather, Erastus Post Stocking, who'd been born in 1825 in New York State's Madison County. Erastus came into Ohio from New York in the mid-1850s, most likely by way of the Erie Canal. In Ohio he married Mary Jane David, sixteen years his junior, and sometime later they came north by oxcart to White Cloud, Michigan.

One bright, fall Saturday, tired of hanging around my sister's office at the college, I took the bus down to Lafayette Square in the center of Buffalo. The library was a grand, noble, behemoth of a place, designed in 1887 by the famous American architect, Cyrus Eidilitz. Although I didn't know it at the time, I would be one of the last patrons in that awe-inspiring place. The old library would be replaced a year later by a new one that looks like an office building. I found the book in the rare book collection. It wasn't in the general circulation section. I had to read it in a special room of the library under supervision. It was a thin, mildewed, ancient copy with the liver-spotted pages falling out.

The book recorded George Stocking as an immigrant to Connecticut in 1633. He came from Suffolk, England, during the chaotic period leading up to the English Civil War. He was labeled "a Dissenter from the King and a Nonconformist," like you'd put a label on a jar of home-canned pickles. For the first time it occurred to me that maybe my rebelliousness was genetic. Stocking means a measure of standing timber ready for harvest, a "stock," as you would have "stock" in the stock market on Wall Street, or as you would have "stock" in the stock pot on the back of the stove for soup. It means "to take stock" of something or to "take the measure" of something.

The Old English *stucca* means a trunk or log of a tree. The Stockings, including my father and his father and his grandfather and perhaps all the way back to Suffolk, were lumberjacks. They were ordinary people, not rich or royal. George, who died in America at the age of one hundred and three, was illiterate and signed his name with an 'x.' He had worked as a surveyor so he must have known numbers. It was still early times for reading. The name Stocking is recorded in a survey of English land owners in 1086.

People always seem to describe the New World as a wild and forbidding place, but if you think about it for a minute, for a tree cutter four hundred years ago, any forest would have been pretty much like another. There weren't any airplanes or roads. Everything was field and forest, with a bit more of the latter than the former. A cottage of hand-hewn timbers in Suffolk would have been little different from a cottage of hand-hewn timbers on the Connecticut River; and in Connecticut, the hunting and fishing would have been better.

When George Stocking came to America, the idea of the king's so-called Divine Authority ever residing in ordinary, untitled men, much less there being any respect for the individual rights or personal liberty of such men, was new. Women and their children had no rights and were the property of the men to whom they were assigned through birth, marriage or purchase. If I had been a woman in that time, I think I might have opted for a frontier outpost, simply because I would have been more needed and would have had more value. My husband would have had to think twice about the way he treated me since it would have been difficult to find a replacement.

The English ballad about Geordie, the lad who was hung for killing the king's deer, had its origin in the reality of a time, not so long before George Stocking came to America, when English law decreed that all the deer belonged to the king and his friends. Geordie's fellow outlaw, Robin Hood, famous for robbing from the rich and giving to the poor, was real, too, in some fashion, or we wouldn't have the story of it. Even four hundred years ago the old ideas about natural inequality still held sway. In Roman law the status ladder was: slave, freeman, land holder, warrior, citizen, and ruler. In the Hindu caste system it was: untouchable, laborer, farmer, artisan, soldier, royalty, and priest. In English society it was: riffraff, military recruit, worker, craftsman, merchant, nobility, and king. (Women didn't exist, really, nor did children.) These ideas about natural inequality, and the hierarchies built into everyday reality, were only beginning to change, and ever so slowly, when George Stocking got on a boat for America.

England isn't very big. It's roughly the size of Michigan. And, like Michigan, you're never more than sixty miles from a view of the water. Michigan's a peninsula. England *was* a peninsula. Eight thousand years ago England was a European peninsula called Doggerland, a swampy wasteland that probably wasn't used for agriculture and might have been good only for hunting and fishing. Then glaciers melted, the sea rose, there seems to have been a tsunami, water rushed into the riverbed of what is now the English Channel, and Britain became an island.

Some ancient people in England three thousand years ago raised the stones at Stonehenge—perhaps stones brought by a tsunami or a glacier or, more fancifully, flown through the air by Druids; nobody knows for sure—and also, for reasons no one knows, made a four-hundred-foot-long chalk horse, or what people guess is a horse, because it's got a beak so it's not exactly a horse, on a hill near Uffington in Oxfordshire. They were up to stuff, those folks who lived around there, but nobody knows what.

These are the two things I learn on the Internet about Suffolk County: the Magna Carta was signed there, and there had been a ship burial, like the ones in Scandinavia, at Sutton Hoo on the Deben River. Pieces of that old ship from fourteen centuries ago are in the British Museum. I know, because one day I got off the tube at Russell Square and went to see them in their temperature-and-humidity-controlled glass case. They were pretty far gone, the ship's pieces, not much there after all that time.

The British Museum is a wild place, like someone's crazy aunt's attic, crammed with stuff from all over the world, much of it looted during the heyday of British colonialism. It takes up an entire city block and is several stories tall. It holds the Rosetta Stone, kind of a metaphor for the place itself.

I like London. I like the restaurants where there are young people working from all over the world. I like the signs on the public busses that advertised the 2012 Olympics on one side and, "Some people are gay, get over it" on the other. I like the queen, or her facsimile, in cotton leggings and heavy shoes and her frumpy hairdo, parachuting into the Olympics. I like the Olympics opening with all the nurses on roller skates pushing hospital beds around in honor of Florence Nightingale. I like London's yellow-haired mayor, Boris Johnson, bicycling madly about town like a giant Tweety Bird.

I like the dry and subtle English sense of humor. My mother was a teacher of English, and so I've heard the stories, like the one about Thomas More, the man who dared to disagree with King Henry VIII. More said to his beheader, as he ascended the scaffold, "See me safe up: for my coming down I can shift for myself."

I like the honesty of the English lower classes. Nell Gwyn, born in a brothel where she learned the trade from her mother, was a beautiful little girl who caught the eye of King Charles II when she was selling oranges at the theater; she later became his mistress and bore him two illegitimate sons. One day her coachman began to fight a man who had called Gwyn a whore. She got down out of her carriage and broke it up, saying, "I am a whore. Find something else to fight about."

Don't mess with English orange girls. Their stock in trade is the unvarnished truth and a sense of humor on top of it. Gwyn also allegedly said, "Rich people are just poor people with wigs," and to her son, one day when the king visited, "Come here, you little bastard, say hello to your father," whereupon the King gave the kid a title and an estate. Gwyn's pungent remarks aren't recorded in "Bartlett's Famous Quotations" because she was illiterate and couldn't write anything down but people knew, and people told. A Robin Hood type of a different stripe and a different gender, Gwyn left money to the poor in New Gate Prison when she died.

The English like beautiful and outspoken women, starting with Boudicca, who fought the Romans, right up through Margaret Thatcher, who fought the miners, and Lady Diana, who fought for her place in a marriage that, as she said, was "crowded" because it included Camilla, her husband's mistress.

Somewhere I read that the word for the Britons means 'the bright ones,' because of the way they wore their beautifully crafted gold ornaments. I think it's their language that is bright. They were few in number and small in stature. They learned how to do with words, what the Romans only knew how to do with spears.

I like the feistiness in the English language which, thank

goodness, crossed the ocean with them when they came to the New World and reappears in Herman Melville, Emily Dickinson, Henry Thoreau, Walt Whitman, Mark Twain, James Baldwin, Leonard Peltier, Toni Morrison, Alice Walker, Lenny Bruce, George Saunders, Jon Stewart and many others. Authors don't come from nothing. They come from a culture. Shakespeare didn't appear out of nowhere, like Athena from the head of Zeus, full-armored. Shakespeare, and his language, came out of a place where the people said what they thought and said it well enough to stop someone in their tracks and make them think. Nobody exists in a vacuum. The spirit of a writer comes from the people who surround him or her. It's first in the people, in the place they live, and it's in their talk, and then it's in the writer. It gets in there from living. It gets in there from feeling and thinking and talking, and, finally, it's in the writing.

Half the people on the red double-decker busses are from somewhere else. I like that there are all different kinds of people on the bus: different clothing styles, different skin colors, different ages and, from the looks of things, different incomes; and those differences seem to be just fine with everyone. I like a democratic prism.

Most of us on the bus, no matter where we're from, speak English. I think the English people may disappear, once they've intermarried with everyone they've colonized, but the English language is likely here to stay.

Peace Corps volunteers in Thailand were saying in 2006, as we were hearing that the Chinese were gaining global economic ascendancy and would soon surpass the United States, that the next international language would be Chinese, because there are already more than a billion Chinese people, and more every day. But India will soon have more people than the United States and China combined, and many of them, thanks to conquest and oppression, already speak English. Also, no small thing, the Chinese language has fifty thousand written characters, time-consuming to learn how to write, even for the Chinese who can already speak the language, whereas the alphabet for the English language, thanks to the Roman invasion, has twenty-six letters.

At the same time that the English language has a smaller alphabet than most other languages, it has more words than any other language, more than a million. This, too, is because the English were conquered and colonized, not just by the Romans, but by the French, Germans, and Scandinavians; and each time they were taken over they were required, by decree or by the need to conduct their affairs with the people in power, to speak the language of their oppressors. The English had the language of their conquerors shoved down their throats, quite literally. The languages interbred, there in the throats of the English, or in their heads, or something. The Chinese language, by contrast, only has about three-hundred-thousand words, roughly a third as many as the English language.

More words means more ways to say things. Joseph Conrad, a Polish count, and Vladimir Nabokov, a Russian nobleman, chose to write in English, their second language, because there were more word choices and, no small thing for a writer, more readers. Authors may write in their own native language, but once their books are translated into English, they have more readers in English than they ever did in Urdu or Swedish, for example. English is the language of ideas, of world literature, commerce, computers, and international travel. English got the beachhead.

There's something else the English language has that makes it fecund and strong and flexible, and likely to outlast all the other languages, something that has nothing to do with the sheer number of words or the millions of people using it, and that's what I call the Nell Gwyn factor, which is: the freedom to say what you feel and think. Freedom of speech is the foundation of civilization. Shut us up and we're no different than the beasts. If Nell Gwyn had been the mistress of the king of

Thailand, for example, even today, or the lady-on-the-side for a Salvadoran coffee grower or Russian oligarch, she would have been, and would be, "silenced," permanently, for being so outspoken; and she would have known this even before she spoke which is the whole point of silencing people. It's the most used tool of all authoritarian regimes and thuggery in general. The freedom to think is germane to the freedom of expression, and both are essential to speaking eloquently. The English language has that more or less built in to it. It's all of a piece. Speaking well and speaking out are in the same place in the brain.

Westminster Abbey, with all the tombs of all the kings and queens for eighteen centuries, is beautiful. Parts of it were still under construction when Chaucer, in the last years of his life, trying to stay out of the inclement weather, was forced to join the beggars and thieves in the courtyard there. He sent several letters to the Royal Exchequer asking for back wages for his services tending to the docks along the Thames, but no one ever responded. Chaucer finally died in Westminster after a mugging. Only years later did the palace honor Chaucer with a very large, handsome tomb, which was thoughtful of them, but he probably could have made better use of it when he was alive to stay out of the rain.

In beautiful spring weather I cross and re-cross London by subway and bus. It's easy and cheap. They have great maps. They have information kiosks all over the city, staffed by the world's nicest people. I like the names for places: Burned Oak, Picadilly Circus, Knightsbridge, Tower Hill, Pimlico, Hay Market Square, Covent Gardens, Oxford Street, Charing Cross, Aldgate, Newgate, Cripplegate, Shoreditch, and Cockfosters. In London my name isn't the only funny one.

My hotel is on Belgrave Road. It's a little place, cheap and clean with windows that open, in an old, four-story house with no elevator. The stout Scotsman who'd hauled my bag to the top floor the first day, stopping to rest at the third floor landing, finally had to ask what in the world I had in my luggage that made it so heavy. He just had to know. Who could imagine what such an odd, little old woman might have in her duffel? The Elgin Marbles? Gold bullion? Smuggled antiquities? Contraband artifacts? Human organs? Haggis?

"Books," I'd told him, and winked broadly.

He'd nodded sagely, and with a remarkably dead-pan face, said, "Of course, Madam."

Coming from my Peace Corps site in Romania, I'd stopped at Charing Cross on my way into town and gone to Foley's Books with an almost empty duffel bag. I can't live without books. Books are something one can't get in Romania, at least not books one wants. Amazon won't ship books to Romania because the books don't always arrive. Books are too heavy to carry while traveling and so I'd planned to read the books while I was in England and leave them behind. I'd wanted to tell him this, and tell him that I would be able to bring the bag down myself, but because I could see he already thought I was barmy, I'd just smiled and thanked him when we got to the top and, of course, tipped him.

The first morning in the little basement eating room of my humble lodgings, I'm served toast, eggs, bacon, juice, and baked beans. Now I know where my mother got the idea for her bean sandwiches which her children all spurned but which she liked. You probably don't need a DNA test for Englishness if you can eat a bean sandwich. Maybe my mother was English after all.

We all mythologize ourselves, and my mother, to whatever extent she could, saw herself as English. She bought English biscuits in tins with the British flag on them. She quoted Shakespeare by the page. For years I thought Macbeth was some guy who lived in Glen Arbor. When Queen Elizabeth and Prince Phillip sailed through the Great Lakes and their glamorous cruise ship passed for an hour or more in front of our home's long wall of picture windows looking out over Lake

Michigan and Sleeping Bear Bay, my mother watched with joy and pride, dabbing her eyes. There was the Queen!

I was young, but I thought her love of the Queen was odd. Wasn't that the queen of the country America had fought during the Revolutionary War? The country of those frightful tinned biscuits? In fact my mother was not at all English by heritage or anything else. She was at best Scottish and maybe Jewish.

Three families, the Lees, the Cushmans and the Finks, came over from Scotland in the late 1800s. They were peddlers in Scotland, became greengrocers in Canada, and eventually became regular grocers in the United States. My grandfather Lee married my grandmother Cushman. The Lee and Cushman families were close, but my grandparents, Armon Lee and Ruth Cushman, were not. They were estranged and emotionally distant from each other when I knew them, always quarreling, and according to stories my mother told, seem never to have been in love or even respectful of each other. Why had they married? Was it because their families felt that it was important for their children to marry someone Jewish? Was Lee an anglicized version of Levi? And why did my grandfather Lee listen to the baseball game on the radio in the car out under the apple tree in August when it was hot, wearing a hat and a shawl, while also reading the Bible?

My mother kept matzos on a top shelf at Easter and said they were crackers. But if they were crackers why couldn't we eat them whenever we wanted like the other crackers? When her breast cancer metastasized when she was in her eighties, she said that breast cancer was something to which Jewish women were more prone.

I didn't know what matzos were, but I remembered how she'd stiffened when I was little and asked her about them. When I made friends with Jewish students at the University of Michigan, I learned matzos were the unleavened bread for

Passover. I didn't think about matzos again until Madeleine Albright was Secretary of State and reporters uncovered her Jewish heritage. I have no idea if my mother was Jewish; maybe she was mythologizing herself as that, too. What I do know is that she never researched her genealogy or showed any curiosity about it, and she was the kind who would have.

England was the most virulently anti-Semitic country in Europe for hundreds of years. The religious persecution and ethnic bias was, unfortunately for Jewish people there, woven into the culture: a law against money-lending for Christians, combined with other laws keeping Jewish people from doing just about everything else, meant that Jewish people naturally fell into the unsavory occupation of usury or loan-sharking. Jewish people had to wear red hats so people could avoid them.

There were never very many Jewish people in England, presumably because of bad living conditions and murderous attacks, but after an Edict of Expulsion in 1289 there were none, or at least none who were there openly or legally. Many Jewish families went to Scotland during this time since Scotland was less restrictive. Oliver Cromwell changed the law again following the English Civil War. Cromwell allowed rich Jews back into England in 1657, but only because he needed money. Manasseh ben Israel from Amsterdam was one of the people who talked him into this. Shakespeare's single Jewish character, Shylock, in "The Merchant of Venice," a play written sometime between 1590 and 1600, includes many of the negative English stereotypes about Jews. The Nazis put on this play in 1943 as anti-Jewish propaganda.

My father, I'm sorry to say, was anti-Semitic. He would have had no occasion to know anyone Jewish in northern Michigan, but during the Great Depression he had made arrangements with a Jewish vendor in Detroit to sell the Christmas trees he'd grown. It takes eight years to grow a Christmas tree, and they have to be pruned every year of that. My father hired a crew and cut his trees in northern Michigan, rented a semi-truck, and drove five hours south to Detroit's Eastern Market. When he arrived, the man said that Christmas trees weren't selling very well and therefore he could only pay half what he'd promised. My father brought the trees home and burned them in a giant bonfire in the backyard gravel pit.

When my child's Jewish father kidnapped her from the daycare in Manhattan, before this kind of thing was illegal, my father told me to prepare for "Jewish tricks and lies," which, in fact, did follow. My father died soon after and went to his grave with his prejudices intact. If my mother was Jewish, she apparently never told my father. Even if she was Jewish, which we still don't know, if she had ever been inclined to tell him, say in one of those intimate moments in a relationship when we trust completely and want to divulge everything, she would have reasonably enough, certainly after the scary, Christmas-tree-bonfire-in-the-backyard incident, decided against it.

My mother went to London several times to see plays, sometimes taking students, and sometimes, because the group rate made it economical, going with a tour arranged through the National Council of the Teachers of English. Now by some fluke of fate I'm in London, so I decide to go and see what it feels like to go to a play here, the way my mother did.

On Leicester Square in the pouring rain, I get a cheap, last-minute, matinee ticket for *Blood Brothers* and walk a few blocks and wait in the rain until I can follow the others up the narrow stairs to the balcony. There's red velvet everywhere, but the feeling of elegant refinement, something I think I'd always almost unconsciously associated with anything my mother liked to do, is missing. There are no people speaking through their noses; no one in a mink stole with elbow-length gloves; no maids circulating with flutes of champagne. There's a rather seedy feel to it all, or at least an everydayness. It smells like peanuts and beer and wet umbrellas and other humans.

People here are ordinary English folks and a few English-speaking tourists like me. The English appear to be here because they love the theater and, according to London's mayor, Boris Johnson, always have. Johnson writes in his book about the London of Shakespeare's time when a full one-third of the London population, everyone from riffraff to royalty, went to the theater once a month. That's how King Charles II was able to see the orange girl and ultimately court her, too.

Blood Brothers is a musical about two brothers born to a woman too poor to keep both. She gives one up and keeps the other. The one she gives away is raised rich and the one she keeps is raised poor. The one she gives up becomes a clerk and one who stays with her becomes a thief. You wouldn't think people could sing and dance to something so sad, but they do and it's quite wonderful. *Blood Brothers* has been showing for thirty years, but when I see the play it's one of the last showings, at least at the Phoenix.

My father really was English or, more accurately, someone in his family had come from England. Many people thought, just from looking at him, that he was very likely part Indian and maybe part black, but apparently he wasn't, at least if my recent DNA test is any indication. Anything is possible. His family had been in the American backwoods for four hundred years. We know white slaveholders fathered children with their slaves. We know that black and mulatto slaves escaped to the Indian tribes and intermarried. We know the pioneers married the Indians. America is a melting pot, and it's huge. Who can say who's related to whom? Surely there were some French in the mix. What about the Lithuanians?

England, on the other hand, is so small I might be related to everyone here. In a *National Geographic,* I think, I read once about a prehistoric human, maybe Lindow Man, buried in an English peat bog. The DNA test showed that he had the same DNA as the people living in the nearby village. In general, people don't move very far from where they were born.

So one sunny day I get on the train to Bury St. Edmunds in Suffolk where my Stocking ancestors are supposed to have been. Bury St. Edmunds doesn't mean that St. Edmunds is buried there, or that someone wants him to die and *be* buried there. "Bury" is a German word that means berg, or village, so technically it's St. Edmunds-bury or village. King Edmund was killed by Danes in 869 A.D. I wonder if it was my Danish ancestors there who did the killing or my English ancestors who were being killed along with their king. After all this time, I decide, what with the routine rapes carried out by Norse raiders and also with the normal intermarrying in more peaceable times, probably both.

The view out the window is like the Blake poem about "this green and pleasant land." There's been a lot of rain. Everything is beautiful. For part of the way my seatmate is a lorry driver with a Cockney accent going to visit his mum. He says she was a single mom who had him out of wedlock and raised him by cleaning houses. "I can't believe everything she did to keep me and raise me," he says. "Her parents disowned her." I like the open-hearted way he talks and says he loves his mum and can't wait to see her. He shows me the flowers he's bringing her. "My mum loves flowers," he says. I like his honesty about being poor and illegitimate. There's a deep dignity in him. I can understand why the English loved Princess Diana. She was, as in the Elton John song, "a candle in the wind." I like the spunk of the English. They're the same as Americans in that.

My ancestors came to America during the years leading up to England's turbulent Civil War, a good time to leave Suffolk. I can just hear one of my female forebears saying, "Honey, let's go somewhere safe. I think I might be pregnant. I don't want to lose the baby because I'm scared of being attacked or because we don't have enough to eat. I don't want you to die in this fight. Let's get out while we still can. Let's go to America. You know how to cut trees. There'll be a lot of trees in America."

Most of the people fighting in the lead-up to the English Civil War, on all sides, had power. And the ordinary people, my people, the people without power, people who were conscripted against their will, people who didn't have a stake in it, couldn't benefit much, to their way of thinking, no matter who won.

My understanding, and it's sketchy, is that prior to the Civil War-King Charles I was in a tight spot financially and wanted Parliament to get him more tax money. The King cut off the ears of some noblemen. The cutting off of ears was something done all the time but apparently not to noblemen. The noblemen, most of the guys in Parliament since they didn't let regular folks in at that time, took umbrage. Then the King got rid of Parliament. Then the King's men and the former Parliament guys fought. There was a lot of killing all the way around and King Charles I was beheaded. Oliver Cromwell took over, a Parliament guy, a wily power broker who would be beheaded, too, but not until after he was dead. Craziness reigned. King Charles II, the dead king's fifteen-year-old son, hid in a tree and then escaped to Europe. Finally when he was thirty he got to come back to England, that green and pleasant land, and be king.

King Charles II had no children with his lawfully wedded wife but had a lot of illegitimate children, two of whom, bringing us up to date, helped create the bloodlines of Princess Diana. The English keep pretty close track of royal blood, but they needn't bother, at least not when the people are English, as far as I can tell. All the white-skinned people on the train look an awful lot alike, and to an average observer it looks like everybody slept with everybody all the time for centuries.

Four hundred years ago, England was a good place to leave. And since my ancestors left, and therefore survived, I'm alive and able to come back to visit. I like the idea that I might be related to people who created the Magna Carta. When I get off the train it's apparent that I am not going to see much without a car. I see no taxis. I need water and the railroad ticket person tells me there's a Tesco grocery nearby. If I go across the street, and under the railroad trestle, and up the hill a little ways, I'll see it there.

I think maybe in the grocery store I'll see people who look like my father's side of the family. Sure enough, here they are. Here's a man, scrawny and tall and well-muscled, with a high forehead, a long neck, a huge Adam's apple, and a slight over-bite, a man who looks like my cousin Harold. This man is blond and sort of Danish-looking and like me might have been related to the old guy buried at Sutton Hoo. Just before I ask his name, as I trail him myopically out of the aisle with bottled water and into the aisle with laundry soap, the chickens of my ridiculousness, which have been flying dizzily every which way for days, come home to roost, and the hawks of my reasonable-ness swoop down to feast on their weaker cousins, thus restor-ing the balance of nature and the vitality of the hen house.

The question, I see clearly now, is not really where did we come from but what does a person feel drawn to? What does a person choose? I choose William Blake's compassion for har-lots and orphans, Thomas More's sense of humor in the face of death, Julian of Norwich's idea that God is love, Chaucer's way of describing April, and open-hearted lorry drivers with Cockney accents. In the same vein, I choose Walt Whitman, Chief Joseph, Mother Jones, Sojourner Truth, Woody Guthrie, and Marilyn Monroe. Whoever my ancestors were, they have been in America for so long that England has to be an infini-tesimal part of my genetic heritage, and what does it matter? The reality is that we are all ninety-six percent chimpanzee and twenty-nine percent daffodil.

HOME

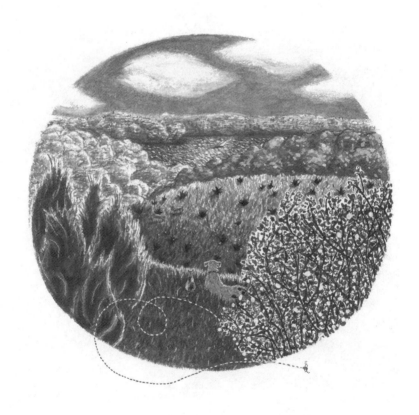

Ono No Komachi

The ad on *craigslist* offers free kittens.

It's one of those downy spring days with everything the softest shades of green and yellow under a pale blue sky. From the big woods behind my house emanates the baby powder smell that comes out of the ground when winter's finally over.

A month earlier, before the leaves were on, I'd adopted a big, ba-rooo hound from an ad on the bulletin board in Anderson's Grocery Store in Glen Arbor. His previous owner couldn't keep him. The lady's husband had had a stroke; she said she was afraid of the dog knocking him over. She'd said the dog liked kittens.

The kitten will be a companion for the hound, I'm thinking, as I drive to an assignation point on M-37 near Grawn. The kitten woman had said it was going to be too hard for me to find her house because there were no house numbers where she lived, so I should meet her at the side of the road off M-37 where there was a house number. She described her car, a big, older model maroon wagon.

It takes a little doing but finally we rendezvous in the horseshoe-shaped driveway of a tin trailer with a mound of slab wood in front of it. She opens the boot of her car and takes out a box of kittens. At the exact same time a huge white dog starts barking ferociously at the loosely closed screen door of the trailer.

"That's a big dog," I say, trying to sound like I'm just making conversation.

"My boyfriend's pit bull," she says in a smoker's husky voice with a hint of southern twang. "My EX-boyfriend, to tell the truth. He's a piece of work, to tell the truth."

"Hmm," I murmur sympathetically, but what I'm wondering is: the boyfriend, or the pit bull?

She is blonde, petite, and perhaps had been very beautiful but her sad, watery blue eyes tell a story of a hard life.

The dog's barking becomes more insistent and I pick up a kitten and say, "This one's great. Thanks so much." I put the kitten in a carrier on the front seat, close my car door and roll down my window. "That's great firewood. Do you know where it came from?"

"Lake Ann Hardwoods," she says.

"I'll give them a call," I say. "Good information. Thanks for the kitten."

Okay, I think to myself, this is okay. My face hasn't been eaten by a pit bull and now I have a kitten, a miniscule ball of fluff that I suspect is much younger than six weeks.

Home in Leelanau County the downy fluffs of the poplar trees along the driveway float everywhere. It's a downy day and my kitten is downy. She's orange and brown and black, a tortoiseshell cat with white paws and a blaze of white on her chest and face. She's all black around her eyes. She looks like a mime, or a geisha with heavily made-up eyes. Something in her walk and the way she moves, it's as though she's on geta shoes, those Japanese geisha platform sandals you can buy in the Tokyo airport. She's a beautiful creature and she seems to know it.

She needs a bath and so I give her one. She loves the warm water. When she is all clean and dry and fluffy again, I slowly feed her some warm milk and introduce her to the hound, named before I got him, a hound-type name, "Blue."

The hound, being a good dog, like in the Joan Baez song, "Oh, Blue, you good dog you," makes no sudden moves. It isn't long before the kitten has curled up next to him, enjoying his warmth. Soon she's sound asleep. Does she make him calmer? It seems so.

By the end of the first day, she has become Ono no Komachi, the famous ninth century Japanese courtesan and poet.

Komachi had been the most beautiful woman in Japan, so the legend goes, and the best poet. "Everyone know about Komachi," according to my friend and neighbor, Suki LaForrest, "Komachi famous. Many story." Suki, now a grandmother, grew up in Japan and it was there that her husband, Jimmy LaForrest, met her and fell in love and convinced her to come back to Leelanau County with him. "Suki was high class," according to Jimmy, "and so beautiful." Although he was a lowly American soldier, he courted Suki tirelessly and finally won her trust. One of the essays in Jane Hirshfield's *Nine Gates: Entering the Mind of Poetry* explores the lore surrounding Komachi.

Komachi was described by one of her admirers as "a woman who was like a rose, if someone had never seen a rose." She was a woman who could so mesmerize men with the subtlety of her words, her understanding of their every thought, and the profundity of her insights about them and the world that they felt they couldn't live without her.

Legend has it that one day Komachi left the palace, only to reappear from time to time down through the succeeding centuries. Sometimes she was an ancient lady emerging from the shadows at the edge of a campfire tended by some weary, traveling soldiers. Sometimes she was pulling in nets at the seashore. Once she was saved from a tsunami. She was in the mountains, astonishing the peasants with her poetry. The stories, never possible to verify, traveled by word of mouth. Remote obscure peoples had seen Komachi dance and sing and recite her poems in the firelight, transforming before their unbelieving eyes into the compellingly mysterious beauty she had once been.

In the 1960s, so one story goes, a young American student went to Japan to perfect his already proficient Japanese language skills and study Zen. In his mountain village there was a beautiful, sixty-year-old female artist. He loved her drawings, he loved the way she moved her hands, and most of all he loved the way she listened to him when he spoke and made brilliant amused and amusing responses that he thought about every night when he was falling asleep, thinking of what he would say to her the next day, to charm her and to impress her.

One day as the young man was walking the lady artist to her mountain home, she said in her honest, charming way, "I think you would like to take me." In the suddenness of the moment, he confesses his ardor and she says, "Then I must tell you I've had a double mastectomy." Instantly the young man's passion evaporates. The next morning he finds a beautiful, black, ceramic bowl on his doorstep. On top is a thin layer of fragile, almost-translucent, pale-pink, almost-white rose petals. Underneath the petals the eager student discovers the bowl is full of dead bees which still hold the faint smell of honey. And the lady has vanished. People tell him, "Komachi."

The Japanese figured out, long before anyone else, that men not only need women, they need brilliant women. Women perceive things differently from men and men need that way of seeing to get a complete picture; and vice versa. Somewhere I read—in Steven Pinker or Noam Chomsky, Steven Jay Gould or Julian Jaynes, *The New York Times* or the *National Enquirer*—a theory about how women taught men to talk. You only need to think about the expression "pillow talk" and your own personal experiences, to know that there might be more than a grain of truth in this.

Men, especially the ancient warriors and kings in myths and legends, tell women things in bed that perhaps they shouldn't. Thus, so the stories tell us down through the ages, beautiful, extremely intelligent and wily females, always in a dangerous game to save their lives, since the time of Ashtoreth, Cleopatra, Olympias, Scheherazade, Boudicca, Mulan, Mata Hari, and Marilyn Monroe, have used feminine wiles to trump male strength.

Blue becomes deeply attached to Komachi. He carries her in his mouth. He keeps her from going into the road. He lets her sleep with him. She likes to sleep between his hind legs, right in his crotch, which would seem to be uncomfortable for him. He looks uncomfortable. Still, he does forebear. Perhaps it is the warmest place for her. Perhaps he doesn't want to disturb her.

Not long after Komachi's arrival in my home, she becomes deathly ill. Perhaps she had been removed from her mother too soon and could not survive on cow's milk and tuna. Animals can't talk, as you're well aware, so it's hard to know what's wrong. She lies so still, I surmise she's dead. For three days she doesn't eat or drink water. Blue sleeps next to the box where, as perhaps we both imagine, Komachi lies dying.

When Komachi is well again, Blue becomes more attached than ever. Blue begins to get better, too, more himself, more self-confident, less demanding. He patrols the property at night. There's a soft June evening at about three in the morning when I hear a whole pack of coyotes in the woods around my house. They're making the high-pitched scary sounds, like bagpipes only shrill, a sound that says, "We're coming for you."

Blue barks that night in a way I've never heard him bark before, and the coyotes stop their killing song and move to more likely venues. The next morning Blue is clearly proud, walking around, stiff-legged, with his head up. "I did it," he seems to be saying. "I took care of those coyotes."

My house is in need of many repairs after two years away in the Peace Corps, and with unfortunately terribly irresponsible renters who took advantage of my being on another continent to be reckless and cause expensive damage. As I can afford it, I hire men to come and make repairs. They are all fine with Blue. He's a handsome dog and men especially seem to like his looks.

Then one day something terrible happens. The young man who's going to fix my computer arrives thirty minutes earlier than I'd expected. Blue is inside the Invisible Fence barking and, instead of waiting, the young man breezes past him up the walkway. Blue bites the young man's hand, a nick, a warning bite, like being stuck by a rose thorn. But the young man is terrified, and goes immediately to the police.

That's the end of Blue. I later learn from the man at the Animal Control that Blue had been an abused dog, the dog of a close relative of the woman who had put up the ad to give him away. She had been too embarrassed to tell me the whole story. I'm sorry for Blue and I'm sorry for Komachi who's desolate without her dog.

I love all animals. All those years of traveling, in tough lonely places, I promised myself I would get a cat and a dog when I got home.

In Turkey people love cats for their gracefulness and intelligence. They find them beautiful, like living art. In Romania, people love dogs for their sweet patience and loyalty, as if they were people. I agree with both views.

Christopher Isherwood, the writer, and his partner, artist Don Bachardy, were gay in the 1950s, in the years before it was okay in this country. So in their correspondence Isherwood took on the persona of a horse. Bachardy took on the persona of a cat. Their letters were filled with terms of endearment like Worshipped Glossy Hoof and Dearest Raggledub; and Beloved Catkin and Angel Sweetcat. I am not making this up. As in many gay relationships, one person was male and one person was female, a phenomenon on which, so far, neither the likes of Noam Chomsky or the *National Enquirer* has been able to shed any light. I'm fine with gayness, lest you think otherwise, and now, more recently, transgenderedness, but wouldn't it be far out to be trans-specied?

Komachi and I go through a time with just each other, but it's not the same for her as having Blue. She needs to be adored. Cats do well with being worshiped, as the Egyptians discovered long ago. Dogs like to have a purpose. There's some crossover, some overlap, but not much.

In October, I call another ad on *craigslist*. This is for a shepherd-collie mix, a dog that an assisted living place near

Cadillac is giving away. I'm the first person who has called, they say on the phone, and yes they can hold the dog for me until Monday. I work weekends as a server in a winery, I tell them, and Monday morning will be the first time I'll be able to drive to Cadillac.

All weekend I think about the question I hadn't had the temerity to ask on the phone: why are you giving this dog away? I knew they wouldn't tell me the truth over the phone and simply by asking the question I might lose my place in line.

Early Monday morning I drive along sleeping Lake Michigan, through a waking Traverse City, and then through the brilliant orange and red fire-colors of autumnal back roads all the way to Kingsley and then to the far side of Cadillac off M-115. When they bring the dog out, an old dog they say is ten but who looks more like twenty, a dog variously called Dixie, Daisy or Dusty, I pop the question.

"She came in with someone who passed," the tired attendant says. Her shift is about to end. "But then she seemed to be able to tell when someone was about to pass and wouldn't leave their side. The last time, she wouldn't let the Emergency Medical Technicians (EMT) near a woman who'd had a stroke."

In Cedar, where I stop at Pleva's on the way back to get welcome home hot dogs and bones for the dog, I see a friend and tell her I have a new dog. She crosses the street and looks into the back seat.

"She looks sad," she says.

Well, I explain, she was the death-watch dog, the hospice dog at a long-term care facility, so of course, it would wear on one.

When I get Dixie home, I show her the kitten: your new job, I say. This is your responsibility. The kitten understands instantly but the old dog is like, "I don't know if you got this about me, but my time card's all filled out."

Komachi has to train Dixie to be her nanny. After a few days, Dixie is as tolerant and attentive as Blue had been. Because this dog is a female, she has actual nipples, non-functioning, but there. Amazingly, she even tolerates the kitten's instinctive nursing on her. Technically, the kitten is too old to nurse, but in the real world she still needs to go through all the stages of growing up before she can become a cat.

Winter, as any resident of the northwest coast of lower Michigan who lived through the winter of 2013-2014 knows, engulfed us. As the snow falls, the kitten grows into a young cat. When spring comes and the snow melts, Komachi discovers the out-of-doors. She discovers hunting.

Another dog comes into our life, a female puppy named Happy. This time Komachi is the one who is stand offish. She hisses and arches her back and runs away. The puppy pursues her, not to eat her, as perhaps Komachi's instincts had warned her, but only to lick her face and play chase.

Cats are much more athletic than puppies and much smarter about running and hiding. If the cat goes under the car, the puppy can't imagine where she is. If the cat goes up a tree, the puppy is disconsolate. If the cat does a feint, running first in one direction and then turning suddenly and going in the other direction, the puppy never, ever anticipates it, no matter how many times the cat plays this trick.

It must be boring for Komachi to play chase with Happy. She looks bored; but long-suffering. Who else is she going to play with? The old dog is too old and I'm not interested.

The day I know Happy has won Komachi's friendship is the day Komachi brings back a living mouse for Happy. This is not so easy. Komachi has to climb an eight-foot, outside ladder up to a garage window, carefully keeping the mouse in her mouth but not killing it, and then she has to leap down several feet to the garage floor, still not dropping the mouse, and lay it at Happy's feet.

Happy is mystified by the mouse, but bless her heart, makes a polite show of interest. Golden retrievers have really good social skills.

Happy and Komachi now have a ritual exchange of affection. Happy obliges Komachi with soft bites, a kind of adapted play-wrestling that is gentler than what dogs ordinarily do. Komachi, a sensual creature like most cats, loves to be petted and fondled and accepts this physical attention from the puppy as a manifestation of unconditional love, which it is.

Indian Summer on South Manitou

If you want to know what the world was like two hundred years ago, go to South Manitou Island some nice Indian Summer day. Take the ferry out of Leland on the northwest coast of lower Michigan, about three hundred miles north of Chicago. Be prepared to be transported back in time to a place with no air pollution, no sound pollution, and no light pollution.

Fall colors on South Manitou arrive about two weeks later than the fall colors do on the mainland. This is due to the moderating effect of the surrounding waters of Lake Michigan which still retain the summer's warmth. Autumn arrives just a little later, and lingers a little longer, helping to create the feeling that you've entered a time warp.

Once you've docked and walked a short distance away from the others who were on the boat with you, all you will hear is the sound of the wind and the waves. The air will be so clear and sweet you will instinctively breathe it in as an elixir. If you stay the night, the only light will be from the moon and stars. South Manitou is new, relatively speaking, eleven thousand years more or less since the last glacial period, so new some days it seems you can smell the ice melting. A more pristine and beautiful place can scarcely exist anywhere in the world.

Archeological records show that South Manitou was a stopping-off place for Native Americans who used it mostly for seasonal fishing. Starting in the 1600s, French Canadian voyageurs in thirty-five-foot-long cargo canoes heaped with furs, overlapped with and were eventually replaced by tall sailing ships in the 1700s loaded with lumber, which in turn overlapped with and were replaced by steamers in the 1800s full of immigrants which, in turn, were replaced in the 1900s by diesel ships hauling iron ore. All these vessels could be seen at different times in the island's history waiting out storms in the large South Manitou harbor.

"In the landlocked heart of our America," Melville writes in 1851 in *Moby Dick*, "those grand freshwater seas of ours have drowned full many a midnight ship with all her shrieking crew." The November storm of 1913, the worst Great Lakes storm ever, was a hurricane with whiteouts, thirty-five-foot seas and ninety-mile-an-hour winds. It killed two hundred and fifty people, sunk nineteen ships, destroyed nineteen others and caused, by today's measure, one-hundred-and-fifteen-billion dollars in damage.

The day before I went to South Manitou there was a ferocious storm and the ferry out of Leland, the Manitou Island Transit, stayed in the harbor. That night I was afraid my trip would be cancelled. But the next morning dawned bright and clear and the lake was blue and calm. Now on the boat I'm sitting next to an elderly couple from Ohio. "My husband's family used to come to Crystal Lake after the [Second World] War," the woman tells me, "when just the wives and children came during the week, you know, because it was cooler out of the city, and the men came up on weekends and brought all the groceries." She shakes her head. The changes in her lifetime have come so fast, she seems to be saying, that it makes one's head spin.

In the early years of shipping on Lake Michigan, South Manitou was the first stop after Mackinac Island for people on their way to Chicago. "Beyond South Manitou there was no sure shelter and [with steamers] the captain had to order aboard enough wood for the entire run to Chicago," writes George Hilton in *Lake Michigan Passenger Steamers*. "A captain had to rely on traditional predictive devices such as the color of sunsets, behavior of birds, and the presence of rings around the moon to make his calculations whether he could safely run the two hundred and sixty miles."

William Burton was the island's first white resident, arriving in about 1835 to provide cordwood to the steamships. In its heyday South Manitou had a fluxuating population of an estimated one to three hundred, but when the steamers switched from wood to coal in the 1880s, the economy died. The National Park Service took over in 1970 and by that time almost everyone was gone and the five thousand acre island began quickly to revert to its prehistoric self.

Once off the ferry the older people and the people with children stay for one of the tours and the young backpackers and hikers melt away into the interior. In the tour's hay wagon, I'm sitting next to a young family from Grand Rapids. The father served as a medic in Afghanistan and Iraq. He says he wants to teach his children two things: to love being outside and to help others. He's starting with baby steps, like the tour, but eventually will do more rigorous wilderness camping with his kids because he wants them to acquire solid, outdoor coping skills. Eventually he wants to take his family on church missions to Latin America and other places so his kids can learn not only the rewards of camping, but the rewards of extending a helping hand to their fellow humans, learning a different but maybe even more important coping skill.

South Manitou is relatively flat. There is some height at the far south end of the island where we go to see the wreck of the Francisco Morazan, but it's really dune and bluff, similar to what's exactly opposite in the Sleeping Bear Dunes. I grew up above Sleeping Bear Bay, and through the telescope on our dining room table we watched a November storm in 1960 that caused the wreck of the Morazan. We were relieved to learn over the next few days that all survived.

I knew an old Indian man, Archie Miller from Peshawbestown, who took his kids to South Manitou one summer for a *Swiss Family Robinson* adventure. They lived on tinned chicken that washed ashore from the Morazan, "square chicken," as Archie described it, and fresh fish from Florence Lake. They stayed in an abandoned farm house. "We had everything," Archie said, "Stove. Kitchen utensils." At night the kids complained about spooks in the house so he told them they could sleep outside. "They came back in because of the mosquitoes," he said. "Guess they preferred the spooks."

Archie took them up into the dunes to see the Valley of the Giants. They slept there on a full moon night when the petrified trees made deep shadows. "I said, 'Kids you gotta see this.'" Archie'd worked most of his life in the woods cutting trees. As a child he'd been taken from his parents and placed in the Catholic orphanage in Harbor Springs. "They came around with a big buckboard," he said. "Gathered up all these kids. I was only five. They beat us if we spoke our own language. I'll never forget the sound at night of all of those little kids crying for their parents." He ran away multiple times, as did many of the children, trying to get back home. I remember him shaking his head and saying, "Amazing we survived." Archie was a naturally joyful person who'd learned that without joy, you die. Joy was what he wanted his children to experience.

My father took us to South Manitou one week at the end of May in 1952 so we could see the ring-billed gulls hatching. I remember how cute the baby gulls were, and also, how smelly the nesting area was, because when the gulls didn't hatch, the eggs rotted on the shore. I also remember endless fields of wild strawberries. The strawberries were bigger than on the mainland, and much sweeter. My father was logging off the island so we went a few times. He showed us red-orange lilies in bloom in the dunes. Wild lilies bloom singly. These were scattered at some distance from each other through the sparse grass of the rose-gold dunes, like little flames. The intense beauty of those fire-red lilies blazing against a blue sky stays with me still.

One of the men who worked for my father cutting trees was Ray Welch. He'd had an Aunt Martha who'd taught school on South Manitou. Ray said she regularly walked home to the mainland, across the ice, two or three times a year. Ray was a taciturn man and what he was leaving unsaid, and this was his peculiar style, was the fact that the ice didn't always freeze thick enough in all places to support the weight of a person.

Charles Anderson, son of an island farmer, wrote in his memoir, "The winter of 1917 was very cold." By February 10, they'd had no mail or supplies for six weeks. His father decided they had to hitch the horses to the sleigh and try to make the trip to the mainland. "The going was good until they came to the channel that the ice cutter, the Ann Arbor #6, had made going to North Manitou with hay for the starving cattle." His father put planks across the water, Anderson explains, but the first horse to cross "got excited and stepped off...." The other horse pulled the first one out and the family returned to the island and, successfully, made the trip the next day.

On South Manitou there was a woman who'd come in the early 1900s from Germany, Bertha Peth. She'd lost her family at some point. She survived by gathering ginseng, an herb which could be sold, and also by roaming the beach collecting corks from the fishing nets. "She would get from three to five cents for the aluminum corks," according to Anderson, "and for the wooden—one cent."

Islands have a unique ecology. One of the reasons Indians had only seasonal camps on small islands is that they couldn't count on there being enough game to feed everyone. European immigrants, too, in the long span of time, were only on South Manitou for about a century. Mammals, other than the human ones, have also waxed and waned. There were foxes on the island in the 1970s, perhaps having crossed the ice from the mainland, but they died out for lack of food. Right now there's a plethora of chipmunks. The chipmunks are so tame they'll eat out of your hand, which is great fun for children.

A trip to South Manitou isn't just another activity on the list for tourists, it's time travel. Since our grandparents' day, the number of people on the planet has doubled, tripled and quadrupled in increasingly shorter and shorter periods of time, going from one billion in 1800 to a projected nine billion by 2050, and maybe three times that by 2100. Google, "global population" and "pollution" and "world resources" sometime if you want to give yourself a good fright. Yes, you can take your kids to Disney World and that's fine. But, the way things are going, Disney World looks like it'll be there for a while yet; and South Manitou, with its clean air and quiet nights, might become a distant memory in the very near future. So go now, before it disappears.

Unnatural Phenomenon

When dolphins wash up on shore in significant numbers, we suspect there's something happening wrong in the ocean. It's just not what we expect. It's not a natural phenomenon. We may not know what it is exactly, but we guess that, whatever's happening, however unknown or unknowable to us, it's got to be about more than dolphins simply taking a notion.

Why don't we have the same common sense intuition about the children at the border?

We've all seen the pictures: children, endless numbers of them, peering wanly out of a dusty group of urchins who have just arrived near a chain link fence, or lined up on the floor in neat faceless rows under foil blankets, like so many child-sized, foil-wrapped entrees.

They have come by the hundreds from Central America, an estimated fifty-seven thousand such children. Four decades ago, according to Oscar Martinez, a Salvadoran journalist writing in *The Nation* in August 2014, our government supported the wealthy oligarchs and their military dictatorships; poor peasants revolting against starvation wages and oppression, were forced to flee from Honduras, El Salvador and Guatemala. Some of these found work as members of gangs in American cities. Arrested and returned to their home countries, "they found [their] countries devastated by war and poverty," according to Martinez, "with thousands upon thousands of corruptible and abandoned children" to recruit for new gangs.

These are the children at the border, according to Sonia Nazario writing in *The New York Times* in July 2014. These are the children of the drug wars. They have come to the United States to escape murder, rape, and conscription by the cartels.

In an alternative view the border children, like kittens dropped off in the night or babies in baskets on our doorsteps, have been sent by irresponsible parents into the United States in order to take advantage of our largesse. An anti-immigration crowd in Oracle, Arizona, holds up signs proclaiming, "You are not welcome." These American citizens, except in the rare event they're of American Indian ancestry, are themselves invariably the offspring of immigrants, but see nothing hypocritical or aberrant in despising other immigrants.

When a boatload of Jewish refugees came to our shores in 1939 during the Second World War, President Roosevelt's government turned them away. Anti-Semitism in the United States, like the anti-immigration sentiment that exists today, was strong enough that Roosevelt took the route that was most immediate, convenient, and politically expedient. Government casuists in 1939 parsed their reasons: the nine hundred and thirty seven refugees were not refugees but tourists. They could not enter the United States on tourist visas because they had no return addresses.

Captain Gustav Shröder, given the Order of Merit by the Germans after the war and posthumously named as one of the Righteous among Nations by the Israelis, considered running aground in Florida and allowing his passengers to escape, but U. S. Coast Guard cutters kept him from doing so. Returned to Europe, an estimated one-quarter to one-third of the passengers died in concentration camps.

In the confusion of the moment, whether we're talking about children at the border in 2014 or a boatload of Jewish refugees in 1939, it's often easy to get bogged down in the economic or legal constraints. It was argued then, and is being argued now, that the refugees don't have the right documents or we don't have enough resources for them.

One needs only to think back to Jonathan Swift's 1729 satiric essay, *A Modest Proposal*, to think twice about purported legal and economic arguments. Swift, as you may recall, suggested that problems of poverty and orphans could be solved by passing a law mandating raising the children as food. Thus people would have enough to eat and the problem of the unwanted children would be solved.

In 1999 I worked with homeless children in Richmond, outside of San Francisco. This was one of the poorest regions of the Bay Area. I taught writing in the Palo Verde Elementary School on Saturday mornings as part of a program called Community Works.

My first morning I was early and wended my way through garbage-strewn streets, past rag pickers pushing rickety grocery carts scouting for returnable bottles and scrap metal, past the evening's revelers and drug dealers making their tipsy way home, past a few children up early, one little boy and a slightly bigger boy inexplicably beating a brand new, bright red bicycle to death with baseball bats.

The Palo Verde School was surrounded by a high chain-link fence plastered with refuse. At first I thought it was strange that no one had removed the garbage, but then I saw that the school was next to a garbage dump. It would have been a never-ending job, cleaning up the trash, so they just left it there.

The school itself was one of those solid, 1940s-era, thick-walled schools with cool, high-ceilinged hallways and polished wood floors. The director of the program was a tiny, competent, white-haired Mormon lady, Evelyn, who had been doing it forever. Her office, next to the nurse's station, was behind an iron grill, like a bank teller's grill in an old western town.

Evelyn decided to put me in the library, a large room with low tables and soft lighting, hidden in the bowels of the building. She wanted me to be safe from the roving gangs of older children who sometimes roamed the school to steal the juice boxes and snacks of the younger children.

That first Saturday morning, about a hundred children found their way into the hidden library. They spoke many languages: Hindi, Chinese, Portuguese, Mon, Swahili, Thai, Tagalog, half a dozen varieties of Spanish, and Black English in a dialect that was sometimes unintelligible. It was like the Tower of Babel in there. I couldn't teach. All I could do was play games with them.

At the break at 10 A.M., I found my way out of the maze of hallways and back to Evelyn's barred window. "I can't do this," I told her. No way could I teach a hundred kids with a dozen different languages.

"Don't worry," she said calmly. She had heard this all before. (Evelyn would die soon after I finished there.) "There will be fewer each time."

I thought about this on the way back to my library hide out. *Fewer each time.* And what happens to the children who stop coming? This was my first time working away from northern Michigan. In the years to come, unbeknownst to me then, I would teach in El Salvador, Guatemala, Thailand, and Romania, third world countries with unspeakable poverty and crime, but I would never get over *fewer each time.*

In a month I had about twenty students, more or less, not always the same students. Even with the different languages, it wasn't as hard as I'd thought it was going to be. I had pattern poems in all the languages and between the games, the snacks, the improvisational theater (I brought costumes), the drawing and painting, the time passed pleasantly.

Two little Hispanic girls from someplace like Guatemala or El Salvador, a younger sister and an older sister, always sat together and never smiled and never wrote or made pictures. They came every Saturday. They didn't cause trouble, but they also didn't participate. They were a mystery to me.

One Saturday after the class ended, I caught up with Evelyn and told her I was concerned about these two little girls. I couldn't get them to engage. She said, "Neighbors called protective services because the girls were screaming every night." It turned out the girls were having nightmares. They had watched their father tortured to death in front of them. Their mother had escaped to California, but the girls were still so traumatized they could not, or would not, speak.

At the same time that I was working with children from the streets and homeless shelters of Richmond, I was working with the most violent inmates at the San Francisco Jail in a program called Resolve to Stop the Violence (RSVP). The jail was the land of bad childhoods. One man's father had tried to kill his seven children after his wife died giving birth to my student, the child he blamed for his wife's death, a child who would become as an adult male, and why are we surprised, a violent criminal.

Most of my jail students were black, Native American and Hispanic. The connection between the damage caused originally by slavery, genocide and oppression, and then passed from generation to generation in a horrifying legacy of dysfunction, poverty and illiteracy, was inescapable. These were the dolphins washed up on the shore.

The trouble in the ocean is our culture's historic lack of support for families and children and a belief that the resulting riff-raff can be put behind bars. We've created a society with more people in prison than any other country in the world, spending more to incarcerate a person for a year than it would cost to send that same person to Harvard. If the same money we now spend on prisons were spent on family maternity and paternity leave, if parents didn't have to work three jobs in order to support their families but instead could spend time with their children, it would save billions. Children who are not cared for often become dysfunctional and this, in turn, leads to violence.

Children who are forced to witness terrible violence never get over it; those children do not just fade away. They grow up and, short of some miraculous transformation where they fall in love, find a good job and create a decent life, commit violence themselves. They shut down emotionally and so lack awareness of right and wrong. Violence, to those who've grown up with it, is a way of life. Killing, so I was told, gets easier with time.

The path from terrible childhoods where kids witness terrible violence—or it's perpetrated against them—to drug addiction, finding work as hit men, death and/or prison was pretty clear in my mind. Knowing I had little chance of turning around the lives of violent adults in the RSVP program, I tried harder with the children at the Palo Verde School. I was willing to make a total fool of myself if I could get a smile out of a child.

The kids responded positively to my goofy costumes: a red wig, a full purple skirt with pink sequins. One day I came in sunglasses that had windshield wipers. I talked funny. I used different voices. Another time I wore a tiara with blinking lights.

My Spanish was so bad that if I really wanted to see the Hispanic kids rolling on the floor, holding their sides, laughing, all I had to do was try to speak Spanish. One day I noticed that I drew a slight smile, very slight, from the bigger Hispanic sister. The smaller sister, I learned, had such a stiff facial expression because she had a metal plate in her face. I never knew why.

I was always noncommittal with my students, half-pretending that I didn't know they were there. Of course I did know they were there, but I'd discovered that if I was too apparently aware, it made students withdraw.

On a gray November morning of the California rainy season, I had the students draw a picture of a starry night, using Van Gogh's *The Starry Night* as an example. If a person can get an image then the words will follow. We drew stars all morning. Then after the break I passed out pattern poems about stars in as many languages as there were.

Estrella is the word for star in Spanish. For the first time I saw that the younger Hispanic sister was writing. This was an astonishing turn of events, which I purportedly ignored. I hadn't known she could talk, much less write.

At the end of the class I gathered up all the work and put it in my bag. I didn't even glance at the younger sister's writing. As soon as the students were gone I pulled out her work—for all I knew she had been scribbling nonsense—and read, "*Cuando estoy triest, me imagino que tengo espiritu de mi.*" I knew enough Spanish to make out, "When I am sad, I imagine I have a spirit inside of me."

That afternoon, as I drove back over the St. Raphael Bridge into Marin County, west and then north out along the high coast road above the Pacific Ocean, and finally down into the cove near Stinson Beach where I lived, I thought about what had happened, trying to figure out why.

That evening, when people were out on their decks, I gave the poem to one of my neighbors, a bilingual social worker, to translate. The poem described a star, "brighter than all the others" on a cloudy night, a star that "seemed to reflect all the happiness inside me" that came out of the sky and into her being, "like a many-colored butterfly" and also like something that had been there before but that she had forgotten. It was "the star that illuminates all the obscure and silent night." It was "the spirit inside of me."

"She had a breakthrough," my neighbor said in amazement, after she translated.

How or why, neither of us knew.

This I do know, we each have a spirit inside of us. I knew it before that day, but it was confirmed by what I saw in the younger sister. We fail to honor this spirit in ourselves and others at our peril. It's not so much what will happen to the children if we send them back, but what will happen to us? Do we want to be seen by history as like the people who watched the trains of children headed to Auschwitz and looked the other way? When do we become complicit? When we know something bad is happening, and can do something about it, and don't. That's when.

Children who are malnourished and mistreated become adults. Short of tagging them with computer chips, like animals, or simply raising them for food, as Jonathan Swift suggested, or flat-out genocide, they can end up anywhere. There's no escaping anything anymore; and when we adults close our eyes to the harm being done to children, we become changed, less human, more brutal.

Herman Hesse, the German philosopher and writer, said that every so often in our evolution out of the primordial muck, we must look back down the long, dark, narrow, winding way, and see how far we have come, and keep going, trying to become better human beings.

Evolution is not just about having an opposable thumb or being able to walk upright. Evolution is also about not sacrificing your child on the mountain; and, bringing us up to date, knowing that there is no difference, in terms of sacrifice-ability, between your child and your neighbor's child.

Evolution is about becoming more intelligent and compassionate. It's about sharing resources fairly. It's about recognizing that we are all better off when we are all better off. Caste, class, race, age, gender, and borders are just ancient, ridiculous, outdated ways of thinking that were used to justify some people having more while other people had less.

The idea is to be more evolved, not less evolved. We must care for those children at the border, not just because it's the right thing to do, which it is, but because if they are returned to the violent places from whence they came, they are very likely to become part of that violence and this will come back to haunt us, not just in our consciences, but in reality.

Any child who is loved and cared for—fed, sheltered, educated and told every day in every way that he or she is valued and wanted—is better for all of us. Any child who isn't cared for is worse for all of us. There are no more borders.

My Country

You don't really know where you're from until you've been somewhere else and come back. That's because anything is only itself in relationship to some other thing. A day is only a day in relationship to the night. An apple stands for every fruit until you've tasted a mangosteen. America isn't America until you've been to El Salvador.

Growing up above Sleeping Bear Bay I had some gut-level love of country that was mostly inarticulate and inchoate, the way you love a new puppy. My love of America had something to do with the beauty of Lake Michigan from the top of the dunes and the man who ran the barbershop in Empire, Mr. Lambkin, who did not know me except as a reckless nine-year-old out on horseback in a pelting April rain, who lifted me from my horse and put me into his old, blue, boiled-wool, World War II sweater to ride back to Glen Arbor. The sweater weighed like iron and he must have thought, if nothing else, it would anchor me to the saddle. He said I could bring the sweater back sometime.

My childhood was lucky, with a freedom that in retrospect was unusual. I could go anywhere, anytime, and I did. I played in the ice caves alone. I read in the barn loft, thrilling to the sound of the rain on the tin roof and the lightning and thunder outside. The hidden, fragrant arbutus under its rust-spotted, leathery leaves, when the snow was barely melted, was magical since I discovered it when I was alone. I can still call up the taste of wild strawberries in the spring and the days picking them in the hills above the bay after the ice had melted, the wind off the water smelling like fresh-cut cucumbers.

I sang *My Country 'Tis of Thee* in the old, red brick Glen Arbor schoolhouse in Mrs. Andreson's class, my heart swelling with emotion that came from I know not where. For years the song was conflated in my mind with *America, the Beautiful*, my imagination unconsciously substituting the pink arbutus and the blue-green waters of the lake for the purple mountain majesties and amber waves of grain.

As I got older, I thought about what I was singing. When the song got to "land of the pilgrim's pride, land where our fathers died" I thought about all the Indians who had been killed by all those pilgrims—and vice versa—and what about the black people who didn't seem even to be in these songs? At first unconsciously and then consciously, Woody Guthrie's, *This Land is Your Land*, became my alternative national anthem.

I didn't leave the continent of North America until I went to El Salvador to teach at a private school for the children of the ruling oligarchs. Two tours in the Peace Corps, in Thailand and Romania, followed.

You'd walk into a school in any of these places and ask, "Where's the library?" and like as not, if they even had one, you'd be shown to a small, dirty room with moldy books in heaps on the floor and mostly the books were in some language other than the one spoken by the people there, books that were not interesting even in the other language which was of course incomprehensible to the children who were supposed to be the grateful recipients of the books.

People talk about the horrifying poverty in third world countries, but it's not the poverty that's scary, it's the lack of easy talking and thinking. The United States has all too often been complicit, unfortunately, with tyrants and bad governments; we seem to like freedom at home but to like dictators everywhere else, perhaps because they're easier to control.

There were rumors that the United States government had covert sites for dark operations, called black-op sites, in both

Romania and Thailand, when I was there between 2006 and 2012; and now those rumors have been confirmed. There, according to the United States Senate Intelligence Committee's "torture report" released in December 2014, our government did terrible things to suspected terrorists, some of whom turned out to be innocent.

The problem with torture by our government isn't just the torture. It's that other things that our government does, good things like the Peace Corps, are then suspect. It's about being hypocritical. It's about being a wolf in sheep's clothing, not something you want your government to be; not something you want to have any part of if you're thinking straight.

In El Salvador in the 1980s, according to virtually all sources, the United States took the side of the wealthy ruling families against the poor peasants, supposedly in the fight against communism but in fact to support any and all forms of capitalism, and even trained their military at the School of the Americas in Fort Benning, Georgia. Money, corporate money, whether it's a banana company or an oil company, is often behind our government's policies.

Alexis de Tocqueville admired our civil society, but even in 1830 when he visited and did the research for his nine hundred and fifty-two page tome, *Democracy in America*, he was worried about our greed and thought that, if left uncurbed, it would be our undoing.

But my government is not the same thing as my country. A government, any government, but especially my own, is a huge, unwieldy bureaucracy with different policies at different times, depending on who gets in and who's shoved out. It can depend even on whims. A government bureaucracy is a thing where the left hand often does not know what the right hand is doing. My government is not my country.

My country is the American people. My country is people like Big Annie Clemenc in Calumet, Michigan, who, during the miners' strike of 1913, wrapped herself in the American flag and walked out to the soldiers sent by the government and said, "Shoot this, boys, if you want to shoot something."

My country is the young teacher from Louisiana taking his students to the Museum of the Revolution in San Salvador, getting fired and crying, not because he got fired but because El Salvador was so messed up. The night before he goes back to New Orleans, I find him standing outside my door. He's holding his pillow, and proffering it toward me. "I want you to have this," he says, laughing. "In case you need a pillow to cry on."

My country is some scrawny, old man standing by the side of the road outside Poughkeepsie with a sign that protests the war in Iraq and nobody even knows the old man is Pete Seeger.

When Seeger was before the House Un-American Activities Committee in 1955, he said, "I am not going to answer any questions as to my associations, my philosophical or religious beliefs or my political beliefs, or how I voted in any election, or any of those private affairs. I think these are very improper questions for any American to be asked, especially under such a compulsion as this." A lot of people named names and gave up their friends including some people you'd never expect like Frank Capra and Elia Kazan. They were afraid.

Of course Pete Seeger was afraid, too. During the Civil Rights movement when southern sheriffs turned dogs and fire hoses on children, Seeger was teaching an audience how to sing, *We Are Not Afraid*, and he said, "You are afraid, but you sing it, 'We are not afraid.'" Being afraid and doing the right thing anyway is called courage.

Seeger paid a big price for his courage; he and his music were black-listed for decades. Sixty years later, at Madison Square Gardens in a celebration of Seeger's ninetieth birthday hosted by all his fellow musicians, Bruce Springsteen said, "You outlived the bastards, Pete."

America is the way people talk. It's the young man fixing my roof who says he needs "a phoneless cord" and could I hand one up to him? It's the old lady in Tom's West Bay supermarket who offers me the empty cart she's returning, in place of the one I'm stubbornly trying to wrestle loose. I finally succeed and say, feeling a bit foolish because she's been watching me the whole time, "It would have been smarter to take yours right away." And she says kindly, in the same kind way she'd offered me her cart, "Peoples are always late getting smart."

During the Second World War, out in the French countryside near Lyons, Gertrude Stein wasn't homesick until the American soldiers came by and she couldn't get enough of their American talk. And it wasn't just their talk, it was their American-ness, their saying anything they wanted to with their humble, backwoods grammar and a sweet unselfconsciousness.

It's the self-deprecating sense of humor. It's Gary Snyder and Peter Blue Cloud in the High Sierras on a hot summer day painting the one-room school house in their little mountain community, and Gary says, "Peter, why are *we* doing this?" And Blue Cloud answers, deadpan, never looking up from where he's dipping his brush into the paint bucket, "*Noblesse oblige.*"

Americans volunteer. Americans are generous. Americans pay for the person behind them at Wendy's. Sometimes they call this *noblesse oblige.* They think it's hilarious.

Walt Whitman figured it out, and he didn't even have to leave the country to do it. "This then, is what you shall do," he wrote. "Stand up for the stupid and crazy, give alms to everyone who asks, love the earth and the sun and the animals, despise riches, devote your income and labors to others, hate tyrants, argue not concerning God, go freely with powerful uneducated persons and with the young and with the mothers of families..."

I love my country and I'm not ashamed to say that.

Kindness

Before you know what kindness really is
you must lose things,
feel the future dissolve in a moment
like salt in a weakened broth.
what you held in your hand,
what you counted and carefully saved,
all of this must go so you know
how desolate the landscape can be
between the regions of kindness.
How you ride and ride
thinking the bus will never stop,
the passengers eating maize and chicken
will stare out the window forever.

Before you learn the tender gravity of
kindness,
you must travel where the Indian in a white
poncho
lies dead by the side of the road.
You must see how this could be you,
how he too was someone
who journeyed through the night with plans
and the simple breath that kept him alive.

Before you know kindness as the deepest thing
inside
You must know sorrow as the other deepest
thing.
You must wake up with sorrow.
You must speak to it till your voice
catches the thread of all sorrows
and you see the size of the cloth.

Then it is only kindness that makes sense
anymore,
only kindness that ties your shoes
and sends you out into the day to mail letters
and purchase bread
only kindness that raises its head
from the crowd of the world to say
it is I you have been looking for,
and then goes with you everywhere
like a shadow or a friend.

—Naomi Shihab Nye